Country Visions

We work with leading authors to develop the strongest
educational materials in geographical sciences, bringing cutting-edge
thinking and best learning practice to a global market.

Under a range of well-known imprints, including Prentice Hall,
we craft high quality print and electronic publications which
help readers to understand and apply their content, whether
studying or at work.

To find out more about the complete range of our
publishing, please visit us on the World Wide Web at:
www.pearsoneduc.com

Country Visions

Edited by
Paul Cloke

Harlow, England • London • New York • Boston • San Francisco • Toronto • Sydney • Singapore • Hong Kong
Tokyo • Seoul • Taipei • New Delhi • Cape Town • Madrid • Mexico City • Amsterdam • Munich • Paris • Milan

Pearson Education Limited
Edinburgh Gate
Harlow
Essex CM20 2JE
United Kingdom

and Associated Companies throughout the world

Visit us on the World Wide Web at:
www.pearsoneduc.com

First published 2003

ISBN 0130 89601 2

British Library Cataloguing-in-Publication Data
A catalogue record for this book is available from the British Library

10 9 8 7 6 5 4 3 2 1
07 06 05 04 03

Typeset in 10/12pt Sabon by 35
Printed and Bound in China
SWTC/01

For Viv, Liz and Will with love

Contents

List of contributors

Simone Abram	Department of Town and Regional Planning, University of Sheffield
Cynthia Anderson	Department of Rural Sociology, Iowa State University
David Bell	School of Humanities and Social Sciences, Staffordshire University
Michael Bell	Department of Rural Sociology, Iowa State University and University of Wisconsin-Madison
Catherine Brace	Department of Geography, University of Exeter
Michael Bunce	Department of Geography, University of Toronto (Scarborough)
Carl Cater	Department of Geography, University of Reading
Paul Cloke	School of Geographical Sciences, University of Bristol
Deborah Dixon	Institute of Geography and Earth Sciences, University of Wales, Aberystwyth
Mark Goodwin	Institute of Geography and Earth Sciences, University of Wales, Aberystwyth
Julian Holloway	Department of Environmental and Geographical Sciences, Manchester Metropolitan University
John Horton	School of Geographical Sciences, University of Bristol
Owain Jones	School of Geographical Sciences, University of Bristol
Mark Lawrence	Department of Geography and Political Science, Bemidji State University
Jonathan Murdoch	Department of City and Regional Planning, Cardiff University
David Sibley	Department of Geography, University of Hull
Louise Smith	Thomas Cook, Peterborough
Nigel Thrift	School of Geographical Sciences, University of Bristol
Michael Woods	Institute of Geography and Earth Sciences, University of Wales, Aberystwyth
John Wylie	Department of Geography, University of Sheffield

List of figures

Acknowledgements

As always, the production of a book manuscript is underpinned by the invaluable efforts of key people 'behind the scenes'. I want to thank in particular Theresa Andrews in the Bristol office for her work in organising and administering this book as it came together. I also want to acknowledge the efficiency with which Karen van Eden of Pearson Education has nurtured the book through to its publication.

The publisher is grateful to the following for permission to reproduce copyright material:

Figure 4.8 from *In Search of England* (H.V. Morton, 1927), Methuen Publishing Limited; Figures 11.2 and 11.7 from Shotover Jet, New Zealand; Figures 11.3 and 11.4 from Queenstown Lake District Council (QLDC, 1998); Figure 11.6 from Queenstown Rafting, New Zealand; Figure 16.1 from Dr Steph Mastoris.

Still Life in the Nearly Present Time (N. Thrift, 2000), article reprinted with permission from Sage Publications Ltd, © Sage Publications Ltd, 2000).

In some instances we have been unable to trace the owners of copyright material, and we would appreciate any information that would enable us to do so.

Paul Cloke
Bristol, 2003

CHAPTER 1

Knowing ruralities?

Paul Cloke

Moving beyond the rural idyll

This book is about exploring different ways of knowing rurality; of under-standing the countryside. Somewhere deep down in the early twenty-first century psyche there seem to remain longstanding, handed-down precepts about rural areas, marking them as spaces enabled by nature, offering oppor-tunities for living and lifestyle which are socially cohesive, happy and healthy, and presenting a pace and quality of life that differs from that in the city. Such precepts provide cartographies of identity, encapsulating for some a repository of norms, values and treasures which both illustrate and shape what is precious in a nation, a region or a locality. They also raise up a 'voice', as self-appointed guardians of that identity insist on prescient narratives of how to preserve the country from threat or harm. Equally, these country precepts are plundered by multifarious commercial interests seeking to cash in on the psychological comfort or cache inherent in rural imagery in order to commodify seemingly any product, any time, anywhere.

These knowings of the country are often, somewhat loosely, given the overarching categorisation of 'idyll'. Rurality is idyllic, we are told. You can't get away from it. The long fingers of idyll reach into our everyday lives via the cultural paraphernalia of film, television, art, books, magazines, toys and traditional practices. We are brainwashed from birth by idyllic representational values which present a cumulative foundation for both reflexive and instinctive reactions to rurality. Almost without realising, it seems, we learn to live out these knowledges in perception, attitude and practice. Country visions in this light become unthinking reproductions of received meaning, of hand-me-down identity, of acceptable practice and conventional attitude. And while it is all too easy to satirise and parody these aspects of the so-called idyll, it is very much more difficult to reject them altogether. As the geographical spaces of the coun-tryside in nations such as England become territorially confused, it is the *social* space of rurality – fuelled as it is by many of these idyllistic precepts – that is the centripetal force that continues to emphasise the attraction of the category 'rural' or 'countryside' in the discourses of everyday life. Representations of rurality remain a significant feature in the spatialisation of everyday discourse, and therefore remain a legitimate focus for investigation in rural studies.

However, the various visions and arguments expounded in this book deploy different properties to reach a common conclusion: we *must* go beyond cultural constructions of idyll in order to find new ways of knowing and under-standing rurality. There is some common ground here from which to launch dif-ferent visionary glimpses of the countryside. First, rurality is not homogeneous – different countrysides are different. Over time, rurality has been conflated with agriculture and forestry, natural beauty, representational scenery and settlements, and timeless values. In the British context, there is a world of dif-ference, however, between the 'metropolitan' ruralities in the green belts sur-rounding the major cities and remoter more peripheral ruralities. Cross-cutting these distinctions are others, identifying for example the 'differences' of Celtic nationhood in Wales and Scotland and the cultural and landscape specificities of, say, Yorkshire as opposed to East Anglia. Local-scale differences abound within these 'regions', and taken to the level of the individual it is clear that two people living next door to each other can offer totally different appreciations of 'their' countryside. Such contrasts are further exaggerated in spatially more diffuse nations such as the USA, where to suggest that rural New England is 'like' rural Iowa, or rural Texas, or rural California is to deny the essential intra- and inter-diversity of non-urban territories. Equally in many of these examples, the handed-down cultural precepts are far from idyllic. As Bell (1997) has shown, many of them are represented as settings for rural 'horror'.

Secondly, rural areas are dynamic not static. The seeming timelessness of the country is belied by the changes demanded by the globalised food industry, the increasing mobility of people and production, the niched fragmentation of consumption and the commodification of place. In some cases this has resulted in a blurring of the apparent boundaries between rural and urban. Cultural urbanisation covers most rural areas in the developed world. Out-of-town shopping malls bring the city into the country, while boutique urban villages do the opposite. The knowing introduction of specific flora and fauna into urban developments emphasises how nature can be brought into the city com-munity, while the development of self-contained retirement or 'sunset' com-munities in rural areas serves to manufacture city communities in the extensive spaces of nature. All this and more renders the rural–urban distinction indi-stinct. New regions focus on the hybrid relations between cities and surround-ing areas; new information technologies permit the traversing of time–space obstacles; new forms of counter-urbanisation result in spatial cross-dressing both by the arriving in and leaving of places.

Thirdly, the dystopic character of rural areas is being increasingly recogn-ised. The idea of idyllic rurality, with it own country voice with which to lobby for distinct rural futures, has tended to render invisible the seamier side of rural life. For example, the cultural constructions of rurality which associate rural England with some form of arcadian and pastoral idyll have exerted a pervasive yet obfuscatory influence over the ability of decision makers, urban residents and rural residents to recognise the existence of poverty in the midst of that idyll. Similar socio-cultural barriers exist to the recognition of homelessness in rural areas. In a recent study of rural homelessness in England, Paul Milbourne, Rebekah Widdowfield and I concluded:

> First, homelessness has been assumed in many key discourses to be spatialised and 'in place' in certain urban settings . . . Second, homelessness is assumed to be 'out-of-place' in certain kinds of rural spaces. Rural homelessness, therefore, represents a transgression where the doxa does not conform to the weight of the socio-economic expectations. Moreover, rural homelessness as transgression marks the boundary of in-place and out-of-place homelessness. Following Sibley, we can identify the countryside as a purified space where boundaries are policed and where the rejection of difference is embedded in the social system (Cloke *et al.* 2002, 74).

Knowing the rural through idyllic representations, then, not only hides social problems such as poverty and homelessness, but also establishes a political and cultural expectation of orthodoxy which actively seeks to purify rural space from transgressive presences and practices.

Notwithstanding these connections between idyllisation and the invisibility and impossibility of social problems in rural areas, the smiling 'happy face' mask of country living is beginning to slip. Crime and drug addiction, for example, are usually constructed as city problems, yet there is now a determined trickle of evidence that rural life is little different in these respects, even if some rural residents are (or want to portray themselves as) unaware or indifferent to these issues in their own back yard (Figure 1.1). Even more inescapable are the environmental disasters which have cropped up in rural areas. The foot and mouth epidemic which consumed much of rural Britain during 2001 was a stark reminder that the countryside has another (non-idyllic) face. Vivid imagery of the funeral pyres of culled livestock dominated the news media. Spaces normally used to escape from city life became no-go areas, as an ideology of right-to-roam in the countryside was transformed into a pragmatics of exclusion. As a result, previously 'idyllic' landscape scenes were stripped of their essential animal context, and hidden away from much public view, with disastrous consequences both for the rural economy and, temporarily, for rurality itself. Elsewhere in the developed world, rural areas are regularly beset by forest fires, tornadoes, drought and significant environmental pollution, each equally capable of bringing disaster to both the image and the practice of rural living.

The heterogeneous, dynamic and dystopic characteristics of rural areas (Figure 1.2) suggest a number of important questions about ways of knowing rurality. The risk of knowing the country through the medium of socio-cultural construction is that significant agency and practice will thereby be ignored. It

Figure 1.1 'Not so very pastoral' (Willson 1996).

Figure 1.2 A dystopic countryside: John Goto's 'Deluge' (Goto 2001).

is worth emphasising the truism that rural areas are not merely blank canvasses on which to paint socially constructed meanings. Indeed the heterogeneity of a particular area is integrally bound up in the co-constitutive agency of humans and non-humans. Rural areas are not just known differently, they are also performed differently. To know rurality, to understand the countryside, full account has to be taken of the embodied practices of people in relation to the potentially transformative agency of animals, plants, weather and technology. It is these networked comings-together that both bring characteristics to rural places, and indeed characterise these places.

The country and hybridity

Over recent years, social theorists have pursued two very important and inter-connecting themes in the reformulation of 'agency': the hybridity of relational agency; and the performance of embodied practice. In each case, there has been a deconstruction of previous dualistic thought. The first addresses the nature–culture binary. Donna Haraway, for example, in a seminal statement which combines eco-feminism and the sociology of scientific knowledge, has insisted that nature is a multi-dimensional tangle of the political economic, technical, textual, mythic and organic, involving actors 'who come in many and wonderful forms' (1991: 63). This observation has been influentially taken up in the formulation of Actor Network Theory (ANT) which recognises the agency of non-humans as well as humans as essential elements in how the natural and the social flow into one another. It is these mixtures of nature and culture – or hybrids – which permit agency to be viewed as being spun between different actants, rather than being manifest as some kind of solitary intent. These hybrids are mobilised and assembled into associative networks in which the collective capacity for human/non-human action is expressed.

ANT has provided an excellent framework for mapping the combined and networked agency of a collective of different actants. It has also provided a convincing account of how all manner of things constantly combine and recombine in the formation of the functioning world (Thrift 1999). It is less useful, however, in the recognition of how these coming-togethers can have qualities, or have qualities brought to them. To bring understanding to this idea of place-formation, and to related questions of how places are experi-enced, there has also been a turn to the notion of *dwelling* which describes the complex performative achievement of heterogeneous actors in relational settings in time and space – an embodied, co-constituted habitation of the human and the non-human (Ingold 2001; Jones and Cloke 2002).

The second theoretical reformulation of agency addresses the body–mind binary, asserting that the body is both active in the formulation of knowledge, and legitimate as a source of such knowledge, given that it is the body which represents the essential human capacity to animate and be active in the world.

Macnaghten and Urry (2001), for example, describe how embodied practices can co-relate with the natural terrain and weather conditions to produce performed agency in countryside places. These practices:

> happen in the 'outdoors', in the fresh air, where there is something about hot or cold or wet or dry 'air' that is thought particularly bracing or refreshing or rejuvenating. Such fresh air drives the body to do things or go to extremes that singularly contrast with some aspects of everyday life. Importantly, though, some of these practices become so central to people's lives that they in turn become their 'everyday', that is, when and where people actually feel at home on a wet hilltop . . . up a sheer rock face . . . on a nudist beach . . . when wandering through a dense wood . . . and so on (2001: 2).

The turn towards embodied practices and performance emphasises a being-in-the-world rather than a viewing of it. As such, there has been an interest both in conscious reflexive awareness, and in non-cognitive dimensions of embodiment. For example Edensor (2000) discusses walking as a reflexive practice, while Thrift suggests that walking can become

> a means to contact the Earth, to be at one with 'nature', even to be deemed therapeutic. It becomes a means of gathering stillness, without having to stay still, a means of contemplation and mystical communion to be found within the body (2000: 46).

Recognition of the embodied self, therefore, opens up ideas about places, countrysides, which can be known through embodied practice, both through time-deepened regular cohabitation, and in the fleeting, the momentary, the instinctive. The nature of rurality is seen as able to contextualise attempts to stimulate new corporeal sensibilities, and an approach which focuses on being-in-the-world can draw attention to the mystery, spirituality and ghostliness of rural places.

These theoretical accounts of hybrid ruralities offer substantially new country visions. The previous dominance of political–economic structures and socio-cultural constructions might be regarded as destabilised by any insistence that the primary focus should be on complex hybrid mixes of people, animals, plants and things. The non-human, or in-human, countryside assumes a greater importance in this scheme of things, and the concomitant emphasis on embodied practice makes for an intimate understanding of different ways of being in the hybrid countryside. Possibilities also arise here for greater sensitivity to the floating signifiers of nature and rurality – the sensuous or scary intimations of places, and their possibilities for becoming.

Ultimately, however, there are likely to be widely differing reactions to these theoretical moves. Some will want to reprise longstanding questions and set them against these different theoretical environments. For example, how does the recognition of hybridity and embodied practice help to address issues such as social exclusion or spatial purification? How do these different ways of knowing rurality suggest answers to issues of political or ethical priority?

How do they equip us to do anything about anything? These are simple but potentially critical questions. Clearly there will be some wish to superimpose socially motivated constructions back onto the complex hybrid world. ANT *has* pointed to potentially political and ethical processes of enrolment and mobilisation of particular networks. Is it possible to deploy this knowledge on behalf of the powerless? ANT has also highlighted the relational networks involving animals and plants. How does this help provide a suitable ethical framework for these relations? Dwelling has sponsored the imagination of a marvellously complex and interrelated world of co-constituted performance and place-making. How can this embodied, co-constituted habitation be used to help those who most need help? And how do we prioritise such need, especially given the widening of scope to include the non-human more fully in the analysis? It could be that these different ways of knowing the countryside can be used to point to its importance as a context of therapy, of self-fulfilment and of the stimulation of new corporeal sensibilities. Maybe the answers to these questions of powerlessness reside in the spiritual realm as well as the political world, and that an affect of some hybrid ruralities is to evoke just such spiritual riches. It seems inevitable, however, that in order to address these difficult questions, political and ethical constructions will have to be brought back into this picture of how rurality is known, and that other forms of hybridity – a hybridisation of different *theoretical* approaches to knowing the rural – will be necessary to complete the focus of being-in-the-world. Such theoretical hybridity offers an opportunity to make most use of those key ideas about the making of connections between worlds, and more completely to view the countryside as a means of performing difference.

Reading country visions

What follows is a collection of invited essays, each of which in some way tackling the question of how rurality, and its countrysides, can be known. There is no attempt here to bring together like-minded authors so as to develop a singular approach. Indeed, the book should be read as a series of glimpses into the nature of rural areas, each carrying a different understanding of what *can* be known, and what *should* be known. The difference of the rural is clearly highlighted in these essays. Authors bring different agendas and emphases to the book in their attempt to open out new knowledges and ways of knowing. Some write about research which has a rural focus. Others are using the rural to focus their research, finding in the countryside – its nature, its people, its places – a grounded inspiration for ideas, particularly around issues of embodiment, dwelling and performance. Yet others centre their interest on the natures to be found within the country rather than on rurality itself. Other differences will become equally apparent. Some authors insist on the necessity of new theorisation, while others are more content to be patiently critical of existing theoretical under-standings. Some access the country via cultural representations in maps, books and films. For others it is practices and performances which characterise rurality, and bring characteristics to it. Together, the essays mark a polymorphous inter-vention into debates about rural areas. They beg questions about how to read, analyse and write about the country; they challenge conventional wisdoms about how to think about and categorise rurality. And in the end they raise, some-times implicitly, crucial questions about the heterogeneity of the countryside, how it works for its actors and how it might work better in the future.

The book is organised into three groups of essays, the first of which opens out different ways in which the country is represented and envisioned. Ways of know-ing here suggest action metaphors for knowledge – reproducing, gazing, map-ping, representing and viewing the rural. Michael Bunce (Chapter 2) addresses the reproduction of rural idylls, suggesting that the values that sustain the rural idyll indicate a profound and universal human need for connection with land, nature and community. As people become increasingly separated from these experiences, the psychology of connection, and lost connection, emerges as a nostalgic construction of rurality which acts as a foundation for sustaining images and attitudes which impinge on its current social, economic and environmental role. Bunce rejects any assumption of a monolithic rural idyll, but argues that the many different rural idylls converge around a normative, nostalgic, over-arching ideal which is firmly bedded in social and economic structures.

The socio-economic embeddedness of constructions of rurality is taken up as a theme by Simone Abram in Chapter 3. She argues the existence of a system-atised 'gaze' which represents the social organisation of the concept of 'rural', and which determines much of the contemporary politics of development in rural areas. However, at the same time she problematises this gaze, showing how different organised views of rurality serve to empower and disempower different actors. Abram grounds these themes in a study of a village in rural Buckinghamshire, tracing the specificity of the gaze to place(s), and suggesting that the everyday local commentary on people's surroundings is a significant contributor to the conjuring into existence, maintenance and reproduction of a particular regard for the rural. This localised prompting of the 'gaze' is a neglected but crucial element in the generation of constructions of rurality, for where there are mismatched notions of local rural space, the contestation of the gaze can provoke sustained and often bitter political controversies over land use and development.

Catherine Brace (Chapter 4) explores the generation of a particular country vision in a discussion of the literal and symbolic mapping of rural England in the 1920s and 1930s. In her unpacking of these mappings, she shows how con-temporary ideas about the countryside are deeply embedded in the past, and how contemporary ways of knowing and imagining rurality are replete with historical ideas, images and motifs. Using a detailed study of representations of the Cotswolds, she demonstrates how the depicted landscapes both provide a shape and a substance to the imagined community of the English nation, and present exemplars of moral order and aesthetic harmony. The current meanings and ideologies which are culturally attached to the countryside, she argues, are often predicated on just such (taken for granted) ideas about rural England, which have a provenance and a history which require careful, political, scrutiny.

In a study of the storybooks produced for children in post-war Britain, **John Horton** (Chapter 5) also emphasises an enduring, even stubborn presence of countryside ideas and ideals, such that many of the most durable and stereo-typed representations of the countryside can be traced to the literatures of childhood, and by implication of parenthood, when old classics are reread, and new literatures encountered through the process of reading to the next generation of children. Yet Horton shows how these supposedly enduring ideas actually represent a continual flux of representation, as at different times and within different genres, different stocks of representations/texts/images have been made available constituting particular parameters through which differ-ent generations are enabled to envision countryside differently.

Difference in representational meaning is not merely temporal. In Chapter 6, **Mark Lawrence** draws clear distinctions between American and British visions of rurality drawn from the translation of Jane Austen's novels as films. He shows how the complexes of meaning in the films orbit themselves in simula-tions rather than re-presenting the reality of places, thus overwriting the real with the hyperreal by organising thoughts and responses around codes of recognition, behaviour and judgement that are detached from the specific referent. Jane Austen's novels position the reader/viewer somewhere between the subtlety of lived experience and its disappearance in the simulations of her settings when adapted to film. The films are productive of a permanently liminal state of an incessantly self-absorbed present, and this Lawrence argues, presents very considerable challenges in recognising, and heeding neglected voices in the countryside.

The second group of essays addresses a range of ways by which the country-side can be known and understood through practice and performance, by embodying, performing, spiriting, sexing and adventuring. What these chapters have in common is a desire to move beyond representation in order better to gain purchase on what it is to know, experience, understand and perform differ-ent ruralities. **Deborah Dixon** (Chapter 7) takes as her theme the embodied work practices of women crab pickers in Eastern Carolina. She shows how, for both tourists and residents, it is the performance of bodily practices that animates the landscape, and the ways in which the working women invest mean-ing in their embodied practices emphasises the importance of lived experience in the knowing of place and people. Her analysis also clearly demonstrates the links between bodies and the economic structure which is capitalism, drawing attention to the inequalities which are maintained through the processes by which identities are constructed and bodies are shaped. Activities in the Eastern Carolina crab houses are both gendered and racialised, to the detriment of par-ticular individuals. By bringing to light the bodies of women crab pickers, Dixon looks beyond the tourist gaze on rurality and traces their absence from other, more readily accessible representations of people and place. She also traces how their presence invests both local and wider space with different embodied meanings and animations.

John Wylie bases Chapter 8 on a fleeting visit to Glastonbury Tor in Somerset, in order to illustrate the possibilities of writing performatively about (rural) landscape, and to present a critical grounded exploration of ideas of dwelling. He articulates a theoretical shift from knowing a landscape by viewing it, to knowing a landscape by being in it. Landscape is thus a milieu of involvement, although Wylie argues against any new binarism between vision and embodiment which risks defining the body as somehow non-visual. He also insists that dwelling be regarded as the milieu for material cultures and ways of being that are productive of multiple spatialities and temporalities – it must enable the register of the transient and the fleeting as well as the enduring.

Glastonbury is also the subject of **Julian Holloway**'s enthnography of spiritual seekers (Chapter 9). He explores how this part of rural Somerset is represented and practised as a sacred space, with the surrounding landscape believed to hold mystic energies, and the space being constructed, perceived and sensed through a range of embodied practices. Holloway deploys non-representational theorisation to acknowledge how the alternative spiritual community of Glastonbury is produced through affective and sensual embodied relations. He suggests that rural landscapes are increasingly becoming spaces for the enactment of these alternative spiritual lifestyles. However, this spirituality is more than just a question of visiting the countryside in order to consume its sacred benefits. What the Glastonbury study suggests is a search for a re-enchanted embodied corporeality that apprehends rural space as sacred without recourse to representation, myth or symbolism.

David Bell's account of male same-sex desire in the USA (Chapter 10) also explores issues of embodied practice in rural settings. He presents four different scene/sites in which particular embodiments of male homosexuality interconnect with distinct constructions of rurality, and demonstrates how the material and discursive constructions of 'homosexuality' and 'rural' come together in complex and sometimes contrary ways. Bell describes two intertwined motifs: the *homosexual rural*, denoting an idyllic place in the homosexual imagination, and the *rural homosexual*, indicating the embodied life experiences of men with same-sex desires who come from and/or live in rural places. These motifs are densely woven together, their weave suggesting lives lived at the complex intersection of the material and the symbolic.

Finally in this group of chapters, **Carl Cater** and **Louise Smith** (Chapter 11) explore the commodification of rural places as space of adventurous activity. Their approach is to advocate a more active, embodied and sensuous understanding of the consumption of the countryside. They direct attention, therefore, both to the commodification of rural places, and to different ways in which spaces can be opened out so that particular activities can be intelligently informed. Cater and Smith base their studies on Queenstown, New Zealand, the self-styled 'adventure capital of the world'. They show how the hosts, the tourists and the town itself perform to commodified roles, and how adventurous embodied practices offer new ways of accessing nature within and outwith us. Such re-connections have the potential to challenge dominant views of the countryside, presenting instead both a contested zone which is open to multiple experiences, interpretations and behaviours, and a contested construction of the body. Beyond the idea of the body as a compliant receiving receptacle there is potential for new and less restricted forms of pleasure in the countryside.

The third group of chapters specifically addresses the issue of providing newly envisioned ways of proceeding with studies of the rural. There is a wide range of perspectives here. **David Sibley** (Chapter 12) writes on the psychogeographies of space, exclusion and rurality. He explores some of the tensions between mobile 'othered' groups, and those who construct static and bounded understandings of the English and Welsh countrysides; tensions which underpin the production of exclusionary geographies of the rural. In his study of how mobile groups such as gypsies and asylum seekers are rejected by rural communities, he detects a determination to cling to a vision of rural space as homogeneous and harmonious – a vision which as he points out has never existed in anything other than symbolic terms. Anxieties are betrayed by such spatial categorisations, thus achieving a 'splitting' of things and spaces which need to be re-connected if social justice objectives are to be achieved. Sibley argues that there is still much to know about these split ruralities.

Another potential vision for the knowing of the rural is discussed by **Cynthia Anderson** and **Michael Bell** in Chapter 13. They chart the meteoric rise of 'social capital' as a way both of recognising the value of social relations and of envisioning ways of improving the quality of life in rural communities. Anderson and Bell present a strong critique of the conceptualisation and practice of social capital. In their view, the concept calls attention to real and important phenomena, but its significance is exaggerated as a means by which a remedy can be found for major social problems. They warn against making a pact with the devil by adopting economistic language and knowledge which potentially reinforces the very cultural trends that researchers have long sought to intervene with and change. We need always to be wary, they indicate, of damning ourselves with our own good intentions.

Similar concerns have not yet beset the recent initiatives in the study and understanding of rural governance. As **Michael Woods** and **Mark Goodwin** point out in Chapter 14, the theorisation of rural policy and governance has proved both fruitful and influential in the current dynamism of rural studies. Their chapter reviews key changes both in rural government and policy, and in the ways in which these changes have been made sense of. As they observe, concepts such as regulation, governance and governmentality have been *applied to* rural concepts rather than being *developed within* them. The danger, then, is that somehow 'urban' ideas will be imported to somehow 'rural' situations. The opportunity, however, is for rural studies to contribute to the further development of these theorisations. In both cases, the call from Woods and Goodwin is for rural researchers to engage more directly with the original theoretical writings on governance and regulation, and in so doing to exploit the possibilities offered by rural areas as laboratories for innovative and influential work on governance and policy.

In Chapter 15 Jonathan Murdoch envisions how the countryside can be co-constructed from knowledges of hybrid networks and the extensive self. He demonstrates a new way of talking about the rural and the countryside – a discursive mode which combines 'social' and 'natural' perspectives in order to know the rural as a hybrid space which mixes up social and natural entities in creative combinations. Rurality, therefore, is also hybridity, co-constructed by humans and non-humans, bound together within complex interrelationships. Moreover this hybrid countryside is defined by networks in which heterogeneous entities are aligned in a variety of ways, giving rise to slightly different country*sides*. Murdoch's argument, then, is that there is no single vantage point from which the whole panoply of rural relations can be seen. However, it is still possible to talk about *social* constructions of the countryside, just as it is still sensible to discuss rural *natures*. The countryside continues to be shaped by social processes, it is just that these processes are more than just social. Equally the shaping by natural processes is more than just natural. Social identity, then, is realised through linkages with heterogeneous entities.

Owain Jones in Chapter 16 envisions a countryside which is known, at least in part, in terms of the geographies of the relational agency of animals. He illustrates how animals are integrally bound up with cultural formations of the rural, but that the embodied presence of these animals is often hidden from analyses of rurality. Jones acknowledges the strides made by deploying ANT to the relational agency of human and non-human actants, but expresses concerns about how the natures, roles and fates of animals are conceptualised within ANT. He argues for a reconceptualisation of animal presences and geoethics through the idea of dwelling, which permits an encounter with the 'otherness' of animals, and especially with the ways in which they dwell in creative ways which are outside human enrolment and often in conflict with human-centred networks. The significance of interweaving rurality and animality will depend on the ability to account for these othernesses of animals, the (un)ethical geographies of the interrelations concerned, and the ways in which animals dwell benignly or bitterly in the rural context.

Finally, **Nigel Thrift** (Chapter 17) offers a view of the nature of rurality which escapes the pitfalls of representational thinking. He presents nature as a complex virtuality to be experienced through contemplative practices which allow an expansion of the awareness of present time and place/space. In particular he points to the mystical qualities of nature which can be nurtured as part of a larger political project to renovate and value bare life through immersive body practices. Thrift's approach exposes the 'moment' of nature, and suggests that inhabitation of the moment can be a significant re-embodying of nature; he warns that capitalist super-nature can tune our bodies to an economy of naturalised experiences, but offers hope that heightened participation in bare life can also occur in the myriad activities which exist at the edge of the economic system, thereby offering an alternative biopolitics of considerable relevance for the future consideration of the embodied countryside.

The essays in *Country Visions* remind us that rurality can only ever be a partly connected multiplicity which can be known only partially and from multiple standpoints and experiences. Rather than being seen homogeneously from one particular viewpoint, the countryside needs to be pieced together, recognising the heterogeneous networks and dwellings which constantly realign and become in a variety of ways, resulting in changing and different country-sides. Embodied practices criss-cross and characterise these forms. Social constructions zoom overhead, bringing political and ethical frameworks which may or may not connect with the ethical sensibilities of corporeal performance. The hope is that the chapters of *Country Visions* will open out the knowledge of significant agency, practice and performance in and of the rural. Perhaps these chapters will also bring to the fore the need for more significant and subtle interconnection between more 'knowing' ruralities, and other important knowledges relating, say, to the politics of social and natural justice, and the ethics of otherness and difference.

References

Bell, D. 1997 'Anti-idyll: rural horror', pp. 94–108 in P. Cloke and J. Little (eds), *Contested Countryside Cultures*, Routledge, London.

Cloke, P., Milbourne, P. and Widdowfield, R. 2002 *Rural homelessness*, Policy Press, Bristol.

Edensor, T. 2000 'Walking in the British countryside: reflexivity, embodied practices and ways to escape', *Body and Society*, 6, 81–106.

Goto, J. 2001 'High Summer', *Portfolio: The Catalogue of Contemporary Photography in Britain*, 33, 4–11. (Goto's series of photographs can be viewed at *www.johngoto.org.uk*.)

Haraway, D. 1991 *Simians, Cyborgs and Women: The Reinvention of Nature*, Chapman and Hall, New York.

Ingold, T. 2001 *The Perception of the Environment: Essays on Livelihood, Dwelling and Skill*, Routledge, London.

Jones, O. and Cloke, P. 2002 *Tree Cultures: The Place of Trees and Trees in Their Place*, Berg, Oxford.

Macnaghten, P. and Urry, J. 2001 'Bodies of nature: introduction', pp. 1–11 in P. Macnaghten and J. Urry (eds), *Bodies of Nature*, Sage, London.

Thrift, N. 1999 'Steps to an ecology of place', pp. 295–322 in D. Massey and J. Allen (eds), *Human Geography Today*, Polity Press, Cambridge.

Thrift, N. 2000 'Still life in nearly present time: the object of nature', *Body and Society*, 6, 34–57.

Willson, R. 1996 'Not so very pastoral', *The Times*, 2 January.

CHAPTER 2

Reproducing rural idylls

Michael Bunce

In late May of 2000, reports began to emerge of *Escherichia coli* contamination of the water supply in Walkerton, an Ontario rural community. As the consequent seven deaths and widespread illness became national headlines, what appeared to shock people beyond the fact of the tragedy itself was that it occurred in a rural area. As *Maclean's*, Canada's national news magazine, put it:

> A picturesque farming community . . . nestled among the rolling hills of south-western Ontario, Walkerton does not look like the sort of place where a deadly pollutant would strike . . . the sparkling Saugeen River meanders through the town and surrounding countryside, a popular region for such recreational activities as fishing and canoeing. Elsewhere, on the area's prosperous looking farms, dairy and beef cattle contentedly graze. Ironically, that bucolic beauty may be at the root of Walkerton's problems; investigators suspect run-off from cattle manure as a possible source of the *E.coli* in the water (Wickens 2000: 34).

Picturesque, farming, community, recreational, bucolic: these are the words of the conventional rural idyll, of the aesthetics of pastoral landscapes, of humans working in harmony with nature and the land and with each other, of a whole scene of contentment and plenty. Applied to Walkerton (which in fact is a fairly ordinary Ontario small town set in a typically functional agricultural landscape, in which cattle are more likely to be in intensive feedlots than contentedly grazing) the language intentionally romanticises the setting to emphasise the sense of threat to rural peace and harmony. But beyond this it assumes that these are the images of rurality with which the average *Maclean's* reader would readily identify. This is hardly surprising because these are also the images which have become so culturally embedded that to describe the real Walkerton would be to challenge the whole history of the rural idyll, and of its significance in shaping the idealisation of countryside in Anglo-American and probably western culture in general. In other words this is how we would expect to see a rural place described, especially when it is in trouble.

There has been such an active discourse in recent years about the role of the rural idyll in shaping contemporary visions of countryside (Bunce 1994; Halfacree 1995; Little and Austin 1996; Mingay 1989; Short 1991; Williams 1973), that the immediate question with which I was confronted in writing this chapter, especially as one of the participants in this discourse, was, what more is there to be said? Well, the *Maclean's* article partially answers that question. Here we are at the beginning of the twenty-first century, with a dominantly urban readership – well-educated, electronically connected, lifestyle-oriented consumers, well aware of how the world is rapidly changing – still clinging to an old symbolic imagery of the rural world. What, if anything, does it signify about the contemporary strength of the rural idyll? How is the rural idyll being reproduced in contemporary culture and what does this imply for the future of rural spaces? Is the idyllic vision becoming universal or should we still be talking, as Cloke *et al.* (1997) have suggested, of a diversity of idylls? Where does it fit into the dynamics of rural–urban relations, and of class, gender and ethnicity? And, finally, in the context of rural disasters such as Walkerton, to what extent is it challenged and reinforced by the realities of rural life?

One simple answer to all these questions could be that the values that sustain the rural idyll speak of a profound and universal human need for connection with land, nature and community, a psychology which, as people have become increasingly separated from these experiences, reflects the literal meaning of nostalgia; the sense of loss of home, of homesickness (Harrison 1982). Tuan has argued that it can also be explained by the essentialism of binary opposition in our lives: life/death, day/night, home/away, mountain/valley, country/city. As urban civilisations reached their zenith the sense of city and country dichotomies became heightened and the sentimental pendulum swung in favour of the country (Tuan 1974). Add to this the thesis that countryside satisfies basic spiritual needs and that its landscapes stand as metaphors for associations buried deep in our memories (Schama 1996) and the rural idyll becomes a natural and therefore inescapable response to the rise of urban civilisation and the separation from daily rural experience that this establishes.

The rural idyll in the rise of urban-industrialism

Nostalgia for pastoral golden ages, the essence of the Theocritan Idylls, is as old as civilisation itself and has proved to be remarkably durable (Williams 1973). Yet this very point reveals that it is also a product of the material changes that have accompanied urbanisation – the establishment of distinct entities of country and city, and the changing socio-economic relations that accompanied this – as well as of the culture of civilisation which could express and manipulate the values that sustain the rural idyll. It is through the complex interaction between these processes over the past three centuries or so that the countryside has come to acquire the symbolic status as the idyllic alternative to urban environments that it now enjoys.

So we are not just dealing with an instinctive reaction against urbanisation but, in the first instance, with sentiments that could only have emerged in the material conditions of the rise of urban-industrialism itself. These produced the social structures and political-economies that redefined rural–urban relations and attitudes to countryside. The massive movement of the labouring classes from the countryside which sustained urbanisation in Britain and North America in the past two centuries involved the substitution of the natural rhythms of farm work and country life with the time and work discipline of the factory system. The reciprocity of the rural community was replaced by the individualism of the urban market place and complete separation from land and nature. However, while this shift from *gemeinschaft* to *gesellschaft* living may have fostered some nostalgia for countrysides left behind, this has to be set against the generally harsh realities of rural life that were abandoned.

The principal contribution of the new proletariat to the countryside ideal is a more indirect one. Its formation was part of a complete realignment of the class system. In Britain, and especially England, it not only solidified the position of the old landed gentry, but it also supported a new bourgeoisie which sought to establish its social status by separating itself from the urban working classes by imitating the lifestyle of the country gentry. Most of the English countryside as it is idealised today was created by the process of enclosure and gentrification which accompanied the spread of landed estates. From this emerged a rural landscape in which the preservation of social status and the creation of landscapes of leisure established perfect conditions for cultivation of the rural idyll. And as the working population left rural areas in growing numbers, the countryside became even more amenable to appreciation for its scenic virtues and for its sense of timeless social order.

The impact of industrialism on North American rural landscapes was quite different. While it supported a bourgeoisie which could set the standards of taste and lifestyle, its effect on rural landscapes was dominated by the progressive and egalitarian ideology of the pioneering yeoman farmer and of the commercial small town (Lemon 1972). And so the landscapes around which any rural idyll could gather were those of the family farm and the productive yet virtuous agrarian economy it sustained. Added to the scale and diversity of North American rural landscapes, this has largely prevented the establishment of any of that sense of an archetypal and universal countryside which is the object of the English rural idyll.

While these contrasts in the rural landscapes that were forged out of the rise of urbanism and industrialism are important in explaining the differences between English and North American idylls (a point to which I return later in the chapter), on both sides of the Atlantic the cultural construction of the rural idyll has followed more convergent lines. In the first place it is important to recognise that it was the new bourgeoisie in the eighteenth century that formed the core of an increasingly educated society, whose attitudes to nature and landscape, reactions to urban environments, in fact their social and aesthetic values in general, were informed by the swirl of intellectual ideas and cultural expression which accompanied the rise of industrialism. Between the middle of the eighteenth and throughout the nineteenth centuries, the fundamental shifts in the understanding and appreciation of nature, the intellectual reappraisal of industrial progress, the philosophy of agrarianism, and the values of romanticism combined to place rural life and landscape on an ideological pedestal.

All this occurred in the context of a huge growth in demand for what today we would call 'culture'. From the mid-eighteenth century onwards, there was a rapid growth in the reading public, stimulated both by the increase in the educated and leisure classes and by innovations in the technology of publishing. This resulted in a radical change in the place of writers and artists in society, who could now reach a wider public (Williams 1960); a literate and culture-conscious middle-class which, from the comfort of its country estates and urban villas, readily consumed an expanding body of literature and art which drew on various versions of the rural idyll.

Underpinning the cultural reproduction of this idyll was a political and philosophical discourse about industrial capitalism itself which dominated the nineteenth century and which has had a remarkably durable influence on thinking about country and city ever since (Coleman 1973; White and White 1962; Williams 1973). In the first instance this was expressed in the broad critique of industrialism, modernism and the general ideology of material progress. From Robert Southey's repeated condemnation of the conditions of the industrial city (Coleman 1973) and William Cobbett's characterisation of London as a 'pestiferous growth' on an otherwise harmonious rural landscape (Cobbett 1912: 43), to John Ruskin's (1866), William Morris's (1891) and Ebenezer Howard's (1898) judgement of Victorian urbanism as aesthetic, social and environmental failures, the intellectual climate of nineteenth century Britain invariably compared the city unfavourably with the countryside. Across the Atlantic, Thomas Jefferson's warnings against the reproduction of the industrial city in the new republic had a profound influence on an enduring American intellectual rejection not only of the city as social organism but also as a threat to democratic stability (White and White 1962).

Anti-urban and therefore pro-rural sentiment, however, was sustained by deeper anxieties about industrialism and modernism which have survived to the present day. One of the central dialectics of modern civilisation, it is a debate which, at its highest philosophical level, sets the ideology of industrial capitalism against that of nature and human spirituality. As industrial capitalism has tightened its grip on life and landscape philosophical doubts have prevailed. In 1830, Thomas Carlyle advanced ideas about the oppressive effects of industrialism which were taken up across the Atlantic by Emerson and with even more enthusiasm by the great guru of modern environmentalism, Henry Thoreau, whose celebrated retreat to the Concord woods symbolised his outright repudiation of the culture of technology (Thoreau 1854). The rejection of industrialism reaches its zenith at the turn of the century in the radical anti-industrialism of William Morris and the Arts and Crafts Movement. 'The leading passion of my life', wrote Morris, 'is a hatred of modern civilisation' (Morris 1891). This is a sentiment which resurfaces again and again throughout the twentieth century in increasingly radical attacks on the whole fabric of industrial capitalism (Shi 1985) from the technocratic dystopias of Orwell and Huxley to the critiques of Daniel Bell and Theodore Roczak.

The alternative for Morris was in the pre-industrial Utopia of *News From Nowhere* (1891), another version of the old Golden Age myth which becomes the ideological counterpoint to industrialism and modernism. And so the rural idyll is also nurtured against a philosophical backdrop of agrarianism and pre-industrialism which praises the virtues of farming and rural traditions. Various strands of agrarianism run as a virtually continuous thread through North American discourses of rurality. From the Jeffersonian idealisation of farmers as the chosen people of God and the foundation of a democratic society to the romantic agrarianism of contemporary proponents of the traditional family farm like Wendell Berry (1977), agrarian sentiment is deeply rooted in American and to a lesser extent Canadian culture (Montmarquet 1989). American agrarian ideology has been closely associated with the Puritan belief in the virtues of simple rural life as against the greed and cosmopolitanism of the city. Presidential candidates are still fond of referring to their farm and rural roots as evidence of their virtuousness. While the British idyll has tended not to include the ideal of the working farm, it has nevertheless been strongly influenced by a broader philosophy of rural traditionalism. While the American version of this is underpinned by Thoreauvian-inspired idealisation of rural simplicity (Shi 1985), British, or rather English, values are embedded in an intellectual nostalgia for an old rural England which becomes the essence of the country itself.

Whether or not, as Martin Wiener (1981) has suggested, the views of Morris and his fellow anti-modernists reflect an ingrained English distrust of the whole notion of industrial progress remains debatable. Yet, what is clear is that the values of the late Victorian and Edwardian English establishment were influenced as much by the writings of conservatives such as G.K. Chesterton and Hilaire Belloc as by the radicalism of Morris. Wiener attributes the attachment to the English countryside primarily to the gentrification of the middle class and its absorption into the conservative value system of the landed gentry. Mixed with the Arts and Crafts-inspired revivalism of country crafts and traditions, this suffused the values of Edwardianism with the belief that the real heart of England lay in a countryside where the old social order and the old ways of doing things could still be found. This became part of the political rhetoric of the nation, the country worth fighting for in both World Wars (Ecksteins 1990) was the England, as Stanley Baldwin was fond of saying, of 'the tinkle of the hammer on the anvil in the country smith, the corncrake on a dewy morning, the sound of the scythe against the whetstone, and the sight of the plough team coming over the brow of the hill . . . for centuries the one eternal sight of England' (Baldwin 1926: 7).

What is remarkable about this way of thinking is how culturally embedded it is. While the specific images may have changed, the general attachment to the idea of the countryside as the real country because it is symbolic of old orders and ways remains strong. The same can be said of agrarianism and its associated extollation of rural life in North America where recurrent stories of collapsing farm economies invoke nostalgic responses for the family farm and the rural community.

With the intellectual renaissance that accompanied the rise of western industrialism also came a rethinking about human relations with the natural world which had a profound influence on the valuation of the countryside. In the eighteenth century, led by the writings of Hume, Kant and Rousseau, new understandings about the interdependency of humans and nature emerged. These were accompanied by a growing interest in natural history. By the early twentieth century the journeys of Alexander von Humboldt and Charles Darwin shed new light on the workings of the natural world. Accompanying the shift towards greater ecological knowledge was a growing appreciation of nature's significance for the human experience. Nature took on sublime qualities, a philosophy that flourished in the rise of romanticism. An explicit reaction against the forces of rational science and economics, the romantic movement saw nature as a spiritual and aesthetic refuge, a restorative for the human soul (Frye 1967). Expressed in the enduring legacy of the English romantic poets – Coleridge, Clare, Blake and, above all, Wordsworth – and in the paintings of the landscape school, the values of romanticism coincided perfectly with the undercurrents of anti-urbanism and rural nostalgia to reinvoke the imagery of the rural idyll and to place it firmly in a picturesque countryside. In the New World a growing nineteenth century reverence for 'untamed' wilderness drew directly on European romanticism, but also took off in transcendentalist directions with the writings of Emerson, Thoreau and John Muir (Nash 1967). But on both sides of the Atlantic, romanticism served to elevate nature to sacred status (Tuan 1974). With new ecological understanding and new perceptions of its inspirational powers the natural world came to be viewed from then on not only as the salvation for the alienating conditions of industrialism, but also as the defining essence of the rural environment. There is a direct line between this and modern environmentalism, which seeks to defend the countryside as the last depository of nature.

Images of rural

The discourses of anti-urbanism, agrarianism and nature that emerged in the nineteenth century have shown remarkable durability, gathering particular strength as the evidence of the failures of the urban industrial system mounted during the twentieth century. My argument here is that, to understand the endurance of the rural idyll, we must recognise the subtle influence of the ideas of these discourses on how people think about the rural. They are the foundation for the cultural construction of the rural idyll, the bedrock for sustaining popular images of the countryside and attitudes to its social, economic and environmental role.

The second chapter of my book *The Countryside Ideal* (Bunce 1994) is entitled 'The Armchair Countryside'. In selecting this title I set out to capture the idea of countryside as something that successive generations have appreciated from the comfort of their urban and suburban homes rather than from direct rural experiences. In the chapter I emphasise three main literary and artistic streams that have served to construct and re-construct mental images of countryside: the green language of the pastoral and picturesque, country life literature and children's literature.

'Green Language' is Raymond Williams's (1973) apt term for the long stream of English pastoral poetry and literature which reaches its zenith in the Victorian rural idyll, but which survives to this day as a popular element of Anglo-American culture (Finch and Elder 1990). Drawn in direct line from the Theocritan and Virgilian Idylls, this becomes the language of the Elizabethan pastorals of Spenser and Sidney which then mutates into nature poetry of Pope, Dyer, Thomson and Cowper in the eighteenth century. A poetic genre which was strongly influenced by the emerging values of the sublime and the picturesque, it is a probably best epitomised by James Thomson's poem 'The Seasons', which for its description of the *natural* tranquillity of the Georgian countryside became a bestseller on both sides of the Atlantic for decades after its publication in 1730 (Hart 1950). Eighteenth century poetry and art combined to foster a public enthusiasm for pastoral landscapes, but it was with the rise of pastoral romanticism that the poetic and artistic celebration of nature captured the public imagination. In all of this there is no escaping the dominant figure of Wordsworth whose celebrations of both the wilder landscapes of the Lake District and the cosier versions of nature set in the landscapes of lowland England not only attracted a huge readership at the time but also became the abiding image of the English countryside for generations to follow.

Wordsworthian imagery is reinforced by a Victorian idyllic tradition which presented a vision of an English countryside of woods, wildflowers, grassy-banks and birdsong. An escapist view of places where modern civilization had not yet reached, it is epitomised in Tennyson's *English Idylls* and by the supremely nostalgic descriptions of Robert Browning in 'Home-thoughts, from Abroad' in which England was an April morning of budding elms and chirping chaffinches on orchard boughs (Hunter 1984). This poetic landscape imagery was matched by the idyllic scenes of water-colourists such as Millais and Holman Hunt whose prints were not only in great demand for living room walls but also illustrated volumes of poetry.

Given the dominance of British settlement, it is not surprising that the English idyll was very popular across the Atlantic (Hart 1950). However, while nineteenth century North American readers enjoyed the imagery of Wordsworth and Tennyson, they were also served an expanding menu of home-grown idylls. Beginning with William Cullen Bryant in the 1820s and culminating over a century later in Robert Frost. American nature poetry has fostered many of the prevailing images of the North American countryside (Stauffer 1974). Bryant's celebrations of the American wilderness combined with the prodigious output of the painters of the American picturesque, led by Thomas Cole, and initiated a successive stream of nature poetry in the works of Emerson, Emily Dickinson and Walt Whitman. But it is Robert Frost who is, without doubt, the best known of all American nature poets (and probably the best remembered of all American poets). His enduring popularity owes much to his portrayal of the rustic wooded landscapes of New England.

The imagery of nature and of natural yet domesticated settings – the essence of the rural idyll – is an enduring theme in English and North American art and literature (Keith 1974, 1980). It surfaces again and again in the poetry and art of the twentieth century: in the Edwardian romanticism of Edward Thomas, in the poems of Robert Frost, in the depictions of Canadian wilderness by the Group of Seven painters.

Running through the long span of nature writing is a lingering sense of potential loss, a valuation of real experiences and a nostalgia for the connections that have been broken. But, if, as many have argued, nostalgia is the essence of the rural idyll, then it is in the depictions of country life that it reaches its peak. In the construction of the English rural idyll this has been dominated by the repetition of images of old social hierarchies. From the country house novels of Jane Austen (see Chapter 6) to the squirearchical world of Anthony Trollope, the portrayal of the English countryside through the lifestyles and residential landscapes of the gentry has retained its popularity to the present day through movies and TV serialisations. This is the England of the country house, the county town and the village, occupied by a contented society which still clung to the old ways and the old rules. This is also the England of Constable, whose portraits of an English rural garden populated by a contented peasantry engaged in rustic tasks has become the derivation for all subsequent sentimentalised pictorial portrayals of the English countryside. And it is the same England of conservative Edwardian writers such as Kipling, Hilaire Belloc and Ford Madox Ford who linked national character with ancient rural virtue (Wiener 1981), a recurrently reassuring myth in turbulent times. In the inter-war period, the fabrication of this myth of a 'timeless realm' (Keith 1988: 130) had become so dominant that it prompted Stella Gibbons to write *Cold Comfort Farm*, an anti-idyll directed satirically at the rural nostalgia of the times.

Central to much of the popular sentimentalisation of English country life has been the village. Hilaire Belloc believed that the true heart of England was the village (Wiener 1981), a sentiment that has been fostered by a seemingly endless output of illustrated volumes about English villages and by the caricatures of village life popularised by H.E. Bates (*The Darling Buds of May*), Laurie Lee (*Cider with Rosie*) and the pseudonomous 'Miss Read'. But for the reproduction of contemporary nostalgia for village life, the most influential medium is radio and television. From the seemingly endlessly-running BBC radio programme, 'The Archers' ('an everyday story of countryfolk') to TV series such as 'All Creatures Great and Small' and 'Heartbeat', the English village soap-opera has a huge following (Phillips *et al.* 2001) which extends across the Atlantic where it fits perfectly with North American romantic stereotypes of the English countryside.

It also fits with the pervading nostalgia of North American country life literature itself. From the early nineteenth century on it is dominated by the mythology of agrarian simplicity and virtue, a theme that is popularised in women's magazines from the *Lady's Book* to *Harpers* which delivered a steady stream of stories set in the cosy world of farm and small town America. From the early twentieth century novels about country folk, the most popular of which must be *Rebecca of Sunnybrook Farm* and Gene Stratton Porter's series of country life idylls, to the romanticisations of pioneer life in TV serials such as 'The Waltons' and 'Little House on the Prairie', the sentimentalisation of the struggle of honest folk on the frontier has made a powerful contribution to the myth of manifest destiny and therefore to the American dream.

Underlying this is a lingering nostalgia for some imagined ideal rural community set somewhere in a post-pioneer past. The most enduring example of this is Canadian rather than American: *Anne of Green Gables*, Lucy Maud Montgomery's story first published in 1908 of a young orphan girl growing up on a farm in late nineteenth century Prince Edward Island. In the countless reissues of the original novel and its seven sequels, as well as the stage and screen adaptations this piece of rural nostalgia has not only become embedded in the Canadian perception of countryside (Prince Edward Island promotes itself this way), but is also enormously popular among Japanese and South Korean readers!

Although popular with adults, *Anne of Green Gables*, like Gene Stratton Porter's novels, were really aimed at a younger readership and so fit into that broader stream of childhood armchair countrysides. This is discussed by John Horton in Chapter 5 so I will not devote much space to it here. Suffice it to say that through what they read, generations of children have absorbed images of a countryside occupied by a variety of anthropomorphised wild and farm animals, of an environmental benign farming overseen by jolly farmers and their wives, and of happy children enjoying free-roaming adventures in fields and woods in which the countryside often transforms into an imaginary place (the latest version of this being the *Harry Potter* novels).

Contemporary communication and reproduction of the rural idyll

In this chapter and in other writings I have emphasised the depth and durability of the rural idyll as a cultural construction which has evolved with the rise of urban-industrialism. That the long history of intellectual, literary and art-istic abstraction of rural life and landscape has embedded idyllic mental images of the rural in Anglo-American civilisation is no longer a matter a debate. What remain debatable and, until recently, largely unaddressed, are questions sur-rounding the contemporary strength and influence of the rural idyll. In the first instance this is a question about how the cultural construction of this idyll translates into values and actions which determine how people will perceive and use the countryside.

To a large extent, much of the imagery is absorbed in childhood. Given the formative significance of the early years, exposure to even small amounts of children's literature must result in the subconscious absorption of stereotypic-ally idyllic perceptions of rurality. Formal education plays a central role in this as it uses books to teach reading and then exposes students to the classics of English literature which unavoidably would include a share of the pastoral poets and the country life novelists. Rural images for generations of urban schoolchildren have been received more through the romantic language of Wordsworth and the distant rural world of Jane Austen than through any direct experience of countryside. And so the rural idyll as abstraction is shaped in young minds and becomes the imagery that most people carry with them into adulthood. For many this may be all that the rural idyll amounts to: an imagery which has filtered into the subconscious to be filed away and only retrieved when the right stimuli, such as Walkerton, come along. When I ask my thoroughly urban and modern undergraduate students at the beginning of my Countryside Conservation course each year what comes to mind when they think of countryside all the predictable pastoral stereotypes come pouring out. Yet few can explain why they say these things.

The other important point about what we can call the classics of the arm-chair countryside is that they are probably far less influential than the contem-porary commodification of the rural idyll. We are now bombarded through all kinds of media with what appears to be an increasingly universal rural im-agery, a veritable countryside industry. First there is the commercialisation of countryside literature, involving both the extensive reissuing of earlier classics of country writing, such as Edith Holden's *Country Diary of an Edwardian Lady*, as well as the proliferation of modern publications on every imaginable countryside topic. On my desk as I write this is a lavishly illustrated book by Roy Strong, entitled *Country Life, 1897–1997: the English Arcadia* (Strong 1996). The flyleaf notes run as follows: 'This is the story of rural life in Britain as seen through the pages of *Country Life*. It is an account of the aims and ambitions of generations of actual and would-be country dwellers inspired by idyllic vision presented by the magazine'.

These kinds of publications, of which there seems to a virtually unlimited output, are part of the nostalgia business, tapping into a growing attraction to rural heritage. They are matched by the proliferation of magazines such as *Country Life* itself, with North American counterparts such as *Harrowsmith*, and *Blair and Ketchum's Country Journal*. The commodification of this sentiment reaches its zenith in the home and garden magazine trade which has adopted 'country-style' as a motif of domestic design. The American monthly *Country Living*, a standard item on the magazine racks at supermarket check-outs, purveys the designer countryside in William Morris prints, pine furniture (Shaker designs are especially popular), dried flowers, heritage paint colours, wicker baskets, patchwork quilts, all set in country cottage-like surroundings. But this in turn is just one piece of a rural nostalgia industry which extends into actual commodities, such as Laura Ashley designs and into the world of advertising and into the images presented by movies and television.

All this suggests a convergence around a thoroughly commodified and even trivialised rural idyll which disseminates universal nostalgic images. Although, as Bell (1997) has urged, we must be cautious of seeing the rural idyll in terms of monolithic and static images, it is difficult to avoid coming to the conclusion that these are precisely the images that are now being consumed by the public. One can even detect a global dimension to this, in other words, the development of an international rural idyll. I am thinking in particular of Peter Mayle and his Provençal series. Mayle's *A Year in Provence* and his subsequent books on the region have sold millions of copies around the English-speaking world (it is just as popular in Canada and the United States as in Britain). What Mayle has done is to wrap all the ingredients of the rural idyll – the pastoral landscapes, the vernacular architecture, the activities of farming, the quaint-ness of rural folk and customs, and above all the food and wine – in a bucolic setting removed from the specifics of the English and North American coun-trysides. Provence becomes the archetypal rural utopia, the imaginary world (most readers will never set foot there) which is the essence of the classical pastoral idyll.

Spaces of the rural idyll

The British invasion of rural Provence, like the search for idyllic residential settings everywhere, raises fundamental questions about the exclusivity of idyllic valuations of countryside especially when it is blended with issues of class conflict and power relations (Harvey 2000). As Halfacree has pointed out, the rural idyll is predominantly about the visioning of the countryside by a hegemonic bourgeoisie (Halfacree 1993). And the real power of this vision is revealed in the appropriation and re-shaping of actual landscapes by this class. The middle class urbanite (i.e. bourgeois) occupation of rural land (and the ruralite collaboration in the process) for country living and for recreation and relaxation, is a process of converting pieces of countryside from landscapes of production to landscapes of consumption. One way of conceptualising this 'amenitisation' of rural land is through Lefebvre's ideas about spatiality in which the transformation of rural landscapes around idyllic expectations

Heterotopia

involves the production and reproduction of rural spaces through new spatial practices (land uses), new representations of rural space (residential design, heritage conservation) and hence of new spaces that represent new sets of values (Lefebvre 1991; Urry 1995). Another way of looking at it is through Foucault's notions of heterotopias, which as interpreted by David Harvey (2000) refer to actual places in which life is experienced differently (as opposed to the no-place of Utopias). So, far from remaining a Utopian vision, the rural idyll is materialised in the amenitisation of the countryside and the countryside becomes, in some sense, heterotopic, a space where alternative experiences are possible.

In the context of idyllic visions of countryside this can mean many things: the country estate, the exurban enclave, the country park, the heritage village, the country inn, the hiking trail, the golf course, the scenery. This suggests, as Foucault intended with the meaning of heterotopia, that the countryside provides spaces which allow us to 'escape the world of norms and structures that imprison the human imagination' (Harvey 2000: 184). And yet so much of the symbolic and the material expression of the rural idyll is all about norms and structures. Even if we accept that there are many versions of the rural idyll, they all converge around a normative nostalgic ideal which is embedded in social and economic structures. In the first place the new countrysides, essentially the exurbanising landscapes of much of rural England and most of the metropolitan regions of North America, are still largely controlled by a white middle class which is reshaping rural spaces around fairly conventional expressions of the rural idyll. This is particularly apparent in the protectionism of the ruralisation process, which establishes a direct link between private and public idylls in for example the designation of heritage districts and collective opposition to internal and external threats to those idylls. While this may not always fracture along new urbanite/old ruralite lines it does represent a hegemonic process which extends to the general campaign for countryside preservation.

The other way in which the rural idyll is all about a normative nostalgic ideal is in the consumption of its commercialised versions. Embedded in the structures of consumerism, the marketing of country lifestyle has become a predictable part of middle class life. It extends to the consumption of restored and manufactured rural heritage in, for example, English rural theme parks such as Marwell in Hampshire. It is re-echoed in the atmosphere and commercialism of 'antiquefied' small-town and village main streets in places such as St Jacobs, Ontario, where Mennonite heritage has become a local tourist attraction (Mitchell 1998). In southern Pennsylvania, this theme extends to a whole region where a large part of the rural economy relies upon the peddling of rural nostalgia through the exploitation of Amish culture (Cong 1994).

This commercialisation of the rural idyll takes place in rural landscapes that are being increasingly normatised by a ruralisation process that is remarkably predictable. Within this there are of course conflicts between different versions of the idyll. But there is also a discernible convergence of interests that mutually reinforce the reproduction of idyllic values of countryside in the landscape.

This is expressed in a new ruralism in which exurbanites, back-to-the-landers, small farmers, rural artisans, countryside recreationists and environmentalists see country life as a heritage package of non-industrial farming, revived rural crafts and traditions, village institutions and protected natural environments. It is in these communities that the contemporary rural idyll finds its most obvious and normative expression and it is these communities where the contemporary cultural reproduction of the idyllic rural myth in its most intense form is most likely to be found.

Idylls and counter-idylls

We are still left, however, with Bell's warning against assuming a monolithic rural idyll. While I would argue the evidence for an increasingly standardised rural nostalgia industry (and Mayle is certainly an industry in his own right), I also recognise the multi-dimensionality of the rural idyll. By this I mean not so much that it takes on different forms of cultural expression but rather that it has varying degrees of significance across populations. Some, perhaps most, people, probably have no sense of and no interest in a rural idyll. For others it represents an image of the countryside with which they readily identify when prompted, but which does not play a significant part in their lives. For yet another group it may influence what they read and watch and the ways in which they decorate their houses. And for some it will translate into action in the search for actual experiences of a rural idyll in countryside recreation or country living. And finally it will persuade some to engage in campaigns to protect the countryside from threats to its idyllic character.

We are dealing therefore with an ideal that operates at various levels of consciousness and action. But we are also dealing with something that is fractured along a number of other lines. In the first place, there are important differences between the English and North American rural idylls. The English idyll is mediated through a strong sense of countryside as a national treasure. When the English talk of *the* countryside they are referring above all to a landscape aesthetic which in broad terms applies or aspires to apply to all rural areas. While much of this has to do with the compactness of the country itself, it is also a product of the processes that shaped the rural landscape and of the nationalist emotions that this landscape stirs. The word 'countryside' has not carried with it the same emotional connotations in North America; indeed, until recently the word itself was little used and had no meaning to most people. Moreover, the very scale and diversity of the subcontinent has defied the development of a single rural idyll. And the values that shaped the rural landscape – utilitarian values of a largely egalitarian and individualistic society and economy of the family farm and small town – were quite different from those that shaped the gentrified landscapes of rural England. Finally, in contrast to so much of the English countryside, landscapes that conform to the conventional aesthetic expectations of the rural idyll are scattered and localised.

So an idyllic view of countryside, indeed a sense of countryside at all, is more likely to reside in New England (especially Vermont), southern Pennsylvania and Virginia than in Indiana and Kansas, and in southern Ontario and Prince Edward Island than in Manitoba or Saskatchewan. And as a cultural construction, the North American rural idyll has been less about a countryside than about the idealisation of agrarian community and the development of the cult of wilderness and forest (Nash 1967; Schama 1996).

More significant than these regional and trans-Atlantic differences however, is the fracturing of the rural idyll along social lines. The recent debates about class and countryside notwithstanding (Hoggart 1997), the evidence for the rural idyll, even of different idylls, as a possession of the white, Anglo middle class is overwhelming. This was pretty well guaranteed by the material and cultural conditions that shaped the abstract idealisation of countryside and reinforced by the ability of this class to translate this into power over the actual rural landscapes and communities. So what of the rest of society? The flurry of recent discussions of how issues of class, gender, ethnicity and age relate to the concept of a rural idyll appears to agree that it has either no significance or has different meanings for the urban and rural poor (Cloke 1997), for ethnic minorities (Agyeman and Spooner 1997), for women (Little and Austin 1996) and for the young (Jones 1997). Agyeman and Spooner point to the sense of alienation on the part of visible minorities when they visit the countryside and of their feelings of exclusion from the profound Englishness of the countryside ideal. In North America, the overwhelmingly urban black and Hispanic populations not only tend to avoid rural living by choice, but are also intentionally excluded from exurban and small town who are not averse to using heritage and agricultural designations to screen out undesirable land uses and therefore undesirable people.

That the rural idyll is challenged by the experiences of rural life has been well illustrated by a number of recent studies. In their survey of women in two English villages, Little and Austin (1996) emphasise the juxtaposition of women's acceptance of the idyllic qualities of the village with the realities of lack of employment opportunities and limited personal mobility. Matthews *et al.*, in a recent study of children's experience of rural life, reveal 'a "darker" rural, where not all children are growing up in innocence within carefree, supportive communities' (2000: 145). The rural idyll then is coming under increasing scrutiny, not only by academics, but also by the more popular media. A flurry of articles challenging the reality of the idyllic countryside have appeared in British newspapers and magazines over the past few years. 'Rural poverty – the ugly secret in Britain's beautiful hillsides' (Colebrook 1999) and 'Not so Merrie England' (Brown 2000) headline two articles sampled from the *Guardian* which illustrate an alternative vision of the countryside. Nor is this restricted to the analysis of deprived and marginalised rural classes, for it is accompanied by the revelation of disillusion amongst new country dwellers.

Oh yes, it's beautiful, unspoilt, exclusive, rich. All the things you want the country home to be. So why isn't it working for me and why would I advise those happy newcomers to proceed with caution? The answer is simple (although it's taken me eight years to work it out): social isolation, boredom and the long, slow death of the spirit due to a lack of stimulation.

So wrote Deborah Bosley in a *New Statesman* article entitled 'Country living stinks' (Bosley 2000). A minority view perhaps, but not a singular one. Studies of those who have sought the experience of the rural idyll confirm that for many the idyll can evaporate quickly in the face of the realities of country living. In a study of recent migrants to rural Montana Jobes discovered that 50 per cent had sold up and left within five years, revealing a high level of what he refers to as 'shattered illusions' about country living (Jobes 2000).

And yet they keep coming to Montana as to other areas around the world where the landscape seems to match the images of the rural idyll. Perhaps it is, as Little and Austin discovered about the rural women in their survey, that they were 'seemingly aware of the limiting nature of the rural idyll' but acknowledged it as a 'small price to pay for a rural way of life as they perceived it' (1996: 18). But perhaps it also reveals the durability of the rural idyll as the dominant country vision. The intellectual challenge to this vision gathers momentum, the popular image of an idyllic countryside is held up to media scrutiny, and rural disasters come one after another. Yet the evidence for a decline in the strength of the vision is scant. Maybe it persists precisely because of the questioning of its validity and the threats to the environment that it celebrates. The rural idyll, in fact, is now embedded deep in the politics of the countryside. While the issues may shift and the strength of the idyllic vision will be challenged from time to time, history tells us that it will continue to dominate the discourse over the future of rurality for a long time to come.

References

Agyeman, J. and Spooner, R. 1997 'Ethnicity and the rural environment', pp. 197–217 in P. Cloke and J. Little (eds), *Contested Countryside Cultures: Otherness, Marginalisation and Rurality*, Routledge, London.

Baldwin, S. 1926 *On England, and Other Addresses*, Philip Allan, London.

Bell, D. 1997 'Anti-idyll: rural horror', pp. 94–108 in P. Cloke and J. Little (eds), *Contested Countryside Cultures: Otherness, Marginalisation and Rurality*, Routledge, London.

Berry, W. 1977 *The Unsettling of America*, Sierra Club Books, San Francisco.

Bosley, D. 2000 'Country Living Stinks', *New Statesman*, 13(611), 29–30.

Brown, D. 2000 'Not so Merrie England', *Guardian*, 15 June.

Bunce, M. 1994 *The Countryside Ideal*, Routledge, London.

Cloke, P. 1997 'Marginalisation, poverty and rurality', pp. 252–71 in P. Cloke and J. Little (eds), *Contested Countryside Cultures: Otherness, Marginalisation and Rurality*, Routledge, London.

Cloke, P., Phillips, M. and Thrift, N. 1997 'The new middle classes and the social constructs of rural living', pp. 220–38 in T. Butler and M. Savage (eds), *Social Change and the Middle Classes*, UCL Press, London.

Cobbett, W. 1912 *Rural Rides*, J.M. Dent, London.

Colebrook, C. 1999 'Rural poverty – the ugly secret in Britain's beautiful hillsides', *Guardian*, 27 January.

Coleman, R. (ed.) 1973 *The Idea of the City in Nineteenth Century Britain*, Routledge and Kegan Paul, London.

Cong, D. 1994 'The roots of Amish popularity in contemporary USA', *Journal of American Culture*, 17, 59–66.

Ecksteins, M. 1990 *Rites of Spring*, Lester, Orpen and Denys, Toronto.

Finch, R. and Elder, J. (eds) 1990 *The Norton Book of Nature Writing*, W.W. Norton, New York.

Frye, N. 1967 *The Romantic Myth*, Random House, New York.

Halfacree, K. 1993 'Locality and social representation: space, discourse and alternative definitions of the rural', *Journal of Rural Studies*, 9, 23–37.

Halfacree, K. 1995 'Talking about rurality: social representations of the rural as expressed by residents of six English parishes', *Journal of Rural Studies*, 11, 1–20.

Harrison, F. 1982 *Strange Land*, Sidgwick and Jackson, London.

Hart, J. 1950 *The Popular Book: A History of America's Literary Taste*, Oxford University Press, New York.

Harvey, D. 2000 *Spaces of Hope*, University of California Press, Berkeley, CA.

Hoggart, K. 1997 'The middle classes in rural England, 1971–91', *Journal of Rural Studies*, 13, 253–73.

Howard, E. 1898 *Garden Cities of Tomorrow*, Faber and Faber, London, 1946 edition.

Hunter, S. 1984 *Victorian Idyllic Fiction*, Macmillan, London.

Jobes, P. 2000 *Moving Nearer to Heaven: The Illusions and Disillusions of Migrants to Scenic Rural Places*, Praeger, Westport, CN.

Jones, O. 1997 'Little figures, big shadows: country childhood stories', pp. 158–79 in P. Cloke and J. Little (eds), *Contested Countryside Cultures: Otherness, Marginalisation and Rurality*, Routledge, London.

Keith, W. 1974 *The Rural Tradition*, University of Toronto Press, Toronto.

Keith, W. 1980 *The Poetry of Nature*, University of Toronto Press, Toronto.

Keith, W. 1988 *Regions of the Imagination: The Development of British Rural Fiction*, University of Toronto Press, Toronto.

Lefebvre, H. 1991 *The Production of Space*, Blackwell, Oxford.

Lemon, J. 1972 *The Best Poor Man's Country*, Johns Hopkins University Press, Baltimore, MD.

Little, J. and Austin, P. 1996 'Women and the rural idyll', *Journal of Rural Studies*, 12, 101–12.

Matthews, H., Taylor, M., Sherwood, K., Tucker, F. and Limb, M. 2000 'Growing up in the countryside: children and the rural idyll', *Journal of Rural Studies*, 16, 141–54.

Mingay, G. (ed.) 1989 *The Rural Idyll*, Routledge, London.

Mitchell, C. 1998 'Entrepreneurialism, commodification and creative destruction: a model of post-modern community development', *Journal of Rural Studies*, 14, 273–86.

Montmarquet, J. 1989 *The Idea of Agrarianism: From Hunter-Gatherer to Agrarian Radical in Western Culture*, University of Idaho Press, Moscow, ID.

Morris, W. 1891 *News from Nowhere*, Routledge and Kegan Paul, London, 1970 edition.

Nash, R. 1967 *Wilderness and the American Mind*, Yale University Press, New Haven, CT.

Phillips, M., Fish, R. and Agg, J. 2001 'Putting together ruralities: towards a symbolic analysis of rurality in the British mass media', *Journal of Rural Studies*, **17**(1), 1–28.

Ruskin, J. 1866 *The Crown of Wild Olive*, H. Altemus, Philadelphia, 1899 edition.

Schama, S. 1996 *Landscape and Memory*, Alfred A. Knopf, New York.

Shi, D. 1985 *The Simple Life: Plain Living and High Thinking in American Culture*, Oxford University Press, New York.

Short, J. 1991 *Imagined Country*, Routledge, London.

Stauffer, D. 1974 *A Short History of American Poetry*, Dutton, New York.

Strong, R. 1996 *Country Life, 1897–1997: The English Arcadia*, Country Life Books, London.

Thoreau, H. 1854 *Walden, or Life in the Woods*, New Haven Library, New York, 1960 edition.

Tuan, Y.-F. 1974 *Topophilia*, Prentice Hall, New York.

Urry, J. 1995 *Consuming Places*, Routledge, London.

White, M. and White, L. 1962 *The Intellectual Versus the City*, Harvard University Press, Boston, MA.

Wickens, B. 2000 'Tragedy in Walkerton', *Maclean's*, **113**(23), 34–6.

Wiener, M. 1981 *English Culture and the Decline of the Industrial Spirit*, Oxford University Press, New York.

Williams, R. 1960 *Culture and Society*, Chatto and Windus, London.

Williams, R. 1973 *The Country and the City*, Chatto and Windus, London.

CHAPTER 3

The rural gaze

Simone Abram

The notion of the 'gaze', proposed by Foucault (1976), suggests that looking is not an innocent pastime. Looking is the active organisation of what we see, and what we see is socially organised, structured through our internal interpretation of the visual stimulus. Vision in 'western' societies is often assumed to be a very immediate sense, free from the interpretative rigours of the other senses. Foucault argued, in particular, that the Classical age was defined by an increasing emphasis on the evidential properties of the visual, or what Jay terms, 'an intensified faith in visual evidence' (1986: 182). Whereas we are very aware of the knowledge required to interpret sounds, language, music, animal sounds, etc., we fall into the trap of expecting our visual interpretations to be universal. Despite the sustained philosophical attack on the illusory nature of sight[1], truth, in our society, is most closely associated with vision; the visual constitutes the ultimate evidence. However, Foucault demonstrated vividly that not only are our interpretations of what we see socially organised, but the focus of our visual attention is defined through collective understanding too. Until the eighteenth century, it was not possible to see mental illness, since symptoms of hallucination, disorder and unrest were, until then, not defined in terms of illness, and would be interpreted as religious fervour, possession, evidence of witchcraft, etc. This notion of 'social construction' is often misunderstood, particularly by positivist scientists, as relating to the elementary philosophical conundrum of whether things exist if we do not look at them. To say that 'the rural' is socially constructed is not to argue that there are no fields or meadows 'in reality'. On the contrary, it is to point out that physical reality exists in leaves and insects, but that the experience of nature is organised socially into concepts such as 'meadow', 'rural', 'animal', 'mineral', etc. Our categorisations of the world are collectively organised and, as such, are subject to change over time and space.

This chapter concerns the social organisation of the concept of 'rural', and of the systematised gaze that determines much of contemporary politics of development. What I wish to do here is to problematise that gaze, with the help of some examples, and open the range of debate about the potential for rural politics.

The gaze

In his study of tourism, John Urry asserted the existence of a particular organised and systematised view exerted upon landscapes or townscapes by those who 'go away' as tourists. In adopting Foucault's analysis of the medical gaze and of the organisation of deviance, Urry suggests that by investigating the 'bizarre and idiosyncratic', we can 'reveal interesting and significant aspects of "normal" societies' (1990: 2). Tourism certainly presents us with a wealth of bizarre and idiosyncratic practices, and many of them are related to the encounter with different kinds of landscape which may be interpreted in relation to landscape 'at home'. One could, indeed, argue that the rise of tourism industries has provided one of the major driving forces for changes to the visual appearance of landscapes, both externally and internally, in terms of changing interpretations of the visual experience. Tourism's obsession with views and sights can be seen to have emerged in the early nineteenth century, following a trend towards what Foucault calls 'ocular obsession'.

Early English tourism was primarily the preserve of young gentlemen scholars (and their tutors) seeking to complete their education (see, for example, Feifer 1985). The precursor to the Grand Tour of Europe that became so popular during the nineteenth century was the voyage of predominantly young male Elizabethans to the various capitals of European kingdoms, in search of knowledge. These young men travelled often with letters of introduction to the courts of Europe, where they would seek education through dialogue and practice, in languages, the arts of politics, and the courtly arts of fencing, dancing, and so forth. The emphasis in these travels was on discourse with the learned; the travel was a means to reach court and the company of nobles. However, during the course of the eighteenth century, in particular, as travel became more popular and more routinised, the emphasis began surely to shift (Adler 1989). By the time Byron began to eulogise the wilderness of Alpine landscapes, the object of the traveller's pleasure was moving securely into the realm of the visual. Feifer notes that by the twentieth century, one of the dominant objects of travel was 'sight-seeing', and tourist merchandising of images of landscapes was well underway.

One can postulate that this transformation was mirrored in the domestic. Whereas prior to industrialisation and enclosures, the dominant experience of the rural landscape was through labour (grazing, pastoralism, ploughing, reaping), experience began gradually to shift to the visual, its ultimate expression being the landscape arts (Green 1995). Indeed, for some the landscape arts themselves have been instrumental in changing the experience of rurality for certain sectors of the population (as Okely argues, 1997). The working land of agriculture was transformed through capital accumulation and conspicuous consumption into the aesthetics of landscape, directly through the transformation of productive landscapes into artistic objects, and through the changing artistic expostulations of writers and painters. Whereas earlier landscape painting had related symbolically to classical or biblical scenes, landscapes became symbols of the power and capital of the wealthy, later taking on a Romantic value of their own in an aesthetic that was then imitated by garden designers.

One might also argue that the transformation was reflected in academic discourses, too. In the geographical emphasis on the 'gaze' of tourism, Veijola and Joikinen argue that the body of the tourist completely disappeared. The experience of tourism is not merely the search for visual authenticity but includes the bodily experience of difference (in some cases, sexually, e.g. Bowman 1996; Leheny 1995; Pruitt and Lafont 1995). Similarly, the experience and imagination of the rural is also far from limited to the visual. People also dwell in the rural in a far more multi-dimensional way. While it is useful to isolate the visual in order to understand its impact on the politics of place, it is a mistake to treat it as if it existed in isolation[2]. Hence, the emphasis within the literature on landscape aesthetics (including the built elements of the 'traditional' landscape – a notion there is not room to investigate here), reduced other aspects, such as the aural in landscape, to incidental qualities. New arguments about the impact of soundscapes on the quality of life have taken a long time to re-emerge as eligible for political consideration, and often only in extreme circumstances (such as the excessive levels of aircraft noise over certain, mainly urban, residential areas). A recent paper from Sweden, for example, argues that we need to reassess our concept of soundscapes and recognise hearing as a way of dwelling, rather than an incidental distraction from seeing (Soneryd 2001). Other comparative examples also exist to indicate that the reported dominance of the visual is neither complete nor universal. Gell's description (1999) of his experiences among Umeda forest-dwellers (in Papua New Guinea) in the 1960s shows how specific our visual domination of experience is. In a world where sight lines rarely extended further than a few tens of metres, what was visible was relatively close. The Umeda were much more aware of their acoustic and olfactory surroundings. Evidence, in Umeda land, was based on hearing, not seeing, and this realisation can be a profound shock to those who have completely internalised the notion of seeing-as-believing.

Gell says rather less about olfactory significance, but as I will argue later in this chapter, contrary to the focus on rural gazes, 'country smells' can be as determinant as sights in the representation of the authentically rural in contemporary England. The shift from aural, embodied and olfactory experience of landscape, towards the dominance of the visual was not exclusive nor complete, even in tourism. However, we need constantly to be reminded that this is the case, as assertions of the visual dominate our political and social organisation. Despite this dominance of the aesthetic, particularly salient in terms of controlling the appearance of 'valuable' buildings, it is the limits to the visual accessibility of landscape which are prioritised through the British planning system. While one can buy property – buildings and land – one cannot 'buy a view'. People move to homes where the view from the window is one of the main features, but they are relatively powerless to protect that view from further development. In this situation, the preference for landscape is not supported by the political system except in 'special' circumstances, but, ironically, these circumstances reinforce the visual priority, through designations such as 'Area of Outstanding Natural Beauty' or 'Area of Attractive Landscape'. Gradation into qualities of landscape beauty indicate the extent of the organisation of the rural gaze into a classificatory principle.

The dominance of the visual in relation to landscape came at the expense of other senses. Just as Foucault argued in terms of the establishment of a medical priority for visual evidence, the visual began to dominate in many areas of western thought. As Jay remarks, 'with the rise of modern science, the Gutenberg revolution in printing and the Albertian emphasis on perspective in painting, vision was given an especially powerful role in the modern era' (1986: 177). Foucault's critique of this dominance entailed a description of how the visual had dominated through science at the expense of other forms of experience. Urry, however, extends the notion of the gaze to include forms of anticipation and pleasure-seeking, played out through consumerism. In this chapter, however, I wish to argue that the dominance of the visual aesthetic in commentary on the rural (and through what could be considered rural-pornography through the pages of glossy 'country' magazines) is, in fact, experienced in an embodied way through a complex web of senses, through sounds, smells, direct contact and social organisation and experience. As Veijola and Jokinen argue (1994), it is time to reconnect the seeing-eye to the rest of the body.

Separating the gaze

One of the reasons why Foucault adopted the concept of the gaze as a socially organised tool was to distinguish between the body and the person. The medical gaze depersonalises the body, making the latter amenable to treatment. In effect, the power of the medical gaze is achieved through the disempowering of the person by exploiting the definition of the body as a separate entity from the person. The person is socialised through ritual (name-giving, education, marriage, etc.), experience, relationships, and so forth. The body is nourished through food and drink, and is susceptible to disease and illness. Through the medical preference for visual evidence, however, the body becomes physicalised and disentangled from its social experience. It must be pacified to be amenable to that most extreme of medical procedures, surgery, where the person is reduced to a pure body, its personality temporarily nullified by anaesthesia. If the medical gaze makes possible the distinction between person and body, what then is the power of the rural gaze? When we look upon the landscape, do we attempt to remove the human experience from the physical aesthetic? What are we making amenable to action, and what kind of action are we exerting by aestheticising the landscape?

I would like to put forward a suggestion about the contemporary discourse of rural crisis that has developed and been elaborated throughout the latter half of the twentieth century. Arguments about rural collapse have centred on the decline of agriculture as synonymous with the decline of the rural. The colonisation of rural England by commuting classes has been described as a crisis of rurality, the loss of rural community, and so forth. Is the agricultural, therefore, the person to the physical body of the rural form? Are those who berate the loss of agriculture for the countryside lamenting the loss of person from the body that lies scarred as landscape? My suspicions are aroused by the lack of lament for earlier transformations, such as the loss of Britain's indigenous forests to shipbuilding some centuries ago. Who, now, laments the ecological ravaging of British highland landscapes by over-pasturing? (Indeed, there is now a movement for the preservation of open treeless moorland.) Those who mourn the loss of pastoral parkland rarely see beyond the recent changes in cultural landscapes to a time before pastoralism. It has become a cliché to point out the Romantic creation of a picturesque peasantry whose passing can be mourned by those who never suffered rural deprivation themselves, but perhaps the defence of contemporary agricultural practice is equally romantic. The recent agricultural crisis associated with foot and mouth disease threatens to destroy much of the moorland of England's most picturesque landscapes, through the extermination of the sheep whose grazing sustains open parkland. The loss of parkland, through loss of sheep, threatens to destroy much of the contemporary English rural economy, not through loss of agricultural income but through the loss of tourism based on 'seeing' (and being in) the characteristic English landscape created by the alliance of grazing animals and farmers. At this point, the domestic rural gaze meets the tourist gaze squarely. In fact, Urry argues that tourism is a way of seeing that can apply to anyone, much as Feifer claims that we are all tourists much of the time through our consumer-nostalgic relation with the world. It is now widely accepted that this tourist gaze is nostalgic. Sightseers may be thought to be searching for some kind of authenticity of the exotic (see Culler 1988; MacCannell 1992), even though this authentic may be a signifier which has no concrete signified. That is, there is nostalgia for an imagined past which often bears only the sketchiest relationship to real circumstances (see Lowenthal 1985). We might argue, therefore, that the tourist gaze upon the rural landscape is one and the same as the rural gaze which aestheticises land uses in a nostalgic way in an attempt to distance it from contemporary capital and globalising processes.

However, this nostalgia needs to be contextualised as part of a wider discourse on ruralism. We need to recognise the extent to which indigenous definitions are adopted by rural commentators and converted into analytical observations. The very term 'rural' has little value as an analytical category, but reflects popular concepts of the division of space. The term 'rural' is useful to think with, because it means something to people as a concept, but not because it has any precise analytic role. What is it, then, that the popular conception of 'rural' denotes? And to what extent have these assumptions been incorporated into analysis? Moreover, how do organised views of the 'rural' differentially empower or disempower different actors? This question can be explored using a case study of contest over land use, in which we can consider the claims and counter-claims of rurality that are adopted by different actors.

Rural, urban, suburban, subrural

Let us consider a 'rural' village in Buckinghamshire which appears to suffer from many of the malaises attributed to contemporary rural England. This description is based on around six months of ethnographic fieldwork based in the village during 1997, and contacts with villagers both before and since then[3]. Fieldwork included living in the village, joining village clubs, attending meetings of various groups, public meetings, assisting at coffee mornings and folk-dances, and interviewing a number of villagers from a wide spectrum of the population. That population has expanded at least five-fold during the twentieth century, although in the last decade or so, as the number of houses has increased, the population has very slightly declined. House prices have rocketed and there is a dearth of affordable or rented accommodation, and traffic levels have also risen along with the number of commuters. There have been struggles over who speaks for the village: is it members of families who have lived there for generations, or is it others who are preoccupied with maintaining and improving the fabric of the village?

While the social organisation of the village has been radically transformed, particularly since the 1960s, this transformation was one of a series of such transformations in the village's history. The population grew during the nineteenth century, only to be decimated by the agricultural crisis later in the century. It grew again when railway workers moved in early in the twentieth century, falling again during the economic decline of the 1930s, and so on, the population increasing particularly dramatically in the 1970s with the building of an estate of around 250 family-houses. Like many commuting districts of the Home Counties, the population has expanded in both size and wealth in parallel with the growth of London as an economic magnet, and the booming of the economy of the South East of England as a whole. The village is a classic site of counter-urbanisation, housing both those moving out of London, and those moving into the South East but reluctant to move right into the metropolis (see Abram et al. 1998). The location of the village on a main railway link into central London has made it extremely popular among those looking for a standard of living unaffordable within the city itself, but this affordability is relative only. Housing in the village may not be in the bracket of west London suburbs, but it is well beyond the reach of local factory workers, for example.

At the same time, the village has probably never been so well serviced as it is now. There are frequent rail links to London and Birmingham, buses to Oxford and Aylesbury, a public library, health centre, three schools, several shops and restaurants, and some hundred clubs and societies ranging from sports groups to elderly-care and Morris dancers. There are also a number of both formal and informal churches (Anglican, Methodist, Baptist, Fellowships, etc.). This is a lively social place, and yet some villagers bemoan the loss of vitality that they remember existing in the village of their youth or childhood. Some resent 'incomers', and some incomers resent later arrivals. It is not the self-defined 'Old Villagers' who resist expansion, though, but those who moved in early in the village's recent expansion, supported by more recent immigrants. The reasons for this difference are related to the different aspirations and imaginations of the village held by the various actors involved in the politics of expansion. We can, to some extent and at the risk of caricaturing certain representations of the village, trace which village is being defended through which gaze.

Before considering various representations, we must acknowledge that these are distilled from a complex and changing pattern of social relations. Simplified for the purposes of analysis, these snapshots of various rural gazes should not be assumed to be constant nor homogeneous, but glimpses at a certain point in time. People living in the village refer to a group of the population as 'Old Villagers', as some of them refer to themselves, but we should not imagine that the discourse of 'Old Villagers' applies equally and universally to all those referred to as such. That is, we must remember that naming is a social process in itself that creates the appearance of social groups. 'Old Villagers' are, thus, difficult to identify by any rigid code, but are those who have some kind of long-standing links with established families. Just as Strathern observed (1981) in attempting to find the 'authentic' residents of another English village, the authentic belonging of villagers recedes as one attempts to capture it. There are families who can trace their predecessors back through several centuries of village residency, expressed in a time-compressed identification with previous generations, as in the following instance:

> We've been in the village or environs since 1546. We know that because in 1977 the year of the Queen's silver jubilee, Eve Maclaughlan, who's a genealogist in the village, she decided to do a family tree of an old family, and she chose ours, so she did all the work for us, which was great, and Mother's got the family tree, wonderfully framed, going back to 1546 . . . we're a farming family. My father was an only child but his father had the farm and I think my grandfather's father had the farm as well in the village.

Here, also, the link with farming the land acts to legitimise claims of belonging to the village. There are others, though, whose families came in the early twentieth century who may still be 'Old Villagers'. The retired schoolmaster who moved into the village in the 1930s and served as one of the village worthies on the parish council in his day, was associated with a vision of the former life of the village as a smaller, more cohesive social place. Those who remember the village before the beginning of the most recent wave of expansion and its transformation from small community remote from the capital adopt a discourse about the village's past and future. This discourse is partly about class distinction, but is itself distinguished by class. The village was never a homogeneous working village, for example. While there was never a resident feudal landlord, there was a yeoman class which bought the land out of manorial ownership around the time of the English Civil War. There were, of course, many agricultural workers prior to the Second World War, and for a short time afterwards. There are still labourers in the village, working at some of the small factories based there, but what has changed is the context in which they are identified. No longer part of a small community where 'everyone knew each other', and where only a few were wealthy enough to paint their houses, now they are a small minority in a very affluent society.

'Old Villagers' included those who were landowners and who have, over the years, prospered through the sale of land for new housing. There is no record of active resistance to expansion on any scale from within the village until a significant number of new residents began to reclassify the value of the old village property in terms of its heritage and architectural value. Then, a small number of 'Old Villagers' joined forces with some of the incomers to campaign for better conservation of the old village, and for new developments to pay attention to the vernacular style of the older village buildings. However, while there have often been rumblings of discontent among certain 'Old Villagers', particularly a group who drink in one of the less elegant village pubs, there has never been outright rejection of housing growth in the village. Whereas in similar villages, workers moved out of old cottages in favour of 'modern' council housing, and cottages were bought up by those wealthy enough to renovate them beyond any state they had ever been in before, here there were many villagers wealthy enough to maintain their cottages and many remain living in the 'heart' of the village. However, rather than defending 'their' village against any outside influence, some 'Old Villagers' welcome change:

> I don't see Haddenham as a museum piece as some people perhaps coming into it new think, 'oh yes, isn't it sweet', you know. Well it isn't sweet any more.

They may also be keen to emphasise the less glamorous side of the village, in contrast with the picturesque Church End with its carefully crafted 'Englishness':

> . . . if you come in the other end, you come down Lower Road, you see council houses first and it's just another place, isn't it? It is quite a mixture of all sorts of different periods.

There is, in fact, disapproval by 'Old Villagers' of the groups of anti-development activists who have moved into the village over the years, revealed through comments such as 'if we'd had that attitude to development, they wouldn't even live here in the first place'. Discontent, however, also takes the form of disapproval of the behaviour of some of those who have moved into the village. One particularly vocal 'Old Villager' complains that so few people walk through the village, instead driving the very short distances between home, school, church, etc. The essence of the 'old village' for him (and others are sympathetic to him) is its social fabric, which holds far more importance than the visual aesthetic of the village. Without active villagers who know each other and help each other, run clubs and social groups, there is no more than a pretty picture. Rich Londoners who drive into the village and lock themselves away behind ostentatious garden gates symbolise this loss of social village-ness. However, even some of the more conservative 'Old Villagers' recognise that without many of those who have moved in over the years, there would be fewer facilities for everyone. It is many of the generation who moved in during the 1960s and 1970s who run day-care groups for elderly people, coffee mornings, and so on.

Among those who moved in during the 1960s was a group of professionals mostly from other non-urban parts of Britain, and including a number of planners and architects, as well as business people. A core group created a 'Village Society' early on with the intention of preserving and encouraging the best of planning and architecture in the village, mainly in response to some thoughtless demolitions and road widenings in the late 1960s. One of their most visible achievements concerned the renovation of the village pond. The village was once renowned for raising Aylesbury ducks. Many householders kept ducks, raising the ducklings at first within the house, and then sending them to the village pond, situated in front of the medieval stone church. In fact, the pond would have been dug out specifically to water the animals that, at one time, grazed on pastures within the village, and was no doubt also used to run carts through to wash their wheels. When mains sewers were installed in the village in 1928, the springline that fed the pond was broken, and it began to drain. By the 1980s it was little more than a bog. Members of the Village Society decided to renovate the pond, sealing it and installing a link through a ball-valve to the mains, to keep the pond topped up in all weather:

> We said to everybody, look, do you want a hole in the ground or do you want a pond? And people did all sorts of things, and we got grants from various people, before the lottery of course. And then I got a contractor from Leighton Buzzard and we dug it all out with a crane and everything, shovel, and we recovered some clay from it, we bought some clay and we got right down to bedrock and then we clayed the bottom and put some polythene in the bottom just to protect the clay, not as a liner, and then some more clay and of course, the thing is, you can't have a pond without a water supply. So in fact, the pond is fastened up to a thing like a lavatory cistern. When the water level goes down, the valve opens and it tops it up.

What they achieved was a picturesque idyll, with church, green and pond, war memorial and remains of an ancient monastery, surrounded by thatched cottages, pubs and old village stores. The setting has been used as a set for television and film recordings, and features on various pictures, postcards and calendars. As the village society member above commented,

Alright, Church End does look a bit like a chocolate box, but you know, it looks like that because people have done something about it, not because it just happened.

This is one rural gaze in action. Not only does the gaze organise the way things are seen, but organises what is deemed appropriate to be seen, and motivates people to change the appearance of the land to conform with their ideals. Some would argue that this vision represents a suburban imagination of rural scenes. However, those responsible for such actions do not consider themselves anything other than rural. This same commentator criticised later incomers for their lack of rural knowledge:

... I was born in a town that was not much bigger than this when I was a boy, so I understand what it's all about, but a lot of people here don't because they've come from principally perhaps from the south of England which is a good deal more sophisticated than my neck of the woods and not all of them understand the country, they don't know one bird from another, they don't know one smell from another really, but it's a pleasant place ...

This particular gaze conceals a body of knowledge about nature and the social, how to interact with neighbours both human and non-human in a proper, rural way. One of the ways to break this moral code is the prioritisation of financial interests over the 'greater good' of the village. Prioritising the value of one's house over the general good of the village is worthy of criticism for precisely this sector of the population that believes in the aims of the village society. Those most eligible for such criticism from commentators such as the retired businessman above were not only some 'Old Villagers' but many more recent incomers, whom he suspects of being more concerned about their own narrow personal interests than in any community-of-interest in the village. Until recently, however, the Village Society was not against expansion of the village. In its early days, members were much more concerned about architectural quality. Another member of the Village Society in its early days reminisced about the construction of a major housing estate in the 1970s:

I can't recall any dispute about whether there was going to be 200 houses, it was just about how they were going to be arranged, we wanted small ones as well as big ones, you know, the usual story and so on.

However, since then, growth has ceased to be a finite step to accommodate population expansion and has become a steady state. Consequently, many of those who were attracted to the village for its 'village feel' are reluctant to see that disappear, as another member commented:

[the village has] almost been a victim of its own success, I think because people when they move here settle so quickly and enjoy it so much, they then feel that there's something precious about it so whatever change may come, they don't want to lose it ...

These Village Society members are well aware of the cliché involved, as one commented:

> [there is] a considerable number of people who think that [the village] should be frozen in aspic at the point they moved in and that has gone from being something which was almost funny to almost a tenet I think now.

Ironically, many of those currently campaigning against further village expansion feel that only they uphold the true interest of the village. A new campaign group was set up in response to proposed new development in the village, heavily criticised by Village Society members as confrontational and unwilling to work with either the District or Parish Council. However, many of the core members of the new group were also long-standing residents, who had similar sympathies with the established group as well as a sense of 'something special' about the village, as one commented in response to a proposal for a new housing estate:

> ... the risk is that it would lose its character and friendliness. It is still a sufficiently charming village that you can walk across it, see people you know, you're not concerned about being attacked, there is the right balance between small shops but without having the major congestion caused by people coming in to shop. It has a good character of its own and the character is exemplified in the picturesque Witchert [mud & straw] walls and cottages and so on in those parts of the village.

This commentator, a village resident for over 20 years, tied together the visual and the social in his interpretation of village character. The picturesque, in this view, is symbolic of the sociality in the village. Seeing the picturesque in a village surrounded by council-built post-war properties is one clear example of the organisation of the rural gaze. This is illustrated in Figure 3.1. All these photographs were taken within the village, but as the above comment demonstrates, some of these views carry greater significance than others and are, in fact, seen more than others. Indeed, many newer residents explained their move into the village as a result of driving into the village past the Church End, with pond, cottages and green, and seeing the 'archetypal English village' as the fulfilment of their desires for a place to live. One such resident who moved into the estate built in the 1970s (mentioned above) explained this as follows:

> ... so I just thought, well, I'll just follow this road and see where it leads to. And, I came in via the church, and it was a sunny day, and I just stopped the car, I mean, it was a good job there was nobody behind me, because I stopped the car and thought 'this is the English village I've been looking for', and didn't look any further ...

In a simple sense, the picturesque symbolises some relatively romantic notions about civilised living, as Lowe *et al.* have pointed out (1995). It does this despite counterfactual information, for example, that drug abuse among

Figure 3.1   Views of the village: which are made (in)visible by the organisation of a rural gaze?

young people is higher in these rural areas than in urban areas. People are 'not concerned about being attacked', although the local policeman moved out after a petrol-bomb was shoved through his letterbox. The gaze on the picturesque which here defines the 'rural' in the gaze, is focused on the reno- vated historical buildings: cottage gardens, remnants of agricultural practice and the surrounding countryside with its woods and streams. The gypsy site, on a small lane off a B-road outside the village, is almost invisible, sheltered by hedgerows from most views (find it among the illustrations on page 42). People do occasionally talk about 'tinkers' in both positive and negative light, although 'problems' are accepted to have been resolved some years ago, and, in contrast, the arrival of travellers provokes much more hostility in the nearby town of Aylesbury, where they are more visible.

Some of those objecting to further expansion of the village were concerned both about expansion and change in village 'character'. These concerns have their focus on two forms of change. The first, as noted, is in village growth. Members of the group believe that the debate about housing sites concealed a definitional change in the future of the village:

> . . . the issue wasn't a housing issue so much as are the planners going to change the village environment and the village that we've lived in for twenty years

since,

> clearly, the planners' intent is for [the village] to become a sustainable small town. . . . It's a matter of time before there'll be a roundabout up at the junction, I think, where Station Road comes in. We will see all the consequences of becoming larger and larger and the planners trying to push more housing and more industry into the village.

The second major concern is over industrial change. Whereas the village has housed small factories since before the Second World War, these were mainly light engineering factories, producing mechanical parts (aircraft wings, hoses, stationery). In the 1960s, the Village Society fought a proposal to build a large paper mill in the village, on grounds that such an industrial plant was inappropriate in the village. In fact, it was this campaign which is sometimes attributed as motivating the foundation of the Village Society. In a curious parallel, in the late 1990s, a large spice-processing factory was proposed to be built in the centre of the village, with consequences that reveal a great deal about residents' appreciation of their environment. Despite objections from villagers, the factory was built. The smells that emanated from the factory were soon felt as repugnant, and 'out of place' in a rural village. Here, in fact, the campaign group was united with the Village Society, in attempting first of all to prevent the factory being built, and secondly in attempting to control the emissions. The campaigner quoted above remarked:

> . . . you can shut your gates to housing, it might even be good for the village, you can't actually tell, but one thing's for certain, if you want to sit out here and have coffee and you've got a pungent smell coming in, that's just not acceptable and that affects everybody, whether you're gardening or sitting outside or opening your window or whatever.

The visual, in this instance, is occluded by the olfactory. The pungent odour that emerges from the factory is not appropriate to the village, where the otherwise pungent smells of agricultural products may be acceptable. The sickly smell is a smell-out-of-place, one that should be found, if at all, in industrial parks, or perhaps in distant spice-lands, but not in an English village. It is not enough, therefore, that the village should look picturesque. It must smell appropriate and sound appropriate too.

According to some 'Old Villagers', in fact, this objection to the smells from the factory represented an organised 'smell', as systematised as the 'gaze' of Foucault's definition. Worse, one argued for example, was the smell of exhaust fumes from the cars of those objecting to the smell from the factory. The factory provided at least some employment for villagers who did not have big, expensive cars, but the objectors did not smell the exhaust from their own cars, nor hear the noise that they made. For some, the rural seems somehow to accommodate modern/technological intrusions in the form of comfort and convenience, such as cars, metalled roads, telecommunications, modern agriculture, but not others: industrial processes with perceptible by-products. The defence of a rural space is concerned with the aesthetic as a symbol for a Utopian, and simultaneously nostalgic, social vision. Although nostalgic, it is not seeking the actual past of the village, where most small-holders were too poor to paint their houses, but a sanitised, picturesque vision, where old houses are renovated to contain modern conveniences, and are spruced up well beyond the state they would have been in when new. This gaze, in other words, is not referential only to the past, but seeks an improved, idealised (and some would say suburban, modern) vision where even ruined buildings are cleaned and tidied. Indeed, current residents generally do not want the agricultural to encroach too closely into the village. Whereas some 50 years ago, pastures were to be found within the village itself, these have gradually been sold and filled in with lavish housing. Animals and crops and even farm machinery are kept well out of the way, and complaints have been made about lorries collecting chickens from the one remaining farm in centre of the village. As one 'Old Villager' from a farming family commented:

> If we ever wanted to annoy people I suppose, we could put pigs back down the yard [giggle]. Which we would be perfectly within our rights to do, but can you imagine, you know, how quickly people would moan about it?

One could argue that this sanitisation of the rural is characteristic of the British rural and perhaps particularly the English. However, objections by 'townies' to cockerels crowing provides a staple story for rural anti-urban tales in many countries, and the 'heritage' mentality with its desire for a cleansed countryside is pervading other European countries as well (see Abram 1997).

Before allowing readers to presume that my analysis of village groups is unequivocal, it should be noted that there are many other readings of social organisation in the village. Although the representation above is easily confirmed (with nuanced differences of definition) within the village, alternative defini-tions also exist. The groups, for example, are not mutually separable, since their membership overlaps considerably. The campaign group member quoted earlier, for example, suggested the village could be divided into wealthy resi-dents near the church, do-gooders with public spirit, young families too busy to get involved, and those that just 'don't really care'. In his typography, the motivations of a new group of protesters, who 'came out of the woodwork' when a field was closed to dog-walkers were merely selfish to the point of being 'laughable'.

His description also reveals that many villagers are most concerned with amenity, but also that they prefer to walk their dogs on land that most resembles urban parkland, rather than through the woods and fields nearby. This, again, indicates a sector of the population which expects their environment to fulfil suburban demands for convenient and sociable dog-walking, rather than the more romantic traditional pastimes of small-holding agricultural rural life. Perhaps the embodied pleasure of walking on a field is more significant to them than any visual aesthetic of 'the rural'. It is when such amenity is threatened that many in the village begin to object to local political plans.

Discussion

There are a number of points to be made about a 'rural gaze'. Firstly, that it is not independent of other sensory perceptions. Secondly, as hinted at above, the gaze is specific to place. That is, it varies with time and space. The situation described above is one case, and although it shares many features with similar cases in England, it should not be generalised in its detail, as Rapport argues (1993). The understanding of rurality in the Auvergne, for example, is not the same as in the Loire, and this is substantially different from notions of rurality in South East England, and so on. The strength of the peculiarly English rural vision is apparent in the preservation of 'conservation areas' under British planning law, where external appearance is highly regulated. Such conservation areas tend stringently to aspire to a previous (if imagined) state of building appearance. Regulations banning the use of modern signage in conservation areas, in a neighbouring village's conservation area for example, hint at an ironic nostalgia for a period less marked by consumer commercialism even though many of the residents have gained prosperity through those very means. In the English case, also, rural conservation areas often aspire to conserve the diversity of building details within a vernacular style, often exhibiting changes in that style over several centuries. There are clearly differences in aesthetic as well as in the political organisation of its enforcement.

A third point then arises, that far from being a purely academic curiosity, the organisation of the perception of the 'rural' has implications for the politics of rural development, conservation or preservation. The villagers described above approach development issues from a completely different standpoint than planners poring over maps, for example. Local Authority planners (at least in the district described above) tend to work to guidelines on a criteria-based rationality. Local planners looking for sites for quantities of housing may mark up criteria for appropriate sites; under current regimes, these include proximity to employment sites, public transport, public services, etc. While they may visit a settlement or know different sites through personal experience, the location of sites is calculated using two-dimensional representations: sites are marked on maps. The map serves, therefore, to distance experience from the rationalities that structure planning, distancing the planner from the various 'ground-level' gazes adopted by local residents. This distancing may be necessary to allow the planner to approach difficult dilemmas of siting controversial developments, but it also means that the planner is gazing on the landscape through the highly distorting medium of the map. The map is not merely a shorthand representation of the world, but is a means to govern the space it refers to, distanced by both time, space and structuring rationalities[4]. It is no wonder, then, that so many rural planning processes involve conflict and dispute given the very different ways of seeing/experiencing the rural that different parties adopt (see Murdoch and Abram 2002). What appears on a map to be a convenient space for building may relate to a landscape attributed with many other values by nearby residents.

The struggle for policies over land use is indicative of the multi-dimensionality of the emotional force of people's connections to landscapes and environments. This ensures that control over land, and landscape, is never static. As with any other form of power, it is constantly re-enacted and struggled over. Consequently, it would be futile to try to define '*the* rural gaze', since we can realistically describe only the areas that people choose to debate or ignore. We can note, therefore, the English concerns with hedgerows and stone walls, with vistas over meadows and pastoral scenes, and contrast this, for example, with the Norwegian concerns over public access to coastal zones, and the taking for granted of open access in non-cultivated areas (which, in contrast, is a distinctly *political* concern in England). Such contrasts, and the contrasts mentioned earlier in the paper, remind us that our experience of the rural, defined as it is through both discourses about the rural and the related ordering of our gaze upon the rural, as much as our embodied experience of rural life, is particular and not general. Our sense of what the rural is, despite the impossibility of defining it in any accurate, let alone objective sense, (who, in practice, adheres to a definition of urban density to define the limits of the rural?) has a set of distinct histories related both to histories of pastoral art and Romantic discourse, and historical political struggles.

However, it is as much the everyday local commentary on surroundings that conjures into existence, maintains and reinforces a particular regard for the rural, as much as the dominating effects of major art works and governmental policy. Residents in the village described above comment to each other, when meeting in the street, at coffee mornings, summer tea parties, etc., on the state of the village. They discuss the wildflowers in the hedgerows, the traffic around the school, the receding grass around the war memorial, the variety of wildlife they have seen in the fields (hares, muntjac deer, larks), the quality of villagers' gardens, litter and graffiti on the village hall. Local painters sell picturesque views of the village, reinforcing the nostalgia for quaint Englishness which helps to uphold the belief in the 'special' qualities of the place. Such background 'babble' of everyday commentary provides the context for larger debates about how to accommodate new housing, whether to rebuild roads, or whether to provide formal meeting places for teenagers, or the location of international airports, motorways or factories. The gaze, then, contributes to a world of understanding about what the 'rural' is, has been, and should be.

This chapter has taken a very specific approach to understanding the rural gaze. It has attempted to separate the academic/political terminology that denotes 'rural geography', for example, from the examination of the notion 'rural' as an ethnographic fact, that is, a concept found in practice and used to structure thinking about the world which can be examined and analysed using in-depth, experiential field research. Rather than pontificate on a general definition of what the gaze contains in the English context, it has used a case study to relate the organisation of lived experience and expectations to a notion of the rural, and to question what the concept of 'rural' is and does in practice. Some indication has also been given of the role of concepts of 'the rural' in political processes, and how mismatched notions of rural space provoke sustained, and sometimes bitter, political controversies over land use and development. I have tried to indicate the extent of the ascendancy of the visual over other senses, but at the same time have drawn the visual gaze back into its relation with other forms of perception, and examined its relationship with a broader discourse about rural life. This indicates, perhaps, a certain ambivalence about the privileging of the gaze over other forms of perception. On the one hand, it is inarguable that the visual has a particularly dominating role in the collective organisation of our perceptions. On the other hand, it seems that this role is deeply meshed with other senses, once one begins to examine, in practice, how people relate their experiences of rurality.

Notes

1. This debate is summarised by Jay (1986).
2. Which Perkins and Thorns (2001) perhaps unfairly blame on Urry's influence.
3. Fieldwork was funded by the Economic and Social Research Council (ESRC) under research award R000222057: *Planning as Metaphor: Mediating Aspirations for Community and Environment*.
4. See Miller and Rose (1993) on the use of technologies to enable 'action at a distance' as a tool of governance.

References

Abram, S. 1997 'Performing for tourists in France', pp. 29–49 in S. Abram, J. Waldren and D. Macleod (eds), *Tourists and Tourism: Identifying with People and Places*, Berg, Oxford.

Abram, S., Murdoch, J. and Marsden, T. 1998 'Planning by Numbers: Migration and Statistical Governance', pp. 236–251 in P. Boyle and K. Halfacree (eds), *Migration into Rural Areas: Theories and Issues*. Wiley, Chichester.

Adler, J. 1989 'Origins of sight-seeing', *Annals of Tourism Research*, **16**, 7–29.

Bowman, G. 1996 'Passion, Power and Politics in the Palistinian Tourist Market' in T. Selwyn (ed.), *The Tourist Image: Myths and myth-making in tourism*. John Wiley and Sons, Chichester.

Culler, J. 1988 *Framing the Sign: Criticism and its Institutions*, Oklahoma University Press, Oklahoma.

Fiefer, M. 1985 *Going Places: The Way of the Tourist from Imperial Rome to the Present Day*, Macmillan, London.

Foucault, M. 1976 *The Birth of the Clinic*, Tavistock, London.

Gell, A. 1999 *The Art of Anthropology*, Athlone Press, London.

Green, N. 1995 'Looking at the landscape: class formation and the visual', pp. 31–42 in E. Hirsch and M. O'Hanlon, *The Anthropology of Landscape*, Oxford University Press, Oxford.

Jay, M. 1986 'In the Empire of the Gaze: Foucault and the denigration of vision in twentieth-century French thought', pp. 175–204 in D.C. Hoy (ed.), *Foucault: A Critical Reader*, Basil Blackwell, Oxford.

Leheny, D. 1995 'A Political Economy of Asian Sex Tourism', *Annals of Tourism Research*, 22(2), 367–84.

Lowe, P., Murdoch, J. and Cox, G. 1995 'A Civilised Retreat? Anti-urbanism, rurality and the making of an Anglo-centric culture' in P. Healey (ed.), *Managing Cities: The new urban context*. Wiley, Chichester.

Lowenthal, D. 1985 *The Past is a Foreign Country*, Cambridge University Press, Cambridge.

MacCannell, D. 1992 *Empty Meeting Grounds: The Tourist Papers*, Routledge, London.

Miller, P. and Rose, N. 1993 'Governing economic life', in M. Gane and T. Johnson (eds), *Foucault's New Domains*, Routledge, London.

Murdoch, J. and Abram, S. 2002 *Rationalities of Planning*, Aldershot: Ashgate.

Okely, J. 1997 'Picturing and Placing Constable Country', pp. 193–220, in K.F. Olwig and K. Hastrup (eds), *Siting Culture: The Shifting Anthropological Object*, Routledge, London.

Perkins, H.C. and Thorns, D.C. 2001 'Gazing or performing? Reflections on Urry's tourist gaze in the context of contemporary experience in the Antipodes', *International Sociology*, 16(2), 185–204.

Pruitt, D. and Lafont, S. 1995 'For Love and Money: Romance Tourism in Jamaica', *Annals of Tourism Research*, 22(2), 367–84.

Rapport, N. 1993 *Diverse World Views in an English Village*, Edinburgh University Press, Edinburgh.

Soneryd, L. 2001 'Hearing as a way of dwelling: implications of a technological understanding of noise', paper to 'Siting Controversies' conference, CEFOS (Gothenburg) 17–20 May 2001. See www.cefos.gu.se/sitingconf

Strathern, M. 1981 *Kinship at the Core: An Anthropology of Elmdon, a Village in North-West Essex in the 1960s*, Cambridge University Press, Cambridge.

Urry, J. 1990 *The Tourist Gaze: Leisure and Travel in Contemporary Societies*, Sage, London.

Veijola, S. and Jokinen, E. 1994 'The body in tourism', *Theory, Culture and Society*, **11**, 125–51.

CHAPTER 4

Rural mappings

Catherine Brace

Introduction

> One icon of heritage has a distinctly English cast. That is the landscape. Nowhere
> else does the term suggest not simply scenery and genres de vie, but quintessential
> national virtues (Lowenthal 1991: 213).

In this section on Representing the Rural, I want to take a historical perspective to explore the construction of a particular 'country vision' through the
literal, visual and symbolic mapping of rural England in the 1920s and 1930s.
In so doing I will examine the link between English rural landscapes and
national identity. Though my title is 'Rural mappings', this is not a chapter about
cartography but uses mapping as a metaphor, as a means of 'comprehend-
ing the contours of social reality' (Smith and Katz 1993: 67)[1]. Using this idea
to unpack the construction and representation of rurality is part of the new
cultural politics which employs a richly spatialised vocabulary of grounding,
territory, exploring, colonising and so on. Such metaphors have proved fertile
means of destabilising supposedly fixed assumptions about identity and social
relations. Just as maps can show the spatial relations between places or locations, the metaphor of mapping can help us to work out the relations between
groups of people and help us to expose and destabilise the unequal power that
different groups have. Spatial metaphors are valued by cultural geographers
and others because of the way in which they can be used to challenge the taken
for granted aspects of social life.

   All metaphors, spatial or otherwise, 'work by invoking one meaning system
to explain or clarify another' (Smith and Katz 1993: 69)[2]. Smith and Katz note
that mapping works as a metaphor in two main ways. First, it can be useful to
define an area of enquiry – especially in cultural geography which has become
highly interdisciplinary and consistently draws on theories and bodies of work
across the social sciences. Second, the act of mapping is an active process
'whereby the locations, structures and internal relations of one space are

deployed in another' – from on the ground onto a piece of paper or computer screen, for example (Smith and Katz 1993: 70). This 'deployment' is important, for it is never a straightforward, literal, automatic process but involves exploration, selection, definition, generalisation and translation of data. The map thus assumes 'a range of social cum representational powers' (Smith and Katz 1993: 70) which have only recently been taken seriously by historians of cartography (see, for example, Harley 1988). Although in the past the claims to authority of maps and map-makers eluded critical scrutiny, recent attention has been paid to the work of the cartographer and the processes of positioning, scale, framing, absence and presence on the map as well as the ways in which maps are 'discursively embedded within broader contexts of social action and power' (Pickles 1992: 193). This extends the usefulness of the metaphor, for mapping speaks to the complex ways in which social relations are made and re-made and how the process of constructing knowledge is partial, contingent and saturated with power. The metaphor of mapping helps us to think through different country visions by calling attention to the existence of multiple and competing discourses of rurality. It also makes it possible to frame questions about both what the countryside represents and how it is represented.

In developing these key ideas, I take as my examples rural England in general and the specific region of the Cotswolds, a district of limestone hills in central southern England (Figure 4.1). The Cotswolds are an interesting example because they are still seen to represent an unspoilt bit of rural England, a prime example of the imagined 'rural idyll' which dominates popular conceptions of the countryside and which is still consistently rehearsed through books, magazines, television and other media and cultural products. Dymphna Byrne, a travel writer for the *Observer*, described the Cotswolds as 'the very picture of a perfect England. Their centuries old mullion-windowed houses with lichen encrusted roofs are part of the national consciousness. They . . . represent a dream of rural England we all want to share' (Byrne 1994: 46). Indeed, many images and ideas from the 1920s and 1930s about the countryside, rurality and Englishness still have tremendous contemporary resonance. Take, for example, the remarks made by the Prince of Wales as he launched a rural action plan to overcome the social and economic effects of foot and mouth disease in rural areas. 'The British countryside' he said,

> is only as beautiful as it is because it has been cared for, and lived in by these people with generations of experience and knowledge. The unique scenery, and the people who live amongst it, are one of the country's most treasured national assets (BBC 2001).

Rather than providing an account which isolates past representations, I attempt to trace the provenance of some of our contemporary thinking. In other words, this chapter offers part of a twentieth and twenty-first century history of ideas about the countryside that sees contemporary ways of imaging rurality to be deeply embedded in the past and that recognises a certain continuity of ideas,

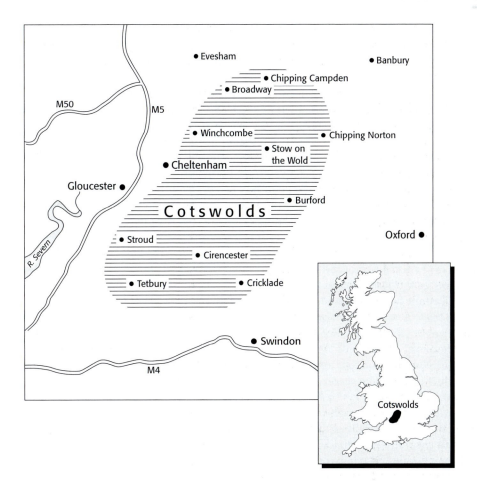

Figure 4.1 The Cotswolds.

images and motifs at work. This is not for a moment to argue that ideas about the countryside have remained unchanged since the 1920s and 1930s, or indeed that these decades somehow marked a clear *beginning* of some kind. It is important, however, to recognise that there is a history behind taken for granted dominant imaginings of the rural that requires critical scrutiny.

I wish to use the idea of mapping in a number of connected ways throughout this chapter. First, mapping stands as a metaphor for the seemingly new discovery and exploration of rural England in the 1920s and 1930s. As I will show, this was a physical discovery by a wave of visitors, daytrippers and holidaymakers and an intellectual discovery by writers, artists and thinkers not to mention an armchair discovery by those who bought books (fiction and non-fiction), magazines and newspapers and who listened to the radio[3]. Second, the metaphor of mapping helps us to think through the marking out of intellectual terrains in that period – especially ideas about the links between countryside and nationhood which were being developed in part because of new intellectual, popular and physical discoveries of the countryside. Third, we can think about the ways in which these ideas came to be mapped onto particular landscapes – in other words, how the countryside, or bits of it, came to represent the apotheosis of rural life and the ideal condition of England.

In what follows, I unpack the literal, visual and symbolic mappings of rural England and the Cotswolds by exploring mainly written and visual forms of representation including travel guides, pamphlets, collections of essays and especially a genre of books collectively known as non-fictional rural writing[4]. This collective term covers everything from personal memoir to topography and the diversity of the genre is characterised by a fascinating mix of political positions on display and the heady combination of historical lecture, humorous anecdote, polemic ranting, patronising pomposity, sentimentality and nostalgia. Although a readily available and widely used source, the important point about non-fictional rural writing, which is often overlooked, is that it is not just *writing*. In the period in question black and white photographs were widely used to illustrate books, and good quality colour photographs also started to be included. This was a significant selling point in the publishers B.T. Batsford's publicity material for the popular British Heritage Series, for example (Batsford *c.* 1939). Books of countryside writing also often included stylised end-paper maps, line-drawings, woodcuts and other types of illustration, not to mention striking dust jackets, like those of B.T. Batsford Ltd and Paul Elek. These visual components of countryside books are frequently overlooked, but should not be for they did not passively illustrate the message of the book but envisioned the countryside for the reader, added imaginative intensity to the text, and above all naturalised a version of rural England in which timelessness and continuity were powerful recurring motifs. If it is possible to think of mapping as a process controlled by conventions, rules of composition, framing, positioning and production then it is also possible to think of non-fictional rural writing in the same way, as a body of knowledge constructed in and through particular ways of seeing and recording with some shared conventions of production and style. As Matless argues, many such sources 'purport to speak with the authority akin to that of the scholar. All suggest being based on careful study rather than speculative musing' (Matless 1994: 11). As with maps, it is important to remain alert to the claims to authority and truthfulness made in non-fictional rural writing and the grounds upon which these claims are made.

Discovering the rural

In this section I want to explore the dimensions of the popular discovery of rural England that took place in the period between the two world wars. This 'discovery' is important in understanding representations of rural England in the 1920s and 1930s because it took place not only in the countryside itself but also between the covers of books, magazines and in other cultural products. Of course, people had been travelling through rural England for many years and writing about their travels (see Bunce 1994 for examples) but in the later years of the nineteenth century and at the beginning of the twentieth century a number of broader changes in society led to much greater use of the countryside as a site of recreation and leisure for a greater proportion of the population than ever before. By the 1870s, bank holidays and half-day holidays on Saturday were starting to be formalised and it became possible, with improvements in the rail network, to use this free time to travel into the countryside from large industrial cities by train, especially with the advent of cheaper fares and special excursion services (Bunce 1994). Organised hiking and rambling excursions were popular, as evidenced by the formation of the National Federation of Rambling Clubs in 1905. However, as Bunce notes, 'as long as people depended upon nineteenth century modes of transportation there were clear spatial limits to their enjoyment of the countryside' (Bunce 1994: 118). The growing popularity and affordability of the car had a tremendous impact on countryside recreation. In 1911 there were 132,000 privately owned cars in Britain. By 1939 this figure had risen to over two million (O'Connell 1998). This made a difference not only to the sheer number of people visiting the countryside but also to the nature of their encounter with it; new pastimes such as motor touring and motor picnicking gained popularity. H.V. Morton noted that the roads of England had 'come alive again; the King's highway is once more a place for adventures and exploration' (Morton 1933: vii–viii). Other forms of motorised transport were also important. In 1923 the Bristol Tramway and Carriage Company Ltd, which operated frequent daytrips to the Cotswolds, announced that

> The advent of the char-a-banc has brought a new joy to the lives of the great mass of people in this country. Not only do these great vehicles enable the onlooker to see and appreciate all that is delectable in the countryside, but they take their passengers out into the fresh air – air that is uncontaminated with factory smoke. We are transported from the prosaic purlieus of the towns to places that are sweet and clean (Bristol Tramway and Carriage Company Ltd 1923: 1).

Travelling through the countryside, observing and recording rural landscapes, architecture, pastimes and traditions became a staple of much non-fictional rural writing in the 1920s and 1930s. This was part of an imaginative mapping of rural England, in which even those who rarely visited the countryside could participate. It is impossible and indeed counter-productive to say whether the massive outpouring of tour guides, rural anthologies, topographical writing, countryside memoir and other kinds of countryside writing between the wars was stimulated by or itself stimulated new interest in coming to know rural England. Nevertheless, a glance around any second-hand bookshop today will reveal the extent of this publishing phenomenon, the importance of which has been recognised in recent scholarship. Gruffudd, for example, has identified the 'growing range of cultural products – travel books, landscape art, popular treatises on rural life, academic studies – [which] contributed to the creation of a ruralist discourse between the two world wars, each stressing the integrity of rural life and landscapes' (Gruffudd 1994: 247; see also Brace 2001).

Methuen, a substantial publishing concern, had popular success with H.V. Morton's *In Search of* Series which started in 1927 and was cheaply priced at three shillings and sixpence per volume (Gruffudd *et al.*, 2000; Rose and Anderson 1991). *In Search of England* – part tour, part personal travelogue – went through twelve editions by 1936 (O'Connell 1998). B.T. Batsford Ltd published 113 countryside books in seven series with over half appearing between 1934 and 1940 (Brace 2001). Between 1933 and 1941 Batsford claimed to have sold about 300,000 books in their British Heritage series (Batsford 1941–45; Table 4.1). The British Heritage series clearly reflected the

Table 4.1   Titles in The British Heritage Series

Title	Author	Date
The Face of Scotland	Harry Batsford and Charles Fry	1933
The Cathedrals of England	Harry Batsford and Charles Fry	1934
The Heart of Scotland	George Blake	1934
English Villages and Hamlets	Humphrey Packington	1934
The Old Inns of England	A.E. Richardson	1934
The Parish Churches of England	The Rev. J.C. Cox and Charles Bradley Ford	1934
The English Abbey	F.H. Crossley	1935
The English Country House	Ralph Dutton	1935
The Countryman's England	Dorothy Hartley	1935
The Heart of England	Ivor Brown	1935
The Spirit of Ireland	Lynn Doyle	1935
The Spirit of London	Paul Cohen-Portheim	1935
The English Castle	Hugh Braun	1936
Seas and Shores of England	Edmund Vale	1936
The Old Towns of England	Clive Rouse	1936
English Village Homes	Sydney R. Jones	1936
The English Garden	Ralph Dutton	1937
The Land of Wales	Eiluned and Peter Lewis	1937
The Old Public Schools of England	John Rodgers	1938
The English Cottage	Harry Batsford and Charles Fry	1938
Old English Customs and Ceremonies	F.J. Drake-Carnell	1938
Old English Household Life*	Gertrude Jekyll and Sydney R. Jones	1939
Prehistoric England	Grahame Clark	1940
British Hills and Mountains	J.H.B. Bell, E.F. Bozman and J. Fairfax Blakeborough	1940
The Greater English Church	Harry Batsford and Charles Fry	1940
English Church Craftsmanship	F.H. Crossley	1941
English Church Design 1040–1540 AD	F.H. Crossley	1945

*This edition is a revision of an earlier work by Jekyll in the English Life Series.

company's history of publishing books on the built environment and architecture by dealing with inns, castles, cathedrals, country houses, villages and so on. Another Batsford series, the Face of Britain, included regional topographies and concentrated on descriptions of landscapes, traditions, settlement, building styles and materials which were also popular themes amongst other publishers (Batsford *c*. 1939; Cook-Batsford 1987).

These coherent series of books say much about the imaginative mapping of rural England, for they offered systematic and almost complete region-by-region or county-by-county coverage of the country. Indeed, the idea of owning a whole series was promoted in the Batsford catalogues. In the 1938 catalogue a promotional photo shows all the books in the British Heritage series racked up on a desk in a study between two book ends (Batsford 1938; Figure 4.2). Three of the books have been taken out of the run and two lie on top of one another, as if just about to be referred to, while the other lies open at the title page. Nearby are a pair of gentleman's reading glasses and a cigarette burning on the edge of an ashtray. It is as if the reader has just been called away and will be back at any moment.

This image works at several connected levels; first, the books, when racked up with their spines showing on a special bookcase which sets them apart from other books, form an attractive, uniformly produced series and suggest pride in ownership. Second, the fact that the reader has three of the books out and is

Figure 4.2 Promotional photograph for Batsford's British Heritage Series (1938).

referring to one of them gives a sense that the series is more than the sum of its parts – a complete guide to various aspects of Britain's, or despite the series title, England's, landscape and (mostly material) culture. The books are not to be seen as individual texts. The appeal of the series is not just based on the uniformity of appearance but also on the sense of connectedness between the subjects. Finally, the books come across as enabling – they enable the reader to travel both mentally and physically while simultaneously educating him and giving him a complete sense of Britain's heritage – and the absent reader is most certainly a man.

Books that eulogised the glories of the English countryside were also a staple of smaller publishing houses such as Robert Hale, which produced two series of Regional Books and County Books, and Paul Elek, which produced the Vision of England series under the editorship of the architect and pre-servationist Clough Williams Ellis and his wife Amabel. Individuals were also prolific: H.J. Massingham, who wrote widely on agriculture and rural issues, was a regular contributor for B.T. Batsford Ltd while writer and broadcaster S.P.B. Mais produced 23 guidebooks for different publishers between 1930 and 1940, among them *This Unknown Island* and *Round About England* (Lowerson 1980). To these concerted publishing efforts can be added the scores of pocket guides, tour books, locally published writing, anthology and countryside memoir and special interest magazines published by cycling and motoring organisations and the Youth Hostel Association. Books, pamphlets and guides published in conjunction with railway companies such as Great Western Railway encouraged the reader to leave the comfort of the armchair and set off on a voyage of discovery around the 'unknown' English countryside (see, for example, Richens 1935).

What version of England was the new breed of domestic explorer encouraged to set off in search of? The range of countryside literature available was, as I have noted, enormous, but Lowerson notes that examples from this genre were 'by no means uniform in direction, structure or quality and were often submerged in a lowest common denominator of popular books' (Lowerson 1980: 260). Yet, representations of rurality in the interwar years from many different sources, often with widely different political intents, are remarkable for their congruity. The dominant motif might be most readily summarised through the phrase 'village England', for these were representations that positioned the village at the centre of rural life, as 'totems of stability and tabernacles of values' (Chase 1989: 132).

The Cotswold village, for example, was an important signifier of the best qualities of the region. Edward Hutton found himself lingering in Lower Guiting because 'the village was so charming, the old cottages so gay and contented, the old manor-house so perfectly at one with the England of my heart' (Hutton 1932: 98). The Cotswold stone lent a uniformity to the appearance of such villages and a great deal was made of the connection between the local geology and the vernacular architecture which seemed to point to an organic relationship between people and place. The Cotswolds were frequently referred to as a 'garden of stone' – a place where the stone has been cultivated into architectural display and the landscape has been cleared, colonised and enabled by hard work, thoughtfulness and skill, in a reciprocal rather than exploitative relationship with the land (Brace 1999c).

Writers such as H.J. Massingham applauded the 'revelation of a local, self-acting society, living by a fixed pattern of behaviour and with its roots warmly bedded in the soil' that he found described in Flora Thompson's reminiscences of village life in *Lark Rise to Candleford* and embodied in the Cotswolds where he lived for some years (Massingham 1942, 1984: 9). The church, the houses and the fields were the three 'anatomical essentials' of every English village, populated by the peasant, the yeoman, the craftsman, the squire and the priest (Massingham 1942: 152). For Massingham and others, the village was above all a symbol of order, continuity, tradition, stability and harmony.

The village was also a popular motif in the work of Brian Cook, who designed book jackets for B.T. Batsford Ltd. On the dust jacket of the *Legacy of England* (1935), for example, the view is framed by trees and shrubbery on the left and the church on the right (Figure 4.3). The lane draws the viewer simultaneously into the picture and the heart of the village. But the position from which this is viewed is elevated, perched high above the rooftops, enabling not just the contemplation of the village but the surrounding countryside. Several of Cook's early dust jackets combined both artistic conventions of framing and composition with conventions of an outlook geography that takes as its starting point the view from an elevated position from which all salient features of the landscape can be observed, described and categorised.

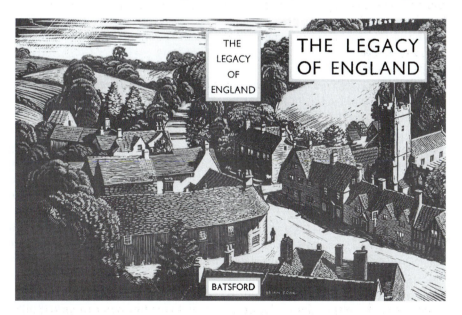

Figure 4.3 *Legacy of England* (1935) dust jacket.

Matless argues that outlook geography – that of pointing and talking on high places – taps into and informs a broader culture of landscape in Britain of which Batsford dust jackets are a part (Matless 1990).

There are strong parallels between Batsford jackets and, for example, Ordnance Survey map covers. The cover for the 1931 half inch map of the Cotswolds featured a rambler using the map as a tool of discovery, used to position himself in the landscape as a discoverer and explorer, not just a casual sightseer (Figure 4.4). There is a sense in which the elevated position encourages the act of survey in two senses; to view and to take stock, both of which have a didactic function. In the explicitly instructive *How to See the Countryside* (1940), Harry Batsford argued that while landscape can be appreciated without being understood, it was best appreciated given an understanding of form and structure (Gruffudd 1994: 256). The elevated position works to make form and structure more apparent; to give the very best vantage point for the act of discovery and enlightenment that awaits the reader between the covers of the book. But as much as the elevated position offered the opportunity to be able to see more clearly, the act of seeing was remarkably proprietary and reactionary, enabling the appropriation of the English rural landscape – to see the order of things as they were, are and should be. Whereas the outlook geography inspired by Patrick Geddes sought to understand the community and its habitat and their interrelations to point the way towards a more rational material and fuller spiritual expression of mankind (Matless 1992), Cook's imaginative mapping constructs a conservative vision of rural England. The villages look inward to the main street or the green, nestled in a valley, overseen by the manor, surrounded by fields, in an organic relationship with the landscape – constitutive of the scene rather than disrupting it. There are few people, and even fewer signs of progress or modernity: no new roads, no pylons, no unsightly building.

The elevated position also allows the viewer to be distant from dissenting voices or contested interpretations of either rural landscapes or the nation. Further, the surveying gaze indicates objective detachment, reinforcing the authority of the claims to knowledge embedded in the images. It was a popular technique of envisioning the rural, even adapted by modern artists like Sven Berlin. His line drawing of the remote Cornish village Zennor, for Peggy Pollard's *Cornwall* (1947), though full of vigour and recognisably modern in its use of perspective and form, takes up a position gazing over the foreground rooftops into the centre of the village, nestled beneath the high ground of Zennor Moor (Figure 4.5).

Photographs used similar techniques of positioning and composition but while line drawings and book jackets could be recognised for their decorative and creative content, photographs were privileged as an accurate and objective means of recording rural England. This claim to truth is important, for as Rose argues, the 'production, circulation and consumption of photographs produce and reproduce the imagined geographies of the social group or institution for which they are made' (Rose 2000: 555). A.K. Wickham's *The Villages of*

The Cotswolds

An Ordnance Survey District Map
on the HALF-INCH Scale.

Price: Three Shillings Net.

PUBLISHED BY THE ORDNANCE SURVEY OFFICE, SOUTHAMPTON.

Figure 4.4 Cover for the 1931 Ordnance Survey half inch map of the Cotswolds. (*Source*: reproduced from the 1937 Ordnance Survey map)

ZENNOR

Figure 4.5 *Zennor* by Sven Berlin.

England (1933) was conceived as an illustrated manual and typography of English villages based on classifications such as geology and place-names and as such contained a large number of photographs. The photograph of Northleach in the Cotswolds, which is taken across the rooftops from a field outside the village, is only one of many examples where an elevated standpoint is employed to look down into the village (Figure 4.6). The view from ground level looking up the village street was also a popular composition. Yet what Rose calls the 'complex practices of observation, production, reproduction and display' are rendered opaque by the pseudo-scientific way in which the photographs are employed (Rose 2000). The B.T. Batsford volume *England in Colour* was warmly praised for the way the photos reproduced natural colours (Bradley Ford 1939). The novelty of good quality black and white and colour reproduction led to a rush of new books almost entirely devoted to photographs of the countryside. Odhams' *British Countryside in Colour* (*c.* 1940) used a combination of black and white photographs and colour reproductions of paintings on nearly every page. For the first time the text became secondary to the envisioning of rural landscapes and culture.

Despite the new methods of photographic reproduction employed, the overall message continued to be conservative, emphasising changelessness and continuity, antiquity, tradition and stability. For *England in Colour*, B.T. Batsford

Figure 4.6 Northleach, Gloucestershire.

employed the most up-to-date and technologically advanced means of reproducing colour photographs, embracing and utilising modern techniques to convey a message about continuity and changlessness. What is important here is not what was included in the photographs but what was left out. People and vehicles are usually absent, as are recognisably new buildings, pylons or any other intrusive markers of modernity. In *English Villages and Hamlets*, Humphrey Pakington used a picture of Denham in Buckinghamshire with the telling caption 'so near to London, yet seemingly so far away' (Pakington 1934: 34). Photographs, like other visual representations, tended to locate rural England at the heart of villages – a village green was a useful signifier of a geographical and spiritual centre but a lane leading into the heart of the village also suggested a homecoming (lanes were hardly ever seen to leave the village in the background of the picture). Among the happy assortment of buildings, all in vernacular styles appropriate to the region, not a discordant note was sounded.

The countryside beyond the village was also important and was represented as a product of centuries of careful, cooperative stewardship. The English rural landscape was, for William Beach-Thomas, 'due to the home and the homestead that were built therein and the farms and gardens that were gathered about them. England is a homeland . . .' (Beach-Thomas 1938: xiv). The narrative device of situating the origins of the contemporary rural landscape in a distant past was a common one in both textual and visual representations which wove together narratives of the past, tradition, history, longevity and continuity (Brace 1999a). The Cotswolds were frequently represented as being a precious survival of an unspecified pre-industrial golden age upon which fortunate writers stumbled just at the moment when it had become helpless to combat the relentless march of progress and modernity (Brace 1999a). Locating the Cotswolds in the past constituted a deliberate and conscious setting apart and privileging of older versions of England from contemporary ones. Throughout the interwar years, the Cotswolds were continually 'discovered' as an exceptionally complete and undisturbed example of the best of 'old' England. As Potts shows, 'a common notion of the making of the English landscape . . . was that the tidy humanised views were the accumulated work of centuries of Englishman's labour going back into prehistoric times' (Potts 1989: 176). This labour was often embodied in the figure of the hearty agricultural labourer working the land with old-fashioned tools, as in the decorative title-page engraving of Blandford Press's *Countryside Mood* (1943; Figure 4.7).

Such a powerful and consistent message of tradition and stability was reinforced by the inclusion of end-paper maps in countryside writing. These were mocked up to look antiquated and were virtually useless for anything except decorative purposes in most cases. The end-paper map for H.V. Morton's *In Search of England* (first published 1927) used a hierarchy of place-name fonts that grouped Salisbury and Dorchester with Manchester, Birmingham and Leeds (Figure 4.8). This is an England of villages, market towns and cathedral cities, not of great Victorian industrial centres. Between the settlements are trees and hills. Mermaids and monsters share the seas with sailing ships, canvas billowing, evoking a bygone age of British seafaring and exploration. When Morton went in search of England, he was also searching in the past as well as making explicit a link between the nation and the rural. It is to this link that I now turn.

Countryside and nationhood

In an age of destruction there is a re-awakened interest in the things that endure. The hills, fields and rivers of England touch the hearts of us all because they offer normal living and the natural joys of earth . . . The picture of England stored in most minds is the serene, satisfying countryside (Harman 1943: 5).

Richard Harman penned his introduction to *Countryside Mood*, an anthology of rural writing, in 1943 in the midst of the Second World War. The book offered a selection of work by authors 'intimate with the true England' – among them Adrian Bell and Henry Williamson – and Harman was in no doubt about where that true England was located. His introduction went on:

Figure 4.7 *Countryside Mood* (1943) title page engraving.

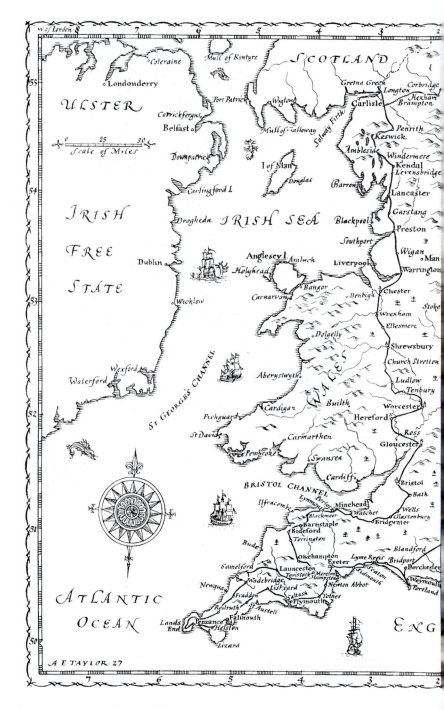

Figure 4.8 *In Search of England* (1927) end paper maps. (*Source*: © Marion Wasdell and Brian de Villiers)

A Map of England

Route followed is indicated by the black line

> Set right across the scene there is the romantic legacy left to us by history and the time-honoured traditions found in rural life. These things, and the quality of the individual lives which have built up the national character, constitute the England we hold in our deepest thoughts and affections. Always, these are the simple things – the unspoiled scenes, the simple lives, the steadfast homes, and the unshakeable faith (Harman 1943: 6).

It would be easy to dismiss Harman's intensely patriotic rhetoric as a piece of crude propaganda writing. Yet Harman was repeating sentiments that had been rehearsed many times as part of the mapping out of the link between English national identity and rural landscapes, life and culture in the 1920s and 1930s. The discovery of the countryside was accompanied by a discovery of the soul of the nation.

Over recent years scholars from a range of disciplines have recognised that landscapes are very important to the constitution of national identity. As Daniels argues, particular landscapes 'give shape to the imagined community of the nation' (Daniels 1993: 5), providing exemplars of moral order and aesthetic harmony. Representations of the Cotswolds were mobilised to precisely this end in the interwar years. A regional aesthetic was constructed which positioned the Cotswolds as the apotheosis of English life and culture. In the Cotswolds, Massingham claimed to have found the perfect landscape of the mind and claimed that 'the satisfaction was ultimate; one wanted no more of English land than this scene' (Massingham 1932: 248).

H.V. Morton – he of antiquated end-paper maps – reflected on this discovery of the essence of the nation in his bestselling *In Search of England*:

> The writer on England to-day addresses himself to a wider and more intelligent public than ever before. And the reason is, I think, that never before have so many people been searching for England. The remarkable system of motor-coach services which now penetrates every part of the country has thrown open to ordinary people regions which even after the coming of the railway were remote and inaccessible. The popularity of the cheap motor-car is also greatly responsible for this long-overdue interest in English History, antiquities and topography. More people than in any previous generation are seeing the real country for the first time. Many hundreds of such explorers return home with a new enthusiasm (Morton 1933: vii).

In this passage England and the countryside are conflated. When Morton speaks of people actively searching for England, he is not talking about searching in cities but in the countryside. Seeing the real country is seeing the real England for, as Charles Bradley Ford confidently noted, 'the English have always been a rural nation at heart' (Bradley Ford 1939: 5).

It should be clear, not only from these two authors, but from other primary source material discussed in this chapter, that rural landscapes and ways of life became powerful icons of Englishness in the years between the two world wars. Part of the explanation lies in the way national identities are constituted.

Recent scholarship has demonstrated that national identities are complex, shifting and dynamic rather than stable and homogeneous (Brace 1999b). National identities are no longer considered to be unchanging entities, an attachment to which is a natural result of having been born in a particular place. Rather, national identities are viewed as cultural artefacts, promoted and spread through a whole range of institutions, events, symbols and cere-monies. Smith lists, among these cultural artefacts, flags, anthems, parades, coinage, passports, war-memorials, folklore, museums, oaths, popular heroes and heroines, fairytales, national recreation, legal procedures, educational practices and military codes (Smith 1991), to which we could add landscape. National identities are constantly in a process of being made and remade, especially at times when they are threatened. Not by accident, then, were new terrains of debate opening up about the nature of the English national identity in the interwar years. Indeed, it only becomes clear that representations of rural England had a greater political purpose when we discover what they are set against. England was being thought about, written about and talked about at great length and across all kinds of mediums from newspapers to novels, precisely because the integrity of the so-called national culture was seen to be vulnerable to unacceptable change and modification.

There were many stimuli to these debates. Heavily influenced by a develop-ing ruralist discourse in the late Victorian and Edwardian eras, First World War propaganda had positioned rural landscapes as something which summed up what it was about England that was worth fighting for, something uniquely English that struck a chord with every Englishman (Howkins 1986; Wiener 1981). This sort of imagery persisted, and was subtly reworked through the 1920s and 1930s to repel domestic and international crises such as the depres-sion, the General Strike and the threat from Nazi Germany. Early in the Second World War, B.T. Batsford managed to convey the impression that the project of publishing countryside writing throughout the 1930s had been part of a patriotic master plan:

> During the last few troubled years, Batsfords have gradually been building up a list of cheap, well-illustrated books which, in words and illustrations, give a true picture of the land whose freedom we are defending to-day: its fine traditions of craftsmanship, and the life and work of its countryside, evolved through centuries of peaceful endeavour (Batsford 1940: 9).

The books were to provide comfort and inspiration to the public. 'The Britain they present' ran the advertising copy, 'the Britain of field, hedge and coppice, of villages and farms, of time-mellowed, historic buildings and ancient cities and towns, will be increasingly cherished by thinking people at a time when all it represents is at stake' (Batsford 1940: 9). Though the company referred to Britain, it is significant that the vast majority of their books dealt with England.

Other threats to national identity that were identified were more insidious. Lowerson notes that between the wars the urban area of England and Wales increased by about 26 per cent including the construction of four million new houses (Lowerson 1980). Books such as *England and the Octopus* (first published 1928) and *Britain and the Beast* detailed the problem:

> [T]he march of an inglorious suburbia across our countryside . . . the marring of vista upon vista, where country still remains, by the erection of unsuitable buildings, by thoughtless felling of trees, by Philistine methods of road-making and road-widening – in short the blighting touch of the townsman upon the country (Boumphrey 1938: 101).

While anti-urban sentiment was nothing new, the threat to the countryside and to a specifically English way of life that was keenly felt and widely talked about was the uncontrolled spread of what Matless calls 'an England in-between of suburb, plotland and ribbon development' (Matless 1998: 32). What was under construction was a moral geography which positioned rural England in general and regions such as the Cotswolds in particular in opposition to unacceptable aspects of life in England. The tranquillity and harmony of the Cotswold village was mobilised against ribbon developments, and the 'invasion' of red brick and jerry building that epitomised the 'in-between England'. Massingham's fears for the integrity of rural life and landscapes were dramatised by new buildings in Bourton-on-the-Water where, he noted, 'the clash between the harmonies of the traditional Cotswold houses rising flowerlike from their Cotswold earth and the abrupt dissonance – cacophony indeed – of those warts of the speculative builder which, I suppose, the railway has brought to Bourton' (Massingham 1932: 248). The language is of contagion, disease and disfigurement. Ancient is juxtaposed to modern; natural and harmonious to unnatural and brash; the ripe mellow colour of the indigenous stone – hewn by the hands of a Cotswold mason – to the jarring red bricks churned out by a Midlands factory.

The integrity of rural life was vulnerable to dislocation from not only new settlements and new buildings but also new kinds of people coming to the countryside, and the countryside changing to accommodate them. Here the imaginative mapping of rural England by visitors and book-buyers and the evolving discourses of nationhood overlap. At precisely the moment when countryside writing was reaching a peak of popularity, serious and far-reaching questions were asked about what writer and philosopher C.E.M. Joad called 'the untutored townsman's invasion of the country' and the consequences for England (Joad 1938). Visiting masses were seen to despoil what they came to admire by roaring through beauty spots in fast cars, dropping litter and seeking out the heady entertainment of the newly established ye olde tea-shoppe instead of enjoying the countryside in a peaceful, contemplative way (Brace 2000). The paradox was summed up by Charles Bradley Ford who, having noted the essentially rural character of the English people, also observed that 'with the improvement of transport the Englishman is only reverting to type again – but at the expense of that hitherto secure escapist paradise, the countryside' (Bradley Ford 1939: 5). Indeed, some of the anxieties about popular discoveries of rural England centred on fears for the character of the nation: that England's people were distant from the countryside that defined them. As John Lowerson has put it 'how sharp had become the notion that the townsman, the weekender, was not necessarily the angel of culture' (Lowerson 1980: 261).

It is clear that part of the process of mapping out the nature of Englishness also entailed constructing a moral geography of places which were signally un-English, like jerry-built suburbia, and people who were out of place like the charabancers who unfeelingly grubbed up the bluebells in a Cotswold wood, to the disgust of a farmer who shot out the tyres of their bus (Massingham 1932). But this vilification of problem people and places was only made possible by the corollary; the search for and valorisation of untouched, unsullied places that epitomised the things about Englishness which were so valued. In other words, the discursive mapping of English national identity was accompanied by the projection of these ideas onto particular landscapes which came to represent the ideal condition of England. The Cotswolds stand as an example of the way in which very specific sets of ideas about the proper order of things in the nation, and the proper balance between urban and rural were mapped onto a material landscape. This is not to make an exclusive claim for the Cotswolds – many parts of rural England were claimed in the same way. Cotswold writing – and indeed, regionally-specific non-fictional rural writing from all over the country – cannot be disentangled easily from writing about rural England and nor should it be, for the attempts to capture the essence of the region and map its moral geographies in the 1920s and 1930s were also attempts to construct a perfect England deemed to be preserved there.

Conclusion

Countryside writing, poster art, map covers, book jackets, line drawings and engravings, end-paper maps and anthologies of rural poetry and prose were just some of the means through which rural England and English national identity were mapped in the 1920s and 1930s. In this chapter I have used the notion of mapping as a means of exploring intellectual and popular discoveries of the countryside, debates about the nation and the ways in which certain landscapes were appropriated as icons of Englishness. It is important to remember that these three ways in which rural England was 'mapped' are connected in complex and shifting ways. Unpacking historical representations of the rural is not always a straightforward task and I have only begun here to called attention to early twentieth century knowledge making by pointing to the means through which certain ways of coming to know the nation became popularised and embedded. However, the job of exploring historical geographies of knowledge and representations of rurality remains an important one, for such mappings have endured in the imagined landscapes of contemporary rurality – for example in the pages of *Country Life* and derivative rural magazines, on television and radio – and are continually evoked in discussions about the future of rural England and the development of appropriate policy vehicles. Contemporary representations of rurality that are often predicated on seemingly taken for granted ideas about rural England have a provenance and a history that requires critical scrutiny. Ultimately the act of representation is not neutral, but political.

Notes

1. Daniels and Rycroft (1993) point to the way in which metaphors of mapping are used to a similar end by Alan Sillitoe in his novels to make sense of working class geographies of Nottingham.

2. For a cautionary discussion about taking spatial metaphors for granted, see Smith and Katz (1993).

3. It is important not to make a false distinction here. Writers, artists and thinkers could also be visitors, daytrippers and holidaymakers, readers and listeners.

4. A significant but under-researched source are radio broadcasts from the period.

References

Batsford, B.T. 1938 *Batsford Books on Britain*, B.T. Batsford Ltd, London.

Batsford, B.T. *c.* 1939 *Batsford's Catalogue of Publications*, B.T. Batsford Ltd, London.

Batsford, B.T. 1940 *Batsford's Autumn Books and War-time Reading*, B.T. Batsford Ltd, London.

Batsford, B.T. 1941–45 Batsford Books 1941–1945, B.T. Batsford, London.

Batsford, H. 1940 *How to See the Countryside*, B.T. Batsford Ltd, London.

BBC 2001 'Prince unveils rural action plan', http://news.bbc.co.uk/hi/english/uk/ newsid_1452000/1452105.stm, 24 July.

Beach-Thomas, W. 1938 *The English Landscape*, Country Life Ltd, London.

Boumphrey, G.M. 1938 'Shall the towns kill or save the country?', pp. 101–12 in C. Williams-Ellis (ed.), *Britain and the Beast*, Reader's Union by arrangement with J.M. Dent and Sons Ltd, London.

Brace, C. 1999a 'Looking back: the Cotswolds and English national identity, *c.* 1890–1950', *Journal of Historical Geography*, **25**(4), 502–16.

Brace, C. 1999b '"Finding England Everywhere": regional identity and the construction of national identity 1890–1940', *Ecumene*, **6**(1), 90–109.

Brace, C. 1999c 'Gardenesque imagery in the representation of regional and national identity: the Cotswold Garden of Stone', *Journal of Rural Studies*, **15**, 365–76.

Brace, C. 2000 'A pleasure ground for the noisy herds? Incompatible encounters with the Cotswolds and England, 1900–1950', *Rural History, Economy, Society, Culture*, 11(1), 75–94.

Brace, C. 2001 'Publishing and publishers: towards an historical geography of country-side writing, c. 1930–1950', *Area*, 33(3), 287–96.

Bradley Ford, C. 1939 *England in Colour*, B.T. Batsford Ltd, London, first published 1937.

Bristol Tramway and Carriage Company Ltd 1923 *Bristol Motor Coach Tours and Omnibus Services from Gloucester*, British Publishing Company, Gloucester.

Bunce, M. 1994 *The Countryside Ideal: Anglo-American Images of Landscape*, Routledge, London.

Byrne, D. 1994 'Travel Cotswolds' *The Observer Life Magazine*, 14 August, p. 46.

Chase, M. 1989 'This is no claptrap, this is our heritage', pp. 128–46 in M. Chase and C. Shaw (eds), *The Imagined Past: History and Nostalgia*, Manchester University Press, Manchester.

Cook-Batsford, B. 1987 *The Britain of Brian Cook – a Batsford Heritage*, BT Batsford Ltd, London.

Daniels, S. 1993 *Fields of Vision*, Polity, Cambridge.

Daniels, S. and Rycroft, S. 1993 'Mapping the modern city: Alan Sillitoe's Nottingham novels', *Transactions of the Institute of British Geographers*, NS18(4), 460–80.

Gruffudd, P. 1994 'Selling the countryside: representations of rural Britain', pp. 247–63 in J. Gold and S.V. Ward (eds), *Place Promotion: The Use of Publicity and Marketing to Sell Towns and Regions*, Wiley, Chichester.

Gruffudd, P., Herbert, D.T. and Piccini, A. 2000 'In search of Wales: travel writing and narratives of difference', *Journal of Historical Geography*, 26(4), 589–604.

Harley, J.B. 1988 'Maps, knowledge and power', pp. 277–312 in D. Cosgrove and S. Daniels (eds), *The Iconography of Landscape*, Cambridge University Press, Cambridge.

Harman, R. 1943 'Foreword', *Countryside Mood*, Blandford Press, London.

Howkins, A. 1986 'The discovery of rural England', pp. 62–88 in R. Colls and P. Dodd (eds), *Englishness – Politics and Culture 1880–1920*, Croom Helm, London.

Hutton, E. 1932 *Highways and Byways in Gloucestershire*, Macmillan and Co, London.

Joad, C.E.M. 1938 *The Untutored Townsman's Invasion of the Country*, Faber and Faber, London.

Lowenthal, D. 1991 'British national identity and the English landscape', *Rural History, Economy, Society, Culture*, 2(2), 205–30.

Lowerson, J. 1980 'Battles for the Countryside', pp. 258–80 in F. Gloversmith (ed.), *Class, Culture and Social Change – A New View of the 1930s*, Harvester Press, Sussex.

Massingham, H.J. 1932 *Wold Without End*, Cobden Sanderson, London.

Massingham, H.J. 1942 'Village bedrock', *Gloucestershire Countryside*, 4(7), April–June, 152–3.

Massingham, H.J. 1984 'Introduction', in F. Thompson, *Lark Rise to Candleford*, Penguin, Harmondsworth, first published 1939.

Matless, D. 1990 'The English outlook: a mapping of leisure, 1918–1939', pp. 28–32 in N. Alfrey and S. Daniels (eds), *Mapping the Landscape – Essays on Art and Cartography*, University Art Gallery, Nottingham.

Matless, D. 1992 'Regional surveys and local knowledges: the geographical imagination in Britain, 1918–1939', *Transactions of the Institute of British Geographers*, NS17(4), 464–80.

Matless, D. 1994 'Doing the English village, 1945–1990: an essay in imaginative geography', pp. 7–88 in P. Cloke, M. Doel, D. Matless, M. Phillips and N. Thrift *Writing the Rural*, Routledge, London.

Matless, D. 1998 *Landscape and Englishness*, Reakiton, London.

Morton, H.V. 1933 *In Search of England*, Methuen, London, first published 1927.

O'Connell, S. 1998 *The Car In British Society: Class, Gender and Motoring 1896–1939*, Manchester University Press, Manchester.

Odhams *c.* 1940 *British Countryside in Colour*, Odhams Press Ltd, London.

Pakington, H. 1934 *English Villages and Hamlets*, B.T. Batsford Ltd, London.

Pickles, J. 1992 'Text, hermeneutics and propaganda maps', pp. 193–230 in T.J. Barnes and J.S. Duncan (eds), *Writing Worlds: Discourse, Text and Metaphor in the Representation of Landscape*, Routledge: London.

Pollard, P. 1947 *Cornwall*, Vision of England series, C. Williams Ellis and A. Williams Ellis (eds), Paul Elek, London.

Potts, A. 1989 '"Constable Country" between the Wars', pp. 160–86 in R. Samuels (ed.), *Patriotism: The Making and Unmaking of National Identity: Volume 3: National Fictions*, Routledge, London.

Richens, F.R. 1935 'The unknown Cotswolds', *Great Western Railway Magazine*, XLVII(5), 265–68.

Rose, G. 2000 'Practising photography: an archive, a study, some photographs and a researcher', *Journal of Historical Geography*, 26(4), 555–71.

Rose, J. and Anderson, P.J. (eds) 1991 *Dictionary of Literary Biography: Volume 112: British Literary Publishing Houses 1881–1965*, Gale Research International Ltd, London and Detroit.

Smith, A.D. 1991 *National Identity*, Penguin, London.

Smith, N. and Katz, C. 1993 'Grounding metaphor – towards a spatialized politics', pp. 67–83 in M. Keith and S. Pile (eds), *Place and the Politics of Identity*, Routledge, London.

Wiener, M. 1981 *English Culture and the Decline of the Industrial Spirit 1850–1980*, Penguin, Harmondsworth.

Wickham, A.K. 1933 *The Villages of England*, B.T. Batsford Ltd, London.

Different genres, different visions? The changing countryside in postwar British children's literature

CHAPTER 5

John Horton

Introduction

[T]aking children's fiction as my ostensible subject, I have also been intent upon a wider and more impalpable subject: the nature of popular culture and the way these particular forms of the social imagination try to fix admired social values in a story, give them place and name and continuity (Inglis 1981: xi).

Anyone interested in how ideas – political ideas in the broadest and most important sense – are fostered and grow up in a society cannot afford to neglect what children read (Dixon 1977a: xv).

This chapter concerns the representation of 'countryside' – that most stubbornly resilient and ideologically freighted of ideas (Bell and Valentine 1995; Daniels 1992; Kinsman 1995; Valentine 1989) – in storybooks produced for children in postwar Britain. It is written from three frustrations. *Firstly*, that despite promising introductory gestures (Bunce 1994: 62–54; Houlton and Short 1995; Jones 1997: 161) made as part of a 'rather furious engagement with . . . representational texts . . . which reproduce constructions of rurality in popular culture' (Cloke 1997: 372) during the 1990s, there is a continued paucity of new empirical research or critical writing on contemporary children's literature, in which representations of rural places, people, events and practices are remarkably, disproportionately present (Hunt 1995: xi). *Secondly*, a frustration that academic engagements with the texts, narratives and representations made available for (us as) children have too often been predicated upon (and reproduced) a limited – some would say perniciously conservative, blinkered, 'distinctly backward-looking' (Tucker 1999: 221) – conception of 'Children's Literature'. Time and time again, the especial significance of a modest canon of 'classic' texts written for young children (Enid Blyton's *Famous Five*, Beatrix Potter's stories, A.A. Milne's *Winnie-the-Pooh*, Kenneth Grahame's *Wind in the Willows*, Arthur Ransome's *Swallows and Amazons* and Richmal Crompton's *William* stories) has been recognised. Notwithstanding their undeniable, continued significance, this has meant that a small exclusive shelfful of books has, in effect, come to stand for 'Children's Literature' *per se* (and thus a few evocations of rurality have come to stand for '*the* represented countryside'). Meanwhile many, many children's books (and represented ruralities) have been cast outside the acknowledged canon. So consequently, *thirdly*, moves to unpack the rural idyllicism of 'Children's Literature' are too often utterly, frustratingly, ahistorical, failing to recognise that 'children's literature' is ever-changing, never complete, that 'change . . . is probably [its] only meaningful conceptual "absolute"' (MacCann 1989: 1). That is, they say very little about how 'the represented countryside' has changed, as new literary rurals for children have been imagined, produced and circulated, while older ones have been reworked, recirculated or effaced. Nor do they have much to say about how books written for children, and representations within them, 'are not part of our culture by chance' (Watson 1992: 14), but emerge(d) from spatially, temporally particular means and relations of production (Hall 1980) in which 'a whole industry full of people making a living from the interchange: author, illustrator, publisher, printer, agent, wholesaler, retailer, . . . teacher and librarian . . . even writer of critical essays' has always been implicit (Mackey 1998: 153).

This chapter aims to address these frustrations, and reassert that anyone interested in how (a particular, exclusive, exclusionary, English version of) the rural is rendered evocatively, imaginarily, effectively 'idyllic' cannot afford to neglect contemporary children's literature. It aims, also, to begin removing the blinkers hitherto characteristic of many academic engagements with children's literature. While acknowledging the continued importance of 'classics', it will draw the reader's attention to some as yet overlooked – particularly more recent, and emergent – literatures and representations of the countryside in British children's literature. It will focus attention, too, upon an important difference: between *representations* of rurality (the texts, images, artefacts and narratives themselves), and the '*systems of visualisation*' (the material structures, guidelines, rules, protocols and practices governing and constituting those representations (Woodiwiss 2001: 3)). The chapter unfolds chronologically, historicising postwar representational practices and products as effects of socio-historic 'extraliterary cultural formations', articulated in and of 'curious and wonderful convulsions in the literary, moral and social landscapes . . . a complex business' (Blishen 1975: 9). The narration of this complex business is part oral history (it is hung loosely from anecdotal recollections of three children's librarians from one of the UK's 166 Public Library

Authorities) and part archival. It identifies four historically distinctive postwar systems of visualisation, which in turn effected four postwar 'genres' of represented countryside, as follows.

1945–1969: 'classic' representations of countryside

I mean really, everything started anew after Second World . . . War . . . Pretty much every library and every school had to go about the business of acquiring a new stock of books . . . It's no exaggeration to say that most institutions had to totally replace their stock . . . Beggars couldn't afford to be choosers, they just bought whatever was published in bulk (Mrs A).

The end of the Second World War is widely posited as a watershed after which, in a very tangible sense, British children's literature began anew. After national paper shortage and print rationing during the war years, and the destruction of many publishers' stocks and printing plates in bombing raids on London, the vast majority of children's books had fallen out of print (Gray 1982: 26). In the economic and legislative preconditions of late 1940s Britain, there was unprecedented demand for children's books because 'money for public and school libraries [flowed] freely under the Labour government' via policies supporting 'National Reconstruction' and mass literacy. This demand was augmented by overseas orders, particularly from the United States 'where Lyndon Johnson's campaign to create the Great Society put children's reading at the heart of government policy' (Reynolds 1998: 2). So British 'children's literature' was literally, materially recreated to meet this demand, almost exclusively in the form of long-running, 'pocket book' series which could be quickly and inexpensively mass produced, and systematically promoted (Kamm 1970: 32). As printing presses rolled anew, there was a need for reflection upon each out-of-print title, since 'a conscious decision had to be taken as to whether it was worth the cost and effort of setting up in type and republishing' (Gray 1982: 26). Many titles deemed out of date in their setting, themes and attitudes were never republished, while those befitting the prevailing 'propitious melding of mood, talent, technological development, and opportunity' (Reynolds 1998: 2) were published, purchased and made publicly available to an unprecedented extent. In practice, this meant 'a sudden rush of nostalgia for rural life', for – as in the immediate aftermath of previous British crises – 'pastoral attitudes were reasserted with intensity', and wholesome stories of law-abiding heroism in gentle rural settings came to proliferate in the series which collectively constituted this 'new Children's Literature' (Hannabuss 1977: 128, 127).

A list (Whitehead *et al.* 1977: 125–9) of the hundred most widely read 'juvenile fiction' books in British public libraries in 1969 illustrates both the predominance of series publication, and the prevalence of representations of countryside in this 'New Children's Literature'. Books from seven different series of books by Enid Blyton constitute two-thirds of the list. Individually and collectively these books – written between 1938 and 1944, and marketed as series with distinctive, oft-imitated branded dustjackets – 'painted an idyllic vision of rural England and hearty Englishness' based upon views, settings and experiences from and around Blyton's home at Green Hedges in Beaconsfield, Buckinghamshire (Liukkonen 2000: 1). In the most widely read of the series, 'The Famous Five' (21 books), Blyton and the illustrator Eileen Soper portrayed rural England as a milieu of isolated farmhouses, country lanes, wild-flower meadows, patchwork fields, hills, moors, hedgerows, haystacks, windmills, lakes, streams, waterfalls and coastal paths (where the water always 'shines as blue as cornflowers'; Dixon 1977b: 55), country houses, romantically ruined forts, caves, smugglers' coves, trapdoors and secret passages, steam trains, scarecrows, gorse bushes, cows pulling up grass and evocative place-names (Tally-Ho Cottage, Appletree Farm, Owl's Dene, Buttercup Farm, Holly lane Cottage, Smugglers' Top, Billycock Hill, Mystery Moor, Demon's Rock, and so on). Across this backdrop, 'the Five' – Julian, Dick and Anne, their cousin Georgina and her dog, Timmy – spend summer holidays camping (hampers full of boiled eggs, chocolate eclairs and lashings of ginger beer), hiking, riding ponies and bicycles, solving problems, having adventures and encountering intemperate rogues, travelling folk, circuses, escaped convicts and greedy speculators. Blyton's other popular series essentially re-presented this imagined rural geography, and this narrative premise with slight twists and different names. Her 'Farm Series' (5 books) portrayed 'snobby town cousins' newly entering this pastoral idyll, coming to 'delight in helping out, learning all about and adapting to farmlife . . . and life in the country' through horse riding, haymaking, mucking out, and mucking in together, becoming 'better people for having their corners rubbed off' (Forsyth 1989: 4). Her 'Malory Towers Series' (6 books) portrayed a girls' boarding school – 'a big, square-looking building of soft grey standing high up on a hill . . . with four rounded towers and scaling green creeper [conjuring] up images of old-time castles' – and follows four pupils and their 'games, lessons, quarrels, rows and . . . lively adventures' (Forsyth 1989: 6), at school, and their picnics, midnight feasts, swims in 'cornflower blue' pools, horse rides and tennis and lacrosse games in the surrounding countryside. In 'the Noddy Library' (24 books) Blyton and her collaborator, the Dutch artist Harmsen van der Beek, rendered the English countryside as a colourful 'Toyland' through which Noddy drives, his head nodding, his bell ringing and his car 'parp, parping', along country lanes, past hills, meadows 'all full of flowers and little butterflies', more 'cornflower blue' lakes, cottages, steam trains and dark woods, encountering his friends Big-Ears, Mr Plod, Tessie Bear, The Tubby Bears, Bumpy-Dog as well as villainous golliwogs. The other listed Blyton series stick closely to the 'Famous Five' format. In the 'Family Series' (14 books) different groups of young people (and their pets) in 'typically Blyton-esque' rural settings' (in Under-Ridge village, on Buttercup Farm, in Redroofs cottage, in a caravan, at the seaside, in a hollow tree) 'learn the value of sticking together like a family' through stories with 'particularly strong moral and religious tones' (Forsyth 1989: 54), while the '*Mystery Series*' (15 books) describes the adventures of the 'The Five Find-Outers' – 'Fatty', Laurence, Margaret, Philip, Elizabeth and Fatty's Scottie dog Buster – as they help the bungling local policeman Mr Goon solve mysteries (a disappearing cat, a missing necklace, a burnt cottage, 'a strange bundle', spiteful letters and so on) in their small rural English village of Peterswood, and the '*Secret Seven Series*' (16 books) followed a 'secret society' of friends (themselves '*Famous Five*' readers) – Peter, Janet, Colin, Barbara, Pam, Jack, George and Scamper the dog – as they solve crimes and raise money for good causes in and around the rural village of Brameley.

Behind Blyton, the most widely read 'juvenile fiction' writers in 1969 were Beatrix Potter, Anthony Buckeridge and Arthur Ransome (with eight listed books each). Each, in their way, wrote brand-able pocketbook-size stories set in (a very particular version of) the English countryside. Potter's series of whimsical storybooks (19 books, 1902–1913) about diminutive young anthropomorphic woodland animal characters – notably Peter Rabbit, Benjamin Bunny, Jemima Puddle-Duck, Mrs Tiggy-Winkle the hedgehog, Mr Jeremy Fisher the toad – were written about animals encountered on the author's numerous holidays to the village of Sawrey in the English Lake District and set in an idyllic countryside milieu based upon, and illustrated with, miniature reproductions of Potter's own pastel and watercolour paintings of views of and from Sawrey. As many biographers have suggested, this world of fir trees, bakers' shops, prettily decorated country kitchens inside hollow trees, cucumber frames, gooseberry nets, rabbit burrows, mill ponds, decorum, courtesy, family values and community, 'where the sun always shines and colours merge gently into each other, [e]verything is neat, ordered and flourishing, adorned by flowers and set against a lyrical backdrop of mountains' might be read as a projection of Blyton's own rural idyllicism, a reaction to her 'lonely, isolated' urban upbringing, where 'pet animals and the Lakeland countryside where she spent her holidays, were lifelines to a more fulfilled existence than her boring life in London could ever offer' (Tucker 1981: 60). Similarly, Arthur Ransome's '*Swallows and Amazons*' series (13 books, 1930–1934) which describe the Walker children's holiday adventures and boating expeditions – stories of genteel leisure broken only by trips to collect fresh milk from an obliging farmer's wife, meetings with friendly charcoal-burners, the tickling of trout, and the collecting of fox-moth caterpillars, where nothing goes awry which cannot be righted by a picnic feast of eggs, rice pudding, brown bread, seed cake, apples, strawberry ices, bath buns, parkin, rock cakes, ginger-nuts or chocolate biscuits – on and around 'Wild Cat Island' in the Lake District, represent Ransome's childhood memories of escapist family holidays from Leeds, 'by train to Greenodd, complete with their belongings packed into a large tin bath, and then by cart along the valley to Lowick and, finally, to Nibthwaite, on the shores of Coniston Water' (Thomsen and Thomsen 1996). Likewise, Anthony Buckeridge's '*Jennings*' series (22 books, 1950–1977) re-presents the author's nostalgia, relating the adventures and japes of Jennings and Darbishire, two young boys at 'Linbury Court Prep', a boarding school in the fictional village of Dunhambury, in rural Sussex, were written for and about pupils Buckeridge taught at Ramsgate Preparatory School in St Laurence's, also in rural Sussex, wistfully articulating the author's belief in a 'a gentler and simpler age before life became complicated and the certainties of the world as we knew them were swept away' (Welsh 2000). Similar sorts of rural idyllicism are predominant in the remainder of the 'most widely read' list, which includes Richmal Crompton's '*William*' series (38 books, 1922–1970), which 'provides a unique portrait of the changing landscape of a typical English village' as a backdrop to 'the pranks and scrapes of . . . this tousle-headed, snub-nosed, hearty, loveable imp of mischief' (Schutte 1993: x), the '*Jill*' series (9 books, 1962–1969) by Ruby Ferguson – 'the Enid Blyton . . . of pony stories' – which 'taught us girls . . . exactly how to ride and care for a gymkhana pony, even if only in theory' (Cridland 1999), A.A. Milne's *Winnie-the-Pooh* series (2 books, 1926–1928) with their famous anthropomorphic animal cast at home in 'informal and inconspicuous . . . wooded English countryside . . . without so-called "progress and development"' (Richards 2001: 1) – based upon Ashdown Forest, East Sussex – familiarly illustrated by E.H. Shepherd, Rev. W. Awdry's *Railway* series (26 books, 1945–1972) nostalgically based upon steam trains which once ran on the Great Western Railway near his rural vicarage in Box, Wiltshire, as well as Kenneth Grahame's (1908) *Wind in the Willows*, Johanna Spyri's (1884) *Heidi*, Frederick Marryat's (1840) *Children of the New Forest*, Johann David Wyss's (1912) *Swiss Family Robinson* and Lucy Maud Montgomery's (1908) *Anne of Green Gables*.

Despite relatively various authorship, the storybook series from this 'Golden Age of children's literature' are remarkably similar in their envisioning of England's countryside (or, more precisely, a particular nostalgic version of countryside characterised by the absence of anything other than happy, white, chivalrous children growing up in happy, patriarchally organised families in idyllic, homely rural settings) as unquestionably *the* idyllic place for childhood. This literary conceit (essentially the assumption that all children – not just those 'with affluent parents well able to afford ample leisure both for themselves and for their children' – had access to leisure time in open countryside and could 'generally expect and manage to have as good a time as possible' (Tucker 1993)) was sustainable because 'producer and consumer were a mirror image of one another' (Leeson 1985: 129). However, this state of affairs did not last forever.

1970s: 'politicised' representations of countryside

In the 1970s I was committed to . . . a thoroughly necessary censorship . . . It was as if, all at once there were suddenly like-minded people in high places . . . we all knew one another. I mean we'd all been to university together, we all went to the same conferences, we were part of the same network . . . [and] we were all very angry about the sorts of books on the shelves . . . Ask anyone from that era and they'll tell you what it felt like to see children confronted with stuff that was quite alien to them . . . [W]e were quite active in acquiring books which reflected multicultural society in a more balanced and accurate way and provided role models to children who maybe didn't have any visible role models. And at the same time, we were quite active in getting rid of some of the stuff from the bad old days . . . It was an exciting time, there were suddenly no sacred cows, and it was suddenly okay to say 'this book is crap, this book is offensive, and this book is offensive crap' . . . Maybe we didn't change the world, but if you look at the sorts of books which became popular around then, I think you'll agree we really made a difference (Mrs B).

British children's literature 'entered the 1970s almost as it had the 1940s and 1950s' (Phillips 2001: 130). The three-decades-long predominance of the 'classic' canon was eventually unsettled by economic and political developments external to publishing. In the early 1970s, 'the economic recession arrived, mainly as the result of the oil crisis and industrial unrest, with inflation at 15%' (Murison 1988: viii), so after 30 years' expansion of publishing sector there was trouble in the marketplace. International recession, coupled with 'the costs of maintaining huge warehouses full of books sold nation-wide from one or two centres of production, had an alarming effect, [and] high interest rates took their toll', presenting publishing houses with 'enormous problems which undermined their reprinting and backlist policies built up over decades' (Leeson 1985: 140). The major British publishers of children's literature were increasingly driven 'to depend upon borrowed money to service the storage and turnover of their incredibly varied produce . . . to boost turnover, not simply to raise profits, but to pay the bank', and driven to 'shorter print runs . . . and a feverish interest in best-seller flagships for their sales campaign' (Leeson 1985: 172). In temporary crisis, publishers with established reputations for quality children's books became increasingly 'susceptible . . . to complaints from pressure groups' (Yates 1980: 182).

Coincidentally, legislation introduced by the 1964–1970 and 1974–1976 Wilson governments provided unprecedented funding, autonomy, licence and political gravitas to an expanded public library sector: this legislative turn is widely imagined as the beginning of a 'New Criticism' of children's literature (Murison 1988: viii) enacted by a 'new generation' of public sector professionals recruited (see WCC 1978: 20–21 on the tacitly politicised and self-perpetuating nature of this recruitment) from a cohort of university gradu-ates educated at 'a time in . . . which the fight for social justice [was] gaining momentum around the world' (WCC 1978: 26). Through a proliferation of new informal discussion groups (Marxist/Leninist, feminist, and postcolonial flavoured), reading circles, journals, newsletters, pressure groups, unions, professional bodies, conferences, community projects and collectives[1], this 'new generation' advanced a radical, revisionist critique of existent children's literature. It was argued that whereas Britain had changed beyond all recognition since 1945 – becoming a multi-cultural, postcolonial, ex-hegemon as a result of New Commonwealth immigration and the fall of Empire – British children's literature had changed very little. Since collections bought in the immediate postwar years still constituted the core of most school and library collections, 'books written for an earlier generation whose social and racial attitudes [were] reprehensible' were predominant (Ray 1979: 59). It was argued, moreover, that as one of 'the arsenal of weapons used by the dominating group to maintain its favoured position' (WCC 1978: 13), children's literature was inevitably, inherently saturated with 'insidious . . . cruel and hurtful stereotypes . . . or fallacies' (Klein 1976: 300), offering children (overt or covert) 'lessons in prejudice which . . . predispose them to become prejudiced individuals', effectively 'distort[ing] their perception of world relationships, and . . . foster[ing] the development of irrational complexes', particularly racism, sexism and elitism[2] (WCC 1978: 5, 9). So as strategically important objects in class struggle, the empowerment of women and racial equality books written for children were to be contested and reclaimed by a 'New Criticism' which – *contra* a prevailing 'reverential unanimity . . . [and] adulation of writers verging upon voyeurism, [and] judgements of books based on uncritical sentimentality' (Robbins 1970b: 5) – would 'launch a sustained and collaborative enquiry into the institutionalised fantasy which fiction is' (Inglis 1971: 60), offering 'serious, sustained criticism of literature written for children . . . to help establish and develop exacting and appropriate standards of judgement' (Robbins 1970a: 6). In practice, this 'altogether different approach to children's literature . . . putting the content before the form' (Dixon 1982: vii, 5), took the form of a drawing up of prescriptive guidelines to be applied to storybooks to judge their (in)appropriateness with respect to illustrations, stereotypes, tokenism, storylines, relationships, roles, loaded words, and so on (e.g. Stinton 1979). An array of (overt and covert) tactics[3] were mobilised when books fell foul of these guidelines, effectively making offending titles absent from library and school bookshelves (and thus, effectively, from contemporary children's literature *per se*) in the hope that they would be 'consigned to oblivion' (Edwards 1979: 3).

Most texts made absent in this way were precisely those in which 'classic' representations of countryside were prevalent. Indeed, most of the aforementioned 'classics' of children's literature became the New Criticism's *causes célèbres*, newly open to critique for their 'overwhelming and mind-crippling indoctrination' (Dixon 1982: 14), precisely because of their over-representation of pastoral 'idyllic' themes, settings and images, which were quite at odds with the lived experiences of most British children. Thus, Enid Blyton's storybooks were made absent from libraries and school bookshelves throughout Britain, for her 'colourless, dead and totally undemanding, . . . sociologically middle class-based . . . conformity to the most narrow, establishment-type beliefs, practices and values', for her stereotyping of the poor, the working classes, the disabled, gypsies, circus people, foreigners and the Welsh, all of whom appear 'submissive to their natural masters, deviant [and] . . . all rather less than human' (Dixon 1977b: 54–55, 69), for her 'sicken[ing] . . . consistent picture of jolly, priggish, snobbish, sexless mini folk' (Tindall, in Tucker 1975: 193), for her 'promotion of ideas of colonialist oppression in the Third World' (Kuya, in Gray 1982: 85) her 'tendency towards to fascism' and for her '[inability to] tell a story without enemies' (Watson 1992: 19). Beatrix Potter's books suffered a similar fate, being branded 'rather thin . . . ludicrously over-rated', 'emotionally retarded' and 'quite nauseating' for the way in which they 'implant or reinforce an unachronistic [sic] view of society' based upon 'upper-class . . . attitudes towards animals – that one loves them but . . . they are also killed – and towards the concept of a hierarchical system . . . – that there are gardeners and washerwomen in the natural order of society' (Richardson 1977: 175–6)[4]. Arthur Ransome's books were made absent for being 'too middle-class, written about privileged children whose parents could afford to take them on long holidays and provide them with boats' (Thomsen and Thomsen 1996), for their 'misogynistic fantasies' (Tucker 1981: 215), as were Buckeridge's 'Jennings' series, being 'books that present only a traditional role for women, and praise their domestic accomplishments, their timidity, their gentle appearance and manners, and fail to portray initiative, enterprise, physical prowess and genuine intellect' while valorising 'boyhood' (Zimet 1976: 74), Grahame's Wind in the Willows for being 'an exhibition of property owning hatred and fear' (Leeson 1977: 10), and so forth.

To a great extent then, the 'New Criticism' effectively removed many 'classic' representations of rurality from the available canon, as all but the most popular abruptly fell out of print. In their stead, a newly politicised children's literature (characterised by numerous one-off publications – often specifically written to fit the 'New Criticism's' prescriptive guidelines – instead of series publication) was actively promoted through organised story times, 'recommended' reading lists for parents and children, prominent displays in libraries, and so on. As is clear from lists of recommended books for children used by public and school librarians during the 1970s, representations of the country-side were largely, purposefully, absent from this new canon.

Where the countryside was represented, it is clear that these were rural visions purposefully written to be radically different from the 'classics', 'convey[ing]' certain . . . anti-sexist, anti-racialist, anti-classist morals in a fairly clear and direct way' (Edwards 1979: 4). Firstly, rural settings formed the backdrop of a number of new books explicitly recommended for their representation of gender equality. For example, Gunilla Wolde's (1974) Thomas Bakes a Cake illustrates the familiar iconography of family life in a cosy rural household with two twists: Thomas is shown enjoying baking a cake, with help from his father – and the book includes a cake recipe which fathers are encouraged to make with their children – and contains frank depictions of breastfeeding and nudity. Similarly, Margaret Mahy's (1974) The Witch in the Cherry Tree, recommended as 'a gentle antidote to the . . . sexist elements in fairy tales' – for 'the witch stereotype is . . . a manifestation of sexism and we ought to do something about it [and] this book shows how we can make a start' (Dixon 1982: 38), narrates the story of a genial, bungling, somewhat maternal woodland witch's friendship with a small boy named David, who learns to appreciate his mother through this friendship, and decides to help her in the kitchen of their English rural home. Other books recommended for their radical gender equality with rural themes included Munro Leaf's (1967) *The Story of Ferdinand* (a bull – 'one of the earliest sex-role rebels'; Dixon 1982: 34 – who prefers to lie in a meadow smelling flowers rather than fighting), Marjorie Darke's (1975) *What Can I Do?* (in which a young girl named Alice, bored with dolls, sewing, pastry making and playing in fields, decides to help her neighbour working on his car, doing repairs, getting covered in oil), and Russell Hoban's (1978) *Best Friend for Frances* (in which a gendered world of anthropomorphic badgers – where there are 'boys only' games and 'girls only' games – unites in preparation for a picnic).

The countryside features *secondly*, in new books recommended for their representation of racial equality. On one hand, there were parables about racism and reconciliation with rural settings, such as Michael Foreman's (1981) *Moose* (in which a anthropomorphic bear and eagle habitually hurl sticks, stones and insults at each other, until a moose caught in the crossfire collects the objects thrown to build a 'mooseum' and 'amoosement park' where all the woodland animals – including, on the last page, Bear and Eagle – gather together, singing songs, eating and playing games). Similar parables and settings appear in Michael Foreman's (1967) *The Two Giants* (in which two giants living peacefully amidst beautiful coastal pasture and wildflower meadows come to blows over a found seashell, but must pull together when storm floods threaten their home), James Cressey's (1976) *Fourteen Rats and a Rat Catcher* (in which an old lady and a family of rats put aside their differences when the forest cottage in which they live is threatened) and Eric Carle's (1978) *The Bad Tempered Ladybird* (in which a ladybird taunts and challenges larger and larger animals to fight, until he gets his come-uppance and is forced to learn how to share). On the other hand, books set in non-English countrysides were recommended, including Christine Craig's (1970, 1971) *Emanuel* books (stories about a young boy's everyday adventures in a rural Jamaican village, amongst cocoa trees and colourful parrots, flowers and fruits), Paul Goble's (1979) *The Girl Who Loved Wild Horses* (a book drawing upon traditional Navaho legend and art, about a young Navaho girl who dwells peacefully among wild horses) and Jane Hollowood's (1969) *Maggie in the Snow* (in which 'almost uniquely' a gypsy family are depicted as human beings 'just like us really'; Dixon, 1982: 19).

Thirdly, several books recommended for their parables about class had strong countryside themes, such as Alexei Tolstoy's (1969) *The Great Big Enormous Turnip* (in which an old farmer's vast vegetable can only be harvested through a communal co-operative effort – involving his family, villagers and farm animals – in which ultimately the farm mouse's contribution makes all the difference, and which culminates in an enormous communal meal), Anthony Browne's (1977) *A Walk in the Park* ('about the sad waste of a class-divided society'; Dixon 1982: 19, in which stereotypical landed and labouring families are brought together and have great fun after their dogs Victoria and Smudge play together, to each family's initial disapproval, while out walking on the village green), and Binette Schroeder's (1980) *Florian and Tractor Max* (in which Florian the farm horse and Max the shiny new tractor must learn to cooperate, and become friends by working towards a common end, when they get stuck in a muddy field).

Fourthly, storybooks sympathetic to 'some of the kinds of complex family situations that . . . perhaps did not exist in quite the same way ten or thirty years [previously]' (Klein 1977: 80) proliferated, sometimes with rural settings or themes. They included Felicity Sen's (1975) *My Family* (about 4-year-old Janey's rural life with her father and brother in the aftermath of her parents' divorce and her mother's departure, relating their quiet, tender relationship, games of snakes and ladders, puppet-making, candle-making, and work on the farm and in the farmhouse kitchen together), Ivor Cutler's (1971) *Meal One* (about the happy, loving relationship between Helbert and his single mother, in which they play football, fighting and hide-and-seek in a plum tree orchard), Margaret Mahy's (1974) *Stepmother* (in which Jenny, whose mother died when she was very young, dreads the arrival of her new stepmother, but bonds with her while picking parsley in her cottage's herb garden), Rolf Knutsson's (1970) *Torkel* (about a little boy who lives on his recently divorced father's farm), and several books by Evaline Ness, like 'The Girl and The Goatherd' (1970) and 'Sam, Bangs and Moonshine' (1971), which describe rural children's lives in the aftermath of parental death or divorce. Many lesser-known titles which deal frankly with issues such as smoking, drinking, drug use, disability and premarital sex were also published at this time.

In all these books, the rural came to function as a neutral, inactive background to a series of emancipatory, politicised narratives and representations. However, as extraliterary formations shifted once more, so did the prevailing representation of English countryside.

1980s: 'reactionary' representations of countryside

There's no doubt that in the '80s that the publishing industry fell back into bad ways. A lot of them were of the mind that they could publish whatever they wanted, to make a quick profit, and bugger the consequences . . . Our hands were tied, there was nothing we could do (Mrs B).

For most commentators the 'New Criticism' of British children's literature ended abruptly on 3 May 1979, with the election of Margaret Thatcher as British Prime Minister. Under three successive Conservative parliaments the public sector in general, and public libraries in particular were increasingly 'marginalised in terms of government's perception of their role, and of course with that came starvation in terms of funding' (Dunne 2000: 1). In effect, these changes produced a publishing scene similar to that of the 1950s 'Golden Age'. Increasingly limited public sector funding meant that fewer books ended up on library or school shelves, so the private purchase market – a sector tradition-ally dominated by conservative, middle-class readers – came to be of much greater importance. Meanwhile the dissolution of specialist public sector posts, rendered public sector intervention practically non-existent. At the height of Thatcherism, in the absence of contestation, 'publishing houses grotesquely swollen through the effort of swallowing up rival imprints . . . put their ener-gies, their sales teams and their market research departments behind . . . books such as *You Can Do the Cube!* And the *Fighting Fantasy* series' (Reynolds 1998: 3). The children's literature thus effected was founded upon a strongly critical withdrawal from the 'New Criticism' (seen in retrospect as at best a comical and overly earnest embarrassment, and at worst, as pernicious 'heret-ical, simply . . . unwarranted and malicious . . . attacks from the "loony left"'; Suhl 1985: 3), coupled with an enthusiastic embrace of free market economics (or at least a helplessness in the face of them), a sense that some stories, themes, settings are just 'naturally popular' (Tucker 1981: 6), that literature and its consumption should be 'free range', for 'after all who would not want his or her child to read the *best* books?' (Waterland 1992: 161).

In practice this meant a wholesale (re)turn to 'classic'-esque representations of the English countryside. The literature of the 'New Criticism' all but dis-appeared, as titles were dismissed as a 'wave of salacious or near-pornographic novels blessed by the critics' (Wynne-Jones, in Gray 1982: 85), 'a tsunami of dirty realist books that outdid themselves in telling children about the nastier, more nauseating aspects of human nature' (Forsyth 1989), and dropped from publishers' lists (mostly remaining out of print ever since). In their stead, pub-lishers eagerly republished new editions of many series which had fallen out of print under the 'New Criticism'. Through the machinations of increasingly complex agglomerated multinational systems of popular cultural production, these cash cows were reinvented and repackaged, and endlessly republished, reconfigured and recirculated as mass-mediated intertextual complexes of texts, toys, games, merchandise, ornaments, etc. Thus Blyton's *Famous Five* series was republished in a blaze of publicity in both 1979 (to accompany a tele-vision adaptation of the series by Children's ITV) and 1996 (accompanying a second Children's ITV serialisation, subsequently syndicated worldwide, and supported by audiocassettes, card games, a weekly magazine, a PC game, and a Christmas annual, etc.), while her *Noddy* series was republished in 1991, adapted as series of 20 animated films by the BBC (supported by a remarkable breadth of merchandising, syndicated to 40 countries worldwide, and repack-aged as 40 episodes of *Notions, Oddities, Doodads & Delights* by PBS in the USA). Likewise, there were new editions of Milne's *Winnie-the-Pooh* books in 1983, 1988 and 1992 (during which time *Winnie-the-Pooh* merchandise became almost ubiquitous in Anglo-American popular culture as, on one hand Disney purchased rights to Milne's characters, and subsequently used them in television shows, films and merchandising and, on the other hand, imagery and extracts from original texts were mobilised in a whole range of quite different nostalgically appealing cultural objects), Awdry's *Railway* series in 1991 (supporting the first broadcast of *Thomas the Tank Engine and Friends*, an animated children's ITV television series, subsequently syndicated to 40 countries worldwide, reworked as *Shining Time Station* by PBS in the USA, and which spawned a further 40 *Railway* books written by Awdry's son, Christopher, and a whole host of merchandising), Crompton's *William* series in 1994 (supporting a six-part BBC television series), Grahame's *Wind in the Willows* in 1986 (supporting a 16-part ITV animation series), Buckeridge's *Jennings* series in 1990 (indeed, after a 20 year hiatus, Buckeridge began writing new *Jennings* titles in 1991), and so on.

These same complex, iterative, multinational systems of cultural production constructed numerous new marketable, quickly produced, intertextual franchises, which have since been accepted as new 'classics' of children's literature, and in which 'classic-esque' representations of countryside predominate, and indeed, which often pay homage to themes, icons, settings and scenarios of earlier classics). Thus this period saw the emergence of *Postman Pat* (the kindly, community-minded 'postie' who serves the fictional rural English village of Greendale who, from 1978 appeared in 200 storybooks by John Cunliffe, 26 animated Children's BBC films – subsequently syndicated worldwide – merchandising, advertising, place promotion and popular discourse), *The Animals of Farthing Wood* (an animated production by the BBC/European Broadcasting Union televised worldwide in 1993, based upon Colin Dunn's series of seven storybooks (1989–1992) relating the journey of a gang of anthropomorphic woodland animals whose woodland home is jeopardised by encroaching development to an idyllic nature reserve, written and reworked as a series of TV spin-off storybooks by the same author in 1994), *Brambly Hedge* (a series of four books about the idyllic hedgerow lives of diminutive fieldmice written by Jill Barklem in 1980, adapted as animated Children's BBC films in 1996, though more widely 'consumed' as Royal Doulton China figurines and patterns, embroidery patterns, images on address books, diaries, shampoo, soap sets and a popular series of sheet music for recorder). Other 'new classics' included *Percy the Park Keeper* (a series of seven storybooks about a park-keeper and his anthropomorphic animal chums, written by Nick Butterworth from 1989 to present, broadcast as a series of four animated Children's ITV films in 1996), *Katie Morag* (a series of nine storybooks about a little girl's life on the remote Hebridean island of Struay, written by Mairi Hedderwick between 1984 and present), Kim Lewis's *Friends* series (written 1990–1997, about different young children's idyllic, nuclear family farm lives) and many other reassertions of a 'classic-esque' version of literary countryside.

So in hindsight, the abiding characteristic of much British children's literature of the 1980s and early 1990s was 'its conservative nature, its resistance to change, its adherence to the pastoral idyll that looms behind so much of children's literature'[5] (Russell 1998: 32).

1997– : 'new' representations of countryside

Suddenly . . . there's a lot of money going pouring into children's literature and libraries and schools libraries. It really is a case of 'New Labour, New Literature' (Mrs C).

Tony Blair's election as British Prime Minister in May 1997 has come to be imagined, perhaps somewhat romantically, as a watershed in the postwar history of British children's literature, ushering in (another!) rejuvenated 'New Children's Literature'. Since 1997, there has certainly been an ongoing critical questioning of certain legacies of Thatcherism, coupled with and enabled by a surge of funding for (and political discourse emphasising the importance of) the public sector professionals and institutions responsible for popular access to reading (Dunne 2000: 1). This extraliterary formation is said to have constituted (yet another) 'New Criticism', characterised by collect-ive interventionist moves to 'assume nothing . . . to embark upon a dialogue rather than a monologue with young readers' (Marley 2000: 3), to ' "find books for the audience" rather than "find audiences for the books" ', without 'coarsen[ing] into didacticism and becom[ing] paralysed in an unintended propagandist posture' (Library Association 1997: 11). This reassessment, coupled with the way in which 'now, perhaps more than ever, the scene is set for small publishing houses to think big and sell big', so children's literature is more than ever characterised by diversity, novelty, unexpectedness, creativity and playfulness in form and content (Marley 2000: 4) has afforded some new, ongoing moves with relation to the representation of countryside.

Firstly, there has been a raft of books that *demystify* the countryside, rendering ostensibly idyllic rural settings as fearful, traumatically dystopic landscapes where hard lessons about life, death and nature must be learnt. Nowhere is this more stark than in three acclaimed, bestselling children's books by Michael Morpurgo who, having been a Blitz evacuee from London during 1940, and having run the Farms for City Children charity since 1976, represents the countryside in a manner particularly sympathetic to the experi-ence of non-rural 'outsiders'. *Sam's Duck* (1997) tells the story of a young inner urban schoolboy's school trip to a farm – depicted as a dark, damp men-acing landscape which makes him long for home – and his attempts to rescue a duck destined for sale at a farmers' market. The book is unusually frank in its depiction of contemporary productivist agriculture, particularly the ways in which animals are reared, kept, bred, born and exchanged. Morpurgo's *The Silver Swan* (2000) narrates a similar story, of a young boy's relationship with a swan on the loch near his idyllic rural cottage home. As the story unfolds, and the swan is mortally wounded by a hungry vixen and eaten by her cubs – this idyllic lochside landscape is unmasked as a brutal, bitterly wintery, natural landscape of predation, death, loss and anxiety. Thirdly, *Out of the Ashes* (2001) tells the story of a young girl living on a Devon farm with her 'pet' lamb in the midst of a foot and mouth epidemic which draws closer and closer to the acreage owned by the girl's parents – depicted frankly by illustrations of culled livestock, blazing carcasses and weeping stockmen – until the symptoms appear in one of their cows. Morpurgo's sometimes dystopic demystifying representation of countryside is echoed by other acclaimed contemporary children's authors, such as Kathy Henderson (whose *The Storm* (1999) depicts a fearful wintry storm raging over a secluded coastal community), Suzanne Fisher Staples (whose *Storm* (1999) depicts an idyllic lakeside community descending into a spiral of racism) and Nina Bawden (whose *Carrie's War* (1973, republished in 1999) narrates the occasionally idyllic but mostly miserable experiences of Second World War evacuees in their temporary rural homes).

A *second* raft of popular recent children's books *romanticise the urban*, imbuing inner cities with all of the idyllic characteristics of peace, community and proximity to Nature so familiarly imagined as 'rural', depicting cities as spaces of potential cosy, authentic, fondly remembered idyll. For example Bernard Ashley's (1999) *Growing Good* is the story of the transformation of a patch of derelict inner-urban wasteland into a community garden, where old, young and every conceivable urban subculture come together on their allotment plots. And this theme of reclaiming a particularly urban notion of 'idyll' for the urban, by representing cities as enchanting, potentially idyllic places is also a feature of work by other acclaimed contemporary children's authors, such as Vivian French (whose *Oliver's Vegetables* (1997) depicts a similar inner urban 'allotment idyll') and Malorie Blackman (whose *Dizzy's Walk* (1999) depicts a dog's walk through a 'municipal park idyll' and along a diverse, richly communitarian inner urban high street).

Thirdly, many new children's books imagine a *child-centred countryside* and 'portray children exploring life and reaping the benefits of a community . . . [making] distinct contributions' (Strehle 1999: 220) as well as their own playful, 'childish' imaginary geographies. Thus authors such as Nick Sharratt represent the rural with attentiveness to the small scale and the child's-eye view: Sharratt's (1999) *My Days Out* depicts 'the countryside' not as an overarching, transcendental thing in itself, but as a sequence of minute engagements, encounters and interventions enacted by the small boy at the centre of the story, so 'the countryside' is represented as a scaled-down milieu of earthworms, puddles, falling leaves and snowflakes. Moreover, authors such as Julie Lacome write this scaled-down rural in a manner attentive to the imaginary geographies made by children with(in) it so, in Lacome's (1997) *Walking Through the Jungle* for instance, the sights, sounds and experiences of being in an overgrown corner of countryside are depicted through the eyes of a child delighting in imagining snakes, tigers, elephants, lions, monkeys and crocodiles looking for their tea.

And *fourthly*, there is an increasingly large emergent literature which celebrates rural idylls which are culturally, geographically or qualitatively very different from those predominant in 'classic' representations of the rural.

Joyce Carol Thompson's acclaimed *I Have Heard of a Land* (1998) romantic-ally portrays an African/American pioneer woman staking a claim for free land in Oklahoma, a land of red earth, cottonbud trees, children playing on home-made swings, and cooperation among blacks, whites and native Americans. This move – persuasively locating idyllic rurality *anywhere but* white middle class English village life – is a common feature of work by acclaimed contem-porary children's authors such as Mary Hoffman (whose *Grace and Family* (1992, republished 1999) depicts a schoolgirl's visit to her father's home in a Gambian village, and her eventual joy in this idyllic environment of communal cooking, eating and dancing, among crocodiles, watermelons and a backdrop of African scenery) and Carmen Santiago Nadar (whose *Marita* (1998) depicts a young girl's idyllic village life in Puerto Rica 'up in the highlands where butterflies fly . . . , where sunlight sparkles the day and sugarcane reaches the sky', among rainforest, waterfalls, flamingos, rainbows and fresh grapefruit).

Conclusions

This chapter offers glimpses of some of the ways in which, at different historical moments, in different ways, for different reasons British children's literatures have been constructed differently and the countryside has been fixed, inscribed, given place and name and identity differently. On one hand this has been a matter of acknowledging that, in spite of manifold postwar historical, socie-tal, political, economic, cultural shifts, 'the countryside' has been stubbornly, disproportionately present in literature (made available for) British children throughout, to the extent that it remains relatively unproblematic to argue that to think of many, many classics of children's literature 'is to think of rural landscapes' (Jones 1997: 161) and that 'many of our most durable and stereo-typical images of the countryside come from the literature of our childhood' (Bunce 1994: 63). And yet despite this stubborn fixity of representation and this recurrent nature of themes and texts made available for children, this chapter has also been the story of represented countryside in flux, a history of the representation of countryside moving through at least four (overlapping, contestable) genres as, at different times, different stocks of representations/ texts/images have been available, constituting parameters/resources through which different generations (made) able to envision countryside differently.

On reflection, it is telling that some of these genres were easier to narrate than others. There is a coherent pre-existent body of texts, critical tools and biographies upon which to draw when approaching what I have called the 'classic' and 'reactionary' genres, but a critical silence exists around the politi-cised countrysides of the 1970s, and the emergent representations of the late 1990s and beyond. Perhaps this is a matter of timing, since academics 'relish the chance to return to . . . popular themes and attitudes that used to be found in their fiction' (Tucker 1999: 221), and those nostalgic for the literature of the late 1970s and later are simply not yet in positions of academic gravitas. Or perhaps it reflects the comfort of contributing to a critical exchange that has already begun, the way in which, with the 'classics' 'there is a reasonable amount of material to lean on, and the book's canonical status means that they can use the vocabulary of conventional criticism [so] nobody asks awkward questions about whether the book is worth studying' (Hunt 1992: 9). Or perhaps it is a matter of reputation, a sense that 'to write about new authors is risky', an 'unwritten need to be taken seriously' (Wilkie 1998: 17), or that 'there is more to be said – and more solidly *intellectual* things to be said – about the "serious" authors' (Hunt 1998: 10). Whatever, I would assert that now more than ever, there are many many more country visions in circulation – in children's literature and elsewhere – than is presently acknowledged. I am left with an abiding sense that 'we critics have lived through a revolution and do not yet know what to say about it – or even have a vocabulary with which to talk about it' (Hunt 1998: 12).

Notes

1. For example, radical journals (e.g. *Children's Literature in Education*, *Children's Book Bulletin*, *Dragon's Teeth*, *Signal* and *School Library Review*), collectives (e.g. Children's Rights Workshop, Spare Rib, the Other Award, Writers and Readers Publishing Co-operative, NAACP, Young World, Federation of Children's Book Groups, Federation of Worker Writers, Community Publishers), professional bodies and conferences (the meeting of 220 teachers, librarians, publishers, academics and writers at the 'Recent Children's Fiction and its role in Education' conference held in August 1969 at St Luke's College, Exeter is widely cited as a pivotal moment) proliferated during this period.

2. For example, different empirical studies conducted during the 1970s give the male:female ratio of characters in British children's literature under-eights as anywhere between 3 and 95:1, while the presence of non-white characters in the same books was stated as between 0.8 and 1 per cent (Zimet 1976: 53).

3. Anecdotally, it seems that the tactics of children's and schools' librarians included banning certain titles outright (many books which fell short of prescriptive criteria – particularly those demonstrating anti-Semitism or derogatory racial signifiers – were apparently discarded automatically on the basis of a single complaint), making titles absent in more subtle ways (for example, not replacing worn out copies, placing titles 'behind the counter', waiting for the paperback editions – 'reprinted with revisions' in response to complaints about first editions – before acquisition, or limiting contentious material to one copy all effectively made titles absent from bookshelves) and, importantly, circulating scathing accounts denouncing popular books as racist or sexist, urging other libraries and schools not to purchase them.

4. These criticisms were invariably supported by a demonisation of Potter herself, glee-fully highlighting the way in which 'her early life was starved of affection, and she was clearly emotionally retarded' (Richardson 1977: 177), her obsessive taxidermy – she was 'herself quite able to skin a dead specimen and then boil it down to pre-serve the skeleton' (Tucker 1981: 60) – her self-proclaimed role as colonial propa-gandist (in her autobiography she wrote 'I do not write merely to entertain . . . My public do not possess matured minds – what is said to them in books they are apt to believe and follow, for they are credulous and immature. Therefore I am also a teacher and a guide (I hope) as well as an entertainer and bringer of pleasure . . . [Q]uite apart from my millions of English-speaking readers, I have to consider entirely different children – children of many other races who have my books in their own language. I am perforce, bringing to them the ideas and ideals of a race of chil-dren alien to them, the British. I am a purveyor of those ideals all over the world, and am perhaps planting a few seeds here and there that may bear good fruit'; in Dixon 1974: 43–4), and her 'hilarious entry into the 1910 General Election. She cam-paigned for the Tory Party's policy of protection, in her case to stop cheap dolls from Germany underselling her home-produced products. The pamphlet outlining the fate of "Poor Camberwell Dolly" ends up with the . . . cry "it is uphill work, trying to help folk who will not help themselves. Why should *I* bother myself about the British workman, if he prefers free trade?" ' (Richardson 1977: 177).

5. The point here is more than merely aesthetic. The way in which English is repres-ented as a cultural 'idyll' *matters*, because those who are systematically excluded from such 'idylls' 'are excluded, to a large degree from the nation itself' (Kinsman 1995: 301) and indeed, recently acclaimed children's authors such as Farrukh Dhondy and Jan Needle have spoken of their initial hesitation during the 1980s of writing for children 'because of an inner conviction that children's literature was about "other people" ' (Leeson 1985: 152–3).

References

Bell, D. and Valentine, G. 1995 'Queer country: rural lesbian and gay lives', *Journal of Rural Studies*, **11**, 113–22.

Blishen, E. 1975 'Introduction', pp. 9–12 in E. Blishen (ed.), *The Thorny Paradise: Writers On Writing For Children*, Kestrel: Middlesex.

Bunce, M. 1994 *The Countryside Ideal: Anglo-American Images of Landscape*, Routledge, London.

Cloke, P. 1997 'Country backwater to virtual village? Rural studies and the "cultural turn" ', *Journal of Rural Studies*, **13**, 367–75.

Cridland, C. 1999 'Pony Books: A Brief Introduction', http://www.penrithcity.nsw.gov.au/usrpages/collect/ponybook.htm

Daniels, S. 1992 'Place and the geographical imagination', *Geography*, **77**, 310–22.

Dixon, B. 1977a *Catching Them Young 1: Sex, Race and Class in Children's Fiction*, Pluto Press, London.

Dixon, B. 1977b *Catching Them Young 2: Political Ideas in Children's Fiction*, Pluto Press, London.

Dixon, B. 1982 *Now Read On: Recommended Fiction For Young People*, Pluto Press, London.

Dunne, J. 2000 'Children's libraries in the 21st century', *Youth Library Review*, 28, 1–6.

Edwards, P. 1979 'The new criticism of children's literature', *Librarian*, 4, 1–7.

Forsyth, K. 1989 'Sunny Stories Shine Through', http://members.ozemail.com.au/~kforsyth/enid_blyton.htm

Gray, S.G. 1982 *The Blyton Phenomenon: the Controversy Surrounding the World's Most Successful Children's Writer*, Andre Deutsch, London.

Hall, S. 1980 'Encoding/decoding', pp. 128–38 in S. Hall, D. Hobson, A. Lowe and P. Willis (eds), *Culture, Media, Language*, Hutchinson, London.

Hannabuss, S. 1977 'What we used to read: a survey of children's reading in Britain, 1910–1950', *Children's Literature in Education*, 26, 127–34.

Houlton, D. and Short, B. 1995 'Sylvanian Families: the production and consumption of a rural community', *Journal of Rural Studies*, 11, 367–85.

Hunt, P. 1992 'Introduction', pp. 1–17 in P. Hunt (ed.), *Literature For Children: Contemporary Criticism*, Routledge, London.

Hunt, P. 1995 'Introduction', pp. i–xiv in P. Hunt (ed.) *Children's Literature: An Illustrated History*, Oxford University Press, Oxford.

Hunt, P. 1998 'The silence of the critics', *Children's Literature in Education* (NS), 29, 9–12.

Inglis, F. 1971 'Reading children's novels: notes on the politics of literature', *Children's Literature in Education*, 21, 60–75.

Inglis, F. 1981 *The Promise of Happiness: Value and Meaning in Children's Fiction*, Cambridge University Press, Cambridge.

Jones, O. 1997 'Little figures, big shadows: country childhoods', pp. 158–79 in P. Cloke and J. Little (eds), *Contested Countryside Cultures: Otherness, Marginalisation and Rurality*, Routledge, London.

Kamm, A. 1970 'Children's book publishing and the educational market', *Children's Literature in Education*, 3, 30–40.

Kinsman, P. 1995 'Landscape, race and national identity: the photography of Ingrid Pollard', *Area*, 27, 300–10.

Klein, N. 1976 'Growing up human: the case for sexuality in children's books', *Children's Literature in Education*, 25, 80–84.

Klein, G. 1977 'School guidelines and multi-ethnic Britain: some guidelines', *School Librarian*, 24, 300–03.

Leeson, R. 1977 *Children's Books and Class Society, Past and Present*, Writers and Readers, London.

Leeson, R. 1985 *Reading and Righting*, Collins, London.

Library Association 1997: 11.

Liukkonen, P. 2000 'Enid (Mary) Blyton (1896–1968)', http://www.kirjasto.sci.fi/eblyton.htm

MacCann, D. 1989 *Social Responsibility and Librarianship*, McFarland, London.

Mackey, M. 1998 '*Little Women* go to market: shifting texts and changing readers', *Children's Literature in Education* (NS), 29, 80–84.

Marley, A. 2000 'The lads and dads experiment', *Youth Library Review*, 28, 1–8.

Murison, W.J. 1988 *The Public Library: Its Origins, Purpose and Significance*, 3rd edn, Clive Bingley, London.

Phillips, R. 2001 'Politics of reading: decolonizing children's geographies', *Ecumene*, 8, 125–50.

Ray, S. 1979 *Children's Librarianship*, Clive Bingley, London.

Reynolds, K. 1998 'The silence of the critics', *Children's Literature in Education* (NS), **29**, 2–5.

Richards, C. 2001 'A Short History of Pooh and Winnie', http://www.pooh-corner.com/pooh.html

Richardson, P. 1977 'Miss Potter and the little rubbish', pp. 173–8 in N. Tucker (ed.), *Suitable For Children? Controversies in Children's Literature*, Sussex University Press, London.

Robbins, S. 1970a Editorial, *Children's Literature in Education*, **1**, 5–7.

Robbins, S. 1970b Editorial, *Children's Literature in Education*, **2**, 5.

Russell, D.L. 1998 '"The city spreads its wings": the urban experience in poetry for children', *Children's Literature in Education* (NS), **29**, 31–42.

Schutte, D. 1993 *William the Immortal: an Illustrated Bibliography*, Schutte, Hampshire.

Stinton, J. 1979 *Racism and Sexism in Children's Books*, Writers and Readers, London.

Strehle, E. 1999 'Social issues: connecting children to their world', *Children's Literature in Education* (NS), **30**, 213–20.

Suhl, I. 1985 '"Doctor Dolittle" the great white father', pp. 3–9 in Council on Inter-racial Books for Children (eds), *Racist and Sexist Images in Children's Books*, Writers and Readers, London.

Thomsen, P. and Thomsen, D. 1996 'Arthur Ransome: a Biography', http://www.arthur-ransome.org/ar/arbio.html

Tucker, N. 1975 'The Blyton enigma', *Children's Literature in Education*, **19**, 191–7.

Tucker, N. 1981 *The Child and The Book: a Psychological and Literary Exploration*, Cambridge University Press, Cambridge.

Tucker, N. 1993 'Arthur Ransome as a Children's Writer', http://www.humboldt1.com/AR/literary/tucker2.htm

Tucker, N. 1999 'The rise and rise of Harry Potter', *Children's Literature in Education* (NS), **30**, 221–34.

Valentine, G. 1989 'The geography of women's fear', *Area*, **21**, 385–90.

Waterland, L. 1992 'Ranging freely: the why and the what of real books', pp. 160–71 in M. Styles, E. Bearne and V. Watson (eds), *After Alice: Exploring Children's Literature*, Cassell, London.

Watson, V. 1992 'The possibilities of children's fiction', pp. 11–24 in M. Styles, E. Bearne and V. Watson (eds), *After Alice: Exploring Children's Literature*, Cassell, London.

WCC 1978 *Racism in Children's and School Textbooks*, WCC, Geneva.

Welsh, G. 2000 'Jennings today', http://www.linbury-court.co.uk/html/jennings_today.html

Whitehead, F., Capey, A.C., Maddren, W. and Wellings, A. 1977 *Children and Their Books*, Macmillan, London.

Wilkie, C. 1998 'The silence of the critics', *Children's Literature in Education* (NS), **29**, 15–18.

Woodiwiss, A. 2001 *The Visual in Social Theory*, Athlone, London.

Yates, J. 1980 'Censorship in children's paperbacks', *Children's Literature in Education*, **39**, 180–91.

Zimet, S.G. 1976 *Print and Prejudice*, Hodder and Stoughton, London.

The view from Cobb Gate: falling into liminal geography

CHAPTER 6

Mark Lawrence

Introduction: the background of the foreground

My principal aim in this chapter is to use the translation of Jane Austen's novels to film as mass entertainment to focus on several important shifts in recent cultural geography, in particular regarding differences between American and British visions of 'rurality' (Cloke *et al.* 1994). Rurality is a term that includes not only such stereotypical rural spaces and places as farms and a farming landscape, but also processes of change in the negotiation and appropriation of supposedly 'rural' lifeways (Cloke and Little 1997). For example, economic restructuring of rural areas involves increasing industrialisation of the countryside, while new rural settlement patterns due to exurbanisation have occasioned socio-political realignment. Likewise, the cultural reinvention of the countryside has found new forms in ecotourism, 'new age' occupation of idealised spiritual landscapes, reorganisation of ethnic geography, and of course in filmic renderings (Lawrence 1998). Inasmuch as the rural is not only a zone for the contestation of meanings, but also an active agent in their negotiation, we ought therefore to speak of rurality rather than simply about particular rural locations. Austen used the manor house, garden park, farm cottage and seaside resort just this way, to enervate particular kinds of interaction between her characters rather than simply arranging backdrops for dialogue and narration:

> [Her] villages and the neighbourhoods of which they form part never are isolated. Their contacts with the outer world, especially the more sophisticated world of London and the watering places, always form a vital part of the plot and machinery of the novels and still more of their moral themes, especially through the contrast between smart, worldly values and the appeal of quiet friendships and the stability of settled families. For her the small neighbourhood is not a vignette with the background faded out, but a focus, or a nodal point from which lines radiate into the wider society (Harding 1998: 50).

At first glance, that Austen's novels hold appeal for contemporary movie audiences may seem remarkable to many observers, since surely only the smallest fraction of those who go to theatres or rent videos of her stories converted to film actually live in nineteenth century gentry landscapes in the South of England. Her 'green fields and cream teas' (Weldon 1995: H24) have been linked to the geopolitical evolution of the British overseas empire (Ferguson 1998; Stewart 1993), but it is clear there's a certain domestic gravity to Austen's geographical imagination, its arc always curving back to a Kellynch or Mansfield Park or Pemberley. This is reinforced in recent film adaptations, as in the voiceover that opens the 1996 screenplay of *Emma*: 'In a time when one's town was one's world, and the actions at a dance excited greater interest than the movements of armies, there lived a young woman who knew how this world should be run. . . .'

Despite the global reach of Pax Brittanica, this is geography of local encounter and limited scope. Even when Austen provides touristic views, her characters' attention is focused on highly foregrounded details of the scene before them. In Elizabeth Bennet's early encounters with Pemberley, broad views of the grounds and surrounding landscape are always firmly anchored by the presence of the great house itself. Or (in one of many scenes missing in Emma Thompson's celebrated film version of *Sense and Sensibility*), Edward Ferrars' zeroing-in on details within the immediate scene considered unworthy of attention by Marianne Dashwood when she aims to have him scan a wider landscape:

> 'Now Edward,' said she, calling his attention to the prospect, 'here is Barton valley. Look up it, and be tranquil if you can. Look at those hills! Did you ever see their equals? To the left is Barton Park, amongst those woods and plantations. You may see one end of the house. And there, beneath that farthest hill, which rises with such grandeur, is our cottage.'
> 'It is a beautiful country,' he replied, 'but these bottoms must be dirty in winter.'
> 'How can you think of dirt, with such objects before you?'
> 'Because,' replied he, smiling, 'among the rest of the objects before me, I see a very dirty lane.'

By contrast, even with the formal closure of the frontier, Americans persistently register their landscapes as vistas. America is a society of immigrants; a society obsessed with the automobile and no less transporting technologies as television and the modem. The trajectory of a receding (or at least constantly rebounding) horizon recalls de Tocqueville's warning made as early as the 1830s (1959: 340):

> [Americans are] a wandering people whom rivers and lakes cannot hold back, before whom forests fall and prairies are covered in shade; and who, when they have reached the Pacific Ocean, will come back on its tracks to trouble and destroy the societies which it will have formed behind it.

Nonetheless, there has recently been a remarkable intensification of interest in the more sedentary and literally pedestrian scenes of Austen's England. While seven British reproductions of Austen novels were filmed between 1970 and 1986, six more appeared just in 1995 and 1996, all wholly or in part as American projects (Troost and Greenfield 1998: 1–2). Moreover, the Austen phenomenon has rapidly taken on global proportions – all available copies of *Sense and Sensibility* were sold out in Taipei the day it was announced Ang Lee would direct the novel's 1995 film reproduction.

What sense can be made of this apparently newfound interest in Jane Austen, and what might an answer to that question say about the roles of contemporary media in producing an increasingly mutable geography of social relations? At the outset, a difference between scenes and scenarios becomes especially important to appreciate, since when novels are filmed it is imperative to find the best possible locations for shooting particular sequences of action. Such persistent retreat – from actual circumstances to their selective reappearance in writing and then again to the reappearance of that fiction in still another form on film – detaches representations of the rural from the material reality of specific places. Complexes of meaning no longer re-present the reality of a place, but instead orbit themselves in what Baudrillard calls 'simulations' (1983a), overwriting the real with the 'hyperreal' by organising our thoughts and actions around codes of recognition, judgement and behaviour that are no longer attached to a specific referent. Not that today's hyperreality is without historical precedent. Tennyson's is perhaps only one of the most famous experiences of an earlier mode of simulation:

> He was led on to Lyme by the description of the place in Miss Austen's *Persuasion*, walking thither the nine miles over the hills from Bridport. On his arrival he called on Palgrave, and refusing all refreshment, he said at once: 'Now take me to the Cobb, and show me the steps from which Louisa Musgrove fell.' . . . Palgrave himself added, 'the persons she created in *Persuasion*, Tennyson remarked as we were returning, were more real and living to him than Monmouth and his followers, whose landing-place on the Western side of the Cobb we had just passed' (Lane 1986: 105, 106).

Still, for Tennyson (and today's Austen purists), there are actual places like the Cobb to which their fascinations about fiction can adhere. But for most of us, ontological or epistemological significance is no longer assigned to things except by reference to congeries of images, metaphors, stereotypes and trends episodically presented by electronic media (Adams 1992). Indeed, since directors may choose locations that have no actual connection to the stories they are adapting for the screen, the cultural consciousness shaped by television and the movies has already produced a displaced history in the appearance of cowboys and Indians in Austen's Devonshire countryside (Cloke *et al.* 1994: 170–71).

But film does more than use geographical imagination to simulate. It also realigns our geographical sense of self by relocating us in a 'liminal' space.

Liminality is that condition of being between the normative and everything eclipsed by it, of being at the border of the everyday and the unexpected. Liminal experiences such as rites of passage assist us in gaining new under-standing not of the rules governing social interaction as much as the ways in which they are naturalised beyond notice *as* rules. This is what Austen's heroines manage that their friends and neighbours cannot. Like Anne Elliot, some have their outsider status thrust upon them even before the narrative begins, while others like Emma Woodhouse inadvertently engineer their own relocation into a space of liminal perspective while working hard to remain within the borders of social expectation. As Anne Elliot suggests about Lyme Regis after Louisa Musgrove's fall from the Cobb, the power of the symbolic can be greater than an abrupt rupture in the spatial practices usually associated with a particular place: 'One does not love a place the less for having suffered in it, unless it has been all suffering, nothing but suffering' (*Persuasion*: 193). Still, ethnographic accounts of liminal experiences always presume the return of the outsider to the company of the society she has had a chance to re-view. But a film's hyperreal sense of place can leave us stranded, failing to complete the circuit from unacknowledged experience of what passes for normalcy through the exceptional distancing effect of liminality and back again to reinvigorated appreciation of the everyday.

Moving targets: thinking about film and new visions of rurality

Understanding how experience of simulated geographies in films effects this unredeemed liminality requires focusing not on relationships between charac-ters on screen as much as on relationships between the film and its audience. Bachelard insisted that 'Images excite us – afterwards – but they are not the phenomena of an excitement', claiming that the 'transsubjectivity of the image . . . cannot be determined once and for all, for the poetic image is essentially *variational*, and not, as in the case of the concept, *constitutive*' (1994: xvii, xix). Thus, while using period costumes and settings seems to lend an air of accuracy to film portrayals of Austen novels, such a tactic is neither guaranteed to produce its intended effect nor even necessary. As the successful mutation of *Emma* into *Clueless* suggests, while the filmmaker's image 'is not an echo of the past. . . . through [its] brilliance . . . the distant past resounds with echoes, and it is hard to know at what depth these echoes will reverberate and die away' (Bachelard 1994: xvi, xix).

In the media studies perspective called transactionalism 'The underlying premise is that a juxtaposition of ordinary events against extraordinary events enhances the involvement of the viewer in the narrative' (Aitken 1991: 115; Aitken and Zonn 1994). Rather than emphasise the transsubjectivity of the image, the 'image-event' (Worth 1969, 1981) that facilitates communication between films and audiences is assumed to have 'the same signification for the organism which produces it that it has to other organisms stimulated by it' (Aitken 1991: 116). Transactionalism revisits Eisenstein's notion (1943, 1949) that 'elements of a production could be arranged in a formally determinable order so that a viewer would be aroused ("shocked" in Eisenstein's terminology) in precisely the intended manner and to the intended degree' (Carroll 1980: 9).

But in a hyperreality, it is unimportant that image-events are always understood in the same ways and with the same intensities by everyone encountering them; what matters instead is endless disturbance of any dichotomy of the ordinary and extraordinary. This is arguably one of the principal reasons Austen's voice attracts our attention, inasmuch as she volatilises the normal, opening up every condition of the acceptability of custom for debate. Film versions of her stories appeal in apparent relevance of their themes to our 'ordinary' existence even as they supposedly portray 'extraordinary' situations.

Nonetheless, from a transactional perspective 'The impact of an image-event is based upon violating everyday expectations and thereby heightening the involvement of the audience with the film. As such, the portrayal of unusual imbalances and unique transformations between people and environments constitutes an important component of good cinema' (Aitken 1991: 106). Careful attention to a geographical imagination is important here because in order to make a meaningful impact 'the view of landscape presented to a spectator by a film must differ from the perceptual image received in direct experience' (Aitken 1991: 107; cf. Zonn 1984). However, direct experience of rural landscapes central to Austen's geographical imagination is rare for today's primarily urbanised audiences, to say nothing of our twenty-first century distance from the historical context of which those landscapes are part. Their rural sites (fishing villages, peasant cottages, ancient abbeys, manor houses far from city centres, etc.) can exist beyond the reach of history, carrying 'a precious melody from the regions of forever to the present' (Gruchow 1988: 10).

Even if the current spate of Austen films really manages to portray 'unusual imbalances and unique transformations between people and environments', violation of expectation may have a soporific rather than stimulating effect:

> Most of the films sanitize the novels from which they've been adapted, transforming the irony and satire of Austen . . . into narratives and images that commit themselves primarily to depicting pleasant, elegant surfaces. What the audience sees is a world of stately houses with servants and formal gardens, country dances and picnics, Byronic men on horseback and luxuriant green meadows (*Cineaste* 1997: 1).

Even making effort to avoid producing such effects comes too late, those appreciative of a novel's ironic voice more prepared to focus on the lovely scenery when the story is put on screen:

> The BBC . . . has collaborated with Sony in an ungraceful adaptation of
> *Persuasion* (in their attempts to purify the movie of Hollywood sheen and give
> it an air of naturalism, the producers . . . have too zealously ripped away the
> romantic gauze: the distressing results are an unappealing Anne Elliot, a pock-
> marked Captain Wentworth, a greasy-locked Benwick, and a slovenly-looking
> Lady Russell) (Allen 1995: 15).

It becomes difficult to locate transactionalism's imbalances and transformations because it is no longer easy to define the unusual and unique, the shift in
media from print to film entailing the 'privileging of audience approval over the
written text' (Collins 1998: 82). Today's audiences, directors, producers and
critics have been conditioned to use and accept a rhetoric 'that seems to equate
films set in the nineteenth century with the nineteenth century itself' (Collins
1998: 81). Worse, it allows critics to complain that films such as the 1995 BBC
production of *Persuasion* 'nudge . . . a little further into the nineteenth century
than the sensibility of Jane Austen belongs' (Alleva 1996: 16) despite the fact
that Austen's fiction is suffused with Romantic conceptions of narrative.

Implicated here are the very technologies involved in a filmmaker's efforts to
make over mere images as 'image-events'. The increasing artificiality of light
from the 1820s onwards emphasises the 'autonomisation' of sight, 'divorcing
it from the necessity to refer to specific spatial locations' (Thrift 1994: 203;
cf. Crary 1990; Schivelsbuch 1988). Arguably, this generates a kind of neurotic
claustrophobia relieved by voyeuristic onscreen experiences of Austen's largely
pre-industrial landscapes. In post-industrial landscapes of permanent illumina-
tion and increasingly digital mobility, each place appears much like every
other, so presentations of less typical landscapes charm with the possibility of
restoring a geography replete with unique (i.e. not instantly retreaded) encounters of the heart. Paradoxically, the descendents of nineteenth century technologies of light, most notably television and film, which originally 'produced
a new regime which permitted new types of image, new forms of fantasy and
desire, new forms of "experience which (did not need) to be equated with presence"' (Game 1991: 147) now assist the simulation of presences more intensely
experienced than is otherwise explicitly the case.

Especially for audiences outside Britain, mechanisation of sight produces
experience of liminality. Film renditions of Austen's landscapes are simultaneously 'so *cozy*' (*New Yorker* 1995: 56), yet for foreign viewers still part of a
geographical imagination that has not been challenged by an autonomous
interior presence. Austen's West Country, for example, is already inhabited by
the presence of an indigenous nationalism that gains no visibility in reproductions of her novels for American audiences. The Dorset of *Persuasion*, after
all, is the country of Monmouth's landing in 1685 and the Bloody Assizes that
followed, not to mention home to the Tolpuddle Martyrs, the six agricultural
workers whose deportation to penal Australia for unlawful assembly in 1834
marked the birth of the world's first trade unionism movement. Today, even as
devotees of Austen scour the countryside trekking after her characters, the

Heart of Dorset Group offers Tolpuddle Farm Holidays and a Martyrs Museum opened in 1934 on the centenary of the group's exile to annually observe the progress made towards improvement of labourers' rights. If these other opportunities to tell stories about private lives burdened by public circumstances do not disturb the tranquil picture we have of rural Dorset from reading or watching Austen, it can be mentioned that close to Tolpuddle is Bovington, where the Tank Museum gives regular firepower demonstrations for tourists. Nearby Wareham hosts a collection of Lawrence of Arabia's personal effects (he was stationed in Bovington when he was killed in a motorcycle accident after the First World War). For that matter, there's always the Donkey Sanctuary near Sidmouth not far from Lyme Regis providing refuge for British beasts of burden at the end of their working lives. The point here is that the Austen phenomenon (largely an effect of American interest) is not an interest in the richly textured real geography of Dorset (or *Sense and Sensibility*'s Devon), but instead an interest in imaginary geographies especially replicated by one film after another.

The persistence of pastoralism

Still, even were it true that Americans are drawn to Austen's landscapes as some sort of nostalgic recollection of bygone countryside, what did that rural space look like originally? This is not an easy question to answer, not least of all because it is difficult to ask in an unbiased manner. Burns argues that 'pastoral inventions' deployed since the mid-nineteenth century to make sense of American rural spaces and places 'keep alive a vision of an America that almost never was, is not, and never will be' (1989: 337; see also Williams 1973). This is the case even despite indications of a quite ancient tradition of pastoralism (Halperin 1983; see also Empson 1950; Kermode 1952; Poggioli 1975). To be sure, a strong reason why so many were willing to risk transatlantic voyage was because in the Old World the habit of 'Being close to nature was not romantic; it was only destiny' (Burns 1989: 4). That the 'picturesque' was in vogue when Austen wrote did not keep her from addressing this underlying reality, for even when Marianne Dashwood tries to instruct Edward Ferrars on appreciation of the countryside, she has to admit that

> admiration of landscape scenery is become a mere jargon. Everybody pretends to feel and tries to describe with the taste and elegance of him who first defined what picturesque beauty was. I detest jargon of every kind, and sometimes I have kept my feelings to myself, because I could find no language to describe them but what was worn and hackneyed out of all sense and meaning.

Still, the onset of the Industrial Revolution was felt in rural areas in the Georgian emphasis on enclosure (Reed 1983). This was the beginning of a process of rationalising the landscape in a way that limited the possibilities of negotiating meanings other than in terms of what was fashionable, even in the face of the everyday reality of places. By contrast, the peculiar opportunities available to those settling the immense territory of young America had the effect of keeping the reality of the countryside significantly (though never entirely) free of efforts to define it in any static manner. Under such circumstances, there have always been layers of the imaginary as regards to how rural spaces in America have been viewed, entered and transformed into distinct landscapes associated with ease.

Of course, such attachment of comfort to life in the countryside was not new. In the Europe abandoned by settlers of the American frontier, artificial working villages had been established for the sake of aristocratic amusement (Johnstone 1938: 232–3), the rural even then subjected to simulation in its early form as replication and resemblance in the production of 'bucolic rococo' (Johnstone 1938: 231). Writing of the connections of 'Turnips and Romanticism', Johnstone (1938) noted that the eighteenth century fascination with the rural (in opposition to the city) was anticipated and influenced by prior economic transformations of agriculture. However, today's economic transformations have de-emphasised the material context of Romantic conceptions, even as the ideal at the heart of those conceptions is revived (not incidentally, by way of film adaptations of Austen novels).

In all of this, it is important to get a sense of the transitions through which a noticeable return to nature has gone. As in the verse of James Thomson recalling Maro singing for the Roman Senate (Zippel 1908), the 'traditional' agrarian philosophy traced back to the likes of Cincinnatus praised the rural hero for whom power was an obligation seriously assumed and dutifully relinquished. But the agricultural enthusiasm of the later eighteenth century (which Johnstone terms 'georgic') converted this pastoral tradition into the ward of an elite for whom power was a privilege automatically – and thereafter more dramaturgically – assumed, while never relinquished (indeed, any efforts toward that end were usually ruthlessly suppressed). In other words, the Romantic imaginary encompassing the rural made of it a self-conscious, intentional reproduction. Johnstone (1938: 232) reminds us for example that 'In 1768, the Dauphin . . . plowed a famous furrow with a beribboned plow at Versailles. A year later his brother-in-law, the Emperor Joseph, performed a similar ceremony in Moravia.'

Under such pressures, the individual since Austen's time therefore needs ways to invest circumstances with significance both in advance of and in the midst of their regulation by society. This suggests that Austen films are popular at least in part precisely because her characters manage to achieve communion even under the full glare of relentless social scrutiny. In this regard, Kristeva (1984) has teased out important differences between meaning and what she terms 'chora'. She insists that the semiotic arises prior to the assignment of meaning, that communication is not conducted exclusively through the use of the symbolic. The semiotic is the minimally significant organisation of 'drive activity', and the notion of chora describes the 'nonexpressive totality formed by the drives and their stases'. The purpose of articulating distinctions of this sort is to register the ability of consciousness to exploit the semiotic without of necessity having to authorise the symbolic. The subject exists not only (or actually not even) in terms of immediately present relation to the world, but rather with the strength of regard for a future which is unforesee-able and toward the opacity of which the subject need not feel antagonistic (Castoriadis 1987). Thus, the presence of drive activity in the symbolic means that communication need not be limited to the taking of *positions* but includes development of open-ended 'rhythmed' *lines* and *flows*.

This offers a valuable insight into the nature of the filmic experience of Austen's landscapes, since the only minimally pronounced, half-spoken, or even unspoken moments of character interaction in the novels already matter in many respects a great deal more than does anything explicit. For instance, following the incident at Lyme, Anne Elliot and Captain Wentworth speak together 'in spite of [her] formidable father and sister in the back ground' (*Persuasion*: 191), the Captain's news of Louisa Musgrove's engagement to Benwick the channel along which so many other kinds of signals pass between he and Anne at last. Anne's suggestion that Louisa and Benwick will make a good match draws a response from Wentworth notable at least as much for what he does *not* say, especially given the focus of Anne's assessment of the exchange afterwards:

> His choice of subjects, his expressions, and still more his manner and look, had been such as she could see in only one light. . . . sentences begun which he could not finish – his half averted eyes, and more than half expressive glance, – all, all declared that he had a heart returning to her at least . . . (*Persuasion*: 195).

A language of lines and flows emphasises the use of movement in such passages, impulses tracing through space without the need of – or, as Austen understood so well, precisely because of the need to *avoid* – the hurtful absurd-ities of the straitjacketed conversational formalities of eighteenth century gentry society. Needless to say, the immediate emphasis of film is also on movement, on the use of space to retrieve the vitality of chora from the review of socially instituted codes of critique. In this sense, film is arguably a more appropriate medium for Austen than is print – scenes of previous chapters can be assayed again and again by simply turning back the pages, whereas the insistent pressure of a film is on passage from start to finish through a narrative. Without resort-ing to such devices as voiceovers to privilege audience access to a character's thoughts – and for that matter, even *if* such devices are used, I suspect – the deployment of setting becomes anything but a neutral means of assisting in Austen's distinction of all that personally makes sense and all that interferes with it in the name of social sensibility.

Except that in using setting in this way, films never accidentally foreclose certain kinds of critique, but instead empower particular modes of perspective to the exclusion of all others. This is especially the case as regards the deployment of landscape as an active force in shaping evaluations of character, plot and the possibility of letting an author's fiction carry a director's message to a film's audience. Ellington (1998: 108) understands this well when she observes of two filmic renditions of *Pride and Prejudice* that:

> Not only is our understanding of character dynamics within the films dependent upon our understanding of the dynamics of landscape, but the English landscape and ideas of England presented in both films subtly alter our concept of England and Englishness. . . . [T]hese films argue for a British heritage of art, people, and, especially, landscape that is worth preserving; productions of Jane Austen . . . benefit from an ecocritical reading which can place filmmakers' use of nature and landscape in the context of the current nature conservancy movement.

Yet Ellington goes on to suggest that the relatively greater attention given to depictions of landscape over people and social issues 'are powerful assuagements for the middle class because they reinforce the centrality of a middle-class perspective and exclude any elements, such as visual images of the poor, that might unsettle a middle-class viewer.' Momentary opportunities for progressive ecocritical consciousness are insufficient in the face of what Ellington sees as the ideological purposes of 'the new conservatism of both Britain and America.' But in my view, such assumptions are too simplistic. To be sure, the nationalist presence is easy to find in Austen, as in *Emma* (p. 358): 'It was a sweet view – sweet to the eye and the mind. English verdure, English culture, English comfort, seen under a sun bright, without being oppressive.' Or again, from a letter to her brother Frank in 1813: 'The idea of a fashionable bathing place in Mecklenburg! How can people pretend to be fashionable or to bathe out of England!' (quoted in Lane 1986: 11)

I would rather revise and elaborate Ellington's view to recognise that claiming any view as conservative (or liberal) is to assume that there is still a *real* object to which the significations of a viewpoint are attached. Instead, we need to appreciate that, especially in the production of films, the depiction of supposedly 'English' verdure is not a harkening back to *actual* landscapes, but to imaginary renditions – a *reductio ad absurdum*. Indeed, the Romantic appropriation of the rural as a source of aristocratic recreational opportunity had already challenged the possibility of sustaining connection with real circumstances (even if only from the medium distance of ideological fetishism). This was accomplished through the distillation of chora associated with country life and labour into symbols proscribing how expression of those energies should be organised and evaluated.

Indeed, from pastoral to georgic, the imaginary of the rural continues to undergo transformation. Now it seems as if the simulation of the pastoral is the necessity of the masses for whom power is a burden that is inescapable (Baudrillard 1983b). It is neither a reality nor a reproduction of the real, but only an invocation of the symbols of the intermediary 'aristocratic' stage. Thus, adherents of a persistent 'agrarian fundamentalism' in support of life in the American countryside (Fite 1981) promote as 'normal' a discourse about rural places and people that divorces social issues from economic issues, assuming that it is only upon the latter that we need to focus (Nunnally 1989: 18; cf. Geertz 1983). Any former co-existence of spatial practices and performative codes associated with the rural started to deteriorate under the force of the Dauphin's plough and has now disintegrated altogether in the proliferation of simulations not needing connection to actual places. Consider the substitution of real farmers before Congressional hearings, for instance, by actors successful at portraying them (Adams 1985). Or again, in the midst of the rural landscape from which I wrote this chapter, the amateur community baseball team in small town Dyersville, Iowa, winds up being hosted in Japan to play against professionals because Dyersville was chosen as the site visited by the ghosts of the game's legends in the Kevin Costner vehicle *Field of Dreams* (Lawrence 1998).

This is what Baudrillard has in mind when he suggests that the 'strategy of the real' now hinges on encouragement of a desire to 're-inject realness and referentiality everywhere, in order to convince us of the reality of the social, of the gravity of the economy and the finalities of production' (1983a: 42). Listen to Lane at the start of her finely detailed account of the connections between Austen's fictional and lived geographies (1986: 13, emphasis in the original):

> . . . I have endeavoured to evoke that [real] environment itself. It takes great effort of imagination to retrieve towns like Southampton or Portsmouth when they were still confined within their medieval city walls; or Cheltenham when it was little more than one long and airy village street, or even London when each district had its own distinctive character. Jane Austen has helped me to visualize this lost, this lovely England – for that, as for so many other pleasures, I am greatly in her debt. This England is, after all, our common heritage; we are just unfortunate that intervening generations have allowed so much to slip away. *We* must be more vigilant over what remains.

In other words, the rural remains real only because of widespread efforts to remind ourselves about it. This is so whether by visiting living history sites, vacationing on working farms and ranches, restoring pioneer camps and mines and abandoned towns, cutting trails in national parks with the Sierra Club, or making and watching movies and TV shows with rural scenarios. Certainly, we may include in this list tours of sites considered acceptable real-life reference points for fictional locations, such as those organised by the Jane Austen Society of North America (JASNA). Partly, such eager activity gains motivation from such sentiments as Lane's that 'Happily, it is not so difficult to recapture Jane Austen's England in the countryside and the villages, so many of which remain largely unspoilt' (1986: 13). Edwards (1985) tours England 'In the steps of Jane Austen', Greene (1988) wants to find the 'Original of Pemberley' in the Duke of Devonshire's home at Chatsworth, and Ellington

(1998: 109) believes 'It would be useful to compare Austen's description with eighteenth-century guidebooks to which she would have had access.' Even so, these efforts seem only to work against themselves. The georgic rural contested the 'distribution of the real' (Baudrillard 1983a: 38) by suggesting that the right of property could be destabilised by its reproduction as a simulacrum. By contrast, the contemporary rural contests neither the distribution of the real nor its production (which is now of particularly manifold character), but the very reality principle which has hitherto been assumed to set it apart as something recognisably distinct.

That American audiences and film production companies especially are drawn to simulacra of 'English comfort, seen under a bright sun' when so few Americans remain in contact with equivalent transatlantic settings surely only emphasises this point. To some, none of this seems surprising, and there are those who flatly insist that to talk of the 'rural' in America or Britain is anachronistic (Hoggart 1990). Kirby (1987) speaks of 'rural worlds lost', and evidence supporting this position would seem to be plentiful insofar as we can speak of a gathering resemblance of city and country, as well as a material (as distinct from an imaginary) history of rural areas as always intimately connected to urban economies (Cronon 1991).

One form of the imagined rural supporting this latter position is the so-called 'Revolt from the Village' which has appeared now and again in American history, but perhaps most strongly during in the first quarter of the twentieth century (Van Doren 1968; Hifler 1969; Jakle 1982: 7–9). Before this, the pastoral ideal had found new ground and new stewardship in efforts to deploy the 'Jeffersonian' vision of an agrarian democracy:

> . . . instead of being a mere fantasy of the privileged and powerful, in which the ideal place represents largely a nostalgic retreat from social reality, [pastoralism] now was a future-oriented, relatively egalitarian, not infeasible vision of liminal possibility (Marx 1992: 213).

But in the Progressive Era's repudiation of Romantic representations of rurality (whether European or American, aristocratic or republican), the best that could be hoped for was that all trace of human spirit in the countryside might yet be rescued by further urbanisation. Frontier and small town life in the United States was conceived of as repressive, ignorantly conformist and hypocritical. By contrast, urbanisation was imbued with a character permissive of experimentation and expression: 'The positive values one *normally* associates with the city – tolerance, innovation, enthusiasm, nonconformity – are products of city life precisely because of the large and shifting populations in metropolitan areas' (London and Weeks 1981: 37–8; emphasis added).

The first long phase of American globalisation had the effect of normalising this big city myth, but with the development of the Cold War this rhetorical bearing was lost. The arms race made urban centres primary targets of mutual assured destruction. The bewilderment of the undeclared war in Vietnam focused attention on cities as the principal staging ground for the youth move-ment's anti-establishment protests. Intersecting tensions regarding race and poverty converted cities into sites of violent unrest. Likewise, after Watergate urban areas were (again) tainted as capitals of only ever corruptible leadership. Thereafter, the American rural briefly seemed to have its own place again, one which the rough facts of economic restructuring and superpower exhaustion have subsequently done much to erode and dislocate.

Still, there is at least a second form of the rural that conditions the imagina-tion of American audiences looking at Austen's landscapes on film. This involves a 'Small Town Mythos' (Jakle 1982: 6–7) in which rural people are not imprisoned in places of limited opportunity. Instead, some now claim the American political establishment has become both city-oriented but exclusive (Lee 1995). This is supposedly a paradox since exclusivity in the American rhetorical tradition has been assigned to a spatially isolated, ethnically homo-geneous and economically centralised mythical small town. That is, to a rural topos, not an urban one that by contrast is the representational parade ground on which one today hears so many calls for increased government-business partnerships. Lee (1995: 57) suggests that 'Ironically, at a time when commun-ication is global, when economic arrangements require people to move far from their hometowns, and the polity is ever more heterogeneous, American politics has returned to premises that equate place and virtue.' More spe-cifically, it is the equation of virtue with *small* and *rural* place, for example the rural small town Arkansas of Bill Clinton's 'place called Hope'.

But what does this rurally based moral community look like – what about it gives the political vanguard reason to believe that it remains the wellspring of 'traditional values'? For that matter, how might answers to these sorts of questions help explain the role of American audiences and production com-panies in promoting the Austen phenomenon?

Frankly, as suggested earlier not everyone views this representation of small town life with an unjaundiced eye. In *Main Street*, Sinclair Lewis wrote of small-town social organisation based on intensely self-repressive conformity of behaviour, the kind of internalised disciplinary techniques or modes of being Foucault much later (1988) related to 'techniques of the self'. Lewis accused the residents of his fictional rural small town, Gopher Prairie, Minnesota of

> an unimaginatively standardized background, a sluggishness of speech and manners, a rigid ruling of the spirit by the desire to be respectable . . . the con-tentment of a quiet dead, who are scornful of the living for their restless walking. It is dullness made God (1961: 154).

Arguably, what is offered by film productions of Austen's novels is revival of a 'rural' sanctuary where intimacy and individuality, not anonymity and conformity, are possible once again. But if, for Americans at any rate, the small town and its more rustic fringe territory have been declared too dilapid-ated to manage such revival, perhaps it makes sense that a displaced rurality

– a simulated English rurality – serves as a substitute more satisfactorily. In such substitution, we move not only into the realm of the ersatz, but also of the liminal.

The unfinished liminal experience of simulation

Helpful here is Lefebvre's analysis of the production of social space as being made up of three coexisting moments (1991). First there is *spatial practice*, related directly to the spatial division of labour promoted by the dominant mode of production at any given historical juncture. *Representations of space* reinforce and naturalise these practices, emphasising, for example, the significance for a particular culture of openness or enclosure, focus on the background or foreground, vertical or horizontal arrangement of elements of the built environment, massive or minimal ornament, etc. For example, Harding (1998: 48–68) speaks of 'distant and nearer contexts' in Austen's fiction, noting the important timing with which each is used to condition the interactions of characters with events and one another. But there are also *spaces of representation* in which dominant spatial arrangements are challenged (as especially in artistic expression).

Continued reference to dominant discourse does not amount to rehearsing surrender to its spatial practices, instead allowing their exploitation to open up novel identity forms. Lefebvre's *spaces of representation* subvert not only identity categories preferred and promoted by dominant spatial practice, but more importantly the whole attempt to engage in categorisation procedures.

As a space of representation – that is, not as a specific rural locale – 'rurality' approximates what Turner (1985) calls a 'liminal space'. After Van Gennep (1960), Turner (1985: 158) notices that as the individual ages, she is socialised to move through 'a series of changes in pragmatic activity and a succession of transitions in state and status'. States and status are characterised by what the individual is expected to do and not to do, and by the depth and facility of her knowledge of the succession of in-group cultures to which she gains admission. Such rites of passage recognise and facilitate the passage of an individual from one cultural state or social status through four principal stages. Initial *separation* from the social group with which one presently identifies is followed by experience of being on the *margin*. After this comes the phase of *reaggregation* into a social group previously inaccessible by the individual, followed finally by a term of *intensification* to acknowledge the unity of the second group's enlarged membership.

The individual occupies what Turner calls the liminal space in the marginalised phase of stage two. This 'liminar' or initiand is 'betwixt and between the positions assigned and arrayed by law, custom, convention, and ceremonial', yet all other populations (still in a normative state) must relate to the liminar under the constraints of these socially organising principles. Similarly, insofar as liminality is part of the transformative continuum from one socially recognised and organised state of being to another, it 'must bear some traces of its antecedent and subsequent stages . . . some symbols must accord with the "manifest" purposes of the ritual . . . But others have the "latent" capacity to elicit creative and innovative responses from the liminars and their instructors' (Turner, 1985: 160). Such use of symbolic gestures to inspire creative adaptation of Austen for film was explicitly deployed in production of the Oscar-winning (and substantially revisionist) *Sense and Sensibility*:

> On the morning of April 19, 1995, as the sun rose over the Georgian facade of Saltram House at Plymouth, a large, cloth-draped table was set out at the entrance to the house and covered with symbolic items, including apples (for safe, smooth shooting), oranges (for luck and happiness), a pineapple (for prosperity), and a bouquet of large redpetaled flowers (for success). The props department handed out incense sticks, and as the smoke curled up into the morning sky, the assembled cast and crew bowed to the north, east, south and west. The camera was dollied in for a blessing, a few feet of film passed through it as part of the ceremony, and only then could Emma Thompson, Hugh Grant, Kate Winslet, and the rest of the cast step on set, and *Sense and Sensibility*'s first day of shooting could begin. This Eastern Ceremony was Ang Lee's idea and is a traditional Buddhist rite known as the Big Luck Ceremony (http://www.hants.gov.uk/austen/story.html#adaptingjane).

A balance of acknowledgement of the purpose of the rite of passage on the one hand but experimentation with novel forms of discourse on the other hand is necessary to ensure that the individual has the strength of will and disciplined temperament to reach the 'reaggregation' stage. This is arguably a definition of the filmgoer's temporary voyeurism (Denzin 1995), but applies in equal measure to the use of the typical landscapes of rurality. In line with Lefebvre's scheme concerning the production of space, rurality is typically taken as 'betwixt and between the positions assigned and arrayed' to dominant spatial practices. It both embraces sites of vestigial wildness and serves as the forward edge of a civilising force, simultaneously productive of zones of historical recidivism but also of rustic retreat. Individuals can be initiated into a new social state of being through experience of rurality, either as difference (for those not familiar with it) or as different kinds of rural experiences (for those already oriented to daily spatial practices emphasising some representation of rurality). By simply being exposed to such differences of type and degree – constitutive as they are of new ontological and epistemological relationships – the individual's knowledge of her ordinary spatial practice and her relationship to it is increased.

This is why so many valorise the 'necessity of empty places' (Gruchow 1988) believed to be found in rural areas. Gruchow laments that human settlement disturbs and displaces what is best about the rural while watching the migration of Sandhill cranes in central Nebraska – a wildness that can be experienced only in a transitory state of being. Speaking about (for?) the migrating cranes, he insists 'The nomad is a visitor, but not a stranger, whose visit is a kind of embrace. I do not mean that it is innocent or without consequences but only that it is temporary. It is a way of taking hold of the land, even of exploiting it, without altering its essential character' (1988: 18). The same could be said of Austen's characters when they traverse spaces of narrative transformation (the Cobb at Lyme Regis is one such site), but also of audiences evanescently occupying the same landscapes watching film adaptations of the stories.

Partly, the experience of rurality as liminal is achieved by filtering out those effects of modern society with which the individual is best acquainted, making them invisible or at least less visible. Doing so allows for a variety of nuanced relationships of human being and natural context, so that upon disengaging from the experience of rurality, the individual is 'reaggregated' into non-rural (though not necessarily urban) society as a member of what for him or her is now a new social category. Concerning the role of rural nature in liminal experience, Gruchow understands that 'I asked of it a certain intimacy, and it spoke to me only of great distances' (1988: 246).

That distancing and the regeneration of identity it can assist is all the more emphasised by American (and other foreign) reproductions and viewings of 'English' landscapes in film renditions of Austen novels. As suggested earlier this is because of late nineteenth century development of technologies of vision:

> [E]lectrification made possible a new kind of visual text. . . . The new rhetoric of night space edited the city down to a few idealized essentials . . . [allowing] spectators [to] grasp the city as a simplified pattern. The major streets stood out in white bands of light, the tall building shone against the sky, and other important structures such as bridges hung luminously in the air. . . . The city center blazed in importance . . . and the corporations erected electrical signs to proclaim their products and their importance (Nye 1990: 60).

Austen's rural England is now viewed as reinforcing a conservative sense of place, but perhaps this is because the option of visiting it is no longer possible in as immediate a mode as before. The novels originally presented such landscapes as liminal zones, spaces of radical transformation, all the more so because those who moved through them did so rather more self-conscious of that possibility than we do now. Consider Anne Eliott musing on autumn in myriad ways on the walk to Winthrop:

> [Her] . . . pleasure in the walk must arise from the exercise and the day, from the view of the last smiles of the year upon the tawny leaves and withered hedges, and from repeating to herself some few of the thousand poetical descriptions extant of autumn, that season of peculiar and inexhaustible influence on the mind of taste and tenderness, that season which has drawn from every poet, worthy of being read, some attempt at description, or some lines of feeling. She occupied her mind as much as possible in such like musings and quotations (*Persuasion*: 107).

Here, too, the landscape is associated with text, but the rhetoric is far from simplified by editing. Instead, in understanding the 'peculiar and inexhaustible influence' of countryside less ornamented and deliberately managed than urban spaces, Austen demonstrates a prescience of Barthes' more postmodern insistence that 'The text is a tissue of quotations drawn from the innumerable centres of culture' (1972: 146). There is always already an element of 'intertextuality' at work in which any given 'reading' of a particular text (even a landscape as a text) forces digression and diversion into explorations of other texts. This is, of course, true of film as well as of print media, but again, the paradox here is that while films of Austen's novels allow us to retreat to a set of less frenetic rural landscapes, such withdrawal into a comfort zone is only possible by deployment of a major form of electrification of the visual as text rather than as experience.

Williams tried to recognise the ways in which a sense of place was organised in a 'structure of feeling' which 'gives the sense of a generation or period' (1977: 131). Thrift (1994) extends analysis of the electrification of the visual as text to claim 'mobility' as the new 'structure of feeling' for our era. In doing so, he appreciates three 'imaginative adjustments' that have occurred since about 1970 (Thrift 1994: 195–7): (1) rise of the artificial environment, (2) a growing disillusionment with the science responsible for that environmental artifice (including (a) rise of 'risk society' (Beck 1992) and (b) hybridisation of Society and Nature (Giddens 1991; Strathern 1992)), and (3) increasing integration of human–machine networks. An original spatiotemporal sense of place was overpowered by the railroad's industrialisation of travel:

> Henceforth, the localities were no longer spatially individual or autonomous: they were points in the circulation of traffic that made them accessible. . . . [P]laces visited by the traveller became increasingly similar to the commodities that were part of the same circulation system. For the twentieth century tourist, the world has become one huge department store of countrysides and cities (Schivelsbuch 1986: 197).

Today, a telecommunicative era beyond the railroad and automobile re-emphasises isolation while also empowering wholly new ways of overcoming it. The Internet is the latest and most powerful medium for facilitation of this re-figuring of relations between enclosure and openness, the ability Harding notices in Austen's landscapes to 'radiate' outward from their local situation. But film and videotape (the privatisation of the theatrical experience) continue to provide important touchstones for understanding how spatialisation of this flexible sort is modified by the modem.

Instructors in the ritual activities of liminality assist visitors to landscapes of rurality. Primarily, these are the institutional actors supporting one or another representation of the rurality, but the same instructive effect can derive from the pressure of mass numbers of individuals engaged in the same transforming experience. Props used to emphasise that experience engage the liminar's discovery of and reaction to such tactically dispersed objects as emphasise representations of local identity, history and aspiration. A 'law of dissociation' identifies the purpose of creating these 'liminal monsters' for instruction of liminars:

> when a and b occurred together as parts of the same total object, without being discriminated, the occurrence of one of these, a, in a new combination, ax, favors the discrimination of a, b, and x from one another. . . . Liminal monsters . . . are compounded from various *discriminata*, each of them originally an element in the common sense construction of social reality. In a sense, they have the pedagogical function of stimulating the liminars' powers of analysis and revealing to them the building blocks from which their hitherto taken-for-granted world has been constructed (Turner 1985: 161).

But though liminal monsters provoke analysis of the taken-for-granted world, Turner understands that 'in another way they reveal the freedom, the indeterminacy underlying all culturally constructed worlds, the free play of mankind's [sic] cognitive and imaginative capacities.' (1991: 576) This ludic element of liminality is found in JASNA tours of Austen country focused on 'Interpretations and Interactions', 'Great Houses & Gardens' and 'Pastimes & Pleasures'. The 2001 tour, entitled 'Jane Austen: Beside the Sea' included a visit to Lyme Regis where JASNA members 'Begin the morning with a walk to the Cobb for readings from *Persuasion* beside Granny's Teeth' (from which Louisa Musgrove so impulsively leapt). Both in the vivisection of lived geography and through the subsequent re-signification of meaning of such discrete sites as the Cobb, JASNA exhibits characteristics of what Turner (1969) called a 'permanent liminal group'. This notion is reinforced by JASNA action to refurbish the rectory bells of St Nicholas Church at Steventon where Austen was born. In many rites of passage, the liminal phase is frequently marked by a suspension or even reversal of taboos and ordinary distinctions. Whereas such deliberate inversion of expectations is usually understood in terms of behaviour patterns, what I am trying to emphasise is that the socio*spatial* context is likewise impacted. Past and present landscapes can be reversed, and the particular and the general likewise mutated out of all recognition.

So analysis of a taken-for-granted world can have the disturbing effect of producing an account not of that reality but only of its own progress in using such a task as grounds for endless self-contemplation. For Gruchow, the experience of rural nature has become equivalent to 'the melancholy of fame' in which, paradoxically, the better one is known *about* the less one is known intimately (1988: 244–5). There is a complex relationship between this and Austen's subtle critique of the social relations of her day. Consider Anne Elliot's claim that there is an important 'art of knowing our own nothingness beyond our own circle' (*Persuasion*: 28). At first, it seems Gruchow and Austen are in disagreement, that for Austen a change of circumstances entails a loss of intimate understanding. But what Austen really understands (and Gruchow probably does not) is that it is possible to have it both ways. It is impossible for Anne to live with the consequences of being thoroughly known *about*, but inasmuch as such knowledge is relational, it ultimately facilitates a more intimate comprehension of Wentworth. Understanding that it is impossible to avoid the fact that the self is always already social, Austen joined von Bülow in appreciating the unexpected advantages that this situation can provide: 'Strategy is the science of military movements outside of the enemy's field of vision; tactics, within it' (quoted in de Certeau 1984: 212).

Thus, since the use of space can no longer be considered merely an effect of social interaction, we should be concerned about the proliferation of simulations of place. For example, the Hampshire County Council promotes a website (http//www.hants.gov.uk/austen/) dedicated to 'Hampshire – the inspirational home of Jane Austen'. Importantly, given the rapid reconnaissance to which most Internet sites are subjected, in the same site Hantsweb connects Austen's 'gift of making the mundane appear bright and interesting' to a similar claim of extraordinary ordinariness for the countryside in which so many of her stories were set:

> Hampshire in 1999, 182 years after Jane Austen's death, is a unique place to visit – no other part of England has so much to offer. It is probably most famous for its wonderful coastline and countryside – the shores of the Solent overlooking the Isle of Wight, the New Forest with its wild ponies and stunning scenery, picture-book villages with thatched cottages and duck-ponds – Hampshire is just waiting to be explored.

That it is a *lived* countryside is hardly to be imagined, since 'A working country is hardly ever a landscape . . . the very idea of landscape implies separation and observation' (Williams 1973: 120–21). Reality acknowledges the 'close, harsh, patient physicality of a peasant's labour *on*, instead of *in front of*, the land' (Berger 1980: 77), so we must suppose that what is to be 'explored' has nothing to do with the terrain of the real but only with the countryside of fiction. Whereas history is often invoked to register erosion of tradition brought about by landscape change, Hantsweb deploys chronology to reinvest the Hampshire scene with the Austen spirit to fortify its insistence that 'no other part of England has so much to offer'. Importantly, there was a strong effort even during Austen's lifetime to produce such a divorce of perspective from reality, as in William Gilpin's decree:

> . . . milkmaids, ploughmen, reapers and all peasants engaged in their several professions we disallow. There are modes of landscape, to which they are adapted: but in the scenes we here characterize, they are valued for what in real life they are despised – loitering idly about, without employment (quoted in Lane 1986: 103).

Baudrillard insists that 'When the real is no longer what it used to be, nostalgia assumes its full meaning. . . . There is an escalation of the true' (1983a: 12).

Thus, even when effort *is* made to remember other presences in the landscapes of rurality, they belong only to other notables. Moreover, their recall is undertaken only to elevate the status of the rest of us who feel otherwise bereft of such scenes and scenarios as rurality is presumed to offer:

> Portrayed in Jane Austen's *Persuasion*, Lyme Regis, Dorset boasts more than its share of writers. The Philpot Museum tells you all about them. John Fowles' *French Lieutenant's Woman* has Lyme written all over it (he still lives here). Henry Fielding caused a scandal here. Beatrix Potter came to stay. So can you!

Conclusions

Landscapes are curiosities – to view one is to look at something simultaneously crafted but apparently natural. Whether through painting, cartographic representation, photography or film, landscape can both obscure and selectively articulate the lived experience and foundational history of those located within the scene. This is true for those who reside or work there, as well as those who are only passing through as tourists or travellers of other sorts – all can have unique insight about a given landscape, but as Raymond Williams suggested:

> Some particular shape: the line of a hedge, the turn of a path round a wood, or in movement sometimes, the shadow of a cloud that bends in a watercourse, or again a sound, the wind in wires, wind tearing at a chimney . . . I really seem to feel . . . these things as my body . . . As if I was feeling *through* them, not feeling *about* them. . . . [Regarding landscapes] there's usually nothing to be said (1979: 97–8).

Ultimately, defining landscapes may be unsatisfying because the real – as opposed to hyperreal – experience of a place involves the inexpressible momentum of complex local history. Jane Austen's novels position us somewhere between that subtlety of lived experience and its disappearance in the simulations of her settings when adapted to film. As Collins (1998: 88) puts it:

> Each time one of her novels is brought to the forefront of twentieth-century popular culture, the renewed interest in her work and times seems to reveal a general desire to learn more about the past. But it is a desire to learn about the past as it relates to the present, and as a result the films are judged not on the basis of their historical realism but on their ability to mould history into a form which is reminiscent of the present. . . . [O]ur society is quickly moving toward a time in which we really don't know much about history.

Or, for that matter, about the multiple, increasingly interconnected human geographies in which history literally takes place. That the simulations broadcast by film renditions of Austen novels are productive of a permanently liminal state of an incessantly self-absorbed *Now* presents us with considerable challenges in paying attention to neglected voices in the countryside (Lawrence 1997).

References

Adams, P.C. 1992 'Television as gathering place', *Annals of the Association of American Geographers*, **82**(1), 117–35.

Adams, W. 1985 'American Gothic: country, the river, places in the heart', *Antioch Review*, **43**, 217–24.

Aitken, S.C. 1991 'A transactional geography of the image-event: the films of Scottish director, Bill Forsyth', *Transactions of the Institute of British Geographers*, **16**, 105–18.

Aitken, S.C. and Zonn, L.E. 1994 *Place, Power, Situation, and Spectacle: A Geography of Film*, Rowman & Littlefield, Lanham, MD.

Allen, B. 1995 'Jane Austen for the nineties', *The New Criterion*, **September**, 15.

Alleva, R. 1996 'Emma can read, too', *Commonweal*, **8 March**, 15–18.

Austen, J. 1966 *Emma*, R.W. Chapman (ed.), Mary Lascelles (rev.), 3rd edition, volume 4 of 6 of *The Novels of Jane Austen*, Oxford University Press, Oxford.

Austen, J. 1966 *Sense and Sensibility*, R.W. Chapman (ed.), Mary Lascelles (rev.), 3rd edition, volume 1 of 6 of *The Novels of Jane Austen*, Oxford University Press, Oxford.

Austen, J. 1985 *Persuasion*, D.W. Harding (ed.), Penguin Classics, New York.

Bachelard, G. 1994 *The Poetics of Space*, Beacon Press, Boston.

Barthes, R. 1972 *Mythologies*, Paladin, London.

Baudrillard, J. 1983a *Simulations*, Semiotext(e), New York.

Baudrillard, J. 1983b *In the Shadow of the Silent Majorities*, Semiotext(e), New York.

Beck, U. 1992 *Risk Society: Towards a New Modernity*, Sage, London.

Berger, J. 1980 *About Looking*, Writers & Readers Publishing Co-operative, London.

Burns, S. 1989 *Pastoral Inventions: Rural Life in Nineteenth-century American Art and Culture*, Temple University Press, Philadelphia.

Carroll, J.M. 1980 *Toward a Structural Psychology of Cinema*, Mouton, The Hague.

Castoriadis, C. 1987 *The Imaginary Institution of Society*, Polity, Cambridge.

Cineaste 1997 'Editorial', *Cineaste*, **22**(4), 1.

Cloke, P. and Little, J. (eds) 1997 *Contested Countryside Cultures: Otherness, Marginalisation and Rurality*, Routledge, London.

Cloke, P., Doel, M., Matless, D., Phillips, M. and Thrift, N. 1994 *Writing the Rural: Five Cultural Geographies*, Paul Chapman Publishing, London.

Collins, A. 1998 'Jane Austen, film, and the pitfalls of postmodern nostalgia', pp. 79–89 in L. Troost and S. Greenfield (eds), *Jane Austen in Hollywood*, The University Press of Kentucky, Lexington.

Crary, J. 1990 *Techniques of the Observer: On Vision and Modernity in the Nineteenth Century*, MIT Press, Cambridge, MA.

Cronon, W. 1991 *Nature's Metropolis: Chicago and the Great West*, W.W. Norton, New York.

de Certeau, M. 1984 *The Practice of Everyday Life*, University of California Press, Berkeley.

Denzin, N. 1995 *The Cinematic Society: The Voyeur's Gaze*, Sage, London.

de Tocqueville, A. 1959 *Journey to America*, Faber and Faber, London.

Edwards, A. 1985 *In the Steps of Jane Austen*, Arcade Books, Ashurst, Southampton.

Eisenstein, S. 1943 *The Film Sense*, Faber, London.

Eisenstein, S. 1949 *Film Form*, Harcourt, New York.

Ellington, H.E. 1998 '"A correct taste in landscape": Pemberley as fetish and commodity', pp. 90–110 in L. Troost and S. Greenfield (eds), *Jane Austen in Hollywood*, The University Press of Kentucky, Lexington.

Emma 1996 Writer and director Douglas McGrath; with Gwyneth Paltrow and Jeremy Northam; Miramax.

Empson, W. 1950 *Some Versions of Pastoral*, New Directions, Norfolk, CT.

Ferguson, M. 1998 '*Mansfield Park*: Slavery, colonialism, and gender', pp. 103–20 in L. Mooneyham White (ed.), *Critical Essays on Jane Austen*, G.K. Hall, New York.

Fite, G. 1981 *American Farmers: The New Minority*, Indiana University Press, Bloomington.

Foucault, M. 1988 'Technologies of the self', in L.M. Martin, H. Gutman and P.H. Hutton (eds), *Technologies of the Self*. University of Massachusetts Press, Amherst.

Game, A. 1991 *Undoing the Social*, Open University Press, Milton Keynes.

Geertz, C. 1983 *Local Knowledge: Further Essays in Interpretive Anthropology*, Basic Books, New York.

Giddens, A. 1991 *Modernity and Self-identity*, Polity Press, Cambridge.

Greene, D. 1988 'The original of Pemberley', *Eighteenth-Century Fiction*, **1**, 1–23.

Gruchow, P. 1988 *The Necessity of Empty Places*, St. Martin's Press, New York.

Halperin, D. 1983 *Before Pastoral: Theocritus and the Ancient Tradition of Bucolic Poetry*, Yale University Press, New Haven.

Harding, D.W. 1998 *Regulated Hatred and Other Essays on Jane Austen*, Athlone Press, London.

Hifler, A.C. 1969 *The Revolt from the Village, 1915–1930*, University of North Carolina Press, Chapel Hill.

Hoggart, K. 1990 'Let's do away with rural', *Journal of Rural Studies*, **6**, 245–57.

Jakle, J.A. 1982 *The American Small Town: Twentieth-century Place Images*, Archon Books, Hamden, CT.

Johnstone, P. 1938 'Turnips and Romanticism', *Agricultural History*, **12**, 224–55.

Kermode, F. 1952 *English Pastoral Poetry: From the Beginnings to Marvell*, Harrap, London.

Kirby, J.T. 1987 *Rural Worlds Lost: The American South, 1920–1960*, Louisiana State University Press, Baton Rouge.

Kristeva, J. 1984 *Revolution in Poetic Language*, tr. M. Waller, Columbia University Press, New York.

Lane, M. 1986 *Jane Austen's England*, Robert Hale, London.

Lawrence, M. 1997 'Heartlands or neglected geographies? Liminality, power, and the hyperreal rural', *Journal of Rural Studies*, **13**(1), 1–17.

Lawrence, M. 1998 'Miles from home in the field of dreams: rurality and the social at the end of history', *Environment and Planning D: Society and Space* **16**(6), 705–32.

Lefebvre, H. 1991 *The Production of Space*, Basil Blackwell, Oxford.

Lee, R. 1995 'Editorial politics and the visions of community: Jimmy Carter, virtue, and the small town myth', *Western Journal of Communication*, **59**(1), 39–60.

Lewis, S. 1961 *Main Street*, New American Library, New York.

London, H.I. and Weeks, A.L. 1981 *Myths that Rule America*, University Press of America, Washington.

Marx, L. 1992 'Does pastoralism have a future?', *Studies in the history of Art 36: The pastoral landscape*, National Gallery of Art, Washington.

New Yorker 1995 'Emma Thompson: A close reading', *New Yorker*, **21–28 August**, 55–6.

Nunnally, P.D. 1989 *Visions of Sustainable Place: Voice, Land, and Cultural in Rural America*, PhD dissertation (American Studies), University of Iowa, Iowa City.

Nye, D. 1990 *Electrifying America: Social Meanings of New Technology*, MIT Press, Cambridge, MA.

Poggioli, R. 1975 *The Oaten Flute: Essays on Pastoral Poetry and the Pastoral*, Harvard University Press, Cambridge, MA.

Reed, M. 1983 *The Georgian Triumph 1700–1830*, Routledge and Kegan Paul, London.

Schivelsbuch, W. 1986 *The Railway Journey: The Industrialisation of Time and Space in the 19th Century*, University of California Press, Berkeley.

Schivelsbuch, W. 1988 *Disenchanted Night: The Industrialisation of Light in the Nineteenth Century*, University of California Press, Berkeley.

Stewart, M. 1993 *Domestic Realities and Imperial Fictions: Jane Austen's Novels in Eighteenth-century Contexts*, The University of Georgia Press, Athens.

Strathern, M. 1992 *After Nature: English Kinship in the Late Twentieth Century*, Cambridge University Press, Cambridge.

Thrift, N. 1994 'Inhuman geographies: landscapes of speed, light, and power', pp. 191–248 in P. Cloke, M. Doel, D. Matless, M. Phillips, and N. Thrift, *Writing the Rural: Five Cultural Geographies*, Paul Chapman Publishing, London.

Troost, L. and Greenfield, S. (eds) 1988 *Jane Austen in Hollywood*, The University Press of Kentucky, Lexington.

Turner, V.W. 1969 *The Ritual Process*, Aldine de Gruyter, Hawthorne, NY.

Turner, V.W. 1985 *On the Edge of the Bush: Anthropology as Experience*, The University of Arizona Press, Tucson.

Turner, V.W. 1991 'Myth and symbol', pp. 576–8 in D.L. Sills (ed.), *International Encyclopaedia of the Social Sciences*, Vol. 10, Macmillan, New York.

Van Doren, C. 1968 'Sinclair Lewis and the revolt from the village', pp. 85–92 in R.J. Giffin (ed.) *Twentieth-century Interpretations of Arrowsmith: A Collection of Critical Essays*, Prentice-Hall, Englewood Cliffs, NJ.

Van Gennep, A. 1960 *The Rites of Passage*, University of Chicago Press, Chicago.

Weldon, F. 1995 'Jane Austen and the pride of purists', *New York Times*, **8 October**, H15, H24.

Williams, R. 1973 *The Country and the City*, Chatto and Windus, London.

Williams, R. 1977 *Marxism and Literature*, Oxford University Press, Oxford.

Williams, R. 1979 *The Fight for Manod*, Chatto and Windus, London.

Worth, S. 1969 'The development of a semiotic of film', *Semiotica*, **1**, 282–321.

Worth, S. 1981 *Studying Visual Communication*, University of Pennsylvania Press, Philadelphia.

Zippel, O. 1908 *Thomson's Seasons*, Mayer & Müller, Berlin.

Zonn, L. 1984 'Landscape depiction and perception: a transactional approach', *Landscape Journal*, **3**, 144–50.

CHAPTER 7

Working with crabs

Deborah Dixon

The where of Eastern Carolina

In the hot and humid months of summer, tourists outnumber the residents of Eastern Carolina by five to one[1]. Mostly they drive south from the North Eastern seaboard or east from the North Carolina cities and towns that stretch inland all the way to the Appalachian Mountains. The numerous waterways of Eastern Carolina make travelling by car a relatively slow pastime, as major roads and bridges are few and far between. But the small ferries that ply back and forth across the rivers and sounds are considered part of the charm of the region, and the leisurely pace allows the landscape to unfold around you as you travel to and from the hotels and holiday homes built along the shorefront.

As is the case with most rural areas in the western world, where agriculture is big business and rural–urban migration has taken its toll, visitors to Eastern Carolina do not see too many people on the road or on the water. What they do see is miles of fir trees and cotton fields, interrupted by abandoned tobacco barns, their red paint peeling in the sun, or the occasional farmhouse set back against a windbreak. Signs along the road offer bacon, eggs, honey and seafood as well as lawn furniture, hunting equipment, cut timber and lobster pots. Jacked-up cars and trucks, hog pens and chicken coops inhabit front yards, while a cluster of benches indicate a roadside barbecue. If you follow one of the dirt tracks leading off from the main road you will more than likely arrive at the entrance to a lumber mill, or in the middle of a small trailer park.

Continue on down the road and you enter one of the numerous small towns scattered up and down the coast, such as Oriental, Beaufort, Swanquarter and Aurora. On Main Street, the courthouse, churches and local bank branches adjoin several real estate offices. If you park the car and walk through the streets of shotgun houses, wooden porches and corner grocery stores, you soon realise (if you haven't already suspected) that in this place race matters as to where residents live, eat, shop and pray. A colour bar still divides these towns into black and white spaces. You might even spot a Mexican food store, and recollect those trailer parks hidden out amongst the fir trees.

Animating the landscape

Given the overwhelming numbers of seasonal visitors to Eastern Carolina it would, perhaps, be appropriate to talk about the ways in which tourism is premised on certain bodily practices, from the relatively passive gaze of the driver and passengers to the more active multi-sensory experience of being in a place that we associate with recreational sports as well as walking, talking, eating and shopping. It could also be argued that the tourist encounter brings into play certain myths and stereotypes concerning how people behave and look. A piratical version of the hillbilly icon, for example, can be found on souvenirs and billboards throughout Eastern Carolina. According to Williamson (1995), the character serves not only as a representation of people and place for outsiders, denoting a lost freedom and independence as well as a backwoods/backwards way of life, it also stands as an ironic comment on urban-based, middle class values for insiders. Hence, he argues, the predominance of this cartoon character tells us something about the expectations residents have of tourists and vice versa.

However, to focus on the tourist encounter is to focus on those people who are 'visibly' animating the rural landscape of Eastern Carolina, in the sense that their bodies are either the source or target of the tourist gaze. What I intend to do instead is focus on some of those people who appear intermittently not only on that tourist horizon, but also in other arenas that lay claim to represent the region, such as historical records, official data sets and popular novels. Specifically, I want to bring to light, as it were, the bodies of women working in the crab houses of Eastern Carolina[2]. Crab processing is a marginal industry by any measure, in that the capital involved, the numbers employed and profits generated are low and in sharp decline. Two years ago there were over 40 crab houses spread over 13 coastal counties, employing between 5 and 200, mostly black and Mexican, women. Currently, only 17 houses remain: cheap crabmeat imports from China, Thailand and South Korea, shipped in by major US food distribution companies such as Phillips and Sea King, have undercut their market. The consensus among crab house owners is that without some measure of government protection, the industry will close down in the near future.

In focusing on these women I want to begin by tracing their absence from these readily accessible representations of people and place. A celebration of the region's male-dominated fishing industry, it is suggested, has foregrounded men's work as central to the development of the region's character and relative success. This association not only privileges a certain form of 'hard' masculinity (hooks 1992) based on physical prowess, it also renders the 'economy' as the key arena within which individuals gain status. In this sense, the relative invisibility of women at work in the seafood sector speaks to a systematic devaluation of their activities.

In order to bring these working women to light, access to the private world of the crab houses must be negotiated. However, rather than use in-depth interviews and observation as a means of assessing their contribution to the seafood sector, it is more productive to step back from the assumption that 'labour' itself is a known and fixed category. Certainly, within the crab houses work is exchanged for wages, but this relationship is merely the entry point for an exploration of how these women are brought together in this place and, further, how their concerted activity has been designated as a 'labour' force. Up until the 1980s, crab picking was associated with household chores and the relationship between managers and pickers was a fairly informal, at times familial, one. The influx of Mexican women into the industry during this decade, however, was presaged on a crisis concerning 'labour.' The subsequent emphasis on efficiency, monitoring and value for money has transformed expectations concerning what it is to work in the crab houses.

This differential understanding of crab picking as an activity indicates the social context within which working bodies are framed, and the relational form of bodies more generally. As numerous geographers have pointed out, we can do more than simply locate bodies, noting their presence or absence from public view. We can go on to explore how and why select aspects of select bodies are rendered visible to the tourist gaze, as well as census data, archives and books, while other aspects and other bodies remain hidden. There is, of course, a history to engaging the body as a significant object of inquiry within geography, but this will not be dealt with here (see instead reviews and critiques in: Callard 1998; Harvey 1998; Longhurst 1997, 2000; Mitchell 2000; Nast and Pile 1998; Pile and Thrift 1995; Rodaway 1994; Seamon 1979; Teather 1999; Valentine 1999, 2001). It is sufficient to note that these disciplinary interjections are themselves embedded in broader academic debates on the appropriateness of placing the human body within a species context (in regard to sociobiology) or a societal context (in regard to, for example, Freudian analysis, Marxism and anti-essentialism). If the latter series of debates can be summed up, the body is accorded no absolute qualities: instead, it is understood to be the physical, chemical and psychical raw material for social and cultural processes and mechanisms. As part of this social existence particular aspects and fragments of bodies are labelled, categorised and valued as organs, fluids, senses, capabilities, emotions and comportments.

Placing the body within a social context, then, is to *decentre* it: the notion of the body as a distinct totality is undermined by an emphasis on its connection to what Massey calls broader networks of social relations and understandings (Massey 1993: 66). As Pile and Thrift (1995: 6–7) note, however, there are diverse opinions on the character of these connections, depending on one's view of how society operates as well as the character of humanity itself. One can view the body as an origin, in that the operation of the psyche produces meaning concerning self and others. Or, the body can be viewed as a medium, in that it provides the means by which access to the world is negotiated. Or, the body can be understood as a destination, in that cultural expectations concerning corporeality and comportment are inscripted onto the surface of the body; more generally, disciplinary techniques concerning the physical and mental development of the self are thought to be instilled throughout the body's parts. The active construction of bodies has particularly excited the imagination of geographers such as Cresswell (1999), Kay (1997), Massey (1996), McDowell (1995), Philo (1989) and Valentine (1999, 2001).

In regard to working bodies, one particular understanding has tended to dominate discussion, namely a Marxist rendering of labour as both *instrumentalist* and *alienating*. According to Krozova (1976), for example, within capitalism the body takes on the function of maintaining itself through production and reproduction. In the process, the range and intensity of bodily experiences are reduced, as well as the expressive capacity of the body. In effect, what Krozova refers to as the 'desensualised' and 'desexualised' body becomes instrumental to the maintenance of labour, and hence to capitalism itself. For Krozova, because this is not the natural state of the human body, physically or mentally, alienation has occurred. Harvey (1998) and Mitchell (2001) note further how abstract labour is extracted from the disciplining, fragmentation and hybridisation of the working body, as labourers undertake increasingly specialised and mechanised tasks. Within this frame of reference, the body is understood to present both opportunity and obstacle to capitalism, in that it provides the means by which value is produced, and yet must also be maintained through the payment of wages (Henderson 1999).

Anti-essentialist renderings of the working body take note of many of the same transformations, and share a common vocabulary, but provide a conceptual contrast to that research agenda outlined above. According to Falk (1994), for example, the working body does undergo transformation, in that there is a shift in the way body parts are used and valued. Within the workplace the mouth, for instance, is generally prohibited from signifying affection (through kissing) or aggression (through biting): these prohibitions in turn privilege speech as an expressive form. Falk also notes the significance of hybridisation, in that the work process is predicated on meaningful connections between particular parts of the body and particular tools. The effect of such work, however, is not instrumentalism and alienation, but rather a complex mix of sensory experiences, including their intensification and diversification, as well as their spatial and temporal displacement from inside to outside the workplace. For Falk, the working body is not somehow reduced through labour: rather, the body remains *eroticised*, in that its sensual existence always approaches, and even demands, social and cultural boundaries on form and expression. Importantly, eroticism as a concept incorporates a spiritual dimension (see Bataille 1962: 15), such that a part of the body generally dismissed in economic analyses of the workplace, and even accounts of the body itself, can be brought into play, namely the soul. Within such anti-essentialist renderings, the body is viewed not as a site of struggle and resistance, but as a continually becoming corporeality. Or, as Doel (1997: 230) more eloquently puts it:

> an assemblage of social apparatuses seizes roughly hewn chunks of flesh, encases them within skin, inscribes them with face and encodes them with the striations of race, ethnicity, gender, sexuality, class and so on and so forth. However, the production . . . is never complete; it is always a work-in-progress and a site of continuous experimentation. Hence the fact that the human subject is always a full body *to come*; it endures without ever existing *as such* [emphasis in original].

In regard to crab picking, then, we can gain some sense of how the working bodies of these women have been invested with meaning by others by virtue of their relative absence from representations that lay claim to present people and place. We can go further, however, and appreciate how the women involved have invested meaning in their body – particularly their hands, voices and souls – through time and over space, and how those meanings have facilitated connections with, and disconnections from, other people and things. Clearly, no account can do justice to the variety of understandings of crab picking that have been produced over time and through space. In light of the above argument on the relational form of bodies, the aim is to highlight how one particular understanding of crab picking – the notion that crab pickers are a labour force – has emerged. In order to emphasise the contingent character of this construct, an alternate understanding of crab picking as work will be reconstructed, one that embeds work within notions of family ties, personal worth and spiritual well-being.

Locating people in the seafood sector

If, as Gibson-Graham (1996) suggests, rural areas are indeed characterised by sharply delineated gendered and racialised assumptions about what kind of labour is appropriate to individuals, and that in such areas these assumptions are likely to be put into practice in the workplace as well as the home, we might well expect the Eastern Carolina seafood sector to be segregated by both gender and race. It might be added that these expectations are embedded in practices that claim to present the area to public view, including the composition of historical reports, the collection, analysis and presentation of statistical data, and the novelisation of people and place. One can trace in such presentations the systematic foregrounding (and simultaneous backgrounding) of particular 'livelihoods'. Not only are particular forms of identity – such as gender and race – assumed to appropriately categorise people and occupations, but some gender and race-laden work activities are accorded more significance than others in the development of the region's 'economy'.

Popular historical accounts of the region, for example, look to the fishing industry as the heart of the economy and, by projection, the community. For Stick (1958), it is the increasing size of the blue crab catch in particular that gives the region a distinct way of life and provides Eastern Carolina a visible place within the national economy. He notes that during the late 1800s, some of the crabs caught up in the fishing nets were eaten or used as fertiliser, but most were thrown away by the region's fishermen. By the 1940s, however, the means by which crabs were caught had changed significantly. Trawler nets were introduced in the Pamlico Sound, while bigger boats were able to carry out more and more crab pots. The catch had increased to the point where North Carolina 'ranked third' on the Atlantic Coast behind Virginia and Maryland. Stick (1958: 228) also notes how in the nineteenth century local 'Negro children' would gather blue crabs and sell them on for 15 to 20 cents per dozen. By the 1950s a complex distribution network had emerged, and processed crabmeat was shipped out to Washington, DC, Baltimore and Boston.

Notably absent from this portrait of a subsistence economy inhabited by Negro children, which is then transformed into a thriving industry, is the actual transformation of the catch into a commodity ready to be sold on the market. In omitting this part of the chain, the people involved in transforming catch into commodity, including crab house owners, managers and pickers, have effectively disappeared from history.

Within the various data sets relating to the seafood sector, a similar absence in regard to the processing of seafood can be traced. Statistics are collected at a number of government levels and cover a wide range of observations including number of workers in a particular occupation, wage rates, fish harvests, value of fish harvests, number of boats and number of work-related deaths. Moreover these data sets are readily available for perusal on the Internet. We can note, for example, that in a good year Eastern Carolina has a blue crab catch of around 60 million pounds (27 million kilograms), valued at $38 million (National Marine Fisheries Service, Annual Landings) and that three-fifths of the crabbers own and operate their own vessels (Bureau of Labor Statistics: Fishing, Hunting and Agricultural Occupations). We can also learn the median earnings of full-time fishermen from the Bureau of Labour Statistics and compare this with the prevailing national minimum wage. The Bureau also produces special reports, and we can learn online that between 1992 and 1996, 18 Eastern Carolina crabbers were lost at sea, making it officially the most dangerous occupation in the United States (Drudi 1998). Some statistics do require more effort, but we can learn through a phone call that there are around 4000 fishermen currently engaged in crabbing in Eastern Carolina (Office of Statistics, North Carolina Division of Marine Fisheries, Morehead NC)[3].

Seafood processing is not counted as a separate occupation by the Bureau of Labor Statistics and so equivalent information is quite difficult to find. In order to build up a profile of this particular part of the fishing sector, one has to be allowed entry into a localised network of professional, familial and social relations and interview crab house managers, as well as senior staff at the

NC Division of Marine Fisheries in Morehead City, all of whom are white and male. Some questions (regarding profits, for example) do not get answered, some information does not exist in a coherent written form (such as the number of crab houses year to year) and some information is patchy (estimates of the number of women employed). This kind of data does, of course, exist in other forms such as tax returns and immigration records, which are not easily, if ever, accessible[4]. In consequence, a large part of the working lives of these women remains hidden from view. As Domosh (1997) points out in regard to secondary sources more generally, the significant point is not that official data sets are more 'accurate' or 'reliable' but rather that they do serve as accessible representations of people and place and that they do highlight particular male-dominated activities. Arguably, then, these data sets embed the view that the processing of seafood is a less significant economic activity than catching it.

In order to explore why significance is accorded some activities over others, we can look briefly at some of the numerous novelisations of fishing folk. In 1988 Glenn Lawson published *The Last Waterman* as a tribute to the tough, hardworking crab fishermen of the east coast. Emphasis is placed on the need to hand down traditional wisdom and knowledge of the area from father to son. As Randall Peffer writes in his book simply entitled *Watermen*

> According to family tradition my colonial ancestors had settled the Eastern shore in the seventeenth century. They were called 'watermen' and they made their living harvesting oysters, crabs, fish and waterfowl. Watermen still dominate life on the Eastern shore . . . (1985: 3).

The central subject about which knowledge accrues is the blue crab, and it is around this particular body that the lives of fishermen are entwined. A similar characterisation of the fearless, independent fisherman and his relationship with the feisty crustacean is celebrated in Warner's 1977 Pulitzer Prize winning book, *Beautiful Swimmers*. As Griffith (1997) notes, fishing is one of the 'primary' activities associated with a physical, risk-taking masculinity, and as such is considered a 'proper' activity for men, alongside hunting, trapping and forestry. There is no similarly visible celebration of an intimate and respectful relationship between women and the crab they are picking meat from, nor the injunction to hand down a crab picking lore from mother to daughter.

Constructing and placing 'labour'

It is quite a task, then, simply to locate and make visible the bodies of these women and the degree of effort required tells us something of the significance and status afforded women's work in the crab processing industry of Eastern Carolina. It is from in-depth interviews with owners and managers, workers and state officials that a history of how particular bodies were clustered in time and space to form a 'labour' force can be pieced together. A more detailed narrative of this history and geography has been presented elsewhere (Selby *et al.* 2001). To sum up the key moments in the emergence of an 'industry', most of the crabs landed at the turn of the century were processed and then sold on to retailers in the North East by the women of the household in order to add to generate extra income. This practice was viewed as a natural extension of the household economy. In the 1930s and 1940s, however, the uniformly white, male owners of established fin fish processing plants took over this lucrative business, utilising their privileged access to credit and workspace. Some owned fishing fleets and brought in their own catch for processing, while the rest entered into informal 'gentlemen's agreements' with local crabbers for supplies.

Women maintained a presence in the industry, but only those related to the owners took on positions of authority, hiring, supervising and paying workers, weighing and packing the meat and organising retail outlets. The majority of women were placed on the work floor and assigned the task of picking meat from cooked crabs. In some crab houses these women were predominantly black, in others white, depending on which racially segregated township the plant was located next to. Both groups, however, were bereft of choices in a region whose residents depended heavily on agriculture and seafood for income and deemed women particularly fitting to the processing of food. For the women involved also, this association with food preparation, as well as the seasonal character of the job and the irregular hours worked, added to the notion that crab picking was an extension of their regular household chores. Crab picking was counted as one of a cluster of activities undertaken to provide for the family (Selby *et al.* 2001), including shucking shrimp, picking cotton and constructing crab pots. Considering the low income levels for the region as a whole, wages were relatively high for this kind of work as crab houses competed with each other for seasonal workers. Those hired could also count on flexible working hours if they needed to go home early to look after children or elderly parents (Mosher 1993; Selby 1998).

In the 1980s a new group were inserted into this already gendered and racialised setting. Concerned at high turnover rates and cheap foreign imports, crab house owners made use of established links with peers in Sinaloa to bring in female crab pickers on H2-B visas[5] during the Mexican off-season. As Mitchell (2001) notes in regard to the Mexican farm workers of California, a seasonal circulation of working bodies, whose primary role is to exchange labour for wages, is thus established such that profits can be maintained. Unlike their agricultural counterparts, however, who work on H2-A visas, these women are not guaranteed reasonable standards of accommodation under federal law. Most of the women share and pay rent on trailers owned by their employers and stationed next to the crab house.

Whereas the local workforce enjoyed an informal relationship with owners and managers, full of shared knowledge and even a sense of mutual loyalty, the presence of Mexican women in the workplace was predicated on quite a different working relationship. This differential rendering of their activity can be appreciated simply by observing the spatial placement of people in the crab house and their outward demeanour. The crabs are cooked in large vats set in one part of the plant and are brought out to a series of long tables in trolleys pushed by local men hired to help out with the heavy work. Whereas the local women all sit at their tables to pick crabs and maintain a constant flow of talk (Figure 7.1), the Mexican women prefer to stand and work in silence (Figure 7.2). Many of the local women wear their day dress to work and a simple apron: most of the Mexican women wear the regulation white t-shirt, hairnet, gloves and rubber boots. The work floor itself is distinguished from the

Figure 7.1   Sitting down to pick crabs. (Photo taken by the author during fieldwork.)

Figure 7.2   Standing up to pick crabs. (Photo taken by the author during fieldwork.)

Figure 7.3   Other residents of the crab house. (Photo taken by the author during fieldwork.)

upstairs (usually panelled) offices where the male owners have their desks. Given the prevalence of an almost mythic association between masculinity and the struggle to reap resources from Nature noted above, it is none too surprising, then, to find that some of the owners devote several temperature- and humidity-controlled rooms in their crab house to elaborately mounted hunting trophies (Figure 7.3).

The hiring of Mexican women has had a significant impact on the way in which the work of local crab pickers has been designated. During the 1980s, when usually high profits took a downward turn, it became commonplace for owners to talk about 'labour' and the problem of maintaining it (Dickens and Stein 1994; Mosher 1993; Ruley 1994; Selby 1998; Selby *et al.* 2001). This appellation, for example, is manifest in the legal context within which crab houses are embedded, as in order for the Mexican workers to gain H2-B visa, their future employers must declare to the Immigration and Naturalization Service that they cannot replace their 'labour' with individuals from the local area. Furthermore, the 'labour'-based relationship established with the Mexican women has become the norm against which other relations are measured. Evaluations based on efficiency and output, as well as value for money, have become commonplace in the selection and monitoring of crab pickers. While the traditional informality of the job is still apparent in the demeanour of local women, the meaning of their work has also undergone a significant shift. If we look at various studies of the crab industry, such as Griffith (1997), Mosher (1993), Ruley (1994) and Dickens and Stein (1994), interview data from local women make it clear that this redefinition of their work is resented. Those targeted for blame, however, are not the owners and management, but rather the Mexican workers who are described as 'displacing' local women.

Giving meaning to the working body[6]

So far, we have looked at the difficulty in locating women's bodies in the seafood industry, in that those presentations most accessible to view, including official data sets, histories and novelisations systematically foreground activities associated with men and masculinity. We have noted how women working in the crab houses are further 'hidden' from view by virtue of the fact that access to them must be negotiated through owners and managers. And, we have begun to examine how meaning is ascribed to the work process by the women who pick meat out of crab shells and the owners and managers of the crab houses within which they work. Traditionally, for local workers, their activity was an extension of their household economy, in that crab picking was one of a number of ways by which they made a living. The introduction of Mexican workers, however, presaged a shift in how crab picking was to be understood. The subsequent deployment of the term 'labour' indicates a much more formal arrangement predicated on the attempt to cleave the exchange of labour for wages from any other social context.

In this section, this construction of working bodies is further explored via an in-depth look at how some of the women themselves ascribe meaning to their work process. In particular, attention is drawn to the meanings invested in the hands, the voice and the soul of working bodies. It is through the signification of these fragments that connections, and disconnections, are enabled with other people, as well as a form of hybridisation. The short, curved knife used to pick meat, and the crab itself, are part and parcel of the activity, and as such are invested with meaning. This understanding of the body at work in crab picking serves as a foil against the more recent and certainly more public view proffered by the crab house owners and managers, wherein labourers produce a commodity for the national market.

Crab picking as work

When asked to tell you about their work, crab pickers look to their **hands** and begin to demonstrate how to pick meat out of a cooked crab. First, the legs are snapped off. Then, the claws are positioned on the table, with the fixed part of the pincher facing up. A knife is inserted gently into the pincher just past the point where it connects to the main part of the claw. The pincher is then pulled down and out, bringing with it the claw meat, which should come out in a chunk. The other legs are then snapped in half at the midpoint of their largest segments and squeezed so that their crabmeat can be extruded. Next, the crab is tuned on its back to expose the apron, located at the base of the shell. A knife is inserted under the apron so that it can be flipped out. Both thumbs are then inserted into this space so that the two shells can be pulled apart. The knife is used once again to scrape out the guts and gills (or 'devil's fingers') that cover the backfin segments. Each shell is then cut in half to reveal two other spaces. The backfin chamber is full of the prized jumbo lump meat, which can be pulled out. The forward chamber has several thin walls of shell, and so the knife must be wielded delicately in order to extract as much 'clean' meat as possible. Usually, this series of manoeuvres will take under a minute. As they talk through the process, crab pickers more often than not go on to tell you how many crabs they can pick in an hour and in a day.

Clearly, crab pickers have invested their own hands with positive connotations of skill, dexterity and precision and are proud of the skill they have developed. But we can gain an added appreciation of the significance afforded this part of their body when we consider how it is prioritised over and above other parts. For several women well past retirement age, for example, crab picking was something they did not for the money but for the enjoyment of it. One of the group insisted on coming in to work every day despite the fact she could not walk and had trouble standing. Another came to work with a broken rib. As other parts of their bodies began to show signs of age and give way, their manual skill became valued all the more, indicating that they were still valuable as workers. 'Jim Paul needs me to work', they declare, even though Jim Paul has switched to Mexican labour some time ago.

Part and parcel of the job of crab picking is the wielding of the knife through and inside the hard shell of the crab. As such, the job is a hybrid one, in that a particular kind of short, curved knife must be deployed and the crab must be dismantled and dismembered just so in order that the job be quickly yet carefully accomplished. Arguably, the knife is more than an extension of the fingers in that even its basic technological character renders the job as a 'skill' as opposed to mere manual labour. The crab, meanwhile, presents both obstacle and opportunity for the worker's skill to be realised. The repeated emphasis on the number of crabs picked imparts a sense of the competition between worker and the pile of cooked crabs stacked in front of them, as well as an appreciation of the money earned from producing so many pounds of crabmeat. A picker considers her work to be good if she can produce between 40 and 50 pounds (18–23 kilograms) of meat a day. Indeed, the framing of this contest is in similar vein to the positive connotations linked with crabbing, in that much is made of the physical and mental toughness required for such a feat: as one woman emphatically declares, 'Men just can't do this kind of work'. Such an attitude not only goes against the grain of popular presentations as to what is considered heroic – catching crabs as opposed to processing them – it also challenges conceptions one might have held on first entering the crab houses that the women working there feel they have been wedged into less worthy jobs.

This latter point can be extended to a consideration of the range of other jobs women recount having engaged in, each of which requires manual dexterity and endurance. Most have been involved in other seafood processing activities, as well as a variety of agricultural jobs from an early age. While much reference is made to the fact that 'there was nothing else to do', this kind of work is considered essential to the provision and maintenance of families and, further, the development of a distinct regional character. While the women note that there are many more opportunities today for their daughters, and themselves, they also bemoan the gradual erosion of a distinct 'down east' way of life. Often, their account of working in the crab houses and the surrounding fields takes on a nostalgic tinge, as they recall that 'we had nothing, but we were happy'. In comparing these accounts with the popular presentations of people and place noted above, what stands out is the centrality afforded families as opposed to the region's economy, as well as a refusal to associate the region's significance with the development of an industry.

The **voice** is also a very significant part of the work process for local women. Talk can always be heard from the crab picking tables, with an occasional snatch of hymn singing. The daily chat that goes back and forth across the table is very much a bonding process between the workers, who often make reference to the fact that their cohorts on either side are also their close friends. It also incorporates, however, the uniformly white crab house owners and managers whenever they are present on the work floor. Moreover, all are referred to by their first names, present or not, and this informality, together with the fact that topics invariably concern local events and people, imparts a sense of shared purpose to the crab house.

Some of the workers are kin to the owners, and so this level of familiarity is unsurprising. Most are not, however, and yet one often hears that this is a 'family' business and that ties of loyalty underwrite their relationship with owners and management. These expressions can even cut across race, with some black women (though certainly not all) expressing a personal tie to owners. Arguably, it is the 'head of family' attitude articulated by the owners through their everyday conversation that is effectively inducing this response. As noted above, for local women crab picking is associated with household chores, and so their talk together while at work is likened to 'a quilting party' or 'a get together'. Within this framing, the owner takes on the role of head of the household, and it is this persona that is manifest in many crab owners when they talk to, and about, their local workers.

This conversational effluvance contrasts sharply with the silence of Mexican women in the workplace. Rarely is a word exchanged between them, while communication with managers and owners is usually undertaken through an interpreter. The content of this is labour-related, such as the expressed need to replace work items, or the requirement that an extra hour of work is needed on the next day. Even when a bilingual manager is hired, the rationale given for this is that any problems with the new labour force can be resolved more quickly. This juxtaposed presence and absence of voice informs us just a little further as to how women view their place within the crab house. Local women project a sense of belonging in the workplace via their conversational ease, while Mexican women are focused on the exchange of labour for wages and, hence, on the physical dismemberment of crabs. It is this mostly non-verbalised relation with owners and managers that is given priority over and against their reluctance to leave their own family in Sinaloa, as well as a feeling of distance from local women and the community more generally.

It is in selective, non-work spaces, such as the trailer, that talk erupts from these women. It is here that the women talk about sending money home so that parents can be fed and children can go to university, or arrange what should be on the shopping list for Saturday. When they do go shopping it is in groups to superstores located miles away, rather than local grocery stores. Most Mexican women will avoid stopping and talking with each other on the street, as there has been a history of local residents calling the police, sure that immoral activities are underway (Dickens and Stein 1994). When they do socialise, most go to Hispanic clubs, of which there are several in the region, and meet up with other friends and family working in Eastern Carolina.

Another interesting contrast emerges through a consideration of the **soul** as part of the working body. The spiritual dimension within which many people construct their identity can be of immense significance in how they then view their work. Often you can hear women singing hymns while working, or quoting from the Bible, and appreciate the sense of belonging to a broader, spiritual community that is projected. The particular religion within which they live, however, also shapes their attitudes concerning the propriety and value of work. Most local workers are Southern Baptist. While in some areas this denomination is viewed as progressive, in Eastern Carolina many church leaders are Moral Majority, and emphasise the rightful position of the man as head of household and the woman as helpmate. This explicitly binary view of what is appropriate to men and women not only facilitates a 'natural' association of women with food processing activities, it also designates their work as secondary to that of the main providers.

Within the workplace, this aural and visual display of belonging in a high spiritual realm stands in contrast with the less visible and certainly less vocal caretaking of the soul by the Mexican women, most, if not all of whom, are Catholic. While in the crab house one might spot a gold or silver cross hanging at the neck, most religious expressions take place inside the trailer, which houses diverse ornaments and pictures, or one of the few Catholic churches in the region. What this presencing of religion in the workplace signifies, then, is the notion that crab picking is more than just a job, it is a means by which women can express their belonging within a community that is underwritten by religious principles. Meanwhile, the relatively covert manner in which Mexican women undertake their faith reinforces their sense of being outside of this community: their religious as well as their social networks are stretched out over space and are explicitly manifest only in those places where other Catholics will be present.

Crab picking as labour

Owners and managers have articulated a shared sense of purpose with their local workers, referring to their business as a 'family' one and engaging in everyday conversation that reinforces a patriarchal rendering of life in the crab house. There is a shared emphasis on hands and souls as part of the work process. And yet, we can also trace the emergence of particular, alternate framings of these bodily fragments that stand at odds with their workers' conceptions, and, further, are partially realised in the bodies of their new cohort of labourers.

Many owners do still talk about their 'family' business when noting the various problems facing its continued survival. However, whereas traditionally this familial association encompassed local workers, the ready replacement of these women with Mexican women indicates that the designation of family is very much centred on bloodline and marriage. The status afforded this new labour group can be gauged from the limited character and scope of their communications with management and owners, as conversations are limited to working arrangements and grievances, rather than general chit chat. The emergent emphasis on family as direct kin can be observed even more clearly in response to closure, as capital is moved out of the crab processing industry and into the hands of sons and nephews who plan to open up more profitable concerns, such as leisure centres and restaurants.

Owners and managers also prioritise the hands of their pickers and the tools they wield. The significance of these bodily parts lies not in the development of individual skill, however, but in the efficient, concerted activity of a labour force. Women are compared and contrasted according to how much quality crabmeat – that is, without shell fragments embedded in it – can be produced in an hour. The goal is to get as much crab meat as possible that looks whiter than snow and feels finer than silk. Those workers who have the best technique with a knife will be hired in the next year. Hence, the competitive aspect of the job no longer pits worker against crab, but labourer against labourer.

Owners and managers are also members of their local religious community, and some take a leading role. A shared embeddedness within a particularly defined spiritual realm connects them to local workers, and simultaneously distances them from their Mexican hires. This distancing, however, seems to go beyond mere religious difference. The key link between crab owners in Eastern Carolina and those in Sinaloa, for example, which initiated the seasonal movement of Mexican women, ensued from a missionary project some of the Americans were participating in during the early 1980s. While this bespeaks a particular attitude towards Catholicism, an interesting question arises as to why no such proselytising takes place in the Eastern Carolina workplace? One can speculate that the Mexican women are viewed as largely out of place, in that while their labour allows crab plants to remain profitable, their social presence is barely acknowledged. Indeed, one can observe and listen to signs of relief in owners and managers whose plants have closed, in that they do not have to worry about what the neighbours think of their hiring Mexican women. Tending to the souls of these women, then, is appropriate only when they are in their place, hundreds of miles away in Sinaloa.

As with the local workers, owners and managers reiterate a close relationship with the crab. Whereas for the pickers the crab is the instrument through which their value as workers is expressed, as well as a defining presence in their evocation of a distinct 'down east' character, the crab is invested with a series of other meanings for those concerned with the continuing profitability of their business. First, the crab is construed as a problem, in that it is subject to the harsh vicissitudes of the weather, particularly hurricanes, and environmental pollution. Just getting a hold of crabs is a constant worry, and owners will send refrigerated trucks miles down coast in the hope of buying a sufficient amount. Many owners, however, will not buy in crabs from outside the United States, and this decision points to a second meaning invested in this crustacean, namely its geopolitical character. These owners will only purchase crabs landed off the east coast because, they say, this is an American industry. This signification has become quite visible in the last two years, as Eastern Carolina crabmeat has been repackaged in red, white and blue and explicitly labelled 'American'. The branding of crabmeat serves more than a patriotic fervour: crab house owners are designated as the caretakers of a domestic industry, and this role has been used in the recent well-publicised (and unsuccessful) appeal to government that crab processing should be afforded protection from cheaper foreign imports.

Arguably, the investment of this kind of meaning in the body of the crab points to a quite contradictory understanding of the 'economy'. On the one hand, crab house owners and managers are focused on acquiring skilled labour in an exchange for wages, a relationship that cleaves the activity of crab picking from any other social context. On the other hand, the crab meat produced is understood to be a vital source of income to the local economy. Within this framing of the situation, the fate of Eastern Carolina is inextricably linked to the fate of its crab houses. At some key point the 'economy' does touch down into the social realm: the point in question, however, is not the actual work of crab picking, but the act of ownership and management. In short, crab house owners and managers consider their own work to be key to the continued well-being of Eastern Carolina. And it is this articulation of the 'place' of the crab industry that has drawn the most scorn. Just as the crab house owners and managers have effected a divorce between 'work' and 'labour', so the advocates of free trade have sought to distance crab meat as a commodity from the social context within which it is produced. According to Rushford (2000), for example, the industry is no more 'American' than any other business: rather, there is simply the continuous production, distribution and consumption of commodities.

Conclusion

While an appreciation of the ways in which working women invest meaning in their bodies strikes a chord with feminist concerns for academia to take note of lived experiences (Massey 1996: 109), or, as Jones *et al.* phrase it, 'bodily experiences spatially lived' (1997: 399), I want to draw a more specific point from this mode of analysis. The emergent discourse of 'labour' articulated by crab house owners and managers actually sits quite comfortably with a particular strain of thought within social theory based on a Marxist reading of the body. As noted earlier in the chapter, within this particular, relational understanding of the construct emphasis is placed on the contradictory role of the working body within the capitalist economy: the body is required for the provision of labour and the generation of value, but is also an obstacle to the full realisation of profits in the sense that it must be fed, sheltered and so on (Henderson 1999; Mitchell 2001). Furthermore, under capitalism the body is rendered as an assemblage of various parts, mental and physical, which are equivalent within the frame of exchange (Callard 1998; Harvey 1998; Krozova 1976; Lefebvre 1991). That is, these parts are rendered distinct, and their material or representational form can be bought and sold within the marketplace. While cultural norms concerning identity forms – such as the categorisation of people according to notions of gender, race and sexuality – also frame how particular bodies, and parts of bodies, are evaluated and shaped (Mitchell 2000: 217–18), this process is inextricably entwined with the economic structure that is capitalism. As capitalism continues to develop and transform, so these forms of identity are renegotiated (Mitchell 2000: 220–21).

Following the feminist argument of Gibson-Graham (1996), I would suggest that such a reading further embeds working women within a discourse that privileges the economy as the key arena within which, and from which, identities are constructed and bodies are shaped. Of course, whether or not this centring of the economy within an explanatory framework is considered productive depends on the perceived need to raise the working class consciousness of these women (in the vein of Harvey 1993) and apprise them of their place as 'labour' in a capitalist economy. I take my own cue from Hacking (1999) on this point, and suggest that a productive goal of analysis is to uncover the social construction of readily proffered norms and assumptions, and in so doing draw attention to the inequalities maintained through this process. In the case of the Eastern Carolina crab houses, this means highlighting how some activities have been, and still are, both gendered and racialised, to the detriment of particular individuals. It further requires, however, that 'labour' as an identity form is understood to be a key construct within the crab processing industry. If this construction is rendered as given or irrelevant, then particular aspects of the working lives of these women will remain hidden within academia, as well as other venues that claim to present people and place.

Acknowledgement

This research was funded in part by a University of Wales – Aberystwyth Research Grant and an HSBC Holdings Small Research Grant (RGS with the IBG).

Notes

1. Although the year-round population barely tops 46,000 people, the area draws nearly 250,000 people each week during the height of the summer season.

2. In utilising such an entry point some issues are foregrounded, while others remain in the background. Questions about sexuality, for example, are not deemed suitable within this setting, while an emphasis on family is unquestioned.

3. Some facts and statistics require even more effort. There has been a recent interest, for example, in making visible the presence of black crabbers (though as yet this has taken the form of school projects such as *Chesapeake Through Ebony Eyes*, accessible at http://www.dnr.state.md.us/irc/boc.html). Griffith (1999, pers. comm.) has also noted the presence of Hispanic crabbers off the east coast, and the anxious response to this from local crabbers.

4. Previously hidden practices – such as illegal wage deductions, unpaid overtime and failure to keep wage records – can also come to light through court cases brought under the Fair Labor Standards Act.

5. The H2 program refers to that part of US immigration law that allows employers to import temporary workers for a short period of time when there is a shortage of local labour. The migrants must work only for the employer who obtains the visa for them, known as their 'sponsor,' while their employer is obligated to have made reasonable efforts to find local American workers, and to provide wages and working conditions for their H2 workers that are at least as good as those offered to similarly employed US workers. The letter after the H2 designation denotes the type of work allowed, as H2-A workers are employed in agriculture, and H2-B workers are non-agricultural.

6. Fieldwork carried out by Emily Selby and myself in the crab houses of Eastern Carolina, 1996–2001 is used as the basis for this section. Those assertions and conclusions drawn from other sources are noted separately in the text.

References

Bataille, G. 1962 *Death and Sensuality: A Study of Eroticism and the Taboo*, Walker and Company, New York.

Callard, F. 1998 'The body in theory', *Environment and Planning D: Society and Space*, 16, 387–400.

Cresswell, T. 1999 'Embodiment, power and the politics of mobility: the case of female tramps and hobos', *Transactions of the Institute of British Geographers*, 24, 175–92.

Dickens, R. and Stein, D. 1994 'The impact of migrant labor on the town of Oriental, North Carolina', unpublished paper, Department of Geography, East Carolina University, Greenville, NC.

Doel, M. 1997 'Bodies without organs: schizoanalysis and deconstruction', pp. 226–40 in S. Pile and N. Thrift (eds), *Mapping the Subject: Geographies of Cultural Transformation*, Routledge: London and New York.

Domosh, M. 1997 'With "Stout Boots and Stout Heart": historical methodology and feminist geography', pp. 225–41 in J.P. Jones III *et al.* (eds), *Thresholds in Feminist Geography: Difference, Methodology, Representation*, Rowman and Littlefield, Maryland.

Drudi, D. 1998 'Fishing for a living is dangerous work', *Compensation and Working Conditions*, **Summer**, 1–5.

Falk, P. 1994 *The Consuming Body*, Sage, London.

Gibson-Graham, J.K. 1996 *The End of Capitalism As We Knew It: A Feminist Critique of Political Economy*, Blackwell, Oxford.

Griffith, D. 1997 'New immigrants in an old industry: Mexican H2-B workers in the mid-Atlantic blue crab processing industry', paper presented at the Immigration and the Changing Face of Rural America Conference, University of Delaware, Newark, DE, 11–13 September.

Hacking, I. 1999 *The Social Construction of What*, Harvard University Press, Cambridge, MA.

Harvey, D. 1993 'Class relations, social justice and the politics of difference', pp. 85–120 in J. Squires (ed.) *Principled Positions: Postmodernism and the Rediscovery of Value*, Lawrence and Wishart, London.

Harvey, D. 1998 'The body as accumulation strategy', *Environment and Planning D: Society and Space*, **16**, 401–21.

Henderson, G. 1999 *California and the Fictions of Capital*, Oxford University Press, New York.

hooks, b. 1992 *Black Looks: Race and Representation*, South End Press, Boston.

Jones III, J.P., Nast, H. and Roberts, S. 1997 'Crossing thresholds', pp. 393–406 in J.P. Jones III *et al.* (eds), *Thresholds in Feminist Geography: Difference, Methodology, Representation*, Rowman and Littlefield, Maryland.

Kay, J. 1997 'Sweet surrender, but what's the gender? Nature and the body in the writings of nineteenth-century Mormon women', pp. 361–82 in J.P. Jones III *et al.* (eds), *Thresholds in Feminist Geography: Difference, Methodology, Representation*, Rowman and Littlefield, Maryland.

Krozova, A. 1976 *Production and Socialization*, EVA, Frankfurt.

Lawson, G. 1988 *The Last Waterman*, Crisfield Publishing Company, Crisfield, MD.

Lefebvre, H. 1991 *The Production of Space*, Blackwell, Oxford.

Longhurst, R. 1997 '(Dis)embodies geographies', *Progress in Human Geography*, **21**, 486–501.

Longhurst, R. 2000 *Bodies: Exploring Fluid Boundaries*, Routledge, London.

Massey, D. 1993 'Power-geometry and a progressive sense of place', pp. 59–69 in J. Bird *et al.* (eds), *Mapping the Futures: Local Cultures/Global Changes*, Routledge, London.

Massey, D. 1996 'Masculinity, dualisms and high technology', pp. 109–26 in N. Ducan (ed.), *BodySpace: Destabilizing Geographies of Gender and Sexuality*, Routledge, New York.

McDowell, L. 1995 'Body work: heterosexual gender performances in City workplaces', pp. 75–95 in D. Bell and G. Valentine (eds), *Mapping Desire: Geographies of sexualities*, Routledge, London.

Mitchell, D. 2000 *Cultural Geography: A Critical Introduction*, Blackwell, Oxford.

Mitchell, D. 2001 'The devil's arm: points of passage, networks of violence and the California agricultural landscape', *New Formations*, **43**, 44–60.

Mosher, A. 1993 'Delicate art, low pay: the legacy of crab pickers in North Carolina', Masters, final project submitted for Masters of Liberal Arts, North Carolina State University, Raleigh, NC.

Nast, H. and Pile, S. 1998 *Places Through the Body*, Routledge, London.

Peffer, R. 1985 *Watermen*, Johns Hopkins University Press, Baltimore, MD.

Philo, C. 1989 'Enough to drive one mad: the organization of space in nineteenth-century lunatic asylums', pp. 258–90 in J. Woloch and M. Dear (eds), *The Power of Geography*, Unwin Hyman, New York.

Pile, S. and Thrift, N. 1995 'Introduction', pp. 1–12 in S. Pile and N. Thrift (eds), *Mapping the Subject: Geographies of Cultural Transformation*, Routledge, London and New York.

Rodaway, P. 1994 *Sensuous Geographies: Body, Sense and Place*, London, Routledge.

Ruley, M. 1994 'On blackwater', *The Independent Weekly*, **29 June–5 July**, 9–13.

Rushford, G. 2000 'Of crabs and motorcycles and the benefits of free trade', *The Milken Institute Review*, **Third Quarter**, 51–6.

Seamon, D. 1979 *A Geography of the Lifeworld: Movement, Rest and Encounter*, Croom Helm, London.

Selby, E. 1998 'Paradise is relative: implications of labor transition in the crab processing industry of Eastern North Carolina', Masters Thesis, Department of Geography, East Carolina University, Greenville, NC.

Selby, E., Dixon, D.P. and Hapke, H. 2001 'A woman's place in the crab processing industry of East Carolina', *Gender, Place and Culture*, 8, 229–53.

Stick, D. 1958 *The Outer Banks of North Carolina, 1584–1958*, University of North Carolina Press, Chapel Hill.

Teather, E.K. 1999 *Embodied Geographies: Spaces, Bodies and Rites of Passage*, Routledge, London.

Valentine, G. 1999 'A corporeal geography of consumption', *Environment and Planning D: Society and Space*, **17**, 329–51.

Valentine, G. 2001 *Social Geographies: Space and Society*, Prentice Hall, Harlow.

Warner, W.W. 1976 *Beautiful Swimmers*, Viking Penguin, New York.

Williamson, J.W. 1995 *Hillbillyland*, University of North Carolina Press, Chapel Hill.

Landscape, performance and dwelling: a Glastonbury case study

CHAPTER 8

John Wylie

In the northern part of Somerset there is a triangular plain, bounded upon two of its sides by the Mendips and the Poldens, and upon the third by the sea. In the centre of this plain rises a strange pyramidal hill crowned with a tower . . .
(Dion Fortune 2000, *Glastonbury: Avalon of the Heart*)

Introduction

When I first sat down to think about the content and argument of this chapter, I struggled. Glastonbury, a small (but famous) town in rural Somerset, in south-west England, with its esoteric bookshops and vegetarian cafes, with its spiritual, mystical tales of King Arthur and the Holy Grail, and its peculiar and affecting landscape dominated by the 'strange pyramidal hill' called the Tor, was a place I had not visited for nearly a year. In the meantime, the thesis of which my research into Glastonbury Tor was part had been completed, and I had moved to a different area of the country. I felt I had lost a sense of how things – beliefs, practices, landmarks – configured together.

So I went back. I drove south to Somerset with mixed feelings: nostalgia, mostly, but also a sense of determination, of being a man on a mission. As always, the task was straightforward: to climb the Tor and spend as much time as I felt necessary on the hilltop, gazing out over the rural landscape. I parked, again, in a country lane not far from the base of the Tor. The bright morning had emulsified into a swelteringly hot and hazy afternoon. Along paths thick with the sticky organic greens of midsummer I walked to the Tor. From the base, its bulk shimmered in the dazed and milky air, softening its strangely regular gradient, and the brief but steep ascent to the top looked for once a little challenging. In the past I'd often lingered in the meadows below before climbing to the top, sometimes I'd circumnavigate the Tor in a slowly rising spiral which would catch the official route about halfway up; but this time I walked straight up without pausing, hunched with my hands clutching the straps of my bag.

By the time the spiralling upward path reached the baking lawn of the summit I was sweating profusely. Across the yellowing acre of grass little knots of people, in twos and threes, lay as if stunned. A few had sought refuge in the cool stone chamber of the hollow tower of St Michael which stands at the centre of the Tor summit. It was unusually quiet: few children, no one singing. Just the restful, tidal swoosh of cars passing along the road far below. In this hush, someone was talking a little too loudly about the Holy Grail. I sat down in an angle of the hilltop and composed myself, gazing out over the circle of countryside which spread out far below. As ever, the view was surprising in its breadth and sweep, but the air, for once, was liquid still.

After an hour or so I could feel myself beginning to be burnt. And I felt sure that coming back had been worthwhile; it was enough at least to get me started. Quickly, soon sweating again, I loped down the sides of the Tor, and back down the livid green lanes to the car. Inside it was unbearable, the steering-wheel almost scalded my palms. After opening all the doors and windows I stood for a few minutes beside the car, looking back at the Tor, which was only a few hundred yards away but already spectral in the haze; then I drove away.

In this chapter, within the context of a discussion of concepts of landscape and dwelling within cultural geography, I want to recount another fleeting visit to Glastonbury Tor. The aim of the narration I wish to present is twofold. Firstly it seeks to explore and illustrate the possibilities of writing performatively about landscape experiences. Secondly, it may be read as a commentary upon recent theorisations of landscape in terms of dwelling and temporality (e.g. Cloke and Jones 2001; Ingold 2001).

The structure of the chapter is as follows. To begin with, I want to discuss a process of 'dematerialisation' of landscape, via a brief discussion of the conceptualisation of landscape within what was once called 'new' cultural geography. The chapter then turns to consider Ingold's (2001) advocacy of a 'dwelling perspective' as an alternative, post-constructionist approach to the study of landscape in particular, and culture–nature relations more widely. While such a perspective opens up distinctive research agendas as regards studies of landscape, nature and rurality (cf. Cloke and Jones 2001; Macnaghten and Urry 1998), I want to suggest that it may be criticised and, hopefully, strengthened, by a discussion of its positioning of dwelling in relation to certain forms of temporality and certain understandings of vision. Following this critique, the chapter offers its rendition of the experience of travelling to the summit of Glastonbury Tor, as an illustration of how landscape, even if conceived of through notions of dwelling and embodied experience, may still be configured in terms of the transient and the visual.

Landscape and representation: metaphor and materiality

In retrospect, the conceptualisation of landscape within cultural geography throughout the 1980s and 1990s becomes at least partly legible as a series of metaphors that express distinctive senses of what landscape is: veil, text, gaze. Considered as 'veil', landscape is understood to function as an aesthetic mask or veneer, occluding and mystifying the reality of underlying social and economic relations (Cosgrove 1985; Cosgrove and Daniels 1988; Daniels 1989), reflecting the longstanding concerns of a British 'cultural Marxist' tradition (Berger 1972; Williams 1973). Considered as 'text' however, the function of landscape is not so much to hide as to construct and express particular sets of cultural meanings (Barnes and Duncan 1992; Duncan and Duncan 1988), even if, following the procedures of structuralist semiotics, the critical reader remains focused upon the task of demystifying discourses of landscape. Considered as 'gaze' (Rose 1993), the point of view shifts somewhat from landscape to the subject who sees/constructs it, a commonly white, usually male and sometimes scientific and imperialist subject, whose gaze expresses binary, hierarchical distinctions between self and other, male and female, culture and nature.

In other words, there are important differences between these metaphors; they spring from different theoretical legacies, they emphasise different ways in which landscape is embedded within western discursive and ideological formations. But I want to argue that they share several common themes and purposes, and that in consequence it is possible to identify a relatively settled understanding of the concept of landscape subsisting within the 'new' cultural geography of the 1980s and 1990s.

A first common thematic here was a definition of landscape as quintessentially *visual*. This is in some ways unremarkable, self-evident even, given that within human geography landscape has commonly been associated with a particular 'area of space' as seen, whether by the eyes of the fieldworker or by the mind's eyes of the regional synthesist. The art-historical bent of many cultural geographies of landscape, moreover, strongly abetted a scopic emphasis though eliding the 'geographical' concept of landscape with the products of landscape art. In fact, within the literatures under consideration, there is a definite sense that landscape art, constructed via perspectival techniques of representation, *is* landscape.

This visual watermark is variously reinscribed within the metaphorical understandings indexed above: landscape as a painterly patina, as a text to be read, as a form of visual desire. The crucial distinction which all share, however, is best described as a focus not upon the 'seen', but upon 'ways of seeing'. Landscape within new cultural geography came to refer above all to the outcome of particular visual processes of description and symbolisation. As an 'outcome' (a painting, a garden, a poem), landscape perhaps retained a certain 'solidity' – it may still be a physical object or environment – but this was a point that could be quickly passed over, for what was crucial were the specificities of the 'ways of seeing' which constitute any landscape's 'meaning'. Within these geographies, landscape was the visual image of cultural meaning; it was therefore both the product and the token of particular cultures, particular knowledges and subjectivities. Cosgrove and Daniels (1988) emphasised that landscape is a 'way of seeing' cognate with the visual gaze of European socio-economic elites. Cosgrove (1985) and Rose (1993) highlighted visual landscape's association with the detached gaze of both empirical and rational science. Rose demonstrated that, as an object of inquiry, landscape is constructed by a masculine, voyeuristic, and narcissistic gaze. Duncan (1993: 140) identified landscape as an 'imperial' gaze, as the visual *modus operandi* of European explorers, artists and cartographers, 'this haughty gaze that has surveyed and appropriated the world'. In these geographies, landscape became the visual medium through which 'critical interpretations' of social and cultural formations could be provided.

This shift from 'seen' to 'seeing' also serves to index a second key alignment between the three metaphorical understandings of landscape which have been outlined: they all saw landscape as being always already a *representation*. Again this is perhaps unremarkable; both geographers and art historians have always sought to describe what a given landscape stands for, in other words what cultures and histories it expresses or symbolises. The distinctive gradient of these cultural geographies, however, lay in the ascending status they accorded to representation and 'representational practices'. On a substantive level, 'landscape' in cultural geography referred no longer to a 'physical environment', but rather to images, paintings, idioms of description in travel accounts. This shift had a methodological correlate, in that the concern of cultural geographers was no longer description, but rather interpretation. Instead of producing 'representations of landscape', cultural geographies of landscape took these as their primary object of concern. And finally, this interpretative turn in terms of method, both heralded and reflected a dominant theoretical stance within cultural geographies, a stance perhaps best described as 'critical constructivism'. This stance held that meaning and knowledge – the discursive essences of the socio-cultural systems which the critic interprets – belong to, and emanate from, the symbolic domain of images, signs, texts, representations. All meaning, therefore, is always already representational. 'All geographies are imaginative geographies', the introduction to an anthology devoted to discourses of travel argued, 'and our access to the world is always made through particular technologies of representation' (Gregory and Duncan 1999: 5).

As Strohmayer (1998: 105–6) commented, 'the constructedness of representations could well be the bond unifying most of the work currently undertaken within geography . . . constructedness thus forms a kind of "pragmatic" response to the "crisis of representation"'. In a slightly paradoxical sense, therefore, the broad critique of mimesis across the social sciences (Clifford and Marcus 1986) resulted in representations and the processes of construction which they reflected and sustained becoming the primary object of inquiry; with representation being positioned as an ontological process human cultures are forever engaged in and produced through.

Landscape was therefore defined as the visual representation of certain subject positions, and as the symbolic expression of relations between subject and object, seer and seen, culture and nature. Yet at the same time, a third unifying characteristic of cultural geographies of landscape throughout the 1990s involved a certain current of unease, an unease produced by a feeling that an exclusive focus upon representation was ephemeral and insubstantial, in that it elided the *materialities* of landscape. This unease surfaces, for example, in Duncan's (1990: 15) 'impatience with groundless idealism. Ideas take place on earth'. It also implicitly informs a review of the literature (Duncan 1995) that contrasts 'painterly' and 'material' approaches to landscape. On the broader plain of landscape conceived as a mesh of 'culture' and 'nature', this material anxiety was been cogently voiced by Demeritt (1994: 172). Drawing a contrast between cultural geography and environmental history, he argued that the metaphorical landscapes of the former have the effect of silencing the 'natural':

> Landscape metaphors of cultural production have, both in theory and practice, served to make nature ephemeral and epiphenomenal. These metaphors treat nature as a blank page or an empty stage on which the drama of culture is written and acted out . . . In moments of metaphorical extravagance the material 'reality' of landscape disappears altogether.

Demeritt's statement may be related to a widespread perceived need for cultural geographers to remain close to the 'ground'. In fact, as Matless (1995: 396), remarked, it was most often voices opposed to the 'cultural turn' that sought to portray culture as 'a realm of representation into which the material world is to be converted and dematerialised'. One year on, however, Matless (1996: 383, emphasis in original), spoke of a desire for 'melded materiality and semiosis', for cultural geographies 'operating less through images *of* landscape, than the tracing of objects and practices (which may include paintings, writings, etc.) *producing* landscapes'.

Though Matless's remarks stressed the possibility of bearing witness to the mutual constitution of meaningful discourse and material practice (a constitution he went on to richly explore in his study of landscape and Englishness; Matless 1998), a perhaps more common response to 'material anxiety' was to position materiality as a 'local' context wherein 'global' discourses are mediated and disturbed. The materiality, the spatio-temporal specificity of landscape thus came to serve not only as a physical anchor of discourse, but also as a site of resistance (e.g. see Dodds 1996; Ryan 1994).

Within such accounts there is a double, dualistic articulation of landscape that remains immanent. On the one hand landscape is a mobile cultural discourse, a way of seeing that seeks to cast its shroud over whatever material local circumstances it happens upon. On the other, landscape is itself these material local circumstances, be they physical, environmental or socio-economic. Given cultural geography's image of itself as a 'critical social science' it might be thought that the materiality of landscape, understood as a 'local' complex of contextual processes and circumstances, would become its definitive hallmark, precisely because material context was, within many cultural geographies of landscape, the very stuff of interpretative purchase, enabling detailed contextual critiques of wider discursive projects. Yet despite this, the sense that emerges from this literature is one in which materiality is positioned as a decidedly secondary characteristic. What is primary, what is held to possess true epistemological significance, is the discursive realm, wherein meaning *first* takes shape, in the process of cultural construction which produces forms such as the 'landscape gaze'. Such forms are, then, the actual objects of critique. By contrast, the material landscape, most commonly reinscribed as 'context', is purely reactive, and possesses only the inertia of substance, as a rock upon which waves of discursive meaning break.

One example particularly helps to clarify the hierarchical duality between meaning/materiality that shaped 'new' cultural geography's understanding of landscape, and cemented its definition of landscape as a discursively constructed visual representation. Duncan and Duncan (1988) use the beliefs of Australian Aborigines to illustrate the interpretative power of their chosen textual metaphor. They argue that 'aboriginal peoples have a set of oral religious texts which are transformed into the landscape' (1988: 122). Thus, for the Aborigines, 'a rock is a rock but also a mythic being' (*ibid.*). Yet this statement perhaps reveals more about the authors' beliefs than the Aborigine's. For it performs, and presupposes, a distinction between, on the one hand the rock's 'rockiness', and on the other its 'meaningful cultural significance'. In the textual approach all 'material objects' must have a '*but also*,' a discursive significance that is anterior to, and constitutive of, their meaning as it occurs through encounter and use. For in itself the rock is regarded as an epistemological nothing which requires the supplement of 'culture' to achieve phenomenal fullness. Meaning, in other words, must infuse the rock from the outside. Meaning must be firstly imagined, before material action is performed.

Landscape from image to dwelling

The above review was deliberately written in the past tense, even though many of the works cited were published only during the last decade. This tense choice emerged primarily from a feeling that cultural geographies of landscape, in many ways central to the 'cultural turn' across human geography, are, almost without comment, slipping out of sight, at least from the vantage point of a still-nascent, further 'turn', away from critiques of representation and towards theorisations of praxis and performance (Nash 2001; Rose 1999; Thrift 1996).

As is maybe often the case, such a shift has a rhetorical component, and it seems to me that 'landscape' is a term which, somehow, has begun to appear inimical, inappropriate, to a focus upon issues of practice, corporeality and performance. However, in their elaboration of the concept of *dwelling*, the writings of cultural anthropologist Tim Ingold appear at the present time to provide one clear passageway between these two idioms.

Ingold's work (1993, 1995, 2001), presents both a critique of the epistemological suppositions of cultural geographies of landscape, and the embryo, at least, of an alternative programme. Citing Cosgrove and Daniels' (1988: 1) definition of landscape as 'a cultural image, a pictorial way of representing or symbolising surroundings', Ingold (2001: 191) states that his aim is to:

> 'Reject the division between inner and outer words – respectively of mind and matter, meaning and substance – upon which such distinction rests. The landscape, I hold, is not a picture in the imagination, surveyed by the mind's eye, nor however is it an alien and formless substrate awaiting the imposition of human order'.

Ingold's citation here locates such geographies with a wider interdisciplinary context embracing archaeology, 'physical' and cultural anthropology and (eventually) philosophy. This, he argues, is a context whose conceptualisation of landscape is bedevilled by a 'sterile opposition between the naturalistic view of the landscape as a neutral, external backdrop to human activities, and the culturalistic view that every landscape is a particular cognitive or symbolic ordering of space' (Ingold 2001: 189). A nature/culture dualism, in other words, continues to shape the meaning of landscape. And one particular consequence of such a culturalist, 'cognitive' (or, more strictly, 'constructivist') approach is the installation of a strict epistemological hierarchy which reductively positions the material aspect of landscape as an inert physicality, a content bereft of form. Thus the irony is that cultural geographies are guilty of the same offence that they tend to accuse landscape, as a particular historical and cultural formation, of committing. Their critique suggests that landscape, as a 'way of seeing', is cognate with a Cartesian spectatorial epistemology that severs subject from object, mind from matter, culture from nature. The problem is that once landscape is understood as being formed, firstly 'in the mind', or within 'cultural discourse', and then projected outward *onto* matter then we are once again firmly in the grip of Cartesian dualism.

Ingold's solution to this dilemma is a (re)turn, of sorts, to phenomenology. In particular he seeks at length to rearticulate the classical Heideggerian critique of traditional spectatorial theories of knowledge, with their 'conception of the human being as an unmoving point of view upon the world' (Mulhall 1996: 39). Through his complex and extensive analyses of being-in-the-world, Heidegger seeks to illustrate how such a subject–object epistemology is secondary to what may be termed 'the directly given and fundamental experience of involvement' (Dreyfus 1991: 42). Thus, in contrast to the disengaged

Cartesian subject, Heidegger presents 'human being' as a way of being which both is, and is exhibited through, ongoing practices. In the most straightforward terms, we skilfully and routinely live through the world without constant recourse to an 'objectifying' stance with respect to the manifold of things and situations we encounter, appropriate and use. The ontological aspect of human being-in-the-world consists of an ongoing absorption in the world, an absorption in which the world does not appear as an 'object' for 'consciousness'.

Following this, Ingold's argument is that rather than offering an holistic explanation of culture/nature relations, the current 'constructivist' incarnations of Cartesianism within cultural anthropology and cultural geography are simply a 'standpoint', extrapolated from an erased 'first order' – a manifold, pre-objective and taken-for-granted *milieu* of practice, in which humans are always already immersed. This 'standpoint' he terms the 'building perspective' (Ingold 2001), tersely summarised as the supposition that 'worlds are made before they are lived in' (Ingold 2001: 179). More expansively, Ingold defines this building perspective as centrally involving 'the premise that human beings inhabit discursive worlds of culturally constructed significance, laid out upon the substrate of a continuous and undifferentiated physical terrain' (2001: 172).

As an alternative to this currently common epistemology, Ingold offers what he terms, again following Heidegger, 'the dwelling perspective'. Beneath the broad umbrella of Heidegger's (1993: 350) initial, open definition of dwelling as 'the manner in which mortals are on the earth', he describes dwelling in terms of practical activity, by both humans and animals, that is rooted in an essential, ontological engagement with the material environment. 'It is through being inhabited', Ingold (2001: 173) writes, 'that the world becomes a meaningful environment'. The dwelling perspective thus focuses upon 'the agent-in-its-environment, or what phenomenology calls "being-in-the-world", as opposed to the self-contained individual confronting a world "out there"'. And in focusing upon the 'agent-in-its-environment, upon ongoing, relational contexts of involvement, the dwelling perspective seeks to deny and dispel the tenets of dualistic thought, the separation of culture from nature, the discursive from the material.

Here, what is especially pertinent as regards Ingold's work is the manner in which he closely aligns such notions of dwelling with *landscape*. Indeed, in some ways he presents the two as indissolubly intertwined, and in doing so seeks to reinforce the overcoming of duality to which the scripting of the dwelling perspective is dedicated. For Ingold (2001: 193) 'landscape is the world as it is known to those who dwell therein', however, and crucially, it may also be defined as 'the everyday project of dwelling in the world' (2001: 191). Landscape is thus presented by Ingold as a *milieu of involvement*: it is neither an environment in or upon which meaningful human practice takes place nor is it simply that practice itself – it is *both*; a material, processual and relational concatenation of forces. Here, landscape is no longer a cultural frame, a 'way of seeing', or a natural surface, an inert terrain; it is instead the ongoing practice and process of dwelling, a way of being that is anterior to such them-atisations, and, crucially, is their condition. As Ingold summarises:

> The landscape, in short, is not a totality that you or anyone else can look *at*, it is rather the world *in* which we stand in taking up a point of view on our surroundings. And it is within the context of this attentive involvement in the landscape that the human imagination gets to work in fashioning ideas about it. For the landscape, to borrow a phrase from Merleau-Ponty, is not so much the object as 'the homeland of our thoughts' (2001: 207; emphasis in original).

Such a theorisation, I would argue, offers cultural geographies of landscape a potential fruitful means of transcending what seems to me to be a conceptual and methodological impasse, one attendant upon discursive solipsism. In the most general terms, it offers the possibility of studying landscape as processual, rather than fixed, as a relation of corporeality rather than a mental construct. It reinstates landscape as a sensuous and material *milieu*. In particular, it gestures towards an understanding of landscape as practised and performed, and itself performative, as opposed to represented or scripted.

At the same time, as a means of gesturing towards how Ingold's (re)conception of landscape might develop, I want to suggest that there are three significant problems subsisting within such a confluence of landscape and dwelling. These problems may be illustrated through the context of Cloke and Jones's (2001) recent discussion of dwelling.

The first issue concerns the potentially problematic relationship between landscape, dwelling and *temporality* which is implicit in both Ingold's recent work and its Heideggerian foundations. Ingold (2001: 190) states that his consideration of landscape in tandem with temporality has the aim of 'dissolving the distinction between them'. To do so, he contrasts the 'abstract' time of chronology and history (as 'constructs' of Western thought) with 'social' time; a temporality grounded in engaged, bodily activity, in which we perceive time 'not as spectators, but as participants, in the very performance of our tasks' (2001: 196). Temporality, for Ingold, is something quintessentially performed, enacted. And so, in much the same way as an ocular, disengaged vision of landscape is replaced by the kinaesthetic involvement of dwelling, the linear, universal time of history is replaced by a temporality phenomenologically grounded in lived, corporeal experiences. The landscape, both the *milieu* and the activity of dwelling, thus becomes ontologically saturated with temporality; the two are fused and indissoluble as a phenomenological 'whole', 'the process of becoming of the world as a whole' (2001: 201).

The difficulty here concerns the precise nature of the temporality which Ingold presents as apt to dwelling. As Cloke and Jones (2001: 661) correctly note, Heidegger's conception of dwelling is at least partly rooted in a 'sinister . . . rustic romanticism'. Dwelling thus tends to be presented in terms of a fictitious, pre-industrial, rural *gemeinschaft*, leading to a view of 'authentic landscapes, or communities, as consisting of diminishing pockets of harmonious, authentic dwelling in an ever-encroaching sea of alienation' (2001: 657). In these terms, dwelling as a concept is at best hamstrung by nostalgia; at worst it installs and maintains a false boundary between the 'traditional' and the 'modern'. Without explicitly confronting this spectre, Ingold appears to side-step it via reference to a cyclical, almost seasonal temporality, one that is 'essentially rhythmic' (Ingold 2001: 196). And these ideas of rhythm and seas-onality are endorsed also by Cloke and Jones (2001: 658), in their advocacy of dwelling 'in a dynamic, time-embedded sense, rather than in comparison with any fixed time-point referencing'. Yet I would argue that a 'rhythmic' temporality may also be quite problematic when presented as an essential accompaniment to dwelling. Aside from the fact that it too beckons us towards a certain vision of 'simple rural toil', rhythm and seasonality are temporal tropes which suggest quite strongly that dwelling is indexed by *duration of inhabitation*. This is especially evident when Cloke and Jones (2001: 654; emphasis in original) speak of dwelling in terms of 'time-deepened experience . . . the experience of rootedness, the richness of things together *over time*'. Dwelling is thus not only grounded within the ambit of a phenomenological, 'social' temporality, it is dependent upon such a temporality, and is accom-plished through it. I would argue that such an understanding of dwelling, as conditional upon duration, significantly narrows the critical purchase and interpretative scope of the concept. Dwelling, as a form of phenomenological ontology, should, by contrast, be the *milieu* for material cultures and ways of being that are productive of multiple spatialities and temporalities, long-standing and momentary, rural and urban, fixed and mobile, coherent and fragmentary. In particular, it must enable the register of the transient and the fleeting as well as the enduring.

The second problem with Ingold's conception of landscape as dwelling, I would argue, is its at least partial eschewing of the *visual*. Ingold is undoubtedly correct to expand the ambit of landscape beyond its 'painterly' definition as a visual image apprehended from a fixed point of view. In a sense, his read-ing of Brueghel's *The Harvesters*, which seeks to distil from the painting the practices, rhythms and routines of an entire way of life, might be understood as a literal exemplification of this expansion. However, the sense remains that the 'dwelling perspective', and notions of embodied practice and performance more widely, in some sense involve a rejection of the visual gaze (e.g. see Coleman and Crang 2002; Macnaghten and Urry 1998). This position is cap-tured well, notably, in Cloke and Jones's (2001: 664) statement that 'dwelling cannot be happily represented or understood in terms of a fixed gaze upon a framed landscape. Rather it should suggest an embodied, practised, contextu-alised melange of experience within that landscape'. The danger here, I would argue, involves the erection of a new binarism between vision and embodi-ment, such that the bodily is defined negatively as the 'non-visual', and any dis-cussion of the visual as a corporeal faculty becomes epistemologically dubious. And again, the ambit of dwelling itself is narrowed by such an eschewing of vision. If the visual is understood as occupying a position 'outside' the landscape, then those who dwell are too easily positioned as being 'within' or 'amidst' landscape, in a sense which once more resonates with tropes of 'rootedness', and the notion that there are ways of life that are somehow 'more' about dwelling than others. I would argue, therefore, that rather than focusing upon a critique of particular cultural forms of visuality, and their association with, for example, discourses of objectivity, control and authority, the task of a dwelling perspective upon landscape should involve a reconfiguration of vision, such that, following Merleau-Ponty (1962, 1968), the activity of gazing is itself understood as a practice of dwelling.

My third and final concern as regards Ingold's understanding of landscape as dwelling is perhaps more general, and I want to raise it here as an issue which requires thought and explication beyond the purview of this chapter. In the simplest terms, how might we develop methods appropriate to a scripting and interrogation of embodied experiences of landscape? This is a question that appears to be a little surprisingly overlooked. The term 'surprising' is perhaps appropriate here, because it seems clear that to adequately conceptualise landscape in terms of dwelling requires techniques of investigation and styles of presentation distinct from the forms of critical discursive examination that are characteristic of current cultural geographies of landscape. In essence, such geographies offer an interpretative schemata, in which the focus is upon *post-hoc* thematisations generated either through interview data or critical reading (see Rose 1999), whereas examinations of what might be very loosely termed 'lived experience' would appear to be more aptly served by an ethnographic, or auto-ethnographic, descriptive approach. However, as Ingold (2001) himself notes, these are techniques already in a sense freighted with the very values and norms of distance and spectatorship which a 'dwelling perspective' attempts to overcome.

In sum, then, while Ingold's reconfiguration of landscape in terms of dwelling offers a potentially fruitful means of reconfiguring cultural geographies of landscape within the ambit of embodied practice and performance, I have argued that much care is needed with the definition of dwelling, so that it operates precisely as a ontological *milieu* of involvement, rather than as a means of delineating what forms of practice count as dwelling. Dwelling, I would suggest, should not be constrained by association with what are quite culturally specific forms of temporality, nor should it become a term constrained by a corporeal vocabulary which excludes the visual. And in a sense beneath these specific points there remains the issue of *how* landscape is to be presented.

In the remainder of this chapter I want to approach these issues by offering a particular account of landscape, an account that briefly narrates a journey to the summit of Glastonbury Tor. This is a journey firstly by car, from Bristol, where I was based when I conducted this research, to Glastonbury, and subsequently on foot from a campsite (where I would later sleep) some two miles from the Tor itself. It is a journey I undertook a total of seven times, hence the account presented here is composite. As stated in the introduction, my aim in recounting this journey is twofold. Firstly this account may be read as a stylistic exercise in *presenting* (rather than *representing*) landscape, an exercise in writing performatively about *milieux* of involvement, which, hopefully, exemplifies Ingold's attentiveness to the sensuous, dynamic and material nature of dwelling. Secondly, I hope, through this account, to (perhaps obliquely) illustrate the criticisms of Ingold's work made above. In other words, by focusing upon a brief, overnight excursion in the country, almost a 'touristic' experience, a trip to the top of the Tor, the aim is to illustrate that practices of dwelling may be brief, may occur in different, momentary ways within different spatial and temporal contexts, and that practices of gazing are practices of dwelling. As opposed to a dwelling predicated upon 'rich, intimate, ongoing' experiences (Cloke and Jones 2001: 651), we might thus offer one lived through the occasional and the transient.

A Glastonbury case study

The road from Bristol to Glastonbury

The road from Bristol to Glastonbury, the A37, outruns the city and sails suddenly into the deep of the countryside, into softly hilly country. A series of peaks and troughs, the course of the road through north Somerset is an affordance. As the car alternately climbs and plunges, so vistas loom and sink. The recumbent fields of the Avon valley, to the east towards Bath, are raised to break into view upon a crest, once, then quickly again, before being sheared off by the planes and angles of the closing foreground on descent. And these vistas slide around the sides of the car, into the narrowing funnel of the visible passed, as the road begins to assume a more definite southerly track.

Settlements make this journey a series of staggered starts. First Pensford, creased around a river on a narrow valley floor, peering through the arches of a high viaduct at the continual snake of vehicles, which concertina with the road's steep fall on approach and then stretch with sudden ductility across and through the village's centre. The road out of town is straight and gradually climbing, through a rare avenue of shielding trees. Clutton, a formless street of detached houses dignified by a sign, comes next, but is soon and easily forgotten on arrival at the village of Temple Cloud. The name helps to at once confer and confirm a sensation of altitude, of buoyancy, which accompanies this section of the road. It seems to travel along a spine, the land sloping gradually away on either side, yet without ever forming the horizon which would give the impression of a plain. The sky dominates. Height without definition or vertigo, therefore, like the view through the cramped window of an aeroplane, only broader, thus more weightless and fragile.

Another crossroads, at Farrington Gurney, momentarily freezes this sensation. A Little Chef. An Esso Snack'n'shop. But then a quick and curving climb seems to cross a geological divide and the road emerges up onto the Mendip plateau. The feeling of altitude now is more earthy: windswept and moor-like. Dry-stone walls pen fields full of sheep rather than cows. The road narrows and gutters, one accelerates and steers like a rally driver. On the horizon the needle of a tall radio mast hovers, its path to and fro across the field of vision measuring the road's deviations from due south. Beyond here, the road takes on a gaudy holiday feel. At Green Ore crossroads a forest of brown tourist signs and B&B premises advertise the proximity of Cheddar Gorge and Wookey Hole Caves. All these urge away from the A37, which hurries forward into a forest before beginning to descend quite sharply, and it falls in successive waves with the pressured, shallowing, downward glide of an aeroplane. Another curve and the trees fall away, and it's surprising how high we are, looking out over a broad regular plain; in its centre Glastonbury Tor.

From a distance of about a dozen miles, from a moving car through flickering branches, the Tor 'stands out' from the plain of the Levels. It stands out, it looks outlandish, a bit 'otherworldly'. The regularity and gradient of its silhouette acts so as to maintain its solidity across the haze of the scene's aerial softening. Various similes come to mind: a pyramid, a dome, a castle, an island, a beacon, a lighthouse.

But maybe some of these namings too easily suggest a distinction between the Tor and its environs. Topographically the Tor dominates the scene, but this domination, this 'standing out' is in fact a *creation*, in the sense that the Tor seems to gather and polarise the landscape, seems to grant it coherence and charm. The Tor 'stands out', but in doing so it becomes the *centre* of the Glastonbury landscape, and a *relation* rather than a distinction is announced. Michell (1990: 3) captures this sense when he writes that the Tor is 'the hub of a great landscape wheel'.

In these terms, the anthropologist Mircea Eliade might probably speak of the Glastonbury landscape as *sacred*. Not because a tissue of myth of symbolism can be extracted from it, but because, from a phenomenological perspective, the mode of being of sacred landscape is to be oriented and organised around a centre. Eliade (1961: 37) dryly summarises this founding ontological process:

> (*a*) a sacred place constitutes a break in the homogeneity of space; (*b*) this break is symbolised by an opening by which passage from one cosmic region to another is made possible (from heaven to earth and vice versa; from earth to the underworld); (*c*) communication with heaven is expressed by one or another of certain images, all of which refer to the *axis mundi*: pillar (cf. the *universalis columna*), ladder (cf. Jacob's ladder), mountain, tree, vine, etc.; (*d*) around this cosmic axis lies the world, hence the axis is located 'in the middle', at the 'navel of the earth'; it is the Centre of the World.

The Tor is such a hub, axis, centre. Like Uluru (Ayer's Rock), like Olympus, Everest and Kilimanjaro, it is a sacred mountain. As the axis and orient of the surrounding environment, it operates so as to draw that environment into a vertical cosmogony. The horizontal levels of the visible Glastonbury landscape are connected by the Tor with the celestial and subterranean realms.

From afar, also, the Tor's 'eye-catching' quality is enhanced by the tower that stands upon the summit, accentuating the vertical dimension of its profile. The darkness of this tower in comparison to the body of the Tor causes it to loom larger in the eye from a distance. This tower dates from the fourteenth century, and is all that remains of a larger chapel dedicated to St Michael, the patron saint of high places. In fact, excavations on the Tor have extracted evidence that the summit has long been a place of habitation and, probably, worship, with grave remains stretching back to the pre-Christian centuries (see Rahtz 1970). But a Tor without a tower is difficult to imagine, because the tower transforms the aspect and affect of the Tor, and by extension the entire landscape.

To explicate dwelling, Heidegger (1996: 354) speaks of a bridge that 'swings over the stream with ease and power'. The bridge does not simply connect the banks of the stream. Through it, the banks emerge *as* banks. 'It brings stream and bank and land into each other's neighbourhood. The bridge gathers the earth as landscape around the stream' (*ibid.*). We might argue that the tower on the Tor works in a similar way. The tower indexes a visible spectacle, yet it also performs the work of gathering which the very idea of a 'spectacle' presupposes. To see it is to be pulled towards it, to feel that one has entered a landscape that coheres of itself, to be drawn into a pattern of activities and postures. The landscape sweeps towards the tower, revolves around it, and a destination has emerged, the terminus of an intention one is carried upon.

Yet as the A37 descends from the Mendips into Wells, both Tor and tower slip quickly from view. Surprisingly, the Tor remains invisible as the road emerges from Wells onto the flat expanse of the Somerset Levels (now we are some five miles from Glastonbury). And this disappearing act is a recurrent feature of the landscape. As the road pursues a flat and straight track across the plain, through the hamlets of Coxley and Polsham, hedges effectively screen the entire view. Even as one passes a sign announcing the entrance to 'Glastonbury: Ancient Isle of Avalon', the Tor remains hidden. The isle consists of a number of small rounded hills; they ripple and shoulder towards the Tor, which is easily the highest and steepest feature. Yet somehow the Tor contrives to lose itself among these skirting folds. As Ashe (1979: 12) says, 'optically speaking, the landscape does not make sense. It is a monstrous refraction. The Tor, so obvious for so many miles, vanishes in the town and hides behind objects far too small to conceal it'. And when from odd angles it is obliquely glimpsed, it appears distorted, an ideal shape now stretched and flattened. Finally turning off the A37, the road to the campsite is a lane that follows the northern 'shore' of the Isle of Avalon. From this lane the Tor seems as far away as ever. As one approaches so it seems to recede, to always skirt the horizon like a rainbow. Turning into the campsite, the peeping tower on the summit shears from view altogether as the foreground closes in.

From the campsite to the 'foot' of the Tor

Deceleration. This journey from Bristol to the top of the Tor is one upon which slowness progressively encroaches. Just as the Tor is first glimpsed, the brakes are applied, and then applied again and again on the winding lane to the campsite, and in the same fashion the walk to the summit starts as a march, becomes an amble, and ends in stillness, lying flat on one's back on the hilltop.

It takes about an hour to select a site, unload the car, stretch the legs, erect the tents, brew some tea or coffee. These activities, on the surface a deflection from the avowedly purposive aim of reaching the summit of the Tor, in fact tend to open up a different relation of dwelling between self and landscape. I would argue that the erection of the tent (the building of a dwelling) does not 'add' to the experience, does not give 'depth and texture' to an otherwise 'shallow' or fleeting vision, does not make one feel 'more connected' with the environment than a camera-toting tourist. Driving the pegs into the ground, muddying one's shoes and knees, does not bring one 'closer' to the landscape 'itself', rather it is a *creative* act that opens up a *new* spatiality and a *new* temporality; as Heidegger (1996: 354) says, it 'initiates the lingering and hastening'. Heidegger's thesis is that building is *already* dwelling, not a means to an end, but an activity which harbours a certain style and potential of being. The camp is not the establishment of a territory, the staking of a claim, but the opening of a *milieu* in which the ascent and return will occur. It is somewhere to return to, somewhere to leave. . . .

Through a gate in the campsite, a gravelled, manicured track leads to a densely hedged and brambled public footpath. So, to begin with, it is a ramble in the country. Often, in the high summer, when this research was composed, the atmosphere was almost absurdly pastoral. The stillness of the air voices the humming of insects in the hedges and, from further off, the deeper growl of tractors gathering hay in the fields. In the heat, the walk becomes an indolent stroll. The path is level, hemmed in, nature at close to hand.

Then after a few hundred yards, the pathway reaches Stone Down Lane, a metalled road which curves up around toward the heart of the Isle. All along this steadily steeper climb, hedges on both sides shield the surrounding fields from view, the world beyond becomes chinks and shimmers of light in the greenery. And as the road gains further upward bent, so it becomes almost like a tunnel. Something changes. There is something about seeing the path going up the hill that changes the way you walk, makes you more strident. Exertion too tends to fix one's eyes downward, hunching into a rhythm for the afternoon swelter, midges, the Tor still invisible, still somewhere over the horizon. Now it is more a trudge than a stroll. Only at this point is the goal of the exercise ever forgotten, as the habitual ambient resonance of depths and surfaces distils into knees, hips and shoulderblades.

Before the path becomes seriously challenging, it levels slightly, and enters a distinctly gloomy glade, into which overhead branches reach like fingers. But on the left hand side of this glade, quickly drawing the eye, there is a rectangle of light shaped by the trees, a classic picturesque foreground opening onto a broad and sun-softened pastoral middle distance.

What is surprising now is the height the path has already reached. Already the width and spread of the Levels are distinctively below, and we are above. From the shadowed glade, the view is a vivid sudden entrance into depth. The view is a moment of focus, and comparative stillness: you compose yourself by taking in what is around you. And this *composure* is an essential aspect of the experience of ascent. Eyes and arms and chest take a position in relation to the landscape below to reach an equilibrium, with hands on hips or head, deep breaths, drinking eyes. The body composes itself by tuning to the elements and levels of the landscape. This composition, moreover, is intimate with the emergence of an idea of coherence and awareness. One *becomes* this individual, this locus, this point of view, in the midst of seeing and framing. With the view, you are composed.

Turning away from this glade, the path continues to climb, and the hedges resume their shielding. With the tunnel-like foliage and the almost-arranged viewpoint, there is maybe a sense of artifice, a feeling of being anonymously guided through an established itinerary. And then, a few hundred yards of climbing later, the hedges fall away, and for the first time the Tor appears, to fill the eye.

For the first and only time it appears alone, framed only by sky and sundered from the surrounding landscape bowl. The Tor now for a few seconds is an object rather than an environment, an object in the sense of seeming to be there *for* a gaze. As such, it shapes and solidifies, for a moment, the ambit of the self, the *for-itself*, so that what remains is already a representation, the sign of itself rather than a witnessed event. And equally, while the tower still beckons, and now figures can be seen on the summit, the Tor is now a challenge as well as a magnet. Starkly upright, it calls forth a response from the suddenly ready body of the onlooker.

At this point the Tor is also revealed as a loci of performance. Figures are scattered over its surface. Dogs drag their owners off appointed paths and into the surrounding fields. Families with children cluster around the ancient ice-cream van which stands perennially by the entrance gate. Tour guides hold aloft crystals for their reverent charges to peer through. Dowsers stutter purposefully past figures in lotus position, eyes shut, legs akimbo. The breeze carries beats per minute and resinous gusts swelling from the gaudy vans of itinerants. And all the while an irregular procession advances up and down the face of the Tor.

Ascending the Tor

From the ground, the Tor rears almost menacingly upward before the walker who approaches it. The climb appears steeper than in fact it is. Approaching it one emerges from the shaded paths, passes through the groups that cluster by the official National Trust entrance gate, and as the ascent begins one feels for the first time the sudden cold breeze always present here. At this point a crucial shift of vision occurs. As if a switch had been flipped, the Tor ceases to be something *looked at* and becomes instead a *process* of looking from. This is not only a question of a shift in sensibility from eyes to legs, from contemplation to action, it is rather a certain involution or folding of the landscape as a whole. The entire journey to the summit is conducted through passages of visibility from which emerge points of view and fields of vision, and with these first few steps of the final ascent the visible landscape which arrows upon the Tor seems to relax its intentions, and settles back into the laying-out of its own visibilities that the ascent reveals.

As one climbs up and around the Tor, the landscape uncoils, it begins to *encircle* as it expands. The sensation of height is considerable, but it is *not* a height upon whose edge one teeters, rather an expanding volume opens to and enfolds the beholder. A relation is formed between the process of elevation and the opening landscape, a relation one is caught in but does not form. Elevation does not straightforwardly *produce* the ever-widening view; these two processes are complementary and necessary to each other. The landscape that surrounds the Tor is not a resultant by-product of climbing it. From the start, an infinity of perspectives sustain the Tor's position as the centre of the landscape, and make it a place where vision dwells.

And equally, the visual landscape that sustains the Tor also sustains the climber. Or in other words it makes one a climber. The heaviness one feels in chest and legs is balanced by a growing lightness, a sense of anchorage being slipped, a feeling of occupying an airy volume of depth and of being lightly supported and elevated *by* the landscape. A double movement occurs, a folding within the landscape like the occlusion of two weather fronts, *from which* one emerges as a viewer, a seer caught up with the horizon.

Finally, the path twists sharply upward, and the exertion and uncertainty felt upon the steeply shelving steps fix one's eyes to the immediate ground. Head bowed, one reaches the summit of the Tor.

On the summit of the Tor: gazing and dwelling

By accident or design, the present path to the summit mostly curls around the Tor's eastern rim, and is thus sheltered from the prevailing south-westerlies. But the summit of the Tor is an extremely exposed spot, and at least a breeze blows across it even on the calmest summer afternoon, the stillest winter morning. But once the body has accommodated the wind, all one's attention is captured by the visible panorama, the innumerable landscape advanced by every point.

I would argue that from the summit of Glastonbury Tor it is possible to speak of practices of gazing as practices of dwelling. In the first place, this visual dwelling does not emerge as a sense of mastery or control, but as vertigo.

This feeling, I would argue, has two related forms. The first is a vertigo of dis-connection. On the summit of the Tor, one is carried 'above', one is no longer 'on the ground'. And yet the summit is revealed as a relatively broad platform, whose borders are rounded rather than sheer. One could never 'fall off' the top of the Tor. The true reason for this feeling of vertigo is the visible panorama itself. The field of vision is unaccountably broader and deeper than the rigour of the ascent would lead one to expect. All its dimensions seem exaggerated. The sensation of height is uncanny: *more* of the visible than there should be. In every direction the recumbent fields of the levels advance into depth. No clear-edged horizon arrests this onward and upward advance, and those who stand upon the Tor see depth in its clarity and inexhaustibility. On the summit the visible world assaults vision. One sees to the limits of seeing, and *this* is vertigin-ous. It is not the vertigo of losing touch with the earth, it is the vertigo of being displaced from 'oneself', from a habit of considering one's sight to be the vehicle of an interiorised intention. To see to the limits of one's vision – to be encom-passed within visible depth – is to recognise that sight is etched out of landscape, rather than the landscape being the product of sight. This is not just an acknow-ledgement of the landscape's material presence, or its persistence beyond the horizon. To perceive is to be already and always caught by dwelling.

The second type of vertigo takes the form of a certain paranoia. I have heard the summit of the Tor might be described as a goldfish bowl. The sense of being 'above' is inverted: now, one is *beneath* the huge arch of the sky, and surrounded on every side by lines of sight; or isolated for inspection like a cell drawn from a Petri dish and placed upon a slide beneath the microscope's lens. But feeling exposed and isolated upon the summit is another way of admitting to an affinity. Merleau-Ponty's (1968: 140) insight was to see that vision was drawn out of visibility, 'this circle which I do not form, which forms me'. The Tor's paranoia rests in the visible, in this abrupt realisation that I am 'one of them', a visible thing. The gift of my vision is granted through embodi-ment, which establishes me in the world. I only see from this visible body. On the summit this reflexive recognition of visibility is sensuous, felt around the torso's twists and neck craning to gaze up at the sky.

These two vertigos gesture toward the intertwining of looking and dwelling. The summit of the Tor opens onto the depths of the visible world – depths from which subjectivity emerges, depths which a gazing subject can explore only as an incarnate, visible being, and not as a disembodied eye.

Only very rarely will a climber find the top of the Tor empty. But although high and wild places are cognate with ideas of the realisation of a self alone, the daily gathering of wildly diverse purposes upon the Tor is seldom an irritation. The summit is not a site of solitary contemplation – it is a social space. By this I mean primarily that it seems to be a place where the individual is *let be*. The others on the summit of the Tor are not distracting objects *for* me, any more than they are isolated subjects whose existence I posit in the moment of their look. *Between* us, in the sociability of our contemplative dwelling, the land-scape surfaces as a style.

But few people spend all their time on the top of the Tor standing upright. On any dry day the tendency is to sit or recline upon the slopes that curve away from the platform of the summit. Sitting or lying down upon the grass transforms both view and viewer. The reclining subject is sheltered and hidden by the folds of the Tor, at once closer to it and less isolated by it. It contains itself more securely than before. And as the body lowers itself to the ground, so a frame seems to slide into place, changing the vertiginous panorama into a picturesque view. This moment of grateful tactility and enfolding enters into a strange alliance with the security and supposed 'aloofness' of viewing from above. The patchwork fields are suddenly a jigsaw. Once I saw a man on the summit pinching the air in front of him with thumb and forefinger. When I repeated these gestures myself, his actions became clear: it was as though sheep and cars and buildings below were miniature, and could be picked up. Sounds emerge softened by the pastoral ambience of the surrounding countryside (the Doppler moan of the cars below like the swell of the tide on the shore). Thought drifts from the landscape while remaining anchored to it, taking its cues from it.

But as evening gathers in the west the summit begins to empty and the contours of the Tor itself begin to fade, until it forms a dark emptiness at the centre of a web of road lights and hamlets. At night, the Somerset Levels, the 'moors adventurous' of Grail legend, come to resemble a Christaller landscape. The descent of the Tor can be quite quickly accomplished. Keeping one's eyes fixed on the often slippery path, one can reach the bottom in about five minutes, be well on the path back to the campsite in ten, and look back finally to see the Tor maintain its visibility: a dark mouth at the centre of the darkening sky.

Conclusion

The purpose of this chapter has been to explicate and examine notions of dwelling in relation to the performance of landscape. To begin with, the chapter sought to detail how cultural geographies of landscape have, in a sense, written themselves into a conceptual and methodological impasse, through their reliance upon a form of discursive idealism for interpretative and critical purpose. Landscape is, of course, a particular, western cultural and historical discourse, a 'way of seeing' even. The difficulty, however, is that in seeking to detail the assumptions, complicities and strategems of landscape discourse, cultural geographies of landscape have, I would argue, tended towards a certain reification of 'meaning', such that landscape appears epistemologically to be a net or shroud of meaning formed within a disembodied precinct of thought and then cast over the ambit of the lived and the material.

This chapter has examined Ingold's (2001) conceptualisation of dwelling as a radically distinctive understanding of landscape. What is particularly appealing about this conception, I would suggest, is the manner in which it presents landscape as a *milieu of involvement*; that is, not as a 'surface' upon which practices of dwelling occur, but as a kinaesthetic medium of practices, an ontological intertwining of human activity, discursive meaning and materiality that precedes and outruns their bracketing and abstraction from each other within a dualistic schemata. I have argued in this chapter that Ingold's work provides a potentially fruitful agenda for cultural geographies of landscape, nature and rurality. At the same time, however, I have sought to register some points of unease, and to offer an account of landscape that inflects some of the suppositions of the 'dwelling perspective'.

Dwelling is a word that undoubtedly resonates with some significant others; with duration, for example, with inhabitation, even with home. As Cloke and Jones (2001: 654) note, dwelling is culturally associated with 'time-deepened experience . . . the experience of rootedness'. But when I returned to Glastonbury, when I sat on the summit of the Tor on that scorching afternoon, I began to think about how dwelling is evident in forms of life that are mobile as well as rooted, in experiences that are occasional as well as longstanding. In other words, I have tried to argue in this chapter that if 'dwelling' is to be the frame through which cultural geographies of landscape are produced, then the term needs to be understood as referring not to certain experiences of landscape, rural, tactile and 'time-deepened' ones. It should instead be understood as the medium *through which* landscape performances are enabled and enacted.

This is not to suggest that certain landscapes are somehow more apt to dwelling than others, that Glastonbury, for example is possessed of some *genus loci* which makes it quite distinctive from more 'mundane' or quotidian landscapes. Instead, in concluding this chapter, I would argue that dwelling, in the sense that writers such as Ingold, Heidegger and Merleau-Ponty have spoken of it, is an ontology that transcends ideas of 'self' and 'landscape', in the sense that it is their condition. Hopefully, my account of travelling to and ascending Glastonbury Tor captures this sense that dwelling underwrites our material, dynamic engagements with landscape, that dwelling is in this sense trans-subjective. Rather than 'personal experiences' of landscape being the means through which dwelling is made manifest, dwelling *produces* landscape experiences, such as the ascension of Glastonbury Tor recounted in this chapter.

References

Ashe, G. 1979 *King Arthur's Avalon*, Fontana Books, London.

Barnes, T.J. and Duncan, J.S. 1992 'Introduction: writing worlds' in T.J. Barnes and J.S. Duncan (eds), *Writing Worlds*, Routledge, London.

Berger, J. 1972 *Ways of Seeing*, Penguin Books, Harmaondsworth.

Clifford, J. and Marcus, G. (eds) 1986 *Writing Culture: The Poetics and Politics of Ethnography*, University of California Press, Berkeley, CA.

Cloke, P. and Jones, O. 2001 'Dwelling, place and landscape: an orchard in Somerset', *Environment & Planning A*, **33**, 649–66.

Coleman, S. and Crang, M. (eds) 2002 *Tourism: Between Place and Performance*, Berghahn Books, Oxford.

Cosgrove, D. 1985 'Prospect, perspective and the evolution of the Landscape idea', *Transactions of the Institute of British Geographers, New Series*, **10**(1), 45–62.

Cosgrove, D. and Daniels, S. 1988 'Introduction' in S. Daniels and D. Cosgrove (eds), *The Iconography of Landscape*, Cambridge University Press, Cambridge.

Daniels, S. 1989 'Marxism, culture and the duplicity of landscape', in R. Peet and N. Thrift (eds), *New Models in Geography, Vol. 2*, Unwin Hyman, London.

Demeritt, D. 1994 'The nature of metaphors in cultural geography and environmental history', *Progress in Human Geography*, **18**(2), 163–85.

Dodds, K. 1996 'To photograph the Antarctic: British polar exploration and the Falklands Islands and dependencies aerial survey expeditions', *Ecumene*, **3**(1), 63–90.

Dreyfus, H. 1991 *Being-in-the-world: A Commentary on Heidegger's Being and Time, Division 1*, MIT Press, London.

Duncan, J. 1990 *The City as Text: The Politics of Landscape Interpretation in the Kandyan Kingdom*, Cambridge University Press, Cambridge.

Duncan, J. 1993 'Sites of representation: place, time and the discourse of the other', in J. Duncan and D. Ley (eds), *Place/Culture/Representation*, Routledge, London.

Duncan, J. 1995 'Landscape Geography, 1993–1994', *Progress in Human Geography*, **19**(3), 414–22.

Duncan, N. and Duncan, N. 1988 (Re)reading the landscape, *Environment & Planning D: Society & Space*, **6**, 117–26.

Eliade, M. 1961 *The Sacred and the Profane*, Harper Row, New York.

Fortune, D. 2000 *Glastonbury: Avalon of the Heart*, Weiser Books, York Beach, ME.

Gregory, D. and Duncan, J. 1999 *Writes of Passage: Reading Travel Writing*, Routledge, London.

Heidegger, M. 1993 *Basic Writings*, ed. D.F. Krell, Routledge, London.

Heidegger, M. 1996 'Building dwelling thinking', in D.F. Krell (ed.), *Basic Writings*, Routledge, London.

Ingold, T. 1993 'The temporality of the landscape', *World Archaeology*, **25**(2), 152–71.

Ingold, T. 1995 'Building, dwelling, living: how people and animals make themselves at home in the world', in M. Strathern (ed.), *Shifting Contexts: Transformations in Anthropological Knowledge*, Routledge, London.

Ingold, T. 2001 *The Perception of the Environment: Essays in Livelihood, Dwelling and Skill*, Routledge, London.

Macnaghten, I. and Urry, J. 1998 *Contested Natures*, Sage, London.

Matless, D. 1995 'Culture run riot? Work in social and cultural geography, 1994', *Progress in Human Geography*, **19**(3), 395–404.

Matless, D. 1996 'New material? Work in social and cultural geography, 1995', *Progress in Human Geography*, **20**(3), 379–92.

Matless, D. 1998 *Landscape and Englishness*, Reaktion Books, London.

Merleau-Ponty, M. 1962 *The Phenomenology of Perception*, Routledge & Kegan Paul, London.

Merleau-Ponty, M. 1968 *The Visible and the Invisible*, Northwestern University Press, Evanston, IL.

Michell, J. 1990 *New Light on the Ancient Mystery of Glastonbury*, Gothic Image, Glastonbury.

Mulhall, S. 1996 *Heidegger and Being and Time*, Routledge, London.

Nash, C. 2001 'Performativity in practice: some recent work in cultural geography', *Progress in Human Geography*, **24**(4), 653–64.

Rahtz, P. 1970 'Excavations on Glastonbury Tor, Somerset, 1964–1966', *Archaeological Journal*, **27**, 1–81.

Rose, G. 1993 *Feminism and Geography*, Polity Press, Cambridge.

Rose, G. 1999 'Performing space', in D. Massey, J. Allen and P. Sarre (eds), *Human Geography Today*, Polity Press, Cambridge.

Ryan, J. 1994 'Visualising imperial geography: Halford Mackinder and the Colonial Office Visual Instruction Commitee', *Ecumene*, **1**(2), 157–76.

Strohmeyer, U. 1998 'The event of space: geographic allusions in the phenomenological traditions', *Environment and Planning D: Society and Space*, **16**, 105–21.

Thrift, N. 1996 *Spatial Formations*, Sage, London.

Williams, R. 1973 *The Country and the City*, Chatto & Windus, London.

CHAPTER 9

Spiritual embodiment and sacred rural landscapes

Julian Holloway

Let us therefore consider ourselves installed among the multitude of things, living beings, symbols, instruments, and men, and let us try to form notions that would enable us to comprehend what happens to us there.

(Merleau-Ponty 1968: 160)

The world in which an act or deed actually proceeds, in which it is actually accomplished, is a unitary and unique world that is experienced concretely: it is a world that is seen, heard, touched and thought . . . I *come upon* this world, inasmuch as I *come forth* or issue from within myself in my performed act or deed of seeing, of thinking, practical doing.

(Bakhtin 1993: 56–7)

Introduction

On the morning of the summer solstice of 2001, approximately 10,000 people gathered at the famous ancient monument of Stonehenge on Salisbury Plain, Wiltshire. As the sun rose over the horizon and between the stones people danced and cheered, remained still in meditative postures, or performed druidic, neo-pagan, Wiccan, New Age or other forms of ritual. The majority there sought to draw upon, in a variety of different ways, the magical qualities that this space and time represented to them. This event not only represented a victory for those campaigning against the 15 year exclusion zone placed by the police and English Heritage around the site on this important date, but also the coming together of a burgeoning community of people for whom such rural sites have a special and, for some, sacred status. This chapter takes another of such sites, Glastonbury in Somerset, and seeks to explore the ways in which it is represented and practised as a sacred space. I hope to achieve this by, firstly, outlining the variety of ways this town and its surrounding landscape is depicted as holding sacred mystical energies, how it carries many historical myths and legends, and how the 'alternative' spirituality community there is represented, both by its members and others, as special and unique. From there I turn to investigating how the rural landscape of Glastonbury, particularly its famous Tor, is constructed, perceived and sensed as sacred through different embodied practices in, towards and with the environment. Using the work of different non-representational thinkers I also seek to understand the way in which both the spiritual alternative community of Glastonbury and a wider movement of such seekers are made through affective and sensual embodied relations. Finally, I seek to provide a way of thinking about the practice of spirituality, which takes it as a comportment, or corporeal style of being-in-the-world, that (re)enchants rurality.

Representing the sacred rural

The study upon which this chapter is based involved an ethnography of spiritual seekers in Glastonbury. With a population of approximately 8000, Glastonbury is situated in the county of Somerset, South West England. Somerset is by most definitions rural, with its national park of Exmoor, three areas of 'outstanding national beauty' (in the Mendip, Quantock and Blackdown Hills) and 5 per cent of its workforce in agricultural employment, compared with the national figure of 2.2 per cent (Department of Environment, Food and Rural Affairs 2002; Somerset County Council 1998). The county of Somerset attracts 2.7 million staying visitors per annum, approximately 0.5 million of which visit Glastonbury itself, with tourism sustaining just over 2000 full-time equivalent jobs in the Mendip District Council area where the town is to be found (Mendip District Council, pers. comm.; Somerset Tourism Partnership 2000). Although it is difficult to estimate, many of these visitors to Glastonbury come (either explicitly as 'pilgrims' or otherwise) to the town for its mythical, spiritual and religious connotations (which I will return to) or to visit the variety of spiritual institutions and shops. The latter are run and organised by the resident 'alternative community' which some estimate to be 1000 to 1500 strong in the town. The respondents who took part in the research would identify themselves with this alternative community. These respondents hold a variety of 'alternative' beliefs concerning the world, themselves and the cosmos. Principally these beliefs can be deemed New Age and to a lesser extent neo-pagan. It is not my intention in this section to describe in detail the contours of these cosmologies (see Greenwood 2000; Heelas 1993, 1996; Prince and Riches 2000; York 1995), but instead to seek to depict how such practitioners represent the rural landscape of Glastonbury as sacred.

However, something needs to be said of what these seekers hold as Ultimate and thus sacred in order to contextualise these representations and also what follows in later sections. Briefly then, those interviewed from Glastonbury's spiritual community hold that humanity has reached a spiritual crisis under the weight of materialistic and disenchanted forms of sociality. Thus the respondents present here are, in a variety of different ways, seeking to achieve a realisation of the spiritual in their personal lives as well as forging new forms of community where the sacred is venerated and fulfilled. In terms of the individual paths towards this goal the aim is to 'become enlightened' or 'ascend'. This results in understanding one's place in a cosmic plan wherein we each have a destiny and justification for incarnating on this earthly plane. To this end a variety of practices are employed, from meditation and different forms of healing, to the divinational techniques of tarot and astrology. Beyond the individual the aim is to achieve a shift in human consciousness so that we come to understand both the deficiencies of our current ways of living and, by jettisoning these, gain from the perceived far-reaching benefits of spiritual forms of life. This desire for change is variously perceived as already happening, will happen at certain cosmically significant dates or needs to be ushered in by connecting the disparate groups practising spirituality to form a network of 'light workers'. In short, the sacred here is something to be realised both beyond the social (a 'vertical' axis of a mystical connection to divine cosmos) and within the social (a 'horizontal' axis of attaining enlightened forms of sociality). Indeed it is the sacred both within (horizontal axis) and beyond (vertical axis) the social that informs the way in which respondents construct and represent Glastonbury.

In overview there are three principal ways in which the spiritual community of Glastonbury represents its sacred environment. The first of these, and probably the most significant of all, is the idea that there is a 'naturally' occurring mystical and psychic *energy* that pervades the landscape. The source of this energy is often attributed to the positioning of Glastonbury on a ley line known as the St Michael ley. Originally simply topographic alignments, the geomantic and psychical characteristics of ley lines have become an important means by which New Age and other spiritual groups imagine sacred space. The St Michael ley is said to be composed on two (male and female) currents of energy that criss-cross along its axis and intersect at certain points, one being Glastonbury's Tor (Miller and Broadhurst 1989). This elevates this natural hill to a site where the mystical (vertical) realisation of sacred spiritual selves can occur:

> There is no mistaking the powerful elemental quality on the Tor. Some would describe it as a whirlwind, a vortex or meeting point of energies in their purest and wildest form. . . . Many visitors to the Tor have had strange psychic experiences including suddenly leaping into the air, feelings of weightlessness and disorientation. . . . People who live in Glastonbury speak of the way they are sometimes impelled to go up the slopes of the Tor, while on other days they would find themselves unable to approach it (Howard-Gordon 1982: 9).

Yet it is not only the Tor, but also the greater landscape of Glastonbury that is said to be a place of special and sacred energies. In particular, it is a space where the transformation of the profane self into the spiritual self can and often occurs:

> JH: 'So this place is a place of healing and learning?'
> BHC: 'Well that's how I see it. I think they're all inextricably bound up together and I think you suffer if you come here (laughs). Things are much more intense here. A lot of people say that because you're living on an energy vortex and things come up very, very intensely it's difficult to avoid them.'
>
> (Interview with Respondent BHC)

As such many go to or are drawn to Glastonbury to begin or further their quest for spiritual enlightenment and, because of the intense and other-worldly energies that animate the landscape, deal with their profane selves. This process of spiritual awakening and epiphany is known locally as having a 'Glastonbury experience', and represents the vertical axis of representing Glastonbury as sacred space.

The second way that Glastonbury is deemed sacred is through the sheer variety and weight of historical myths and legends that are associated with and told of this place. Often this mythology refers to pre-historic and pre-Christian times, where pagan and druidic groups lived in harmonious balance with and spiritual veneration of nature. Consequently, Glastonbury is a significant centre of neo-pagan and Wiccan groups due to its various associations with the Goddess (see Jones 1990). In combination with the legends of antiquity, Glastonbury is often associated with the beginnings of British Christianity. Thus the medieval monastery of Glastonbury Abbey is said to be built on the first site of Christian worship in the UK, founded when St Joseph of Arimathea (Jesus's uncle) visited British shores in the first century AD and erected the 'Old Church' (in some version of this legend his nephew accompanies him during his 'lost years', most famously relayed in Blake's prose). He lands (it is likely that Glastonbury was surrounded by water in the early part of the first millennium) at a hill known as 'Wearyall' in the town, whereupon he plants his staff, which subsequently takes root and become the Glastonbury Thorn, flowering once a year in the Abbey grounds. This legend has a real currency for many both now and in the past, and has been explored and celebrated in a whole host of ways – from Fredrick Bligh Bond's 'psychic archaeology' of the Abbey in the early twentieth century (see Romano 2001) and Jon Michell's (1990) influential reworking of the legend, to the more mainstream celebration by both Catholic and Anglican groups on a yearly basis.

Another and famous association that Glastonbury holds for those who visit and live there, is that of King Arthur. There is not space here to fully explicate the links between this (semi-)mythical warrior King and Glastonbury. However, legend has that this rural landscape is the final resting place of the

King after his last battle at Camlann. Indeed, in a (partially at least) discredited find, medieval monks claimed the discovery of his and wife Guinevere's tomb in the grounds of the Abbey. Furthermore, in Celtic mythology the place of the dead is Avalon, usually depicted as an island, and through various etymological moves (for instance, the ancient Celtic name for Glastonbury is Ynis Witrin meaning 'Isle of Glass') and histories from the Dark Ages (for example, the 'Life of St Collen' of 650 AD) Glastonbury becomes the Isle of Avalon (which is a commonly used name for Glastonbury and its landscape). Of course any association of a landscape with King Arthur requires a concomitant link to the Holy Grail. This miracle-bestowing cup or chalice (even, in some representations a set of cruet) is one that is used by Christ to perform the first Eucharist at the Last Supper. Glastonbury becomes one of the many resting places of this object, sometimes buried beneath the Tor or the aptly named Chalice Hill. Another, less Christianised, version of the Grail legend comes from the sixth century Welsh poem 'The Spoils of Annwn'. Here King Arthur and a band of followers enter the Celtic underworld (Hades or Annwn, ruled by the god Gwyn Ap Nudd) to recover, in this version, a life-bestowing miraculous cauldron and, as we have seen, because of Glastonbury's status as the Isle of Avalon or Celtic place of the dead, once again a mystical and powerful receptacle is said to be buried or can be found there.

While I can give only a 'taster' of the amount and extent of historical mythology of Glastonbury, I hope I have relayed enough to justify the sense that there is almost an excess of history in this landscape. This mapping of multifold history and the temporal reach of some of these representations is something I would like to term *deep time*. The third and final broad thematic by which Glastonbury is represented as sacred refers to a sense of the Ultimate *within* the social. More specifically this involves the representation of the distinctive and spiritually facilitative 'alternative' community gathered in the town. Many of the residents spoken to consider the 'alternative' community different, distinct and special, especially in comparison to other rural towns of a similar size. There is in Glastonbury, therefore, a community of 'like-minded' people attempting to achieve a spiritually meaningful existence. While there are many different types of spirituality being performed there, and sometimes this can be a basis for disharmony, on the whole many see the community as being emblematic of a new way of life. Thus some depict it is as 'a cauldron, a melting pot for allowing a new more sacred human being to emerge' (interview with Respondent BT). Furthermore, it is not only the mystical energies of the landscape that can (potentially) furnish an epiphanal spiritual transformation, but also the community itself, quantitatively via the concentration of healers and institutional geography therein (Holloway 2000), and qualitatively through the enactment of 'different' social relations:

J: '[Glastonbury] is different, people are more likely to talk about important issues. If somebody comes here, we ask them how they are feeling. We're not interested in them saying "alright". If they're feeling really good about themselves then wonderful, and say so, if they're feeling bloody awful then talk about it . . . Yes, if you see a friend in the street you expect to ask how they are feeling, how they *really* are.'

(Interview with Respondent J)

This sense of the Ultimate within the social (the horizontal articulation of the sacred) when combined with the mystical and deep temporality (a vertical articulation of the sacred) maps the rural landscape of Glastonbury and its surrounding areas as sacred.

Embodying the sacred rural

We have now seen how the rural is mapped as sacred by the spiritual seekers in a variety of different ways. In this section I wish to explore the practical, active, sensual or more precisely *embodied* knowledge of the transformative and 'other-worldly' rural landscape that is Glastonbury. Indeed, I would argue that the manner in which spiritual seekers know and understand the rural demands such a focus on corporeality. For one of the predominant encounters spiritual seekers have with the rural is through the notion of an energy that pervades and animates both the landscape and the individual's potentially epiphanal relation in and towards it. Because this energy retains a sense of invisibility while also being (necessarily) graspable and substantial in its varied means of effecting spiritual change, we require an analysis of sacred rurality that takes the sensuous and affective comprehension of the landscape seriously. The spiritual energy of Glastonbury is something felt and sensed. One of the implications of focusing upon the embodied and felt nature of such landscapes is to think beyond ocularcentric theories of landscape as a 'way of seeing' (Cosgrove 1984). Central to the latter is a sense of a disembodied eye viewing the world from a vantage point above or at least higher than what is gazed upon – a visual framing which constitutes and confirms certain ideological and hegemonic subject positions (patriarchal and bourgeois for example). While not wishing to diminish the importance of understanding such powerful gazes, especially in how they subordinate other ways of seeing, here I wish to seek out ways of thinking about landscapes that take all the senses (not just vision) and the kinaesthetic as the manner in which space is known, made, appropriated and transformed. This is what Cloke and Jones call being-in-the-landscape, an embodied embeddedness, such that:

> This is a performed landscape, performed by things and people, and the people mark and map it through their bodies, through their repeated experiences – such as the feel of the pull or push of the hill as they walk back and forth from work to home – (re)making, all the while, the path itself (2001: 653).

This performative and embodied sense of landscape then is central to the examples of spiritual practice and endeavour that follow, as is the sense given here of co-creation of the landscape between people *and* objects/non-humans.

To come to terms with embodiment and corporeality in spiritual constructions of sacred landscapes, non-representational forms of knowledge are the key analytical focus here. In recent years, social and cultural geography has begun and sustained an engagement with such knowledge via the work of thinkers such as Deleuze, Heidegger, Wittgenstein and Bourdieu, among others (see Crouch 2001; Dewsbury 2000; Harrison 2000; Thrift 1996, 2000). Here I wish to trace a trajectory through such work which takes in Merleau-Ponty and Bakhtin, as well as the more contemporary work of the anthropologist José Gil. In a variety of ways these thinkers reject the Cartesian dualism of *mind* as being the only legitimate source of knowledge and *body* as inactive, and indeed unreliable, in the formation of knowledge. Instead, the body must be viewed as not only legitimate and active in the creation of knowledge, but also the basis from which symbolic and representational thought ushers forth. In other words, embodiment, or being a body, is the basis, the existential possibility, for having thoughts, forming representations, exchanging symbolic codes, and so on. Thus:

> Although they cannot be reduced to one another, what we call 'mind' only exists because we have bodies that give us the potential to be active and animate the world, exploring, touching, seeing, hearing, wondering, explaining and we can only become persons and selves because we are located bodily at a particular place in space and time in relation to other people and things around us (Burkitt 1998: 67).

The thinking body as a ground for cognition is given ontological primacy in the process of making sense of the world. Embodiment is a primordial way of being-in-the world that allows other representational forms to be brought into being. As Merleau-Ponty reveals, embodiment is the source of identity and knowledge of the self:

> In so far as when I reflect on the essence of subjectivity I find it bound up with that of the body and that of the world, this is because my existence as subjectivity is merely one with my existence as a body and with the existence of the world, and because the subject that I am, when taken concretely, is inseparable from this body and this world (1962: 408).

To extend this further, it is not just having a body or being in a body that forms the ground for cognitive thought to develop, it is the body's action (hence embodiment) *in and towards* the world that allows representational knowledge to exist. In some senses then an inert or inactive body is not a body at all, in that we, as embodied subjects, only come into being through our grasping and appropriation of the world. This active engagement with the world is not only the source for cognition, it is the source of our very being-in-the-world, our very existence. Concurrently, action, our articulation of the world in which we are placed and of which we make, is inescapable. Perception, for Merleau-Ponty, is embodied action and practice, as we inexorably stand towards, or open upon, the world:

> [O]ur perception of the world is essentially that of an embodied agent, engaged with, or at grips with the world. [The] term 'essentially' . . . is not just that perception depends causally on certain states of our bodies – that I couldn't see if my eyes were not in good condition, or the like. The claim is rather that our perception as an experience is such that it could only be that of an embodied agent engaged with the world (Taylor 1989: 3–4).

In Merleau-Ponty's thinking the body-subject is 'motile' and thus in its movement and orientation to and in the world it makes sense of both its environment and itself, and gives rise to the potential to reflect and represent. In short, 'we *are* bodies and without them *we* would be impossible' (Primozic 2001: 17; original emphasis).

Let us take an example from the spiritual narratives of Glastonbury to see how this notion of action-oriented embodied perception gives insight into the sacred rural landscape:

> V: 'I'm so caught up with doing all the community stuff that I don't have time to think about [the myths and legends of Glastonbury] that much, but still if I'm walking round the Tor or riding around the Tor on the back of a bike or whatever I think wow I live in Glastonbury, y'know, it does hit me. There's *thousands* of years of history and myth associated with the place'.

> (Interview with Respondent V)

We saw earlier how Glastonbury and its environs carries an 'excess' history, myths, legends, fables and symbolism. Such depictions (which can be almost disorienting in their variety and extent) furnish Glastonbury with a historical freight that can be deemed 'deep time' – part of the vertical attribution of sacrality to this landscape. In this example, we see the mobilisation of this temporality and, with the emphasis placed upon 'thousands' of years, a sense of the sheer depth and weight of this time. Here, then, we have representational thinking making sense of an external world, via other referential discourses and textual inscriptions. Yet also contained in this narrative is a revealing sense of an embodied knowledge and action-oriented perception of the sacred landscape. For it is in the respondent's motility in and towards the landscape that provides the basis for the conscious reflection and narrative inscription of the landscape. Thus the appropriation and articulation of the environment through the action of walking or cycling is the inescapable background to memory and imagination. In walking or cycling around the Tor, the weight of deep time is felt and sensed in the respondent's action in and towards the landscape. Through the actuality of somatic practice the Tor is perceived as the site of a certain sacred temporality – it is perceived in the respondent's 'capacity to act in and on it' (Taylor 1989: 9). Therefore, the landscape is known as sacred by the inescapable practice of grasping the world, our embodied articulation as the basis for meaning and thought. Indeed, part of this sensing of the sacred rural is the respondent's own sense of him- or herself doing, here as walking and cycling. Thus the embodied practice of standing towards the world or space in a particular fashion, a corporeal making of the landscape, is felt by the subject. This pre-reflective and kinaesthetic knowledge of practice when combined with the active-practical construction of the world forms Merleau-Ponty's concept of the 'intentional arc':

> *Intentional arc* refers to the way the body is sensed by the person herself, that is, to the configurations of lived significance which constitute the body as unreflect-ively felt; concurrently, it refers to the constellation of impressions that the body resonates towards its living and non-living surroundings (Marcoulatos 2001: 3).

The respondent's motility, action and practice of and in the landscape make the world for him- or herself and bring a tactile sense of memory as myth and legend into being. The sacred landscape of rurality is here embodied, sensual and felt.

Let us take another example, from my participant observation on Glaston-bury Tor to illustrate this further:

> Decide to climb the Tor as the sunset is beginning. About half a dozen people are there on the western side of the tower. Some are sat, some are standing. As time goes on more people appear. Curiously everybody is very quiet (. . .) A young guy, with a big beard, who is holding beads, sits cross-legged next to me facing the sun, breathes deeply and closes his eyes (. . .) I get up and walk through the tower. One of the ladies I passed on the way up the Tor is sat inside with her eyes closed. She has one hand clasped over, but not touching, the other. I catch the glimpse of a crystal in the palm of her lower hand.
>
> (Participant observation 13 November 95)

The Tor, its mythical-temporal freight illustrated in the last example, here is transformed into a time–space for the practice of meditation. Spiritual seekers of many beliefs and faiths use the top of this hill to enact the practices (med-itation, chanting, magical rituals, etc.) through which they hope to achieve connections with a divinity or move towards a cosmic enlightenment, drawing upon the transformative and facilitative energy of the Tor (with the 'deep time' of this space being one element of its agency). Here, again, we have embodied action that articulates and appropriates space. Through bodily postures (sitting cross-legged, clasping hands, closing eyes) and rhythms (breathing techniques, silences), a series of corporeal practices are part of the making of the landscape. As such the landscape is 'perceived' by these embodied subjects, as impressions of themselves and the world around them resonate with and through their action in and towards the environment. The practice of the body forms, with the sense of the body and as its own 'measure', the space of the body, as José Gil has it: '. . . the space of the body is the result of the objectivization of the body in space that itself results from the action of the body – of the singular body, organized in a particular fashion – on space and that finishes up by spatializing space' (1998: 123).

Objectivisation by the body – the sensing, knowledge and spacing of things and their relation, for example – is a process of action which constructs and creates landscapes: embodied subjects are embedded in or 'inhabit' landscapes (Gil 1998: 124). Spiritual seekers thus attend to the landscape through a series of embodied actions that are the space of the body, conceived as a series of relations and practical skills with (the things of) and in the world – or in Gil's terms, 'exfoliations':

> The body 'lives in space', but not like a sphere with a close continuous surface. On the contrary, its movements, limbs and organs determine that it has singular relations with things in space, relations, that are individually integrated for the decoder. These relations imply *exfoliations* of the space of the body . . . [E]xfoliation is essential way the body 'turns onto' things, in objective space, onto living things . . . [B]etween the body (and the organs in use) and the thing is established a connection that immediately affects the form and the space of the body; between the one and the other a privileged spatial relation emerges that defines the space uniting them as 'near' or 'far', resistant, thick, wavy, vertiginous, smooth, prickly (1998: 126; original emphasis).

The exfoliations performed on the top of the Tor are a turning onto, or style of appropriation, where the things of the landscape (the grass, the walls of the tower, the crystals, the sun setting, the temperature of the air, etc.) are sensed or known as spiritually 'energetic'. Put another way, the action-oriented impressions these spiritual seekers attain, as they inhabit this space, is of a cosmic-natural energy that can (potentially) heal and change them. These symbolic relations with the environment, these exfoliations, for New Agers and the like, are felt, they are (somatically) perceived, before (or possibly simultaneously with) their representation/signification. Thus:

> . . . there is a 'logic' 'preceding' the mind that forces it to think according to these types of (symbolic) relations. Now, given that these relations depend most closely on the sensual, that they have an organizing and almost immanent role in the sensual as it is conceived of by the symbolic order, then the agent of this 'logic' must be the body. . . . The body is the exchanger of codes . . . on its own the body signifies nothing, says nothing. . . . [I]f it signifies nothing, then is allows signification to come about (Gil 1998: 98).

Embodied subjects set forth, through practice, symbolic relations with the world that are sensually perceived through the body as the basis for reflection and representation. The body, through its action and practice, is thus the source for sensing the sacred rural landscape.

Actively turning onto objects and non-human elements of the landscape is, concurrently, a turning of the environment onto the body. Thus in the performance of embodied action towards the environment there is a dialectical relation where, if you like, the landscape speaks back to or performs to the spiritual seekers. In other words, we make space as space makes us. If, then, we take embodied action in and towards the world as the constructive background to representational thought, we must recognise and animate in our accounts the agency of the non-human. The latter are not a set of inert things but fields of activity that apprehend us and as we do them: they 'speak quite loudly for themselves' as we speak towards them (Primozic 2001: 63). There is a certain sense of reversibility between the embodied spiritual seeker and the world: a 'continuation' where embodied subject and object 'are in a relation of transgression and overlapping' (Merleau-Ponty 1968: 248). Moreover, this enmeshing of subject and/with landscape is inescapable to being-in-the-world. We are always answerable to the world, there is no (transcendental) position outside the world, for this would return us to the notion of a disembodied cognition and egological view of the subject. As Bakhtin (1990, 1993) has it, there is 'no-alibi in existence', we are always-already in a state of 'non-indifference' to the world around us. Yet this inexorable responsiveness or 'openness' of the embodied subject to the world is (at least) a two-way process (Bakhtin 1984a), for:

> . . . there is no possibility that a given subject can comprehend this world *qua* totality, insofar as we only have access to the existentially and physically delimited horizon within which we perceive, act and think. We can never 'possess' the totality of the world . . . thus our knowledge of the experiential world is always constrained and one-sided (Gardiner 1998: 134).

The implication then is that we are never of the world for ourselves, but of the world for others. This is due to role the other plays in our perception and knowledge of the environment around us: I need the Other in order to create a sense of Self, as the Other possesses a 'surplus of seeing', an 'extopy' or 'transgredience' *vis-à-vis* the Self. For Bakhtin the embodied subject is nothing in itself (Holquist 1990). The alterity and outsideness of the Other is fundamental to the Self, hence 'I cannot manage without another, I cannot become myself without another' (Bakhtin 1984b: 287).

The role, therefore, that others (human/non-human) play in the co-construction of the sacred rural landscape must be stressed. The creation of such landscape is a matter of the push of embodied active subjects and the pull of responsive active others. In the examples detailed here the sensing of the sacred energies of the Tor is achieved through a practical corporeal knowledge *with* the Tor (and the multiple relations that make this space–time) which, in some senses, invites and ushers forth this perception. In this sense the Tor has agency through the embodied agent's practice towards it and also its outsideness and alterity acting as an incitement to remember (myths and legends) and gain spiritually (move toward enlightenment). This transgredience and reversibility in the creation of sacred rural landscapes leads us to Merleau-Ponty's concept of the 'flesh of the world'. Famously, he writes:

> *Flesh of the world* . . . means that my body is made of the same flesh as the world (it is a perceived), and moreover that this flesh of my body is shared by the world, the world *reflects* it, encroaches upon it and it encroaches upon the world . . . they are in a relation of transgression or of overlapping (1968: 248).

In arguing for the active construction by the non-human other in the making of the sacred rural landscape, the notion of the flesh from Merleau-Ponty allows us to think of the time–space of the Tor as pervaded by an immanence that weaves the practices of humans and non-humans together: a unity-in-difference is performed through the subject's and other's possession of a unique and qualified agency in relation to one another. In other words, the practical creation of a sacred space–time is a co-evolution with all that actively consti-tutes it. There is a simultaneous affective co-investment of the qualities and skills of humans and non-humans. Thus the Tor is a field of spiritual potential born out of practice and action, wherein embodied subjects 'reach out to the world, respond to it, actively engage with it, shape and configure it – just as the world reaches into the depths of [the spiritual seeker's] sensory being' (Gardiner 1998: 133).

Articulating a spiritual infralanguage

The alterity that I have argued is essential to the co-evolution of sacred rural landscapes has been, so far, discussed in terms of the active and enticing materi-ality that the non-human environment performs. Put differently, the organic and non-human as actors, have, in combination with the practical embodiment of spiritual seekers, been given prominence. Here I wish to think through, and then draw out some of the implications of, the relations of embodied subject to embodied subject. In part I wish to do this so as to avoid the interpretation of what has gone before as merely being a discussion of how a singular subject relates to and co-mingles with a non-human landscape somehow in isolation from other (similarly located and active) subjects. By doing so I hope also to highlight the importance of the social, cultural and political articulation of spiritual embodiment, and thus recognise the criticisms made of the phe-nomenological approach to the body (particularly that of Merleau-Ponty, much less so Bakhtin). Specifically, this take on embodiment tends to ignore 'the way that the senses and perceptions are formed in a *social world* composed of networks of relations, which, as far as any single individual is concerned, has already been historically constituted by previous generations' (Burkitt 1998: 69; original emphasis). In other words, spiritual embodiment is achieved through both a sensual relation with the alterity of the non-human and through relations to other 'transgriedient' bodies, texts and inscriptions. In a previous paper I have explored how the performance of spirituality is set in and constructs an actor network of institutional space–times wherein prescription and management of what counts as belief are enacted (Holloway 2000). Here I wish to focus upon the orientation of embodiment towards spiritual signification, rather than how different representations are mobilised or managed to define the contours of what can and cannot be said. Furthermore, this argument hopes to move away from the body as simply inscribed by different representations and discourses, in the direction of understanding how the practices and actions of the body are enabled in a certain fashion or style (Dewsbury and Thrift 2000). This hopefully retains the body as an active source in the production of signification, as, once again, the sensual and affective is of such importance to the topologies of spirituality.

To illustrate this I wish to draw upon my participant observation in a 'meditation and healing workshop' run by the *National Federation of Spiritual Healers* (set up by the influential healer Harry Edwards in 1955). This session is held on a weekly and 'open to all' basis in the Federation's centre on the Market Square in Glastonbury:

> The room is relatively small. Around the sides, arranged in a circle, are high backed chairs, all with floral cushions stood up on the back. In the centre of the room on a small hexagonal brown table is a book, into which names are written for 'absent healing', a small purple candle and a box of matches. T is sat next to the window with a large ghetto-blaster type stereo under his chair: the music being played is relatively loud, yet soothing, ambient, melodic and tuneful. I sit where the circle of chairs meet the corner of the room. The room begins to fill up. Soon all the seats are full and about half a dozen have to sit, mostly cross-legged on the floor, around the table. About 35 to 40 are there. A large man sits next to me. He puts the cushion on the floor under his feet (in common with the majority there), opens up the palms of his hands, rests them on his knees and closes his eyes. M from the reception downstairs comes up, gets a chair and completes the circle.

> T welcomes everyone: new, regulars and visitors. He gets up and lights the candle, saying 'I'd like to, as always, dedicate this evening to the Light and the Higher Good for all'. He tells of other 'light groups across the world' and 'the network of light', that is resulting in 'an underground energy emerging'. He explains the procedure for the evening. Firstly there will be a 'guided meditation', which we will leave with 'the sound'. He then will leave us for fifteen minutes for meditation and then bring us out. After this we will send 'light and love to our absent friends, through absent healing'.

> After this introduction the process begins with everyone in the circle announcing their name, in an anti-clockwise direction. T explains that this 'consecrates the wheel of light of us here, in this group'. He instructs us to get comfortable and to let our eyes close, advising that maybe we should straighten our spines to

'let energy flow through us.' The room falls silent and we all close our eyes. I open my palms and lay my hands on my knees. T begins again with a prayer called the 'Great Invocation'. He urges us to become aware of the breath and the energy in the room. He comments on the ebb and flow of breathing, 'Imagine our hearts opening up, and as we breath in golden energy, pouring in, and as we breath out it emanates into the room'. He speaks of the 'heart chakra being the centre', where 'light pours in, into every atom of our being'. He describes the heart as a rose bud, which is 'tight at first' and then opens up to 'receive light'. Welcoming the light into the room, he reminds us of our guardian spirits being present, and how we should ask for the light of the Ascended Masters to be with us. We are now ready to be left with the sound – a 'sacred sound', a 'profound sound', to bring the light into the group. He starts making this sound, which is best described as a one note chant. It begins quietly, builds with intensity, until quite disturbingly loud. Suddenly there is complete silence.

All I can hear is the sound of deep breathing, the odd sniffle and cough, and the occasional burble of somebody's stomach! I'm trying my hardest to concentrate on my breath and to clear the thoughts from my mind. Yet I feel physically uncomfortable: my neck hurts and the chair seems very hard. I open my eyes slightly to see everyone sat motionless. I close them again, drift away and become less aware of those around me – yet I can't help but feel that the time is dragging.

T begins to talk again. He asks us to be aware of the 'energy' in the room, to be aware of our breathing – strengthening the circle of light by taking 'energy' from the person on our left on our 'in-breath' and on the 'out-breath' passing 'energy' to the person on the right. We will then be 'bonding the wheel with love and light'. He pauses and then urges us to send a beam of light out from the 'heart that is Glastonbury', adding that then we will be 'sending light and love along the ley lines to other centres of light – Avebury, Stonehenge, St Michael's Mount, Findhorn', and to 'other light workers' and 'light groups' across the world that are doing the work of the light. Another pause. T begins the 'grounding sound', which is again like a single note chant. I join in with this nearly harmonious sound, but not exactly wholeheartedly. T asks us to slowly come out, 'becoming aware of the room around you'. He warns us not to come out too fast as 'you may not be aware of how deep you went'. After about five minutes everyone seems to be 'out' and aware.

Without doubt one of the principal means by which the somatic is trained here to achieve the appropriate meditative state is through the directives of the workshop leader. To a degree, then, the body is inscribed and made (potentially) productive through the work of certain discursive moves: for example, T's instructions to sit comfortably and to straighten our spines. It is these spoken commands that principally organise and direct the body, and reveal the cultural-political conditioning of the somatic. The ordering of the body in this way helps define what counts as the 'correct' embodied performance that will furnish spiritual enlightenment, and thus facilitate a certain corporeal sensitivity of the sacred. The second set of relations that act to coordinate the form of embodiment appropriate to spiritual knowledge is somewhat less tangible than vocal tuition. I would like to deem this mimetic embodiment (cf. Taussig 1993). The reason I suggest this is because of my own experience during this session. My previous knowledge of 'how' to 'sit' for meditative purposes was somewhat lacking and thus the man who sat next to me, opening his palms and closing his eyes, became something to mime and attempt to reproduce with the positioning of my body – a somatic benchmark if you like. In this sense the embodied practice of my neighbour became something to allude to and articulate through my bodily activity. Indeed, in seeking to understand the relation of embodied subject to embodied subject, one must recognise the alterity or transgriedience of the other that is essential in furnishing this mimetic process. Thus, to perform an understanding of meditative practice and thence derive a form of spiritual individuation, another perspective external to myself is required (Gardiner 1998). Moreover, this knowledge, I would argue, is not achieved by merely directing the body in the appropriate fashion – going through the moves, if you like. There must be a certain kinaesthetic realisation of mimetic embodiment, a feeling of 'getting it right', as one performs the apposite choreography of limbs, posture, breathing and so on (I will return to this point). Spiritual articulation of the world must be accompanied with an unreflective and embodied sense of practical doing. Therefore, the body once more becomes the source for signification or an affective background of sensual knowledge. Through a certain sensing the body knows it has achieved what it set out to prior to the mind's recognition, affirmation or even, in certain cases, doubt or denial of such a success: 'One unthinkingly becomes what one is miming; the reality of the object of one's imitation becomes an aspect on [one's] own reality' (Marcoulatos 2001: 10).

Furthermore, in thinking through the relations between bodies in this workshop one must highlight what can be deemed the sensual collectivity achieved therein. This session involves a quite tangible sense of tactile and sensuous interaction between embodied subjects, that is for the most part non-discursive and non-representational. Certainly, we are compelled at one point to be aware of the energy in the room and to be aware of one another's breathing. Implied in this invitation is a sense of spiritual force generated by collective practice. And as we saw earlier one of the ways in which the sacred landscape is depicted is via a sense of the importance and significance of the community that resides in Glastonbury – the horizontal axis of sacrality. Here bodies coming together and practicing meditation articulates this sense of the sacred rural landscape. Through the active embodiment of the participants in the meditation workshop an affective community is configured which is part of the expression of Glastonbury as sacred rural space. One of the implications of this affective and embodied community can be usefully drawn out via Mellor and Shilling (1997) who seek to trace the changing relationship between forms of embodiment, forms of collective sociality and experiences of the sacred (admittedly in more 'mainstream' belief systems). They argue that, drawing on Maffesoli's (1996) investigation of 'neo-tribes', that there has been a re-emergence, from the denial of the body in the Reformation, of sensual solidarities or 'tribal fealties', which marks 'the resurgence of the "shadow kingdom" of effervescence, and of the sacred as a sensually experienced phenomenon. This means that the experience of transcendence again becomes immanent within bodies, sociality and nature' (Mellor and Shilling 1997: 17). Therefore, it is possible to trace the re-emergence of effervescent and sensuous experiences of the sacred in this example: through embodied performance an immanent sense or feeling of the sacred is realised in the meditation workshop. Indeed, the re-enchantment of spiritual sociality engendered by affective and bodily relations is even extended beyond the confines of the workshop itself to other similar, yet temporally and spatially absent, groups and sessions. The 'emerging network of light' is one that represents, in effect, a spiritual transnational communality born out of the sensuous enactment in and affective connection of similar sessions.

The carnality of the sacred is not only limited here to the realisation of affective communities. In other words, there is also a connection to be made and to be realised here with the spiritually permeated physical, material and rural landscape. Once again, then, we see active bodies involved in the embodied appropriation of the landscape. With this example, we have a more extended sacred geography than just Glastonbury Tor. Here the somatic performance in and towards the landscape articulates the mystery and 'deep' temporality of Neolithic monuments, such as Avebury and Stonehenge, as well as the more contemporary history of St Michael's Mount and affective communities of the famous New Age centre at Findhorn. Following on from earlier arguments, we can suggest that such sites, in their alterity and through the reversibility immanent to the 'flesh of the world', engender an embodied signification. Put differently, the historical, mystical and effervescent communality constructed by the meditative practice is concurrently a pulling or apprehension on the part of such space–times: as the meditators act towards the rural landscape, the rural landscape answers back. This embodied, fleshy and material co-construc-tion of the sacred rural landscape is one where impressions and senses circulate between multifold agents to create an environment where spiritual enlighten-ment can potentially be achieved.

In the workshop we are urged to sense the sacred energy generated by the communal effervescence of the event and we attempt to generate a sensuous connection with sites such as Avebury or communities such as Findhorn. In Gil's (1998) terms, the meditation workshop comprises a series of exfoliations in that embodied subjects 'turn onto' and sense each other, other groups and other space–times. In combination with the other examples presented here, the 'space' of these New Age or neo-pagan bodies can be seen as attending to people, sites and things in a particular spiritually focused fashion. Put differ-ently, these different illustrations reveal a practical and practised spiritual project to embody a sense of the sacred in the world and the rural more specifically. Therefore, the exfoliations of these embodied subjects are series of stances in and towards the world and the rural, constituting a lived spiritual practice. Thus the 'alternative' spirituality discussed here are oriented towards refiguring one's way of life to sense the spiritual and the sacred in all that we do. So sensing the sacred energies of a rural landscape through an embodied knowledge, a corporeal articulation of the sacrality of this or that space, becomes a spiritual endeavour and part of the spiritual seeker's journey towards enlightenment. Through a variety of means, and here I have exemplified both the representational (the discursive inscription of the landscape and the workshop leader's vocal instructions) and the non-representational (embodiment, performative approval and corporeal interaction), these spiritual seekers then are seeking to reinscribe or, more precisely, *re-enchant* the body. Yet this is more than, as mentioned earlier, a mere dictation to the body to do the right thing. It is more because it involves a certain existential endorsement, by which the body senses its achievement of this comportment or style of embodiment, wherein spiritual corporeal knowledge of the world is furnished. This is not an act of refiguration of the body that *then* acts upon the world with the appropriate skills at hand. Rather, as the body is always-already acting upon the world and the world is acting back, spiritual seekers are attempting to realise a transformation of this background to thought such that the world is grasped differently and spiritually. Indeed, this reorientation of exfoliations can differentiate the sacred rural landscape:

> C: Chalice Well type energy is the one I do most resonate to . . . Chalice Well (pause) is the most (pause) I get the most, it's the most sacred place for me, really.
> JH: In what way?
> C: Umm (pause) I just feel there is something of that energy in there.
> JH: Do you feel it?
> C: Yeah, yeah, I feel it's very special for me, whereas if I go up the Tor, I do feel the Tor has got a very special powerful energy, umm (pause) but is a sort of, umm (pause) oh it's difficult to describe energies really (pause) it is a much more male, kind of wild, cutting through energy, whereas the Chalice Well is much sort of softer, receptive, nurturing kind of energy.
> JH: Is it quite difficult to describe those as it were, in a sense, you feel them do you?
> C: Yeah, yeah, I definitely feel them.
>
> (Interview with Respondent C)

Whether the reorientation of the somatic appropriation of the rural landscape is achieved to the extent that sites can be distinguished by their sacred 'feeling', or whether this a general re-enchantment of the everyday such that it is 'felt' differently, the body is here the source of signification. As such we can, following Gil (1998), deem this an (alternative) infralanguage, for it is through the body and its modes of grasping the world that spiritual sense is made of that world. Thus the fulfilment of new spiritual comportments, new spiritual styles of articulating the world, represents reshaping of the actuality of lived embodied existence and corporealised meaning. Indeed, this apprehension of the landscape through a spiritual comportment reveals a somatic mode of sacralised rurality. In other words, rurality in these examples becomes a stylised embodied performance in which spiritual seekers attempt to sense and (re)configure the countryside as sacred through the 'overlapping' of the (active) body and the (non-indifferent) landscape. This spiritual infralanguage represents a (re)enchanted rurality as a spiritual style of being-in-the-world.

Conclusion

In this chapter I sought to explore a number of things relating to the rural landscape. Firstly, I have revealed the various ways in which spiritual groups inscribe and speak of rurality as a landscape wherein spiritual transformation and awakening can occur, whether this be via a mystical connection to the energies that pervade certain rural spaces, connecting to the historical narratives that are told about particular rural sites or through the spiritually supportive communities that have come to live in these spaces. The attribution of sacrality to these landscapes was then explored as something that is embodied, through the corporeal action in and towards the rural, as well as the way in which the environment in its materiality and answerability comprises an active alterity central to the co-construction of sacred rurality. Finally, I turned to examples of how, through different means of somatic reproduction and corporeal knowledge, a wider set of sites and affective communities are being drawn into this sacred topography. Rural landscapes, one could argue therefore, are increasingly becoming spaces for the enactment of 'alternative' spiritual lifestyles. Yet the realisation of this 'alternative' rural spirituality is more than just living in or just visiting the countryside to experience the sacred benefits that can be achieved and consumed therein. Rather, I have suggested here that these different groups are attempting to achieve a re-enchanted embodied comportment or corporeality that, without necessarily recourse to representations, myths or symbolism, apprehends and comprehends the rural and other spaces as sacred. There is then a growing body of people in this country and indeed elsewhere, for whom the rural is not so much a repository or sanctuary of the Ultimate but a space for the realisation of the Ultimate as an existential spiritual way of being-in-the-world.

References

Bakhtin, M.M. 1984a *Rabelais and his World*, H. Iswolsky (trans.), MIT Press, Cambridge, MA.

Bakhtin, M.M. 1984b *Problems of Dostoevsky's Poetics*, C. Emerson (ed. and trans.), Manchester University Press, Manchester.

Bakhtin, M.M. 1990 *Art and Answerability: Early Philosophical Essays by M.M. Bakhtin*, M. Holquist and V. Liapunov (eds), V. Liapunov (trans. and notes), Texas University Press, Austin.

Bakhtin, M.M. 1993 *Towards a Philosophy of the Act*, M. Holquist and V. Liapunov (eds), V. Liapunov (trans. and notes), Texas University Press, Austin.

Burkitt, I. 1998 'Bodies of knowledge: beyond Cartesian views of persons, selves and mind', *Journal for the Theory of Social Behaviour*, 28(1), 63–83.

Cloke, P. and Jones, O. 2001 'Dwelling, place and landscape: an orchard in Somerset', *Environment and Planning A*, 33, 649–66.

Cosgrove, D. 1984 *Social Formations and Symbolic Landscapes*, Croom Helm, London.

Crouch, D. 2001 'Spatialities and the feeling of doing', *Social and Cultural Geography*, 2(1), 61–76.

Department of Environment, Food and Rural Affairs 2002 'Summary of UK Food and Farming', http://www.defra.gov.uk/esg/m_overview.htm. Accessed 27 June 2002.

Dewsbury, J.-D. 2000 'Performativity and the event: enacting a philosophy of difference', *Environment and Planning D: Society and Space*, 18, 473–96.

Dewsbury, J.-D. and Thrift, N. 2000 'Dead geographies – and how to make them live', *Environment and Planning D: Society and Space*, 18, 411–32.

Gardiner, M.E. 1998 'The incomparable monster of solipsism: Bakhtin and Merleau-Ponty', pp. 128–45 in M. Mayerfeld Bell and M. Gardiner (eds), *Bakhtin and the Human Sciences*, Sage, London.

Gil, J. 1998 *Metamorphoses of the Body*, S. Muecke (trans.), University of Minnesota Press, Minneapolis.

Greenwood, S. 2000 *Magic, Witchcraft and the Otherworld: An Anthropology*, Berg, Oxford.

Harrison, P. 2000 'Making sense: embodiment and the sensibilities of the everyday', *Environment and Planning D: Society and Space*, 18, 497–517.

Heelas, P. 1993 'The New Age in cultural context: the premodern, the modern and the postmodern', *Religion* 23(2), 103–16.

Heelas, P. 1996 *The New Age Movement: The Celebration of Self and the Sacralization of Modernity*, Blackwell, Oxford.

Holloway, J. 2000 'Institutional geographies of the New Age movement', *Geoforum*, 31(4), 553–65.

Holquist, M. 1990 *Dialogism: Bakhtin and his World*, Routledge, London.

Howard-Gordon, F. 1982 *Glastonbury: Maker of Myths*, Gothic Image, Glastonbury.

Jones, K. 1990 *The Goddess in Glastonbury*, Ariadne Publishers, Glastonbury.

Maffesoli, M. 1996 *The Time of the Tribes: The Decline of Individualism in Mass Society*, Sage, London.

Marcoulatos, I. 2001 'Merleau-Ponty and Bourdieu on embodied significance', *Journal for the Theory of Social Behaviour*, 31(1), 1–28.

Mellor, P.A. and Shilling, C. 1997 *Re-forming the Body: Religion, Community and Modernity*, Sage, London.

Merleau-Ponty, M. 1962 *Phenomenology of Perception*, C. Smith (trans.), Routledge, London.

Merleau-Ponty, M. 1968 *The Visible and the Invisible, Followed by Working Notes*, C. Lefort (ed.), A. Lingis (trans.), Northwestern University Press, Illinois.

Michell, J. 1990 *New Light on the Ancient Mystery of Glastonbury*, Gothic Image, Glastonbury.

Miller, H. and Broadhurst, P. 1989 *The Sun and the Serpent*, Pendragon, Cornwall.

Primozic, D.T. 2001 *On Merleau-Ponty*, Wadsworth/Thomson Learning, California.

Prince, R. and Riches, D. 2000 *The New Age in Glastonbury: The Construction of Religious Movements*, Berghahn Books, Oxford.

Romano, J. 2001 'The Glastonbury enigma', *Fortean Times*, **143**, February.

Somerset County Council 1998 http://www.somerset.gov.uk/statistics/agriculture %20pages/agriculturehome.htm. Accessed 27 June 2002.

Somerset Tourism Partnership 2000 *Tourism in Somerset – The Facts*, Somerset Tourism Partnership, Taunton.

Taussig, M. 1993 *Mimesis and Alterity: A Particular History of the Senses*, Routledge, London.

Taylor, C. 1989 'Embodied agency', pp. 1–22 in H. Pietersma (ed.), *Merleau-Ponty: Critical Essays*, University Press of America, Washington.

Thrift, N. 1996 *Spatial Formations*, Sage, London.

Thrift, N. 2000 'Afterwords', *Environment and Planning D: Society and Space*, **18**, 213–55.

York, M. 1995 *The Emerging Network: A Sociology of the New Age and Neo-Pagan Movements*, Rowman and Littlefield, London.

Homosexuals in the heartland: male same-sex desire in the rural United States

CHAPTER 10

David Bell

For a few years now, there has been a growing interest in rural studies (as elsewhere) in issues of otherness, marginalisation and exclusion (Cloke and Little 1997; Little 1999; Milbourne 1997; Philo 1992) – a focus on questions such as who belongs in the countryside, and who is made to feel out of place there? There has also been increasing work done on the discursive construction of the rural – on how the countryside is made up in images and ideas as well as fields and farmers (Bunce 1994; Halfacree 1993). These agendas have pushed rural studies in all kinds of interesting directions, one of which has been towards a consideration of sexuality's place in the country. Mainly focused on homosexuality, but with nods to bestiality (Bell 2000a) and naturism (Bell and Holliday 2000), this work has sought to explore both the lives of 'sexual outsiders' in the countryside, and the discursive construction of distinct kinds of 'rural erotics' (see, among others, Bell 2000b; Bell and Valentine 1995; Bonfitto 1997; Cody and Welch 1997; Dews and Law 2001; Fellows 1996; Fone 1983; Kramer 1995; Phillips *et al.* 2000; Smith and Mancoske 1997; Valentine 1997; Wilson 2000). More recently, this has been followed by a focus on the body's place in the country, too, as part of a more widespread 'rediscovery' of the body in the social sciences (see, among others, Macnaghten and Urry 2000b, c). The embodied experience of the rural here reintroduces a material, experiential dimension to run alongside the emphasis on representation found in some work on rural others.

It is to these bodies of work that my chapter endeavours to contribute. My focus is on male homosexuality, expanding on my earlier work on men's bodies, male same-sex sexual activity and rural cultures (see especially Bell 2000b). Most of the work I shall be referring to in this chapter discusses the rural United States. I am mindful of the different meanings and forms of 'countryside' that exist in different contexts, so the arguments that I make here should not be taken as universally applicable. Even within the United States, of course, the rural is far from homogeneous – the West being a very different country from the South, for example – so we need to watch we do not essentialise country folk and places (Spurlin 2000). While I do think that there are some general things to say here, particularly about constructions of the rural and the urban, I would again want to stress the importance of place-based specificity. I am equally mindful of my less-than-comfortable use here of the term 'homosexual' – a term freighted by historical and geographical specificity, an identity rather than a practice. John Howard (1999) uses the term 'homosex' to discuss same-sex sexual activity in his study of Mississippi, but prefers the term 'queer' as a label for his respondents. I feel that queer is equally slippery, despite its well-intentioned inclusiveness, so I go back to the tactic I have used before (see Bell 2000b): to use words such as 'homosexual', 'homosexuality', even sometimes 'gay' quite loosely, at times to describe people who might not self-identify in that way. This may seem like an act of anti-rural symbolic violence, but I do not intend it to be – it is only really an act of writerly simplification. Apologies for its inadequacies, then – I hope they will not detract from the arguments I am trying to make.

I want to begin by describing four vignettes, or scenes, or images: four sites where particular embodiments of male homosexuality (remember: read the term broadly) meet distinct constructions of the rural. These four sites will then form the basis of my discussion, which centres on the discursive and material constructions of 'homosexual' and 'rural', constructions that then come together in complex and sometimes contrary ways. To borrow from Hugh Campbell and Michael Bell's (2000) discussion of rural masculinities (but tweaking it to suit my needs), I want to draw a fuzzy distinction between the *rural homosexual* and the *homosexual rural*, where the former refers to the life experiences of gay men living in the countryside, and the latter refers to the countryside that lives in what Byrne Fone (1983) calls 'the homosexual imagination'. I agree with Campbell and Bell that it is useful to keep these two in dialogue, acknowledging the interplay between the symbolic and the experiential; as they say, 'We can never separate the two entirely: even rural folk have seen *Deliverance*, Marlboro ads, and army training manuals' (Campbell and Bell 2000: 544). David Crouch (1997: 193) similarly notes that '[a]s well as playing with signs of the rural, people [also] participate in the actual materiality and physicality of rural places – the countryside' – and that is very much the doubled approach I want to take here.

Recognising the clumsiness and inadequacy of the terms homosexual rural and rural homosexual, and mindful of exclusions they might suggest, I nevertheless want to use them here as catch-alls to refer to a cluster of same-sex practices and/or identities and/or politics that are located and/or imagined in places that are non-urban – where the landscape is agricultural and/or 'natural', the population relatively sparse, and the settlements comparatively small in scale. Building on my previous work in this area, then, I want here to carry on worrying and whittling at what these things have to tell us about how we see the countryside, how we see homosexuality, and how we see homosexuality in the countryside. I will introduce my four 'scenes' now, and then bounce around the connections they make to the discourses and lives I am looking at.

Scene One: two men are locked in a sexual embrace, clearly having sex, astride a motorcycle in an open, woodland setting. One man is naked, the other dressed in leathers, and both have well-developed physiques. Their moustaches, styled haircuts and hard bodies signify a particular kind of male homosexuality; associated with urban gay culture, with pre-AIDS metropolitan gay life, with the 'clone'. Relocated in this woodland setting, the men appear as day-trippers, enjoying the countryside as a (sexual) recreational resource, having sex in the open air, basking in the tranquillity. We can guess that they have ridden out there on their motorbikes, to enjoy some outdoors sex, like many (urban) men who favour the erotic setting of (rural) woodlands (Lieshout 1995). Wooded landscapes are complex symbols of nature, in fact; as Phil Macnaghten and John Urry (2000a: 168) write, there's a lot to be learnt from looking at 'how specific social groups . . . *engage with and perform their bodies in* wooded environments' (emphasis in original). Here, the woods evoke nature as an erotic topography, but an erotic topography quite unlike those most commonly associated with modern gay life – the bars and clubs of the urban gay scene. The scenario here is depicted in a 1972 drawing by the artist Tom of Finland, well known for his (more-or-less pornographic) drawings and paintings of gay men.

Scene Two: a group of naked men, bodies caked in mud, stands in a tight circle, their arms around each other, faces looking inwards. Some are kissing. The men are improvising a 'fairie' ritual, and the setting is the Arizona desert, summer 1979. It is described by one participant:

> Buckets of water had been brought to a dry riverbed, and soon a great puddle of mud was produced. Cries for 'more mud' rang across the cactus fields as each man anointed the other. Twigs and blades of dry grass were woven through hair, hands were linked and a large circle formed. Coming together, the group lifted one man above it, arms above shoulders, silently swaying in the morning sun (Thompson 1987: 275–6).

A second, similar, scene, this time from 1981 and referred to as 'a dance of the fairies', is also described by Thompson:

> We build a fire near the sweatlodge, in a field above the bubbling springs, and form a circle around it the night of the winter solstice. We evoke the elements, the four directions and then stand awkward for a while. Slowly, some men begin to sing or to join with others in a low rumbling chant. We draw instinctively closer as the sounds grow in intensity and men, young and old together, begin to move. Some break from the circle and dance to shaking rattles and the voice of automatic tongues (Thompson 1987: 292).

The scenes echo those associated with the rituals of the mythopoetic men's movement, and with their reclaiming of 'deep masculinity' through homosocial (but fiercely *heterosexual*) bonding in wilderness settings (Bonnett 1996; Messner 1997). For this movement, the city has feminised men, and nature can remasculinise them – and for the fairies, urban gay culture is similarly rejected in favour of untamed, uncommercialised queer rituals enacted in the wild. The use of mud – natural matter – in these 'rituals' is also sometimes fetishised by groups of urban men who enjoy 'dirty' erotic play in rural sites (as in the British group called 'Slosh').

The fairies' philosophy and practices also echo those lived out by the better-known lesbian feminist pastoralists who established separatist communes and retreats in the countryside, most notably from the 1960s onwards (Valentine 1997). Explicitly rejecting urban life and lifestyles, these back-to-nature movements mobilise a distinct vision of the country as a physically, mentally and spiritually regenerative resource, drawing in assorted ecological and New Age discourses. In the case of the fairies and the 'rural lesbians', same-sex desire and practices are coded as natural, too.

Scene Three: some men who live in rural areas partake of same-sex sexual behaviour *situationally*: they live and work in all-male environments, or in locales where moral prohibition limits opposite-sex contact. This scene of rural male homosexuality is particularly vividly described in the *Kinsey Report*, though the images it conjures are replicated in autobiographical and ethnographic accounts (e.g. Fellows 1996; Howard 1999), and have themselves become staples of gay pornography (Cooper 1986). The gay men's 'bear' subculture eroticises this kind of rural masculinity, too, trading on images of 'poor white trash' (Bell 2000a; Wright 2000). As John Howard notes, the *Kinsey Reports* themselves functioned as a kind of pseudo-pornography, as well as a vital source of scarce information about homosexuality, when the two volumes were published in the United States in 1948. Public libraries have, indeed, long been a vital information resource for sexual outsiders – as well as sites for casual sex (Howard 1995).

Kinsey identifies two distinct types of rural situational same-sex activity: that which takes place primarily between boys in remote rural communities, and that which occurs in all-male working environments. Of the first, the *Report* says:

> The boy on the isolated farm has few companions except his brothers, the boys on an adjacent farm or two, visiting male cousins, and the somewhat older farm hand. His mother may see to it that he does not spend much time with his sisters, and the moral codes of the rural community may impose considerable limitations upon the association of boys and girls under other circumstances. Moreover, farm activities call for masculine capacities, and associations with girls are rated sissy by most of the boys in such a community (Kinsey *et al.* 1948: 457).

These archetypal 'farm boys', then, satisfy their teenage urges with each other (and, as Kinsey also notes, with farm animals) because girls are not available to them. Similarly, the second group discussed by Kinsey practices same-sex activities when it has no alternative, but this type is not age-defined. It is described in one of my favourite passages from the *Report*:

There is a fair amount of sexual contact among the older males in Western rural areas. It is a type of homosexuality which was probably common among pioneers and outdoor men in general. Today it is found among ranchmen, cattle men, prospectors, lumbermen, and farming groups in general – among groups that are virile, physically active. These are men who have faced the rigors of nature in the wild. . . . Such a background breeds the attitude that sex is sex, irrespective of the nature of the partner with whom the relation is had. . . . Such a group of hard-riding, hard-hitting, assertive males would not tolerate the affectations of some of the city groups that are involved in the homosexual [sic]; but this, as far as they can see, has little to do with the question of having sexual relations with other men (Kinsey *et al.* 1948: 457–9).

I have discussed this construction of the rural homosexual in more detail elsewhere (Bell 2000b), where I used shorthands such as the 'priapic hillbilly' and the 'rustic sodomite' and tracked a variety of representations. Here, homosexual activity is coded as natural because it is seen as unrestrained, animalistic, even rapacious (as in *Deliverance*) – these men just want to have sex, and do not much care who or what they have sex with. They are thus naive rather than self-consciously liberated, able to enjoy same-sex sexual activity because they have not been cultured into knowing it is wrong. Here we see a powerful notion of rural 'innocence' emerging – though this is innocence born of backwardness (Binnie 2000).

Scene Four: in the small town of Laramie, Wyoming (pop: 26,000), in October 1998, a 21-year-old student from the University of Wyoming, Matthew Shepard, had been for a drink at the Fireside Bar, and left with two men he'd been seen chatting to. A day later, a passing mountain biker found him barely alive, tied to a fence on the outskirts of town, beaten unconscious. He died five days later in hospital, without having regained consciousness. Two young local men were later arrested, tried and sentenced for his murder. As Beth Loffreda (2000) writes in *Losing Matt Shepard*, his killing crystallised a lot of issues in American sexual politics (and rural politics). Loffreda's book describes the scene of the murder like this:

> [We now know] that Matt Shepard had encountered Russell Henderson and Aaron McKinney late Tuesday night in the Fireside Bar; that he'd left with them; that they had driven him in a pickup truck to the edge of town; that Henderson had tied him to a fence there and McKinney had beaten him viciously and repeatedly with a .357 Magnum . . . [T]he only spots [of his face] not covered in blood were the tracks cleansed by his tears (Loffreda 2000: 1, 5).

The media attention following Shepard's murder painted a picture of Wyoming (and therefore rural America more broadly) as 'cowboy country', as an intolerant, 'backward' place where it is almost impossible to live life as a gay man, and where diverse coping strategies have to be meticulously and unendingly deployed in order to avoid the day-to-day hassles of homophobia as well as (thankfully much rarer) life-threatening situations (Cody and Welch 1997;

Smith 1997). This is, of course, intensely draining and corrosive, so for many 'sexual outsiders' born and raised in such conditions, escape to metropolitan gay communities remains the only liveable option, leading to a sizeable rural-to-urban 'gay migration' (Weston 1995). As an image of what gay rural life is like in America today, therefore, the description of Matt Shepard's battered body has immensely powerful resonances, and has come to assume the status of an icon.

These, then, are my four bodies: Tom of Finland clones, the radical fairies, Kinsey's cowboys and Matthew Shepard. In the rest of this chapter, I want to look in more detail at these embodiments of rural male homosexuality, and consider what they individually and collectively have to teach us about the homosexual rural and the rural homosexual. Let me begin by treating the two separately, before drawing them back together.

The homosexual rural

As already stated, I'm using the term 'homosexual rural' to indicate the imaginative construction of the rural as a particular kind of homosexual space. Most commonly, we can think of this in terms of a queer version of the rural idyll or Arcadia. In this context, Byrne Fone delineates three uses of the homosexual rural in his survey of gay literature:

> 1) to suggest a place where it is safe to be gay: where gay men can be free from the outlaw status society confers upon us, where homosexuality can be revealed and spoken of without reprisal, and where homosexual love can be consummated without concern for the punishment or scorn of the world; 2) to imply the presence of gay love and sensibility in a text that would otherwise make no explicit statement about homosexuality; and 3) to establish a metaphor for certain spiritual values and myths prevalent in homosexual literature and life, namely, that homosexuality is superior to heterosexuality and is a divinely sanctioned means to an understanding of the good and the beautiful (Fone 1983: 13).

The natural or wilderness setting, then, functions as a homosexual Eden, as the prelapsarian and precultural site in which homosexual love may flourish, unhindered by human society's moralities. Homosexuality is here coded as natural, so a natural landscape is its perfect backdrop (see also Shuttleton 2000). Across a range of gay cultural texts, from poems to movies, such motifs recur – and we see them here, in Finland's drawing and in the fairies' gatherings and rituals. Natural bodies (the fairies' nakedness), natural desires, the natural landscape – rather than seeing homosexuality as a 'crime against nature', it is here figured as in harmony with nature.

David Shuttleton (2000) argues that we need to be mindful of the contexts in which particular 'gay pastoral' texts originate and circulate, rather than collapsing them all into a single, transhistorical genre (in the way that Fone perhaps does). That said, there are clear echoes that conjoin them – the fairies explicitly summon up Whitman and Thoreau, for example (Bell 2000b), and Derek Jarman's queer art, movies and journals contain more than a trace of the Arcadian (Parkes 1996). Contemporary rural erotics bear the imprint of past connections, then, even as they rework them – though that reworking may give them new inflections.

Rural folk are sometimes added to the mix here, their lives and bodies connected to nature, the soil and so on – as people equally untouched and unbothered by civilisation's restraints. Agricultural labourers are particularly fetishised in this context, celebrated for their roughness, their manliness, their connection to nature. Rural rough trade, as we might shorthand them, inhabit this homoerotic landscape, from John Addington Symonds' fascination with shepherd boys to the eroticising of the cowboy and the lumberjack on the gay clone scene and in gay pornography today – icons referred to by Shuttleton cutely as 'rural camp'. The appropriation of Kinsey's cowboys into rural camp shows the recontextualisation process at work, their 'situational homosexuality' also coded as a natural thing – if horny men spend too much time together, freed from society's morals, their lusts will find the obvious outlet.

Of course, this re-eroticising of the rural butch contrasts violently with the de-gaying strategies of 'butching up' or 'cowboying up' reported as coping strategies for rural homosexuals fearful of the association of 'sissiness' with homosexuality (Cody and Welch 1997; Wright 1999). As respondents in Fellows' *Farm Boys* (1996) recount, the performance of manliness is often a necessary defence against outing and harassment, in an environment where a powerful hegemonic rural heteromasculinity is omnipresent (Campbell and Bell 2000). Such strategies are also mentioned in press coverage of Matt Shepard's murder, which condense the politics and lifestyles of Laramie to the phrase 'cowboy county'. Shepard's murder, some writers argue, reveals a fear of 'wussitude' that signals the fragility of that same hegemonic heteromasculinity (see Loffreda 2000; Wright 1999). In the writings of gay pastoralists, too, such 'effemaphobia' is a common motif, confirming the association between rural rough trade and manly love, as well as between the sissy and the city:

> Pastoral idealism represents and sustains a private, unselfconscious, non-socially identified and manly notion of homosexuality against which subculturally socialized, gender-transgressive, metropolitan identities are found wanting (Shuttleton 2000: 141).

As I've tried to tease out before, then, rural gay masculinity often gets figured in particular forms – as natural, manly, rough, raw (Bell 2000b). Even the 'fairies', many of whom took to the Arizona desert distinctly metropolitan sensibilities, reconstruct themselves in a version of this, drawing on a queered adaptation of 'Iron John' deep masculinity which rejects the label 'gay' and the culture it has bred:

One of the most remarkable off-shoots of gay liberation . . . has been the emergence of 'radical fairies', a nationwide, grass-roots movement of gay men seeking alternatives within their own subculture and society at large. Many fairie-identified men see little distinction between the two, arguing that as the gay middle class assimilates into the cultural mainstream, deeper inquiries into the predominant structures of state and spirit are being left unanswered (Thompson 1987: 260).

Common motifs, then, work up the homosexual rural as a landscape and an identity, both of which have long lineages and varied manifestations. These in turn have complex impacts on the rural homosexual; if I can recycle and add to a phrase I used earlier, at least some rural folk have looked at Tom of Finland's drawings, or read Whitman's poems, alongside seeing *Deliverance*, Marlboro ads and army training manuals. In fact, as John Weir writes in a diatribe against urban gay politics, there are plenty of 'people with homosexual urges who feel represented more by *Reader's Digest* and *Soldier of Fortune* than by [US gay magazine] *The Advocate*' (Weir 1996: 32). While there are multiple exclusions at work here – around class, race, disability, age and so on – the way that *Advocate*-style 'metrosexuality' fails to represent and include the provincial (and rural) homosexual is particularly significant (Binnie 2000).

What it means to be 'gay in cowboy county', then, cannot be separated from the images and ideas about the homosexual rural. Real lives – and real deaths, such as Shepard's – assume iconic status too, living on in collective memories as well as in pop songs and charitable works (Loffreda 2000). Those images add to, rework, transform the constructions of the homosexual rural in an ongoing process of meaning-making. As Paul Cody and Peter Welch (1997: 66–7) conclude from their fieldwork in Northern New England, '[t]here is a long history of rural gays in this country. It is not as idyllic as Whitman's *Leaves of Grass* implies; however, neither is it as abysmal as urban gay folklore currently suggests'. It is to these life experiences – the experiences of the rural homosexual – that our attention now turns.

The rural homosexual

Talk to gay men here, and you can begin to draw a secret map of Wyoming, one most of its residents would find unfamiliar. There are particular rest stops and scenic overlooks on certain highways where men can find fleeting companionship; the Cheyenne drag clubhouse without a liquor license that had a short, heady life in the early 1990s; the town parks in Powell and Lander that turn 'cruisy' at night; and The Fort, an adult book and video store south of Laramie with private viewing booths. . . .

(Loffreda 2000: 69–70)

This passage, from *Losing Matt Shepard*, paints a familiar picture of rural gay life replicated in a small but growing number of ethnographic and/or life-history accounts, mostly from the United States (Bonfitto 1997; Cody and Welch 1997; Fellows 1996; Howard 1999; Kramer 1995), as well as in the (also small but growing) literature on social service provision for rural gay clients (D'Augelli and Hart 1987; Moses and Buckner 1980; Poullard and D'Augelli 1989; Rounds 1988; Smith and Mancoske 1997). Social and spatial isolation, ambient homophobia, lack of community development, disconnection from 'gay meccas', religious and political intolerance – these are the themes picked up by the research cited here. As should be clear by now, this does not mean that there are no possibilities for acting on homosexual desires in the country:

> The rural for queer Mississippians was less an escape to the seclusion of nature, than a material ingress to a busy network of men. . . . Homosexual meanings and readings, desires and actions, could surface at most any roadside get-together (Howard 1999: 113).

Moreover, a second set of themes emerges in some of these accounts. As Cody and Welch remind us, for example, there are attractions to rural life for sexual 'outsiders', though these may have little to do with sexuality. Among their respondents, gay men who had chosen to move to the country signalled familiar benefits – the fresh air, peace and quiet, slower and simpler pace of life, outdoors recreation, and so on. Others found urban gay culture itself off-putting, preferring the pleasures of a home-based smalltown life. Weighing those positive features against the negatives listed earlier is a bigger version of what Loffreda (2000: 68) calls 'the daily quick math that accompanies gay life' in rural America – the unending calculation of how to act, who to tell, the risks involved in being 'out' (see also Moses and Buckner 1980; Smith 1997). For groups such as the fairies, and their lesbian feminist counterparts, the answer is separatism: elective isolation and self-sufficiency permits the pleasures of country life without the hassles of homophobia (see Valentine 1997). On a smaller scale, a kind of elective domestic isolation often keeps rural gays closeted, their sexuality privatised – not a uniquely country phenomenon, of course, but one that recurs in accounts of rural homosexual life. John Howard's (1999) life histories, in fact, reveal home to be a prime site of sexual experimentation for his sample of Mississippian gay men – not a closet space. Moreover, he warns of over-simplistically seeing rural space as one big closet, arguing that the countryside offers a mix of opportunity and constraint for same-sex desires (see also Fellows 1996). Vincent Bonfitto's (1997) study of the Connecticut River Valley 1900–1970 presents a similarly complex picture, arguing that there were plenty of opportunities for sex for gay men in this part of Massachusetts, and that gay couples established domestic lives with relative ease. However, fear of disclosure or exposure limited public *social* intercourse between gay men, and thus no sense of gay 'community' developed in the area, at least until the political upheavals of the 1960s (brought into the region via its higher education institutions).

Loffreda's 'secret map' of Wyoming is also duplicated in other accounts, most extensively in John Howard's (1999) *Men Like That*, which produces a detailed historical cartography of Mississippian gay existence. Here the rural homosexual in some cases fashions its own version of the homosexual rural, utilising the countryside in imaginative erotic scenarios:

> For those who lived in Mississippi, distinctive features in the rural landscape resulted in particular sexual desires, behaviors, identities, and networks. Queer boys *did it* in abandoned cabins, beside streams, among the trees; in haylofts, in the fields, in ponds; in cars and pickup trucks, at roadside parks, at summer camps; in hotels, bus stations, theaters, bars, city parks, and roadhouses; in prison, in the military; at church, at work, at school, and at home (Howard 1999: 123).

Howard's research stresses the importance of mobility, of transport and especially of the car: often the only way to offset the negative features of rural life is to be able to get to somewhere different, if only for a night. Expansive car-facilitated networks across space can stand in for place-based communities, though they do not easily form the foundation for social and political action. As Tim Retzloff shows, in fact, the car has profoundly reshaped American gay culture:

> The car . . . gave men access to gay spaces both local and distant, became a gay space itself, and helped shape stationary gay spaces as they evolved . . . car cruising, car sex, and homosexually active parking lots all became acknowledged sites where gay and bisexual men could claim public spaces as their own. . . . Often far away from urban areas, these various car-centred institutions provided men with possibilities for homosexual encounters and ways to create gay identities (Retzloff 1997: 243–4).

From Laramie, Wyoming, the nearest place with a 'developed' urban gay scene is Denver, an eight-to-ten hour round trip away. For many rural gays, though, it is more than worth the drive. For those who choose to make the move permanent, the sense of sexual outsiderness is often swapped for the out-of-place feeling of being rural in the urban, of having to let go of heritage and homeland. Nevertheless, those 'farm boys' that had become 'city men' in Will Fellows's (1996) work concurred that the gains outweighed the losses, even if some men found urban gay life difficult to get used to. As Allan Berubé (1996) remembers, for example, arriving in the great gay 'mecca' of San Francisco was a less than Utopian moment for him, since the Castro lifestyle was beyond his meagre economic means, and his 'trailer trash' background excluded him from participation. The homosexual urban, then, exists as an equally mythological site to its rural counterpart, a place made in the imagination and unmatched in reality.

Of course, as noted at the beginning of this chapter in my discussion of Tom of Finland, there's another traffic flow to add in here – urban gay men visiting the countryside. The bikers in Maurice van Lieshout's (1995) Dutch ethnography similarly head for highway rest stops, though they come from all over the Netherlands, and for distinct motives. The rest area they visit, known as the Mollebos, is renowned for its 'leather nights'. Here we have a particular arrangement of Macnaghten and Urry's (2000a) 'bodies in the woods', where the landscape is an erotic backdrop for sadomasochistic leathersex (another scene lovingly recorded in Tom of Finland's illustrations):

> The Mollebos proved to be exciting for gay men as an outdoor facility as well as being a wooded territory. It served for many of them as a sexual Fantasia Land where dreams can come true. The woods met conditions for exciting leather and S&M meetings: an erotically experienced space that suggests adventure, threat, and sensation. . . . [M]any leathermen turned out to be regular visitors, on every occasion waiting for the woods to redeem its promises (Lieshout 1995: 35).

As Lieshout says, urban gay culture has an often ambivalent perspective on public sex activities such as cruising and cottaging, although these practices are nowadays often woven into the sexual landscape in more positive, less demonised ways, even while they remain subject to intense surveillance and policing (Dangerous Bedfellows 1996). In many remote areas, of course, they still often have to stand in for the taken-for-granted trappings of urban gay culture. At the highway rest stop, moreover, we can see the potential commingling of two sexual cultures – the urban homosexuals, for whom the woods are a prime site for kinky sex, and the rural homosexuals, for whom the woods might be the *only* site for any sex. In a neat virtual analogy, Loffreda (2000: 70) finds the Wyoming portion of a certain gay web site populated mostly by 'men from out of state, guys with anatomically impressive handles who are jetting into Jackson for a few days of skiing and sex . . . with the occasional plaintive interruption from a local, wondering where all the gay Wyomingites are'. Like the rustic rough trade beloved of the pastoralists, there is an uneasy feeling of colonisation shadowing this encounter in some critics' readings. However, the Internet is often signalled as another important network that has liberated rural homosexuals from place-bound constraints. Chat rooms for rural gays have proliferated, as have sites for those who make a fetish of the rural. As a helping resource, the Internet increasingly stands in for the public library, as well as providing opportunities to supply vital social services to isolated rural clients (Haag and Chang 1997). It also offers new opportunities for social networking, for accessing pornography, and for making sexual contacts, of course.

One area where social care provision in rural areas has received increased attention is in relation to HIV/AIDS services. Ronald Mancoske (1997) summarises the issues at stake here, noting that AIDS cases are currently increasing in number most rapidly in rural areas of the United States. Kathleen Rounds

(1988) pulls out the challenges to care delivery – geographical and social isola-tion, stigmatisation, community intolerance and so on. Both Rounds and Mancoske focus in particular on the 'return migration' of people with AIDS (PWAs) who had left rural areas because of these problems, but then return 'home' after diagnosis, reversing Kath Weston's (1995) 'great gay migration'. Homophobia and AIDS fears are thus brought into the open in communities where they had previously been invisible by closeting and out-migration. How-ever, the cost of moving home can mean having to be re-closeted. Respondents in Rounds's (1988: 259) study (from an unnamed southeastern US state) said that 'in some families the person with AIDS was allowed to move home only if he agreed to cease contact with gay friends and lovers'. Mancoske (1997: 41) echoes this, writing that '[t]hese migration patterns back to rural areas gen-erate unique psychosocial stresses for PWAs and counseling issues for service providers', before concluding that '[r]ural PWAs seek care less often, later in the illnesses, rely on alternative care providers more often, and experience greater illness-related stigma' (1997: 48). In addition, a study by Poullard and D'Augelli (1989) found that volunteers in rural AIDS prevention programmes often harboured homophobic and AIDS-phobic attitudes. To give just two examples from their survey, 26 per cent of respondents thought that 'homo-sexual behavior between two men is just plain wrong', and 21 per cent found male homosexuals 'disgusting' (1989: 35). Clearly, there are significant issues facing the caring professions in rural AIDS service work.

All of these studies discuss urban to rural return migration as a significant 'problem' facing rural America. Meredith Raimondo (2001) has written an insightful essay focused on these 'new geographies of AIDS', and in particular on the discourses that emerge in the reporting of these migrations:

> In the late 1980s, a series of stories in major daily newspapers took up the theme of AIDS 'coming home' to the American 'heartland' through human interest fea-tures on the return of white gay sons to rural families of origin. For example, the *Los Angeles Times* ran a story that opened this way: 'When David learned that he was going to die, he decided to go home. But when David came home, AIDS came home, too . . . AIDS is killing in the heartland now. It no longer afflicts only nameless, faceless strangers a long way from Main Street' (Raimondo 2001: 4–5).

As Raimondo picks out in her reading of press coverage, a powerful mytho-logisation of the rural as maternal 'home' emerges here – a rural set against the sexually liberalised but uncaring (and diseased) metropolis these men are now fleeing. David Shuttleton (2000), in fact, sees the reprise of nostalgic gay pastoralism as at least in part a response to the AIDS crisis. In the narrative Raimondo highlights, gay men seduced by the city's openness – and driven away by the rural closet – find themselves drawn back home following HIV diagnosis: back to the place they were initially driven from. To accommodate these returners, a mythological home is created, with a welcoming mother at its door, and the incoming men are infantalised and desexualised. A very particular rural idyll thus materialises in these accounts, itself perpetuating both an idea of the rural as a site of 'not-AIDS' and the continuing return migration of ex-rural PWAs.

The press coverage also introduced a familiar AIDS demon to rural United States – the closeted (often married) bisexual man, here a product of rural closeting and a threat to the rural heterosexual population. It simultaneously conjured a further folk devil in the so-called 'AIDS refugee'. These 'refugees' were also fleeing the diseased city, but were not PWAs returning home. In this writing of the homosexual rural idyll, the country is imagined as a place safe from contamination, where sex is not overshadowed by death. AIDS refugees are driven from the (gay) metropolis by AIDS, but rather than being desexualised in/by the rural, they are migrating to the country on the promise of AIDS-free sex. Some gay male pastoral groups mobilise the same motifs of rural purity against urban disease; the Edward Carpenter Collective, based in Scotland, advertised a week-long retreat using the following publicity:

> We will discover an honorable and sustainable way to live intelligent and blissful lives as gay men and to be able to detach from a commercial and predatory gay culture whose deathwish mantra is *Live Fast, Die Young, Be a Beautiful Corpse*.

The closeted bisexual and the AIDS refugee confront such 'heartland' idyllisations of the country, therefore, since they sever the relationship between the rural and 'safety', and refuse the desexualisation at the heart of the 'coming home to die' narrative. As Raimondo makes clear, these complex discourses and movements have forced a major redrawing of the geography of AIDS in the United States. This has had to acknowledge and confront the reality of rural transmission of HIV – something not hitherto considered in either 'stories of the compassionate heartland [or] the rural backwater, [both of which] imagined HIV as an urban visitor' (Raimondo 2001: 9). What we can see here playing out very vividly, then, is the complex commingling of the rural homosexual and the homosexual rural – the invoking of an imagined 'heartland' that can only exist under certain circumstances, and the difficulties that raises for people trying to live under those circumstances. In some instances, maintaining the idyllic homosexual rural means invisibilising certain forms of the rural homosexual.

Conclusion

What I have been trying to do in this chapter is to further explore what happens when two things come together: the 'rural' and the 'homosexual'. I began with four different sites where that coming-together occurs: in the gay pornographic drawing by Tom of Finland; in the rituals of the radical fairies;

in the descriptions of 'situational homosexuality' among rural boys and men found in *Sexual Behavior in the Human Male*; and in the victim of anti-gay murder, Matthew Shepard. These are useful if limited versions of two intertwining motifs from my chapter: the *homosexual rural* (an idyllic place conjured in the 'homosexual imagination' and represented across gay cultural forms) and the *rural homosexual* (the life experiences of men with same-sex desires and/or sexual practices and/or sexual identities, who come from and/or live in rural places). As I struggled to get across, separating these two is an act of over-simplification; one thing I tried to establish was that the homosexual rural and the rural homosexual are densely and complexly woven together. Ideas such as the gay pastoral discussed in David Shuttleton's (2000) work can be traced through cultural texts and life experiences, folding together and working with and against other notions of the rural – as a site for 'natural' love between men, or a dangerous place where backwards intolerance reigns. This should, in many ways, be unsurprising – we live our lives at the intersection of the material and the symbolic, no matter where we live and what texts we have at our disposal. So my concern has merely been with exploring the particular texts and lives (and texts about lives) that I have at my disposal, and that work up their own versions of the homosexual rural and the rural homosexual.

At the opening of the chapter, I made a few observations about exclusivity – by noting the exclusions manifest here. I'd like to echo and add to those exclusions here, as my final points. My chapter has been about the rural United States, but has uneasily totalised that geographical entity. A better Americanist than me could tease out the specificities of the rural West against the rural South, and so on (see Spurlin 2000). I've also totalised diverse activities and identities (and non-identities) into the term homosexual – here I should be more careful to separate self-identified gay men, men who have sex with men, and so on. Kinsey's cowboys are *not* homosexual in the same way that Matthew Shepard was homosexual, for example. I have also tended to keep clear of other axes of identity that clearly cross-cut sexuality and complicate the stories I am telling: what about class, or race, or age, for example? Clearly the middle-class pastoralist has very different experiences from the rural rough he fetishises, for instance, just as the middle-aged gay couple settling down in the country have a life quite unlike a farm-born teenager who sometimes has sex with his male cousins. I should also have spent at least a little time considering the roles of religion in shaping both the homosexual rural and the rural homosexual, especially perhaps in the context of Christianity (see Wilson 2000). Moreover, my focus on male homosexuality has been at the expense of considering the lives and representations of other sexual 'outsiders' in the rural: what could we say about the rural bisexual and the bisexual rural, the transgendered rural and the rural transgendered, and so on (these are picked up in life-history accounts; see Howard 1999, for example). Finally, all this focus on 'others' and 'outsiders' fails to consider hegemonic sexualities – what are we to make of rural heterosexuality? Given the important work on genderings of the countryside, it would be useful to consider notions of heterosexuality and heteronormativity that attach to particular versions of the rural – and that in part produce rural sexual others. Clearly, much remains to be done; I hope that this chapter has in some small way contributed to developing a broader picture of sexuality in the country, for all its limitations.

Acknowledgements

Thanks to Paul Cloke for inviting me into *Country Visions*. Special thanks to Jon Binnie for his very helpful comments on the chapter, and to Meredith Raimondo for her comments, and for sending me her (as-yet unpublished) essay and allowing me to quote from it here. Some first thoughts for this work came into my head at the Rural Economy and Society Study Group conference at Exeter in September 2000; thanks to Jo Little for asking me to that.

References

Bell, D. 2000a 'Eroticizing the rural', pp. 83–101 in R. Phillips, D. Watt and D. Shuttleton (eds), *De-centring Sexualities: Politics and Representations Beyond the Metropolis*, Routledge, London.

Bell, D. 2000b 'Farm boys and wild men: rurality, masculinity, and homosexuality', *Rural Sociology*, **65**, 547–61.

Bell, D. and Holliday, R. 2000 'Naked as nature intended', *Body & Society*, **6**, 127–40.

Bell, D. and Valentine, G. 1995 'Queer country: rural lesbian and gay lives', *Journal of Rural Studies*, **11**, 113–22.

Berubé, A. 1996 'Intellectual desire', *GLQ*, **3**, 139–57.

Binnie, J. 2000 'Cosmopolitanism and the sexed city', pp. 166–78 in D. Bell and A. Haddour (eds), *City Visions*, Prentice Hall, Harlow.

Bonfitto, V. 1997 'The formation of gay and lesbian identity and community in the Connecticut River Valley of Western Massachussetts, 1900–1970', *Journal of Homosexuality*, **33**, 69–96.

Bonnett, A. 1996 'The new primitives: landscape and cultural appropriation in the mythopoetic men's movement', *Antipode*, **28**, 113–22.

Bunce, M. 1994 *The Countryside Ideal: Anglo-American Images of Landscape*, Routledge, London.

Campbell, H. and Bell, M.M. 2000 'The question of rural masculinities', *Rural Sociology*, **65**, 532–46.

Cloke, P. and Little, J. (eds) 1997 *Contested Countryside Cultures: Otherness, Marginalisation and Rurality*, Routledge, London.

Cody, P. and Welch, P. 1997 'Rural gay men in northern New England: life experiences and coping styles', *Journal of Homosexuality*, **33**, 51–67.

Cooper, E. 1986 *The Sexual Perspective: Homosexuality and Art in the last 100 Years in the West*, Routledge, London.

Crouch, D. 1997 ' "Others" in the rural: leisure practices and geographical knowledge', pp. 189–216 in P. Milbourne (ed.), *Revealing Rural 'Others': Representation, Power and Identity in the British Countryside*, Pinter, London.

Dangerous Bedfellows (eds) 1996 *Policing Public Sex: Queer Politics and the Future of AIDS Activism*, South End Press, Boston.

D'Augelli, A. and Hart, M. 1987 'Gay women, men, and families in rural settings: toward the development of helping communities', *American Journal of Community Psychology*, **15**, 79–93.

Dews, C. and Law, C. (eds) 2001 *Out in the South*, Temple University Press, Philadelphia.

Fellows, W. 1996 *Farm Boys: Lives of Gay Men from the Rural Midwest*, University of Wisconsin Press, Madison.

Fone, B. 1983 'This other Eden: Arcadia and the homosexual imagination', *Journal of Homosexuality*, **8**, 13–34.

Haag, A. and Chang, F. 1997 'The impact of electronic networking on the lesbian and gay community', pp. 83–94 in J. Smith and R. Mancoske (eds) *Rural Gays and Lesbians: Building on the Strengths of Communities*, Harrington Park Press, New York.

Halfacree, K. 1993 'Locality and social representation: space, discourse and alternative definitions of the rural', *Journal of Rural Studies*, **9**, 23–37.

Howard, J. 1995 'The library, the park, and the pervert: public space and homosexual encounter in post-World War II Atlanta', *Radical History Review*, **62**, 166–87.

Howard, J. 1999 *Men Like That: A Southern Queer History*, University of Chicago Press, Chicago.

Kinsey, A., Pomeroy, W. and Martin, C. 1948 *Sexual Behavior in the Human Male*, W.B. Saunders, Philadelphia.

Kramer, J.-L. 1995 'Bachelor farmers and spinsters: gay and lesbian identities and communities in rural North Dakota', pp. 200–213 in D. Bell and G. Valentine (eds), *Mapping Desire: Geographies of Sexualities*, Routledge, London.

van Lieshout, M. 1995 'Leather nights in the woods: homosexual encounters in a Dutch highway rest area', *Journal of Homosexuality*, **29**, 19–39.

Little, J. 1999 'Otherness, representation and the cultural construction of rurality', *Progress in Human Geography*, **23**, 437–42.

Loffreda, B. 2000 *Losing Matt Shepard: Life and Politics in the Aftermath of Anti-gay Murder*, University of Columbia Press, New York.

Macnaghten, P. and Urry, J. 2000a 'Bodies in the woods', *Body & Society*, **6**, 166–82.

Macnaghten, P. and Urry, J. (eds) 2000b 'Bodies of Nature', special issue of *Body & Society*, **6**, 3/4.

Macnaghten, P. and Urry, J. 2000c *Contested Natures*, Sage, London.

Mancoske, R. 1997 'Rural HIV/AIDS social services for gays and lesbians', pp. 37–52 in J. Smith and R. Mancoske (eds), *Rural Gays and Lesbians: Building on the Strengths of Communities*, Harrington Park Press, New York.

Messner, M. 1997 *Politics of Masculinities: Men in Movements*, Sage, London.

Milbourne, P. (ed.) 1997 *Revealing Rural Others: Representation, Power and Identity in the British Countryside*, Pinter, London.

Moses, E. and Buckner, J. 1980 'The special problems of rural gay clients', *Human Services in the Rural Environment*, **5**, 22–7.

Parkes, J.C. 1996 'Et in Arcadia . . . Homo: sexuality and the gay sensibility in the art of Derek Jarman', pp. 137–46 in R. Wollen (ed.) *Derek Jarman: A Portrait*, Thames & Hudson, London.

Phillips, R., Watt, D. and Shuttleton, D. (eds) 2000 *De-Centring Sexualities: Politics and Representations Beyond the Metropolis*, Routledge, London.

Philo, C. 1992 'Neglected rural geographies: a review', *Journal of Rural Studies*, **8**, 193–207.

Poullard, J. and D'Augelli, A. 1989 'AIDS fears and homophobia among volunteers in an AIDS prevention program', *Journal of Rural Community Psychology*, **10**, 29–39.

Raimondo, M. 2001 ' "Corralling the virus": migratory sexualities and the "Spread of AIDS" in the U.S.', paper presented at the 'Queering Geographies of Globalization' conference, Center for Lesbian and Gay Studies, City University of New York, 27 February.

Retzloff, T. 1997 'Cars and bars: assembling gay men in postwar Flint, Michigan', pp. 226–52 in B. Beemyn (ed.), *Creating a Place for Ourselves: Lesbian, Gay, and Bisexual Community Histories*, Routledge, London.

Rounds, K. 1988 'AIDS in rural areas: challenges to providing care', *Social Work*, **33**, 218–29.

Shuttleton, D. 2000 'The queer politics of gay pastoral', pp. 125–46 in R. Phillips, D. Watt and D. Shuttleton (eds), *De-Centring Sexualities: Politics and Representations Beyond the Metropolis*, Routledge, London.

Smith, J. 1997 'Working within larger systems: rural lesbians and gays', pp. 13–21 in J. Smith and R. Mancoske (eds), *Rural Gays and Lesbians: Building on the Strengths of Communities*, Harrington Park Press, New York.

Smith, J. and Mancoske, R. (eds) 1997 *Rural Gays and Lesbians: Building on the Strengths of Communities*, Harrington Park Press, New York.

Spurlin, W. 2000 'Remapping same-sex desire: queer writing and culture in the American heartland', pp. 182–98 in R. Phillips, D. Watt and D. Shuttleton (eds), *De-centring Sexualities: Politics and Representations Beyond the Metropolis*, Routledge, London.

Thompson, M. 1987 *Gay Spirit: Myth and Meaning*, St Martin's Press, New York.

Valentine, G. 1997 'Making space: lesbian separatist communities in the United States', pp. 109–22 in P. Cloke and J. Little (eds), *Contested Countryside Cultures: Otherness, Marginalisation and Rurality*, Routledge, London.

Weir, J. 1996 'Going in', pp. 26–34 in M. Simpson (ed.), *Anti-gay*, Cassell, London.

Weston, K. 1995 'Get thee to a big city: sexual imaginary and the great gay migration', *GLQ*, **2**, 253–77.

Wilson, A. 2000 *Below the Belt: Sexuality, Religion and the American South*, Cassell, London.

Wright, G. 1999 'Gay grief in cowboy county', *The Guardian*, Review Section, **27 March**, 3.

Wright, L. (ed.) 2000 *The Bear Book II: Further Readings in the History and Evolution of a Gay Male Subculture*, Haworth Press, New York.

New country visions: adventurous bodies in rural tourism

CHAPTER **11**

Carl Cater and Louise Smith

I would never, ever consider jumping out of a crane at Sainsbury's car park 'coz that's not what I want, it's not about throwing myself off large heights, it's about communing with nature sort of shit you know (Dave).

The increasing popularity of countryside adventures

A cursory look at lifestyle magazines, travel brochures, television schedules[1] bestseller lists[2] and Hollywood blockbuster films[3] reveals how themes of adventure have become prevalent in our everyday life. In short there is a growing recognition that adventure sells. A consequence of this is that experiences of adventure have emerged as increasingly fashionable and desired commodities. This chapter explores the commodification of rural places as activity spaces for a burgeoning adventure tourism industry. In exploring the consumption of adventurous tourism places this chapter also moves towards addressing the lacunae identified by Veijola and Jokinen who bemoan '*the absence of the body* from the corpus of the sociological studies on tourism' (1994: 149). Furthermore, as Macnaghten and Urry suggest, discourses of rural tourism frequently contain 'a number of problematic assumptions based on conceptualising individuals partaking in countryside leisure which produces passive and docile bodies' (1993: 268). On the contrary, using tourists' accounts of experiences of adventure, our intention is to advocate for a more active, embodied and sensuous understanding of the consumption of the countryside.

Tourism is widely understood both as a motif of escape (Krippendorf 1987) and as an opportunity to seek intrinsically motivated goals (Mannell and Iso-Ahola 1987). Shaw and Williams have defined leisure in experiential terms, as 'rooted in enjoyment, well-being and personal satisfaction' (1994: 5). Touristic experiences are becoming more and more influential in modern life because as much of contemporary work seems without clear meaning, leisure time is increasingly the time, and hence creates the space, in which we look for meaning in our lives (Vester 1987; Wang 1999). As a result tourists are increasingly looking for more meaningful experiences when they do travel (Desforges 1998, 1999). Much of the literature has focused on touristic searches for authentic experience, as suggested in the work of MacCannell (1976, 1992) and May (1996) and have been particularly focused on the visual aspects of tourist practices, most notably the *'gaze'* examined by Urry (1990). However, contemporary trends in tourism have highlighted that tourists are searching for more than a visual canvas in their quest for authentic and meaningful experiences. The growth in new forms of special interest tourism emphasises that the contemporary, reflexive tourist is on a quest to participate in a broad range of *embodied* tourism experiences. Tourists increasingly want to experience more than sights; they want action, to be able to 'participate with their own skins' (Moeran 1983: 94). Weiler and Hall (1992) describe the motivations for such tourist activities to be based upon improved physical well-being, social contact, risk seeking and self-discovery resulting from the experience. Whether this is touching a humpback whale's leathery skin, feeling the *g*-forces in a thrilling bungee jump in a spectacular canyon or listening to the moving drumbeat of a native tribal dance, the focus is a deep embodied experience unavailable in everyday life. Touristic experience is no longer just a visual safari.

As a result of these trends, the adventure tourism industry has grown at a very rapid rate. This is significant not only from the importance of the size of the industry, but also in its broader societal impact, particularly as many of these adventurous sports sell an entire lifestyle, epitomised by the continuing vogue for outdoor wear in fashion. Alongside this, and as is illustrated in this chapter, the growth of adventure tourism is also implicated in the changing nature of place and culture. Clearly the term 'adventure tourism' is open to debate for there is a wide spectrum of activities ranging from bungee jumping to mountaineering that have been promoted as adventurous. Perhaps of more importance is the differentiation of these activities in terms of 'thrill value', ranging from 'hard' to 'soft' adventure activities (Cloke and Perkins 1998a[4]). However a characteristic that is common to all forms is that they almost exclusively take place in outdoor natural environments and rural locations.

Adventure and nature

The quest for adventure has always been associated with the natural environment in one way or another, as is borne out by a study of adventurous tales in literature through the ages. In the context of tourism, nature has historically been bound up with the visual consumption and aesthetic judgements of different natures and landscapes (Adler 1989; Urry 1990). Urry argues that this visual discourse stems from the nineteenth century when nature became seen as 'scenery, views, perceptual sensation and romanticised' (1999: 38). In contemporary tourism nature continues to be sold as a spectacular scene that feeds what Urry terms the 'romantic' gaze, where people seek, in their visual consumption, 'solitude, privacy and a personal, semi-spiritual relationship with their environment' (1995: 180). This romantic longing for nature has led to it being framed as a place for refuge, replenishment and relaxation. However, while the framing of nature as a visual scene has dominated tourism practices, there have existed other, more active and engaged ways of communing with nature, which have been severely neglected in tourism research. These practices are important since they carry different meanings for how nature is both interpreted and experienced.

While some individuals may have been content to passively gaze in awe at the wonders of nature, for others, the sights that stood before them initiated a desire to engage with nature in more active ways. Johnston and Edwards (1994) in their account of mountaineering, suggest that interest in the sport emerged in the 1800s when people began to recognise mountains as a source of both pleasure and adventure. Growing interest in 'communing' with nature in this way, led to the rising popularity of combining more general tourism practices, such as sightseeing, with more active pastimes, as is apparent in this extract taken from 1914 tourism promotional brochure for Queenstown, in the South Island of New Zealand:

> Double Cone, the split peak which marks the termination of the gaunt Remarkables, stands over against Queenstown in perpetual challenge to the seasoned climber. The conquest of its 7,688 feet constitutes a long and strenuous day's work, possible only to the vigorous and enthusiastic mountaineer, who will revel in the surmounting of the difficulties (Sinclair 1914: 23).

However, during this era, the consumption of nature in this manner remained confined to those who possessed the skills, desire and money to invest in sometimes risky adventures. For these reasons the active consumption of nature was overshadowed by the predominance of the largely passive tourist gaze (Urry 1990). This has, however, changed with the growth of the adventure tourism and travel industry. Technological developments, modern transportation methods and increased safety have all contributed to the growing popularity of adventurous tourism practices. The allied commodification of adventure has sparked greater emphasis upon, and demand for, interacting with nature in active ways, as suggested by Bell and Lyall (1998: 7): 'Where once commodification was of the vista, or the view translated into a painting or photograph to sell, people now expect to interact with nature in exciting new ways.' The discovery of nature in this manner has lead to it being invested with new meanings where nature is still framed as an entity to be challenged and ultimately conquered, but in a monitored and sanitised setting. In this context, nature is a sight to be both visually consumed and a site to be actively engaged with. The individual does not just search out the most perfect viewing platform, they seek to move within and through the landscape and live out embodied experiences of nature.

Adventurous places

For many contemporary sites of adventurous tourism their reputation carries 'meanings of excitement, thrill, youthfulness (and) freshness' which are communicated through the meanings invested in nature (Cloke and Perkins 1998a: 190). The marketing of places and activities is therefore an important avenue through which they are endowed with anticipatory meanings (Goss 1993; Squire 1994). Through this commodification of place, certain destinations emerge as being 'the opening of a space of places at which activities can intelligibly be performed' (Thrift 1999: 311). As a result of these trends some very strong 'place-myths' emerge which become reinforced through touristic practices. Wilson (1992: 20) discusses how tourism is projected out into nature and then brought back on itself as part of our imaginations. He shows how the Caribbean holiday is a product as well as place, corresponding to an equation of palm trees, sandy beaches, sunshine and a clear blue sea, irrespective of actual geographical location. This applies equally to adventurous tourism, you *can* bungee jump off a crane in a car park, but people would far rather do so off a bridge across a deep canyon with raging rapids below (Figure 11.1). This is the image that is circulated most often, and hence it is the one that the tourist seeks to replicate.

The growing popularity of adventure tourism has lead to the development of so-called adrenaline 'hotspots' around the world. These were listed by the *Independent on Sunday* (14 September 1997) and among others included Queenstown (New Zealand), Cairns (Australia), Victoria Falls (Zimbabwe) and Chamonix (France). These areas have been marked by the media as places where tourists can partake in adventure tourism pursuits in spectacular natural settings. Nature is thus packaged as a spectacular backdrop for these activities. However, the scene is not fixed; it is part of an 'accelerated sublime', as in adventure tourism tourists feel the landscape rushing towards them faster than ever before (Bell and Lyall 1998: 13).

Adventurous places are typically perceived as marginal locations, frequently rural, that form an alternative to the highly developed west. The reality is that these are as much part of the global system as the places where the participants originate, in that they are well served by air links and have the best hotels and nightlife for 'après-adventure'. What is important is that these places 'look' like they are at the 'edge of the world', this look adds to that feeling of adventure without compromising the 'safe' regulatory frameworks that holiday makers have come to expect (Ritzer and Liska 1997).

Figure 11.1   The setting for adventure.

The 'adventure capital of the world'

In order to demonstrate some of the themes that we have suggested above, such as the commodification of a natural setting, the popularity of embodied inter-actions with this landscape, and the reorganisation of place that results, it is necessary to examine one of these adrenaline hotspots. For the purposes of this chapter we shall examine the growth in the self-styled 'adventure capital of the world', Queenstown, in New Zealand (Figure 11.2). Before leaping to the examination of the resort, however, it is necessary to examine some of the national changes that have contributed to its success.

To secure its place as an international tourist destination, New Zealand has pursued a strong tourism growth strategy, with the original aim, set in 1989, of achieving inbound tourism equal to its population of 3 million by 2000 (New Zealand Tourism Board, Annual Report, 1998). A clear branding pro-gramme in place after 1993, aimed at creating an image for tourism as well as New Zealand exports, focused on the unspoiled natural assets of New Zealand while also underlining the global outlook of the 'Kiwis' (Cloke and Perkins 1998a). The results of these programmes may not have been as spectacular as envisaged, as at the year to end February 1999 New Zealand had received approximately 1.5 million visitors. However, New Zealand did experience an inbound tourism annual growth rate of 10 per cent in the first half of the 1990s, which was over twice the global average. More generally, there has been intensive economic restructuring in New Zealand during the 1990s. This has led to the loss of a significant number of jobs in the agriculture industry allied to a massive increase in private ownership and deregulation. To a large extent this restructuring laid tourism at the feet of the regional authorities with the appropriate natural resources. We shall not discuss these changes further other than to highlight that they have both been influential in the growth of tourism in rural locations, although more in-depth accounts may be found else-where (see, for example, Cheyne and Ryan 1996; Kearsley 1997).

Queenstown has been well placed to take up this tourism boom, as one of the country's principal holiday resorts since the early twentieth century. The town's reputation is built primarily on its scenic splendour, although it is interesting to see how even early brochures hint at the wide range of opportunities for engaging with nature that were available in the region, as one from 1914 states:

> Mankind's holiday tastes are as diverse as his business pursuits, but Nature is a never failing storehouse. And surely in no part of New Zealand, nay, of the world, has there been packed into one corner of the storehouse such a wondrous variety of the chiefest delights of nature as is to be found in the neighbourhood of Queenstown' (Sinclair 1914: 5).

Despite pioneering early forms of adventure tourism such as jetboating and whitewater rafting, Queenstown only cemented its adventure credentials with

Figure 11.2 Queenstown, the self-styled 'Adventure capital of the world'.

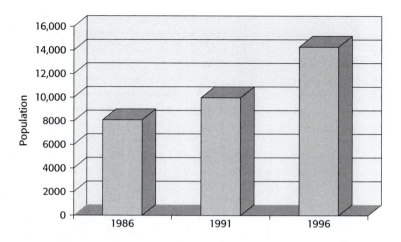

Figure 11.3 Queenstown population growth 1986–1996.

the opening of the world's first commercial bungee jump in 1988. Our discussions with adventure tourism operators have highlighted the importance of bungee as a watershed in the region's tourism development.

It is interesting to observe the resultant changes simply in terms of resident population of the region, where the increase has been meteoric (Figure 11.3). The population almost doubled in the decade 1986–1996, from just over 8000 to approaching 15,000, with a significant proportion of that growth in the latter five years of that period. Most of the residents are employed in tourism (Figure 11.4), with 26 per cent employed in the tourism-exclusive sector of accommodation, cafes and restaurants. If we include cultural and recreational services and retail and transport sectors, which are largely driven by tourism, the percentage rises to nearly 60 per cent directly employed in the tourism industry. It is also worth noting the importance of the construction and property sectors as well, as these too are highly reliant on a buoyant tourism market.

Inclusion and exclusion

However, it is suggested that the practice of adventure tourism creates specific geographies of marginalisation and exclusion in rural areas. At sites of adventurous activity it is usual to observe a placard which sets out an embodied ideal for the participants (Figure 11.5). However, as shown by Cater (2000), participation in adventure tourism is not restricted to the young, white males epitomised by the 'Pepsi-Max' advertisements. In fact participation is much

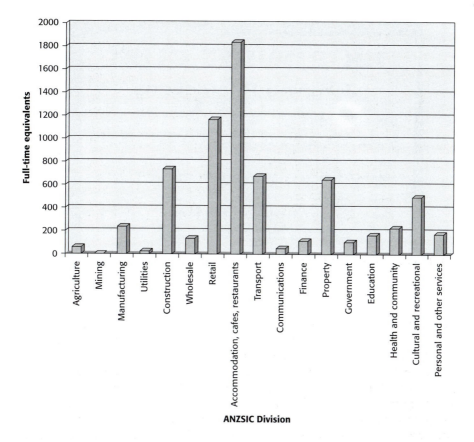

Figure 11.4 Queenstown employment structure.

broader than popular opinion seems to believe, with all ages, abilities and classes participating. Although there are clear masculinities to the promotion of adventure, the performance is just as popular with both sexes, and the average adrenaline seeker is just as likely to be Korean as Californian (Figure 11.6).

Nevertheless there are distinct exclusions as regards the types of country vision that are entertained within the Queenstown tourism product. In addition, the spaces of adventure in which the activities are actually performed are remarkably confined. Locations are carefully sited (and sighted) in order to maximise the potential for scenic backdrops, while maintaining just the right level of access (seemingly adventurous, but not inconvenient). Indeed less spectacular or inaccessible landscapes may be completely excluded because they do not conform to the ideals required by the adventure tourism industry.

Undoubtedly representations of the landscape associated with adventure tourism are dominated by those produced by the Pakeha (white) imaginary,

Figure 11.5   An ideal of embodied perfection for participation in adventure.

whereby the New Zealand landscape was seen as virgin territory. This land was one to be conquered and tamed, and brought within the rationalising gaze of the new settlers. Such a rationale clearly reinforces representations of adventure in Queenstown today. One is encouraged to jump off a bungee constructed along the route of a restored gold mining sluice pipeline; the gold *rush* might be physically different today, but it still contains such motifs as exploiting the rural environment for the fulfilment of personal gain. Aboriginal ways of natural interaction, with a more harmonious view of the environment are conspicuously absent.

クィーンズタウンラフティング

参加注意事項

QUEENSTOWN
RAFTING

皆様のラフティング体験が安全で、かつ素晴しい思い出になりますようぜひお読みください。

Figure 11.6   Global participation in adventure.

Representations of Queenstown

We have argued that the growth of adventure tourism is associated with the commodification of spectacular rural settings as activity sites for adventure activities. In Queenstown, the setting of adventure activities in rural environments has led to the production of what Cloke and Perkins (2002) term a 'designer rurality' where tourists can immerse themselves in nature in fashionable and exciting ways. From our own experience of Queenstown[5], the sheer accumulation of adventure activities in the town creates the feeling of a huge outdoor theme park. These sentiments are apparent in the promotional literature for the destination:

> Welcome to the world's adventure playground for grown-ups. Jetboating, bungy jumping, skiing, white water rafting, parapenting – you can try all of these and more in one place (Destination Queenstown 1998/99: 46).

> This amazing land of mountains, lakes, rivers and forests is home to some of the most accessible adventures on this planet. The region is the Nirvana of outdoor fun (Adventure Capital of the World Group 1998).

Rural spaces within the Queenstown area have therefore been appropriated and commodified into a kind of 'pay and play' attraction with white-knuckle rides set in spectacular surroundings. It is interesting to note that this is made possible by the Department of Conservation, who through a process of concessions allow adventure operations to be established on land set aside for conservation purposes. Since operators are required to operate in accordance with sustainable practices outlined by the Resource Management Act (1991), there is little visible detriment to the environment. However, it may be anticipated that pressure on rural spaces is likely to increase with growing competition for land and escalating tourist participation in these activities.

Although Queenstown is also promoted as a place of outstanding scenic beauty where tourists can partake in more passive tourism activities such as wine tasting and sightseeing, the promotion of adrenaline-inducing activities is so prevalent that the name Queenstown has become synonymous with this type of adventure experience, as Mark Frood of Destination Queenstown, the regional tourism board, suggests: 'There is one thing that can pretty much identify Queenstown and that's usually some shape or form of somebody leaping off a deck with a rubber band tied around their legs'.

Our research highlighted the role of local tourism operators in constructing place meanings both for Queenstown and for the activity sites at which they operated. These localised place meanings are constructed through the representational material for these activities and sustained through tourists' consumption of them. A key theme that emerged from our analysis of the production and representation of these sites is that of the interconnections between adventure and nature. Tourism operators trade on the spectacular rural settings to sell their adventure activities:

> It's more than a jetboat ride, it's a sense of affinity with New Zealand's great outdoors. Navigating deep into the alpine corridor of Mount Aspiring National Park aboard your purpose built Dart River Jetboat will be a new experience for most. The challenging grandeur of the mountains and valleys will leave a lasting impression (Dart River Jet brochure, Shotover Jet 1998a).

However, and in line with Cloke and Perkins, we argue that there is the suggestion that spectacular scenery can be made more so by 'participation in, or watching the participation of others in, adventurous places of natural or historic significance' (1998a: 201). The interweaving of history with nature emerges as a common theme in the representational text for adventure activities, for example Goldfields Jet invites tourists to: 'Experience the rush, Discover the History' (Goldfields Jet brochure, Shotover Jet 1998b).

In incorporating historical elements into the adventure tourism experience the gold-mining history of the area has been romanticised. Heroic accounts are presented to tourists glamorising the idea of 'man' pitting his wits against the forces of nature. Old places and histories are reimagined as adventurous places as tourists are invited to relive the dangers and thrills of a past era. In reproducing these old histories and weaving them into the construction of new adventure landscapes, nature has become imbued with specific connotations. We have already discussed how nature has been activated and re-energised by producers facilitating, and tourists demanding, active as opposed to solely passive ways of engaging with nature. We also argue that through this process nature has been injected with masculine metaphors that stem from 'the adventurous taming of the wilderness' (Cloke and Perkins 1998a: 186) and accompanying this are sexual connotations which derive from a conquest of nature.

Pritchard and Morgan argue that the language of tourism promotion privileges the male, heterosexual gaze. They explore how northern landscapes such as Canada are typically framed as male adventure playgrounds where nature is 'wild, untamed, and often harsh and even penetrative' (2000: 897). Although we recognise that tourism producers, in a bid to secure competitive advantage and tourist interest, construct anticipatory ideas of place and experience that appeal to a wide audience, we do believe that the themes and images used to promote some adventure activities are grounded in a masculinised geography of adventure. We have already suggested that past historical eras, particularly the gold-mining era, are incorporated in the selling of adventure. What is important is that these tales are predominantly focused on man's battle against the forces of nature. In promoting adventure activities these tales are used to enhance the experience of adventure, tourists are invited to relive the experience of a bygone era that is resplendent with masculine references, for example: 'Goldfields Jet takes you in close, to see, touch and feel the remnants of an age where men were men, and gold was king' (Goldfields Jet brochure).

These more explicit references to a masculinised discourse of adventure are supported by a plethora of inherently masculine metaphors demonstrating the conquering and taming of nature that are prevalent in advertising brochures for adventure activities, for example:

> Step across this great frontier and meet the *challenge* of rafting the Shotover River, experience the rugged beauty and unspoilt grandeur of the breathtaking scenery as you *conquer* this wild and untamed river (*our emphasis*, Challenge Rafting).

> Skippers Canyon Jet is the first and sole operator on this wild stretch of the upper Shotover. Jerry Hohneck has successfully *tamed* the mighty 'CANYON OF GOLD', with his help so will you (Crazy Kiwi Combo brochure).

Nature is therefore positioned as a challenge, which tourists are invited to pit their wits against and ultimately tame. In this sense, nature is imbued with feminine characteristics and adventure activities, in their invitation to 'tame' and 'master' nature, acquire sexual connotations. There are also more suggestive ways in which the adventurous experience of nature is likened to sex. For example, Figure 11.7 shows an advertisement for Shotover Jet taken from a

Figure 11.7   Sexually suggestive advertising for a jetboat ride.

Kiwi Experience[6] brochure for New Zealand. The advertisement appeals to the 18–30 backpackers who are the typical Kiwi Experience customers, by using a double entendre, blending colloquial sexual language (Don't Come in the Canyons) with an invitation to experience adventure.

The representational material for Queenstown and for localised adventure activities is therefore implicated in conveying particular ideas about nature and the experience of natural surroundings. While we have argued that these are grounded in a masculine geography of adventure, we are not suggesting that adventure tourism is predominantly undertaken by men, or consumed by men and women in such a way that equates with the readings we have offered of the representational text. In the end how these new rural spaces are interpreted and enacted is dependent both on the anticipation of adventure and the actual performance of it.

Performing adventure

The performance of adventure is an integral part of the experience, and it is perhaps this that is most influential in the new rural character of Queenstown. Although probably less than a third of the visitors to Queenstown will actively participate in an adventurous activity (Berno *et al.* 1996), it is suggested that almost all will spectate, and thus form part of the experience. For example most of the coach tours make a point of stopping at the Kawarau bungee jump on their route into the region, and the provision of large purpose-built spectator platforms provide for this. This performance is not confined to the geographical boundaries of Queenstown either, as the experience is available in a number of 'take away' media formats through which the consumption of performance can be continued. An account of an individual's first bungee jump reveals the importance of the video as a souvenir:

> The video has captured a moment of pure open-mouthed terror. But from the perspective of my safe little flat in London, it is the screams of pure admiration from the onlookers that now gives me the biggest thrill (*Daily Telegraph*, 12 January 1998: 24).

Performing various roles in public space are the dominant way that individuals make sense of their worlds and especially of their own bodies. As Denzin suggests, 'performance is interpretation . . . a performance is a public act, a way of knowing, and a form of embodied interpretation' (1997: 97). Futhermore, these embodied performances shape and are shaped by the spaces that they inhabit:

> The body is entangled with fantasy and discourse; fantasy mobilizes bodies and is expressed through discourse; and discourse, well, discourse is disrupted by

fantasy and interrupted by the body. And all of these relations are articulated spatially; their performance articulates space (Rose 1999: 258).

A frequent comment in interviewing is the desire to achieve the perfect form, particularly where the activity is captured on film or camera. In bungee jumping this may be a perfect dive (Figure 11.1), in other activities the look of confidence and domination in the frame. The look is one of harmonic conquest of the environment, embodying the adventurous ethic itself. As Schiebe states 'The *right stuff* as a concept is bound up with vertigo and transcendence in the escape from earth's bondage. If you have the right stuff you are in harmony with the sublime' (1986: 142). Respondents are undeniably aware of the desire to bring this expression of having the 'right stuff' into their performances:

> Absolutely totally focused to get it right, I wanna go and see it, look at my style. I wanted that good spread thing going, nice little y-shaped descent and that.
>
> Gareth, Pipeline Bungy

> I was trying to act quite cool about it. I must have done, because the bloke said to me 'you're not scared are you?' and I lied and said 'nah', and he said say goodbye to your mates and I said 'see you later lads' on the video, and then when I jump off the bridge I wink at the camera, sound stuff. To be honest, if other people are scared it makes me feel a bit better, cause they are so . . . like her and her mate were really really scared, so that made me feel a bit more in control. If I was the only one who was scared I would have felt pretty fucking panicky. Just before I jumped though, there was a point where I thought this is a little bit stupid, paying to jump off a bridge. When you get up there you have a sudden realisation that you have paid to jump off a bridge and everyone is watching you do it, so you are resigned to the fact, but you do think it is pretty silly!
>
> Anthony, Pipeline Bungy

However, in this recognition of performing bodies it is important not to construct them as somehow passive. Indeed, 'bodies have an undeniable material existence' and as Grosz has argued 'what is mapped onto the body is not unaffected by the body onto which it is projected' (1990: 72). Perform*ing* subjects are 'not just a body being acted upon, but a fractured/multiple agent which is possibly contradictory but always actualising and deforming structural codes; hence elaborating a performance supported by social rituals and exchanges which confirm different personae' (Shields 1991: 269). On the contrary, as Cloke and Perkins point out, 'adventure tourism is fundamentally about active recreational participation, and it demands new metaphors based more on "being, doing, touching *and* seeing" rather than just "seeing"' (1998a: 189).

Tied into these conceptions of looking good are notions of 'looking the part', the classic adventurer. It is clear that in the performance of adventure there is often the requirement to feel that the participant is wearing suitable attire for the experience. Thus the donning of specific *costumes*, or in some case the removal of more 'ordinary' ones, as in the relatively common practice of bungee jumping naked or just in underwear, is a clearly performative aspect of the practice.

> The lifejackets are really just for the photos, I mean yes they would make you float if you did fall out of the boat, but we don't let people fall out of the boat. So the lifejacket is part of the . . . its part of the experience you know.
>
> Nick Flight, Marketing Manager, Shotover Jet

It is clear that the donning of costumes is as much about stripping, meta-phorically, as it is about the wearing, since adventure is about reclaiming a more suspended, liminal identity. Clearly 'the performances characteristic of liminal phases and states often are more about the doffing of masks, the strip-ping of statuses, the renunciation of roles, the demolishing of structures, than their keeping and putting on' (Turner 1986: 107). The fleeting nature of these costumes also bears identification, since these are characteristic of the quick-fix activities under examination, and this corresponds to many other performative genres. As Shields (1991: 269) contends, the 'wearing of different hats' is cen-tral to the articulation of the agency of the body.

It is important to recognise that Queenstown itself performs as is expected of it, and continues to espouse the ideals of adventure 24 hours a day. Nowhere is this as self-evident as in the *après*-adventure establishments of the bars and night-clubs. Even the names seem to confirm an adventurous ethic, with titles such as 'The Edge', 'The World' and 'Surreal'. By their very nature they become places in which triumphant adventurers retire to in order to celebrate the suc-cessful completion of an activity, and in some senses continue the adventure. There may be strong advertising, in the manner in which the dancefloor of one club is emblazoned with the logo of the Pipeline bungee jump. Another nightclub, 'The World' has a central atrium, down which willing partygoers can perform a mini-bungee jump on a special night once a month, organised by the bungee companies.

The place of a rural setting

One of the most interesting observations of our research has been the import-ance of scenery in the practice of adventure. While clearly providing a ready-made environment for the practice of adventure (whitewater rivers, deep canyons, mountains, etc.), it has been hypothesised that a ruggedly beautiful setting is crucial to the attractions of the adventure itself. However, the research in fact points to a far more complicated relationship than this. Participants certainly respond positively when asked about the environment in which the activity is performed with phrases such as 'it's beautiful' or 'it's gorgeous', and are quick to point out the attractions of undertaking in a rural setting:

> Nobody would do this up a river with condos down the side of it, you have got to do it in a natural setting.
>
> Charles, Shotover Jet

However, respondents seem less sure about the actual impact landscape has on the activity itself:

> Its nice, nice scenery, but half the time you don't notice do you?
>
> Scott, River Surfing

> Ah yeah, things like that, beauty, all that, it depends on who you get on the day. I think that's a really small group of people who are interested in that, a lot of people who come, you could put this place in a dump, they wouldn't care you know. It's a big bridge and they are going to jump off it you know?
>
> Stu, Kawarau Bungy

It would appear, then, that landscape aesthetics are important to the practice of adventure, but their relation is peculiar. During the practice of the adventure activity itself, concerns with aesthetics are removed almost entirely. As such it is almost like these attributes are a prerequisite for adventure, but go no further than this, the conditions of a beautiful setting are fulfilled, the box is checked, and the activity can proceed.

These views would concur with the claims made by Hall (1992: 144), that in the practice of adventure tourism the environmental setting takes on a subordinate role. While this setting forms an important backdrop for the practice of the activity, it is the performance of the activity that remains the primary attraction. Perhaps such an acknowledgement is not so surprising if we consider the *place* of the natural setting within the performance of adventure. As highlighted earlier, a significant part of the adventure ethic, at least in historical terms, was the domination of landscape. Paradoxically then, to overstate the importance of nature to the experience would negate the passive role that this conquest demands.

However, the founder of one of Queenstown's main bungee jumps suggests that while the scenic location of adventure activities may have minor importance in the actual practice, it does have a vital role in the memory of that practice:

> I think that a lot of the people who come here to bungy and it's their first jump, they are so focused on that, that they don't actually think about where they are going or what they are going to experience along the way. But when they think back, they have the whole scenery thing, its all value-added stuff.
>
> Andrew Brindsley, Founder, Pipeline Bungy

This sentiment is clearly echoed by the participants, and this is of course far more acceptable to our adventurers, because nature in memory or on a videotape is bounded and commodified:

I mean they have got bungy jumps back in England, but they are off cranes and that, it isn't the same thing is it? You want videos with like the scenery like this.

Shaun, Kawarau Bungy

New rural spaces?

Through this discussion it should be clear that consumption of the countryside in terms of adventurous activity has profound impacts for the understanding of society's relationship with the natural environment. The emergence of adventurous places, where nature takes on characteristics to be tamed and conquered, with the implicit gendering of the landscape in addition to the exclusion of certain 'other' representations of nature is evident. Using Queenstown as an example, we have shown how commodification of the adventure experience has had a major role in establishing the resort and its hinterland as a place synonymous with adventure. The manner in which the hosts, the tourists and the town itself perform to commodified roles is undeniably part of the experience. Tourism to Queenstown is not a new phenomenon, but its character has been changed and supplemented by the growth of adventure tourism. In an average year, over 50,000 tourists do a bungee jump at one of four AJ Hackett sites, a further 15,000 jump at Pipeline, 30,000 go whitewater rafting and over 160,000 do a jetboat ride. These are merely the most popular activities, which are supplemented by a plethora of ancillary pursuits such as river surfing, canyoning, off-road biking, parasailing, paragliding and parachuting. As a result Queenstown represents a rural location that receives over ten times the resident population each year in visitors who will partake in some form of mediated adventurous experience within the locale. It is for this reason then that the town itself is dominated by booking agents, shops, bars and restaurants that extol this adventurousness.

However, to see such destinations solely as a site of commodified adventure would be wrong. As Cloke and Perkins suggested, 'commodification is *one* of a number of processes at play in the creation of place that must be investigated in specific time–space locations at the intersection of the global and the local' (2002: 17). It should be apparent from the discussion that in addition to a mediated interaction with nature, we must also seek to acknowledge the fact that adventure tourism also allows for a deeply embodied individual experience. Perhaps the most valuable conclusion to be drawn from a dynamic conceptualisation of human–environment relationships through adventure tourism is that it does offer new ways of accessing nature within and without us. As Bhatti and Church suggest, 'alongside utilitarian views of nature promoted by capitalist priorities and consumerism there are alternative meanings based on highly personalised re-connections to nature' (2001: 570). It is at the personal level that these experiences are most profound, as is clear from the voices that speak through the chapter. Furthermore these reconnections have the potential to challenge dominant views of the countryside and engage with active embodiment:

> Indeed, the fact that the countryside exists as a contested zone, available to multiple experiences, interpretations, and behaviours, ensures that the potential exists to transgress given, dominant meanings concerning 'what the countryside is', and how one should lawfully and morally behave in it. And, in contesting the construction of one's body as a passive receiving, compliant receptacle lies the potential for free, new and less restricted forms of pleasure in the countryside (Macnaghten and Urry 1993: 268).

Such a phenomenon has, in part, been demonstrated by the complex relationship that the natural setting has to the performance of adventure. Despite this, it is important to give due acknowledgement to the role of nature as a key external actor in adventure. This is emphasised by the examination of accidents in the adventure tourism industry, many of which were caused by extreme weather conditions, although human errors were usually also involved. Indeed, there have been recent concerns over the large influence that the adventure travel industry has over the New Zealand tourism industry as a whole. Although the industry has clearly helped New Zealand inbound tourism to step up a gear, it has a less than perfect record. Accidents such as that in late 1999 when a Japanese honeymooner was killed on the Shotover Jetboat ride, are far from rare. In an 18 month period in the early 1990s no fewer than five tourists were killed in a spate of whitewater rafting accidents. An element of perceived risk is undeniably a fundamental attraction of adventure tourism, but it is still the responsibility of operators to reduce actual risk to an absolute minimum. Tighter regulation is now a reality because of a perhaps too lax attitude in the early 1990s, which should guarantee the long-term sustainability of the adventure travel industry.

In terms of impacts on the greater region as a whole, and indeed the country, it is likely that Queenstown's pre-eminence for adventure tourism has altered the character of many rural New Zealand locations. Many have understandably tried to copy the success of Queenstown by establishing their own adventure products. This may be directly as in Wanaka, a similar resort the other side of the mountain chain to Queenstown, or with more indigenous forms, such as those based in the caves around Waitomo in North Island. It is undeniable, however, that all of these have had considerable impacts in the place-nature of these settlements. Cloke and Perkins (1998b) highlight the example of Hamner Springs, a thermal resort close to Christchurch. The singular presence of an old bridge and a deeply incised river led to the commercial development of a bungee jump, jetboating, rafting and helicopter operations, and its rebranding as 'Thrillseekers Canyon'. Thus the identity and meaning of the place are re-energised and new place meanings are generated by the introduction of adventure tourism. It is for this reason that adventurous representations of the countryside are so influential in emergent country visions.

Notes

1. Sky TV's *Fear Factor* is dedicated to glamorising the rewards associated with an adventurous lifestyle.
2. For example Alex Garland's *The Beach*, and any of Bill Bryson's hilarious tales of adventurous travel.
3. Blockbusters such as *Point Break* starring Keanu Reeves which centres on a surfing subculture, and *Vertical Limit*, starring Chris O'Donnell, which dramatises mountain climbing are excellent examples of how adventure has been glamorised and popularised.
4. Cloke and Perkins (1998a) suggest that soft adventurers are newcomers to adventure activities who want to experience some low-risk activity but also have the comforts of home. Hard adventurers are willing to travel to remote and difficult to reach areas to pursue high-risk activities.
5. Both authors spent six months conducting research on adventure tourism in Queenstown.
6. The Kiwi Experience operates a coach network around New Zealand. It is typically used by 18–30-year-old backpackers and in New Zealand has acquired a reputation as somewhat of an Ibiza experience.

References

Adler, J. 1989 'Origins of sightseeing', *Annals of Tourism Research*, 16, 7–29.
Adventure Capital Of the World Group 1998 *Queenstown: Adventure Capital of the World*. Promotional Brochure.
Bell, C. and Lyall, J. 1998 'The accelerated sublime: thrill-seeking adventure heroes in the commodified landscape', paper presented at conference on 'Practising Places and Tourist Performance', University of Durham, April 1998
Berno, T., Moore, K., Simmons, D. and Hart, V. 1996 'The nature of the adventure experience in Queenstown', *Australian Leisure*, 8(1), 21–5.
Bhatti, M. and Church, A. 2001 'Cultivating nature: homes and gardens in late modernity', *Sociology*, 35(2), 365–83.
Cater, C. 2000 'Can I play too: inclusion and exclusion in adventure tourism', *North West Geographer*, third series, 3(2), 50–60.
Cheyne, J. and Ryan, C. 1996 'The Resource Management Act, a bungy operation and problems of planning', pp. 17–28 in M. Oppermann (ed.), *Proceedings of Pacific Rim Tourism 2000*, Centre for Tourism Studies, Waiariki Polytechnic.
Cloke, P. and Perkins, H.C. 1998a 'Cracking the canyon with the awesome foursome: representations of adventure tourism in New Zealand', *Environment and Planning D: Society and Space*, 16, 185–218.
Cloke, P. and Perkins, H.C. 1998b '"Pushing the limits": place promotion and adventure tourism in the South Island of New Zealand', pp. 271–87 in H.C. Perkins and G. Cushman (eds), *Time Out; Leisure Recreation and Tourism in New Zealand and Australia*, Longman, Auckland.

Cloke, P. and Perkins, H.C. 2002 'Commodification and adventure in New Zealand tourism', *Current Issues in Tourism* (forthcoming).

Daily Telegraph 1998 Throwing caution – and myself – to the wind, *Weekend Telegraph* 12 January, 24.

Denzin, N.K. 1997 *Interpretive Ethnography: Ethnographic Practices for the 21st century*, Sage, London.

Desforges, L. 1998 'Checking out the planet: global representations/local identities and youth travel', pp. 175–94 in G. Valentine and T. Skelton (eds), *Cool Places: Geographies of Youth Cultures*, Routledge, London.

Desforges, L. 1999 'Travel and tourism', pp. 296–304 in P. Cloke, P. Crang and M. Goodwin (eds), *Introducing Human Geographies*, Arnold, London.

Destination Queenstown 1998/99 *Holiday Planner*, Promotional Brochure.

Goss, J.D. 1993 'Placing the market and marketing the place: tourist advertising of the Hawaiian islands 1972–1992', *Society and Space*, **11**, 663–88.

Grosz, E. 1990 'A note on essentialism and difference', in S. Gunew (ed.), *Feminist Knowledge: Critique and Construct*, Routledge, London.

Hall, C.M. 1992 'Adventure, sport and health tourism', pp. 141–58 in B. Weiler and C.M. Hall (eds), *Special Interest Tourism*, Belhaven, London.

Independent on Sunday 1997 14 September, 3.

Johnston, B.R. and Edwards, T. 1994 'The commodification of mountaineering', *Annals of Tourism Research*, **21**, 459–77.

Kearsley, G. 1997 'Tourism planning and policy in New Zealand', pp. 49–60 in C.M. Hall, J. Jenkins and G. Kearsley (eds), *Tourism Planning and Policy in Australia and New Zealand: Cases, Issues and Practice*, McGraw-Hill, Sydney.

Krippendorf, D. 1987 *The Holiday Makers*, Heinmann, London.

MacCannell, D. 1976 *The Tourist*, Macmillan, London.

MacCannell, D. 1992 *Empty Meeting Grounds: The Tourist Papers*, Routledge, London.

Macnaghten, P. and Urry, J. 1993 'Constructing the countryside and the passive body', pp. 89–106 in C. Brackenridge (ed.), *Body Matters: Leisure Images and Lifestyles*, Leisure Studies Association Publication 47, LSA, Brighton.

Mannell, R. and Iso-Ahola, S.E. 1987 'Psychological nature of leisure and tourism experience', *Annals of Tourism Research*, **14**, 314–31.

May, J. 1996 'In search of authenticity off and *on* the beaten track', *Environment and Planning D: Society and Space*, **14**, 709–36.

Moeran, B. 1983 'The language of Japanese tourism', *Annals of Tourism Research*, **10**, 93–108.

Pritchard, A. and Morgan, N. 2000 'Privileging the male gaze: gendered tourism landscapes', *Annals of Tourism Research*, **27**(4), 884–905.

Ritzer, G. and Liska, A. 1997 '"McDisneyization" and "Post-Tourism": complementary perspectives on contemporary tourism', pp. 96–112 in C. Rojek and J. Urry (eds), *Touring Cultures: Transformations of Travel and Theory*, Routledge, London.

Rose, G. 1999 'Performing space', pp. 247–59 in D. Massey, J. Allen and P. Sarre (eds), *Human Geography Today*, Polity, Cambridge.

Schiebe, K. 1986 'Self narratives and adventure', pp. 129–51 in T. Sarbin (ed.), *Narrative Psychology: The Storied Nature of Human Conduct*, Praeger, New York.

Shaw, G. and Williams, A. 1994 *Critical Issues in Tourism*, Blackwell, Oxford.

Shields, R. 1991 *Places on the Margin: Alternative Geographies of Modernity*, Routledge, London.

Shotover Jet 1998a *Dart River Jet*, Promotional Brochure, Shotover Jet, Queenstown.

Shotover Jet 1998b *Goldfields Jet*, Promotional Brochure, Shotover Jet, Queenstown.

Sinclair, W. 1914 *Guide to the Wondrous Wakatipu, 'The Lake that Breathes': An Incomparable Holiday Resort in Picturesque Otago, New Zealand*, Dunedin, Dunedin Expansion League, Dunedin, New Zealand.

Squire, S. 1994 'Accounting for cultural meanings: the interface between geography and tourism studies re-examined', *Progress in Human Geography*, **18**(1), 1–16.

Thrift, N.J. 1999 'Steps to an ecology of place', pp. 295–322 in D. Massey, J. Allen and P. Sarre (eds), *Human Geography Today*, Polity, Cambridge.

Turner, V. 1986 *The Anthropology of Performance*, PAJ Publications, New York.

Urry, J. 1990 *The Tourist Gaze*, Sage, London.

Urry, J. 1995 *Consuming Places*, Routledge, London.

Urry, J. 1999 'Sensing leisure spaces', pp. 34–45 in D. Crouch (ed.), *Leisure/Tourism Geographies; Practices and Geographical Knowledge*, Routledge, London.

Veijola, S. and Jokinen, E. 1994 'The body in tourism', *Theory, Culture and Society*, **11**, 125–51.

Vester, H.G. 1987 'Adventure as a form of leisure', *Leisure Studies*, **6**, 237–49.

Wang, N. 1999 'Rethinking authenticity in tourism experience', *Annals of Tourism Research*, **26**(2), 349–70.

Weiler, B. and Hall, C.M. (eds) 1992 *Special Interest Tourism*, Belhaven, London.

Wilson, A. 1992 *The Culture of Nature*, Blackwell, Oxford.

Psychogeographies of rural space and practices of exclusion

CHAPTER 12

David Sibley

Introduction

In the 1912–1913 issue of the *Journal of the Gypsy Lore Society*, Eric Otto Winstedt describes the movements of a group of Russian *Kalderas* Gypsies through the British Isles during a two year period from 1911 to 1913. 'The first arrivals were Nikola Tsoron, with his sons Nikola and Janko, his married daughters Rupunka and Sophie, their husbands Parvolo Tsoron and Adam Kirpats; his brother Andreas, Worko Kokoiesko and some of [his] relatives, eight families in all, comprising some forty persons'. They had travelled from Marseille to Liverpool by train in May 1911 and first camped in the city on land next to an abbatoir. They subsequently moved across the Mersey to a 'patch of coal dust and cinders' next to a railway line in Green Lane, Tranmere, while some new arrivals found shelter in a drill hall in Birkenhead. In July, one couple with a sick child made a pilgrimage to the shrine of the black madonna of Czestochowa in Poland but returned to Birkenhead about a month later. The group, now about one hundred persons, then began to disperse, seven families moving to Dublin and others to London. In London, some families camped in yards, close to Battersea Park and in Wandsworth, where they were photographed by Fred Shaw (Fraser 1992: 232–3); some rented houses and others camped in a field at Miller's Farm, Beddington Corner, Mitcham. In November 1911, the group camped at Beddington Corner split up. One family travelled to Spain and then to Hungary. Some of the remaining families travelled to Glasgow to be near to relations who had moved to a rural site at Kelvinhaugh, some to Dundee and Aberdeen, and one family to Leek in Staffordshire and to Leeds where they lived in small houses near the centre of the city. Some of this group subsequently moved to Broughton Lane, Salford, before travelling to France and Spain. Others moved to Nottingham, where they were joined by relatives who had arrived from France, and then to Bolton. These internal movements, prompted primarily by the prospects of work but also by family ties and tensions between families, were complemented by international migrations by members of the kin-group during these two years, including journeys from England to Montevideo, Madeira and Montreal. These migrations were probably similarly motivated.

This nomadic narrative suggests an indifference to place but, at the same time, a sensitivity to locale. Essentially pragmatic, these Roma families were looking for land or shelter where the rent was affordable, where they could do business with the locals, and where they would not encounter too many problems with the authorities, particularly the 'sanitary' authorities. They were evidently indifferent, however, to rural or urban stopping places, fields, yards or houses, England or Uruguay. All these sites and places were connected through their complex pattern of movement. As Tim Cresswell (1997) has argued, with reference to De Certeau, the tactics of the nomad stand in contrast to the strategic ordering of space associated with rational governance. For those who try to maintain order, but never quite succeed, movement often registers as transgression, signalling anxiety on the part of the local and national state whose visions of a good society require things to be kept in place. For the nomads described by Winstedt, however, there is no interest in the ways they are classified by others or in where they are deemed to belong. If things did not work out in one place (itself often a reflection of their out-of-placeness, as determined by the local state) they would move somewhere else. For them, stability, order and continuity reside in the family, the kin group and in the re-enactment of the present, not in space or place[1].

In this chapter, I want to explore some of the recent tensions between mobile, 'othered' groups, like the Roma described by Winstedt, and those who hold to a static, bounded view of the English and Welsh countryside, working with the ideas suggested by this introductory vignette. Rural politics are very much influenced by strategic essentialisms, both in regard to people, or cultures, and space and I think that it is important to ask where these ideas come from and how they impact on groups who are seen to interrupt the perceived continuities and stabilities of rural space. In a rural context, some but not all forms of movement have been represented as problematic. The troublesome forms of movement are problematic because they conflict with a conception of rural space as bounded and as possessing exclusive social and cultural qualities. This is clearly indicated in the propaganda of lobby groups for the countryside, particularly the Countryside Alliance (active in England, Wales and Scotland), whose exclusive representation of rural space is described through a discourse of ownership. This discourse suggests a privileged knowledge of the rural economy and society which allows it to judge who are appropriate members of its imagined 'rural community'. Racialised difference, for example, whether represented by Gypsies, asylum seekers or people of South Asian or African Caribbean origin, may be seen as disturbing and discrepant. The issue, from the point of view of those 'defending' the countryside, is essentially a spatial one – it involves resisting what is represented as movement, but only certain kinds of movement, from cities into the countryside, cities being seen as the source of unwanted and alarming difference.

It might be objected that defensive arguments voiced by a small minority of the country's population are nothing to be concerned about. Jock Young (1999: 24) for example, has suggested that:

> David Sibley . . . makes, I believe, the error of believing the rhetoric of the time for the reality. It is easy to mistake the siren voices of basic values for current melody, but they are singing songs that have long been out of fashion, they celebrate a world which will never return, their very insistence is because of incipient failure, they are signs of a world being lost rather than hegemony triumphant.

I would suggest that Young's progressive view is unduly optimistic. In the United Kingdom, centrist and centre-right governments have pandered to the 'siren voices' of the rural lobby in order to demonstrate their conservative credentials and their opposition to any leftwing or anarchist minority that threatens the status quo. This has translated into legislation such as the 1994 Criminal Justice and Public Order Act (effective in England and Wales) which circumscribes the actions of protesters and people who wish to contribute to the creation of a culturally more diverse countryside. This Act effectively reinforced the boundary between the 'rural' and the 'urban' (Sibley 1997). Passed by a Conservative administration, the legislation has not been repealed or amended by the present Labour government, an administration that has also backed away from its promise to ban fox-hunting (an activity cherished by the Countryside Alliance). Rhetoric is important when it resonates with the sentiments of powerful figures in a regime with authoritarian tendencies and, in order to understand conflicting representations of the rural, we need to try to understand this rhetoric. The rhetoric, in effect, produces threatening others who may then become targets for legislation. It also conjures up geographies that reflect deep-seated anxieties about change and social mixing, what I would call 'psychogeographies' because they are products of the unconscious at the same time that they are realised by social and cultural processes. These psychogeographies surface at particular times, when people feel threatened, and, I would argue, they are expressions of more general tendency, described by psychoanalysts in terms of 'primitive' anxieties, that is, anxieties experienced in infancy but never erased in the process of growing up and becoming social beings. Before attempting to demonstrate how psychogeographies are manifest as aspects of social practice and in the production of exclusionary space, I will discuss some of the key arguments of object relations theorists. These are post-Freudian psychoanalysts whose focus is primarily on relations between mother and infant in the first year of life (Kahane 1992). Recently, however, their ideas have provided the basis of social theories (e.g. Young 1994) and, I would argue, they also offer considerable possibilities for deepening our understanding of spatial processes.

Splitting, psychotic anxieties and spatial defences

To begin to understand the tensions that underly the production of exclusion-ary geographies, it may be useful to start with the simple idea of 'splitting'. Splitting is a term used in psychoanalysis to describe the tendency not to recogn-ise the connectedness of objects or, as Segal (1992: 34) defines it: 'an action undertaken in phantasy (in the unconscious) which can be used to separate things which belong together'. This is not necessarily a bad thing. For example, as Segal (1992: 33) comments, 'a phantasy of a nipple which is loving, feeding, creative and good at first needs to be kept quite distinct from phantasies of a nipple which is biting, hurtful and terrifying. Without this splitting, the baby may not be able to distinguish fully between love and cruelty and to feed trust-ingly'. When splitting is carried through into adult life, however, it can be harmful as it distorts interpersonal relations and social relations. As Steiner (1987: 69–70) has argued:

> anxieties of a primitive nature threaten the immature ego and lead to a mobilisa-tion of primitive defences. Splitting, idealisation and projective identification operate to create rudimentary structures made up of idealised good objects kept far apart from the persecutory bad ones. The individual's impulses are similarly split and he (sic) directs all his love towards the good object and all his hatred against the bad one.

The anxieties that the individual is trying to cope with through the idealisation and simplification of object relations include anxieties about chaos and dis-order. These could be included in the category of 'psychotic anxieties', to use Melanie Klein's terminology, and Young (2002) has argued that 'much of what happens in individuals and groups is a result of defences *against* psy-chotic anxieties, so that we do not to have to endure them consciously'. Some psychoanalysts, particularly Lawrence (2002), have used the idea of defence against psychotic anxieties in the analysis of organisations, like firms and public institutions. Lawrence argues that elements of structure, like hierarchies and boundaries, should be seen as a defence against environmental uncertainty (disorder, chaos): 'So there is pressure on managers of institutions to bring into being organisational forms and structures which offer themselves and other role holders a feeling of certainty which in fantasy [conscious imagining] will withstand the environmental uncertainty and banish the psychotic anxieties. In this social arrangement the majority of role holders mutually collude'. Young (2002) suggests that our defences against psychotic anxieties 'act as a powerful break on institutional and social change toward less rigid and more gener-ous social relations between individuals and groups. They diminish mental space . . .'.

Another way of coping, one more hopeful in terms of social relations, is also suggested by Klein. The tendency to simplify and idealise is finally described by her as a characteristic of the paranoid–schizoid *position* which has as its opposite the depressive position. In the depressive position 'conflicts between different parts of the self are no longer solved by splitting and pushing those parts into others, including the good object itself, but by holding them within the self' (Segal 1992: 38). The anxiety now is for the well-being of the object (e.g. the breast or the mother) which, in the paranoid–schizoid position had been split off. According to Lawrence (2002) this could be described as an important developmental advance in that 'it allows for objects in the environment to be recognised as whole objects, containing both good and bad aspects . . . [it is a] position of integration, of responsibility for conflicting emotions and parts of the individual in relation to objects, i.e. *whatever constitutes the Other*' (my emphasis). Individuals may shift between these two positions but, in projecting these ideas on the social plane and using them to understand the behaviour of collectivities, it is possible to see how a group may become fixed in, say, the paranoid–schizoid position through processes of structuration. For example, attitudes, beliefs and anxieties may be reinforced by institutional rules or by laws. As Lawrence puts it 'there is a "rational madness" which suffuses the social configurations which human beings co-construct collectively'. Possibly, this reading of Klein provides another route to understanding what Foucault and, using slightly different vocabulary, Stanley Cohen have described as a carceral society, one that uses both inclusive and exclusive modes of social control in the process of containing and marginalising 'the bad'.

Psychoanalysts increasingly use Kleinian terms, developed in her studies of infant–mother relationships, to describe other states. Kathleen Kelley-Lainé[2], for example, talks of a split-off, lost childhood in describing the experience of exile as a child, changing language as well as country and John Clare[3] has described psychoanalysis itself as 'another country', split off from other discourses; also as an escape but one which helps the analysand to get over an escape. These spatial metaphors, I would argue, can be applied equally to spatial imaginings associated with the social geographies of the countryside, representations that, among other things, signal anxieties about things coming together and things staying apart.

Defending rural space

To illustrate the insistence on separateness associated with the paranoid–schizoid position, we might consider recent statements by the Countryside Alliance which suggest that *their* countryside is split-off from other spaces, particularly cities, the latter being inhabited by people who misunderstand 'rural culture' and who need educating about country life. There is a frequent failure in their propaganda to make connections between the country and the city and a tendency to impose on rural space a false, purified identity. For example, the actor Jeremy Irons, who supports the Countryside Alliance, has suggested that

> [the countryside] is, in modern parlance a balanced ecosystem and our presence here today [at a Countryside Alliance rally in London] is like being a signal. A signal not to meddle for politically correct reasons with that balance. A signal that the voice of rural England will be heard. A signal to leave the countryside alone (www.countryside-alliance.org.uk).

There are frequent references in the literature of the Alliance to 'the way of life of country people' and to the ownership of the countryside by its members. This countryside is even given agency by the chief executive of the Alliance who urges members to 'Listen to *your* countryside' (www.epolitix.com) – my emphasis.

There is a clear implication in the positions taken by the Countryside Alliance that the countryside has to be defended against the politically correct and others who are split-off as bad objects. However, the message is not entirely unambiguous. In a play on a Pepsi advertisement which describes its product as 'Lipsmackingthirstquenching', the Alliance has used the line: 'Bureaucratisedpasteurisedshrinkwrappednannifiedsanitisedhomogenisedsterilisedfreezedried . . . Countryside? It's not too late to act' (www.mediaguardian.co.uk). The suggestion is that the countryside of the Alliance is heterogeneous and it is the state which threatens to impose order and create a homogeneous space, for example, by banning fox-hunting. Also, the Alliance's director of communications, Nigel Henson, has claimed that 'Our march [in London] is not about playing up any divide between town and country but trying to bridge it' (www.mediaguardian.co.uk). The latter quote is in reference to their strategy of advertising their cause in cities but, as with the assertion that the diversity of rural life is imperilled by the state, it does nothing to alter the view that the countryside has a definable *genre de vie* which clearly separates it from the city and metropolitan centres of power. The Alliance might be seen as reactionary, fighting past battles and, if we accept Jock Young's critique, an inconsequential movement, but there is clear evidence that the Alliance's paranoid–schizoid position is echoed in governments' attempts to appease some of the rural population by regulating those who disturb this vision of a sanctified space.

Boundaries and boundary crossings

The bourgeoisie have for a long time signalled their anxieties about movements into *their* rural space by others who bring with them elements of disorder. The familiar coupling of disorder and dirt has been used in connection with the recreational trips of the urban working class into the countryside in the

1920s and 1930s, for example, (Matless 1998) and, in the nineteenth century, the same images were used to denigrate Gypsies travelling in rural England (Mayall 1988). The latter is particularly interesting because modern, negative, reactions to Travellers often include the romantic observation that they formerly blended into the rural scene. This kind of displacement (placing a group in the past) is a common form of distantiation. These responses to Others in the countryside clearly required a vision of order and harmony produced by the work and stewardship of landowners and farmers and the erasure from rural social space of anything discrepant, like the shanty towns occupied by the migrant workers who built the railways, or plotland settlements in the 1920s. The order of this sanitised and clearly bounded space was reinforced by recurrent moral panics which drew a clear boundary between those who belonged and those who did not and the contrasting landscapes of belonging and harmony, and disorder and despoliation. It also required a denial of significant social inequality or the romanticisation of poverty, the rural poor being part of a natural order rather than members of the exploited working class.

This simplified view of the rural is increasingly difficult to sustain. Counter-urbanisation, new rural industries, garden centres, scrap car dumps and pick-your-own strawberry farms make such singular spatial categorisations quite problematic. The British state's role in this regard has been ambiguous. On one hand, it has allowed developments in rural areas which do not fit Jeremy Irons's holistic vision of the countryside, including developments at military installations, such as Faslane and Fylingdales, and asylum seeker detention centres, as well as residential developments for middle class urban commuters. On the other, it has attempted through legislation to secure the countryside for 'the rural community'. It is the latter concern with the integrity of an imagined rural community that betrays the state's anxieties about mobile minorities who may contribute to social tensions and weaken the political allegiance of landed interests and the rural middle class to the government.

Exclusionary practice

Crouch and Marquand (1989: viii) have argued that the control of transgressive others has long been a concern of 'the political class' in Britain, a term that encompasses both rightwing and centrist administrations. The clearest demonstration of this in the recent past was the spatial strategy that framed the public order section of the 1994 Criminal Justice and Public Order Act (Sibley 1997) but earlier legislation has also been used to the same effect. In his speech in the House of Commons introducing the 1994 legislation the then Home Secretary, Michael Howard, talked of the *fear* of mass invasions itself as a justification for controlling movement into the countryside and the Act instituted quite stringent spatial controls which could be employed to police the 'rural–urban boundary'. These measures were directed at Travellers, 'disruptive trespassers' (a category which would include hunt saboteurs and environmental protesters) and people on their way to raves.

While the anxieties of the 'political class' are transparent in the wording of the legislation, the practical consequences, in terms of excluding mobile others from the countryside, are difficult to assess. Most police forces have more to do than control movements into the countryside and the judiciary, in some instances, has been critical of the Criminal Justice and Public Order Act. The legislation has been used to control and exclude, however. A recent example of a punitive use of the Act was the banning of the Horsmonden Horse Fair, a traditional Gypsy gathering in Kent, in 2000. The powers under Section 47 to designate a five-mile exclusion zone, in this case with the help of road blocks and armed police units, were used to enforce the ban (*Travellers' Times* 2000: 9). In 1999, a group of New Age Travellers was arrested near Stonehenge and convicted of taking part in a 'trespassory assembly', applying earlier legislation – the 1986 Public Order Act, Section 14a (although an appeal against this conviction was upheld in the House of Lords (DPP *v* Jones, House of Lords 2 WLR 625, 1999)). At the same time, there have been significant challenges to the Act. Notably, in the year following its implementation, an eviction order on a group of New Age Travellers in East Sussex, using Section 45 of the Act, dealing with aggravated trespass, was quashed on the grounds that the local authority had failed to take account of the primary need for shelter and a modicum of security (Sibley 1997).

The section of the 1994 Act which has had the most serious consequences for Travellers has been that applying to the provisions of Section 2 of the 1968 Caravan Sites Act. Following the Act, local authorities no longer had an obligation to provide sites for Travellers 'residing in or resorting to' their areas and Treasury support for site provision was withdrawn. The only options for Gypsies not already accommodated on a local authority or private site are to apply for planning permission for a site or to move into houses. Since 1994, most planning applications have been for sites in rural areas but the refusal rate has been about 90 per cent (compared with an 80 per cent success rate for all planning applications). As Morris (1998) has pointed out, most people living in houses have no direct contact with the planning system yet Gypsies, who lack access to legal services and credit and have high levels of illiteracy, are expected to surmount all the hurdles erected by the planning system. This system is heavily weighted against them. As Morris (1998: 5) argues:

> In stating that Gypsies should be treated as any other, Circular 1/94 [providing guidance to local authorities in assessing applications for private sites by Gypsies] fails to recognise the influence of often prejudice-based opposition not suffered by other types of applicants, and which stems from a combination of classic racism and lack of understanding of nomadism on the part of the sedentary minority. These factors outside of the system and which influence it, can result in discriminatory treatment of Gypsy attempts at self-provision.

The main hope is that reforms will come through judgments in the European Court of Human Rights which has already adjudicated in a small number of cases involving British Gypsies. One recent case concerned the refusal of planning permission for a Gypsy site on green belt land in Hertfordshire, and a fine for the breach of an enforcement notice, which led to a complaint to the European Commission. The planning inspector, clearly ignoring the judgment in the 1995 East Sussex case (above), refused permission while acknowledging that the family had nowhere else to go. According to Morris (1998), this family has been on the move ever since their eviction and the children have been withdrawn from school. The Commission upheld the complaint. In a second case, Buckley *v* UK, involving a Gypsy woman who had been refused planning permission but who had been offered an alternative site, the European Court of Human Rights ruled that Ms Buckley's rights had not been violated because the local planning authority's interference had been proportionate (that is, while the authority's decision had adversely affected her life it had not been to the extent that it constituted a violation of human rights). Specifically, the European Court was concerned with Article 8 of the European Convention on Human Rights, acknowledging 'the right to respect for private and family life, home and correspondence'. In Buckley *v* UK, there was a *prima facie* case that Article 8 had been violated, however and subsequent cases brought to the Court by Gypsies in England and Wales will be treated on their merits (Low-Beer 2001). One hopeful initiative is the publication in January 2002 of a Traveller Law Reform Bill, based on collaboration by Gypsies, the police, welfare organisations and planners, which would, among other things, oblige local authorities to give planning permission for private, owner-occupied sites and sites with a long history of occupation which presently lack legal status. Housing Associations would be involved in site management and a Gypsy and Traveller Accommodation Commission would be established to assess the need for sites in England and Wales (*Travellers' Times* March 2002). It is interesting that an issue which, at the local level, is primarily about space – the appropriate uses of land as determined by a local planning authority – is judged solely in terms of human rights at the European level, although human rights have also been a significant factor in a few judgments within the United Kingdom since the 1995 East Sussex appeal (for example, DPP *v* Jones, 1999).

Since 1994, we can see the planning system in England and Wales as the main instrument for the defence of rural space against the incursions of mobile pariahs, particularly Travellers. 'The rural community', as imagined by Michael Howard, the Countryside Alliance, and others who hold to a singular conception of rural social space, is necessarily excluding – a number of groups, including semi-nomadic minorities are not recognised as a part of this rural community. Their argument implies that certain kinds of difference are unacceptable and that diversity is something urban and alien. In support of this argument, we could also cite responses to proposals for the settlement of asylum seekers in some rural areas.

Rural asylum and the rejection of difference

In December 1999 the British government initiated a dispersal scheme for asylum seekers, using the argument that concentrations of asylum seekers in some towns had an adverse effect on community relations. Most of the reception areas were urban but there were also some people relocated in rural areas. For example, according to figures provided by the Asylum Seekers Voluntary Dispersal Scheme, by 15 March 2000, while 471 people had been relocated in Yorkshire and Humberside, primarily in cities like Leeds and Hull, 31 had been 'dispersed' to Devon.

Local responses to proposals for rural dispersal have been interesting. Sedgefield Council in County Durham, a largely rural district where the prime minister is the member of parliament, objected that it lacked 'the necessary infrastructure to cope with asylum seekers without back up from welfare agencies'. A housing spokesperson claimed that, because vacant housing was scattered through the district, it would not be possible to settle them appropriately: 'If we were taking any of these people we would need the support services in place to accommodate them. It would not be a good idea to have them dotted all over the place and we have to recognise these people gravitate to where their fellow countrymen and women are' (Hetherington 2001). In this comment, the asylum seeker is, as Kevin Hetherington has suggested in relation to New Age Travellers, a 'blank figure' (Hetherington 2000: 22). Following Michel Serres, Hetherington suggests that the stranger is underdetermined and blank and here the blank begins to be filled in with the assumption that 'these people' will want to live close to each other, something which from the council's point of view is an undesirable and negative quality. The principal objection, however, is that it would be practically difficult to find sufficient housing in the right place and to provide support services.

A second case, in 2000, concerned a proposal by a Baptist charity to house 74 asylum seekers in a former boarding school in the hamlet of Over Stowey, Somerset. This is an area of considerable natural beauty where property prices are very high. The district council (Sedgemoor) objected in similar terms to Sedgefield Council's argument against dispersal, namely, that the remote rural location would make it difficult to provide support services so it would not be able to meet Home Office criteria for asylum seeker settlement. However, the reaction of some residents strongly suggest that they were erecting defences against persecutory anxieties. One resident suggested that 'what people are worried about is the fear of the unknown. There are no ethnic (sic) people in the village and all people have to go on are press accounts of what has happened over the last year in places like Dover. You can understand people's fears' (Gibbs 2000). A less nuanced comment was that 'rocketing crime, begging, racial tension and plummeting house prices could result' (Perry 2000). It would be unfair to represent this case as one involving a complete rejection of difference by an all-white community. Both the vicar and a retired doctor supported the proposal and the district council's rejection of the planning application was overturned at an inquiry. The implication of most negative comments, however, is that a rural area, particularly a wealthy one, is no place for poor people of a different ethnicity – asylum seekers should be accommodated in cities.

One problem with highlighting instances of rural rejection is that it perpetuates the idea of a rural–urban binary and essentialises space rather than drawing attention to the peculiarities of place. It is not the case that cities, generally, are more tolerant and accepting than rural areas. Maybe rural areas in England and Wales are unlikely to accept the settlement of people who are ethnically different, whether sedentary or nomadic, but it is necessary to take account of the class composition and ethnic mix of urban areas in order to understand differences in responses to asylum seekers. Thus, in Leeds, which has a long history of migration from the Caribbean, eastern and southern Europe, south and south-east Asia, there have been no obvious tensions surrounding the settlement of asylum seekers in parts of the city which already have many ethnic groups. In Hull, by contrast, there have been numerous instances of the rejection of asylum seekers. In a four month period during 2001, there were 35 reported incidents of violent assaults on asylum seekers. As a Kurdish doctor at the city hospital commented: 'It's a world of dark looks in queues. I think specially because the asylum seekers shop where the poorest local people shop, and it's the poorest people who feel they're a threat, buying things they want and somehow threatening jobs [although refugees are not allowed to work]' (Wainwright 2001). In Weberian terms, this could be explained as a simple case of closure, as the doctor suggests (Husbands 1982), or of projective identification (Hoggett 1992). It is, however, a local problem for a city which is predominantly white and relatively poor. Rejection of ethnic difference, particularly when associated with the idea of movement – from cities or from somewhere 'distant', such as Kurdish Iraq or Kosovo – is clearly a serious problem for rural areas, but the opposition of rural and urban in framing the problem is not helpful.

Conclusion

Constance Perin (1988: 174) argued that: 'Under the gaze of centuries of civilization are unexamined, if not mediaeval meanings and symbols which maintain and sustain our frightened apprehension of difference'. A determination to cling to a vision of rural space as homogeneous and harmonious, a vision that is obsolete or never existed, is one instance of such symbolism. In this chapter, I have suggested that anxieties are betrayed by spatial categorisations, a 'splitting' of things, spaces, which need to be connected in the interests of social justice. It is equally important, however, not to split off the rural analytically from other spaces where the same defences against persecutory anxieties are manifest. This is a very general problem, illustrated by the popularity of gated communities in the United States and among the middle classes in Latin America, by the opprobrium heaped on Roma beggars on the London Underground by the British Home Secretary, or by opposition to the presence of asylum seekers in Britain, both at the national level and in localities to which they have been directed. In the latter case, it is notable that hostility has been as great in working class urban areas, in Hull, for example, and in middle class rural areas in South West England. Power relations are clearly different in these two cases but attempted distantiation and closure are defensive strategies evident among the urban poor as well as the rural middle class. Ironically, in societies deemed by some to be post-modern, celebrating coming together, fusion and hybridity, fragmentation and barrier erection continue apace.

I would argue that western societies are becoming increasingly insulated and 'capsular'. Lieven de Cauter (2000) suggests that

> Cocooning (an activity for capsular institutions like the nuclear family) is just the sweet glossy magazine word for the hard fact of capsularisation and living. Our daily life can be exactly described as a movement via transportation capsules from one enclave or capsule (home, for instance) to another (campus, office, airport, hotel, mall, and so on) . . . we could say: neoliberal individualism plus suburbanisation of daily life equals capsularisation.

The capsule could be manufactured at any spatial scale – the car, the home, the rural, the nation, etc., because all or any of these spatial categories can be seen to provide security which, as Freud recognised in his essay on the uncanny (1919 (1990)), can never be secure. The drive for security produces threatening others. According to Natter and Jones (1997: 145) 'what may be more helpful just now is a theorisation of categories and subjects that refuses either to subsume difference within the homogenising moment of the category, or to dispense with the category altogether'. Categorisation (in terms of A or not-A) is essential to thought, however, and it is more important that we recognise the political power of some spatial categorisations and challenge them through arguments about social justice and rights, as the European Court of Human Rights has argued.

The Kalderas of early twentieth century Europe, with a precarious hold on patches of ground in Liverpool or rural Surrey, apparently did not have anxieties about spaces of belonging. Their movements cut across the spatial categorisations, across the geographies, of the dominant society. From their perspective, 'the rural' and 'the urban' both had their uses and our academic and political concern with a category such as 'rural space' would probably have been quite puzzling. To legislate to maintain spatial boundaries may be one of the most alienating practices in modern western societies which is, maybe, why we need psychoanalysis, nomads and nomadology.

Notes

1. Indifference to place is not, as I suggest here, universal. There are some sedentary Gypsies who have lived in the same locality for several generations, in parts of London, for example, who are very attached to place. Also nomadic Gypsies have attachments to particular stopping places. Gypsies that I worked with in East Yorkshire, for example, talked about 'the woods', a small triangular piece of land with a few trees at the junction of three lanes, where several of them were born, This site was returned to every year during seasonal migrations, the routes of which varied very little. Clearly, the Kalderas described by Winstedt were much more nomadic and had no long-term association with the places they visited in Britain.

2. Kathleen Kelley-Lainé is a psychoanalyst practising in Paris. Her book, *Peter Pan: The Story of a Lost Childhood* (1997), deals with her own childhood experience as a refugee from Communist Hungary. She emphasises the importance of re-engaging with what was, effectively, a split-off childhood.

3. John Clare is a director of the Multi-Lingual Psychotherapy Centre, London, and has written on the psychogeography of Samuel Beckett. This comment was made in a presentation to the Lost Childhood and the Language of Exile conference, organised by the Imago Multi-Lingual Psychotherapy Centre and the Freud Museum, London, May 2001.

References

Cresswell, T. 1997 'Imagining the nomad: mobility and the postmodern primitive', pp. 360–79 in G. Benko and U. Strohmayer (eds), *Space and Social Theory: Interpreting Modernity and Postmodernity*, Basil Blackwell, Oxford.

Crouch, C. and Marquand, D. (eds) 1989 *The New Centralism*, Basil Blackwell, Oxford.

de Cauter, L. 2000 'The capsule and the network: notes for a general theory', *Conference on Processes of Inclusion and Exclusion in Western Societies*, University of Amsterdam.

Fraser, A. 1992 *The Gypsies*, Basil Blackwell, Oxford.

Freud, S. 1919/1990 'The "uncanny"', *The Penguin Freud Library*, Vol. 14, Penguin, Harmondsworth, pp. 336–76.

Gibbs, G. 2000 'Rural revolt over asylum seekers hostel', www.guardian.co.uk/ Refugees_in_Britain/Story/0, 2763,333134,00.html (accessed April 2002).

Hetherington, K. 2000 *New Age Travellers*, Cassell, London.

Hetherington, P. 2001 'Blair's local council set to reject refugees', society.guardian.co.uk/ asylum seekers/story/0,7991,498044,00.html (accessed April 2002).

Hoggett, P. 1992 'A place for experience: a psychoanalytic perspective on boundary, identity and culture', *Environment and Planning D: Society and Space*, 10, 345–56.

Husbands, C. 1982 'East End racism', 1900–1980, *The London Journal* 8, 3–26.

Kahane, C. 1992 'Object relations theory', pp. 284–90 in E. Wright (ed.), *Feminism and Psychoanalysis: A Critical Dictionary*, Blackwell, Oxford.

Kelley-Lainé, K. 1997 *Peter Pan: The Story of a Lost Childhood*, Harper Collins, London.

Lawrence, G. 2002 'The presence of totalitarian states of mind in institutions', www.human-nature.com/free associations (accessed February 2002).

Low-Beer, R. 2001 *Challenging Gypsy Planning Policies*, Travellers' Law Research Unit, Cardiff; www.cf.ac.uk/claws/tlru/publications (accessed July 2001).

Matless, D. 1998 *Landscape and Englishness*, Reaktion Books, London.

Mayall, D. 1988 *Gypsy-Travellers in Nineteenth Century Society*, Cambridge University Press, Cambridge.

Morris, R. 1998 'Gypsies and the planning system', *Journal of Planning and Environment Law*, 635–43.

Natter, W. and Jones, J.P. 1997 'Identity, space and other uncertainties', pp. 141–61 in G. Benko and U. Strohmayer (eds), *Space and Social Theory: Interpreting Modernity and Postmodernity*, Basil Blackwell, Oxford.

Perin, C. 1988 *Belonging in America*, University of Wisconsin Press, Madison.

Perry, K. 2000 'Go ahead for asylum hostel enrages village', www.guardian.co.uk/Refugees_in_Britain/Story/0,2763,352207,00.html (accessed April 2002).

Segal, J. 1992 *Melanie Klein*, Sage, London.

Sibley, D. 1997 'Endangering the sacred: nomads, youth cultures and the English countryside', pp. 218–31 in P. Cloke and J. Little (eds), *Contested Countryside Cultures: Otherness, Marginalisation and Rurality*, Routledge, London.

Steiner, J. 1987 'The interplay between pathological organisation and the paranoid–schizoid and depressive positions', *International Journal of Psychoanalysis*, 68, 69–80.

Travellers' Times 2000 Traveller Law Research Unit, Cardiff University Law School.

Wainwright, M. 2001 'Hull tested as culture clashes rumble on', www.guardian.co.uk/Refugees_in_Britain/Story/0,2763,426739,00.html (accessed April 2002).

Winstedt, E. 1912–1913 'The Gypsy coppersmiths' invasion of 1911–1913', *Journal of the Gypsy Lore Society*, 6, 244–75.

Young, J. 1999 *The Exclusive Society*, Sage, London.

Young, R. 1994 *Mental Space*, Process Press, London.

Young, R. 2002 *Mental Space*, www.human-nature.com/mental/ (accessed April 2002).

The devil of social capital: a dilemma of American rural sociology

CHAPTER 13

Cynthia Anderson and Michael Bell

Introduction

Rural sociology has never been exactly the most noticed of disciplines in the United States, or anywhere else. Indeed, the social sciences in general cannot be said to carry much weight in general social discussion in America, except in their least social forms: individualistic (and especially biological) versions of psychology and neoclassical versions of economics. The situation is less extreme in the United Kingdom, but the disregard of *social* social science by the public eye is high there as well. Anglo-American social scientists have long envied the attention given their French and German counterparts in their own countries, of course. Perhaps we may make the following extrapolation of Weber's Protestant ethic thesis: the more economistic, and thus individualistic, a national society, the less welcome the insights of the *social* social sciences.

The above is no doubt something of a stereotype of the urbane German and French public, the crass American public and a British public which, as always, is somewhere in between the continents. Nevertheless, it certainly corresponds with the widespread embrace by American sociologists and, to a substantially lesser extent, British sociologists of the breathtakingly economistic phrase 'social capital'. No bit of sociological lingo in recent memory has so rapidly radiated both through the discipline and across the academic divide into common usage by American politicians and policy makers, and into the general public too. The phrase has had less traction in Britain, as we have said, but it has made a mark there as well, in both academic and public spheres.

In the United States, that traction has been nowhere greater than in rural sociology. What we argue in this chapter is that social capital has achieved its current degree of stardom in American sociology because of the hope that, finally, here is a linguistic vehicle for carrying a bit of sociological water to the conceptual deserts of the world's most economistic society. And we argue that social capital has been especially seductive for rural sociologists in America because of the field's historical and financial connection to applied research, and because of hopes that the undeniable public resonance the phrase seems to have might finally give the field the visibility it, like all fields, desires. To use an economistic metaphor, 'social capital' is a linguistic bargain. It remains to be seen if it is a Faustian one as well.

A new academic star

From its development in the post-structural theories of Pierre Bourdieu (1986) and the rational choice perspective of James Coleman (1988, 1990, 1993), the concept of social capital has become a major force in the sociological universe. In the past decade, debates about civic participation (Putnam 1993), community development (Flora and Flora 1993), state–society relations (Evans 1996) and social change (Kolankiewicz 1996) have brought social capital from the halls of academe to policy oriented journals, national newspapers (e.g. *Washington Post*, 1 February 2001), general circulation magazines (e.g. *Business Week*, 15 December 1997), and Internet zines (e.g. *Salon*, 25 February 2000 and 7 July 2000).

Scholarly research on social capital has exploded over the past decade. Type the words "social capital" into the Sociological Abstracts electronic search engine, and you get 655 hits since 1990 (and probably more since this writing). Researchers note, for instance, that social capital increases the education achievement of children (Coleman 1988; McNeal 1999; Morgan and Sørensen 1999), facilitates success for new and second generation immigrants (Lauglo 1999; Portes and MacLeod 1999), impacts career gains (Burt 1992), decreases crime (Kawachi *et al.* 1997), increases status attainment (Dyk and Wilson 1999; Forse 1999; Lin 1999), and promotes economic growth (Fedderke *et al.* 1999). Researchers also argue that social capital affects voluntary participation (Rich 1999; Rotolo 1999; Wilson and Musick 1998) and facilitates rural community development (Flora and Flora 1993). In brief, social capital appears to be a 'panacea for the ills of modern society' (Wall *et al.* 1998).

In American rural sociology, the widespread embrace of the concept registers in journal articles and the goings on at professional meetings. Expand the previously noted Sociological Abstracts literature search to include "social capital + rural" and you get 62 hits since 1990 (again, likely more since this writing) – almost 10 per cent of the "social capital" total of 655. In 1998, there was a special issue of the journal *Rural Sociology* dedicated to social capital, and articles on the subject have been a regular staple of the journal ever since. One recent high-note for social capital within American rural sociology was the plenary speech by Robert Putnam, arguably social capital's leading proponent, at the 2001 annual meeting of the Rural Sociological Society. In addition, social capital has been widely discussed in the Community Development Society, a professional society in which many American rural sociologists participate (Besser and Ryan 2000; Warner *et al.* 1999). However, it is in the peculiarly American institution of 'extension' that social capital has perhaps made its biggest splash. There can be very few extension field workers in the United States who have not, by this time, become familiar with the term, either through 'in-service' training sessions or through the increasing number of extension publications, videos and web sites that argue for the importance of social capital (cf. Iowa State University Extension, 1996; NCRCRD, n.d.).

And, as we have noted, social capital has been widely taken up in policy and political circles across the globe. Central to all the interest in social capital is the view that it has been in sharp decline in the United States and elsewhere for the past 30 to 40 years. The World Bank has even called it the 'missing link' in theories of economic development (Grootaert 1998) and made it one of the centrepieces of its 1997 *World Development Report* (World Bank 1997). Like the extension agents in American land grant universities, development professionals around the world are touting the importance of social capital, giving it equal pride of place with human capital, physical capital, ecological capital, and even financial capital, as in the 'five capitals' model currently popular at Britain's Department for International Development (Carney 1998). Requests for proposals from developing agency after developing agency increasingly speak of their goals in terms of reversing the decline in social capital.

Nowhere has social capital become more common than within policy and political circles in the United States. Politicians at the local and national levels now commonly appeal to the term. A former mayor of our own town, Ames, Iowa, routinely spoke of 'social capital' in his public addresses. Presidents Clinton and George W. Bush have both capitalised on the concept. The image of the lonely bowler – the central metaphor of Putnam's famous paper 'Bowling Alone', and now the title of his 2000 book – inspired passages in Clinton's 1995 State of the Union address. For Bush's inaugural address, advisers consulted on the speech with Putnam and included lots of communitarian words such as 'civility', 'responsibility' and 'community'. The current Bush administration even invited Putnam to advise on its new Office of Faith-Based Initiatives, the controversial plan to turn aspects of government social services over to religious organizations.

Clearly, social capital gets you places.

Just what is 'social capital?'

But we are putting the cart before the horse. Just what is social capital and how has it been applied to the rural?

According to Robert Putnam, in his plenary address to the Rural Sociological Society, the central idea behind social capital is 'the thought that social relations have value'.[1] Other advocates of the term give it a similarly broad, and broadly similar, meaning – albeit with sundry definitions and operation-alisations. Grounded in theories of social exchange (Blau 1964) and social embeddedness (Granovetter 1985; Portes and Sensenbrenner 1993), researchers of social capital typically use the concept to refer to resources that come from the structure of social relationships. Most common definitions emphasise norms and networks that facilitate collective action for mutual benefit, as well as the importance of trust. The metaphor of investment that the term implies also attracts many advocates: that, if you handle social capital right, the more you spend the more you have.

Initial formulations, such as Coleman's influential 1988 article, did not address issues of inequality. But more recent scholars have come to agree that social capital is accessed differently by various individuals, and that there are different forms of and levels of social capital associated with different sets of social relations and institutional environments. Flora and Flora (1993) argue that communities can have horizontal, hierarchical, or no social capital. Woolcock (1998) notes that any given form of social capital confers potential costs as well as potential benefits. Lin (2000) highlights the inequality in social capital, accounted for by structural constraints and normative dynamics of social interactions. Burt (1992) and others argue for the need to distinguish between 'bonding' and 'bridging' forms of social capital, the former being about ties within networks and the latter about ties that connect networks. The distinction between bonding and bridging has become particularly important in recent debates about social capital, as we will describe.

Researchers in the area have typically operationalised social capital through measures of civic participation, informal interactions and social trust. Social capital researchers typically find their evidence in quantitative surveys on topics such as the number of clubs people belong to, the sense they have of the responsiveness and accessibility of government, people's overall sense of trust of others, and such seeming minutia as the number of picnics people go on. There has also been a stress in much social capital work on using longitudinal measures. Of course, you cannot survey people from the past, and consider-able ingenuity has gone into finding measures that were initially designed for other purposes, and reinterpreting them from the perspective of social capital. Putnam (2000), for example, has made extensive use of surveys regularly col-lected by marketing firms of the last several decades.

When you look at these measures over time, virtually all of them are going down. According to Putnam, people in the United States are less inclined than they used to be to leave the house for any reason except work. Americans do not invite friends over as often as in the past, and fewer citizens trust their neigh-bours. Americans have slacked off in terms of volunteer work, and few write letters-to-the-editor or letters to members of congress. Moreover, as Putnam claims, Americans increasingly tend to 'bowl alone'. While the number of bowlers has increased over time and on average – he notes that Americans bowl more often than they vote in congressional elections – fewer bowl as members of a team, in a league. This, according to Putnam, is the epitome of declining social capital.

Outline of the critique of social capital

But not everyone is convinced that bowling teams are the solution to the social ills of America, or anywhere else. Critiques run from the accusation that the concept is theoretically shallow to politically regressive. Most critiques wind up being a mixture of both the theoretical and the political. Edwards and Foley's recent critique of Putnam's *Bowling Alone* is an example of the latter: 'Why the hundreds of thousands of dollars of grant money behind this project?', they write, referring to the financial capital that Putnam had attracted to support his research.

> Clearly, the argument presented in *Bowling Alone* strikes a chord among an over-whelmingly neoliberal elite. The source of our discontent, the argument tells us, lies neither in restructuring, nor in globalization, nor in increasing inequality, nor in anything else related to the go-go economy of the 1990s. If social capital is America's elixir for the 21st century, conservatives of all stripes can take heart that its source lies in civil society, in private initiative and individual disposition, not in public action and government regulations (2001: 230).

In other words, Edwards and Foley find social capital to be conservative in its implications, and argue that social capital theoretically directs our attention away from the structural factors they find most decisive in contemporary social problems. Political doubts also seem to lurk behind the theoretical arguments offered by other critics of social capital, although not always so explicitly. There should be no surprise here, of course. Both advocates and critics of social capital bustle to the topic precisely because of its political implications. What Florence Reece sang in 'Which Side Are You On?' – her classic song of the 1930s miners' movement in Harlan County, West Virginia – applies to the topic of social capital as well: there are no neutrals here[2].

One of the political implications of social capital that has worried a number of critics is that social exclusion may well be a product of high social capital. Certainly, the high watermark of social capital in the United States that Putnam and others often point back to, the 1950s, could not be described as a time of multicultural embrace of the Other. To be sure, people in the United States of the 1950s did indeed go on more picnics, invite their neighbours over for dinner more, and participate in more clubs – the 'animal clubs', as Putnam likes to describe them: the Elks, the Moose and the Lions. But perhaps picnics, dinners with the neighbours and animal clubs were part of the problem.

In other words, not all groups have equal access to social capital. Reserves of social capital are unevenly distributed and differentially accessible depending on the social location of the groups and individuals who attempt to appropriate it. Unequal access to social capital can become self-perpetuating, influencing life chances for individuals and groups. Lin suggests that this happens when 'certain groups cluster at relatively disadvantaged socioeconomic positions, and the general tendency is for individuals to associate with those of similar group or socioeconomic characteristics' – what Lin calls homophily (2000: 786).

A number of critics have brought up this potential negative side of social capital. In a case study of a Southern textile community, Schulman and Anderson (1999) show how a paternalistic form of social capital dominates work and community social relations. They argue that social capital is a context-dependent form of power that can be created, accumulated or destroyed. Thus, instead of providing access to power and voice in decision making, social capital is itself a dimension of the patterns of power that limit access and voice to begin with. This illustrates Bourdieu's (1986) argument that dominant social classes use their privileged access to cultural, human, social and financial capital to make strategic conversions of one kind of capital to another in order to solidify their positions.

Along similar lines, social capital can negatively affect certain groups through downward levelling pressures and group conformity (Portes 1998; Portes and Landolt 1996). Social capital may serve to exclude outsiders, make excess claims on group members, and restrict individual freedoms (Portes 1998). For example, Bregendahl et al. (2000) found that high levels of social capital within a community resulted in high social risk to participants and halted the completion of a controversial project. Where a community values social capital highly and seeks to maintain it, the result may be that controversy is squelched in order not to rock the larger social boat.

More generally, critics argue against the rationalistic connotation that comes from the reliance on economic language. Indeed, most social capital writers have not sufficiently repudiated the rational choice tradition and its limitations (Petrzelka and Bell 2000). In previous work, Bell noted that

> Even with important qualifications, the image remains that of a social actor moved by interests alone. This rational actor follows norms, but only because he or she is constrained to do so. Trust and networks are also necessary for the reformed rational egoist, but the origin of these rest on the self-serving ground of interest (1998: 183–4).

Researchers have argued against using simple measures of social capital, such as social ties, for analysing community relations (Etzioni 2001). In contrast to focusing on outcomes, it is imperative that we address the mechanisms through which communities are created, altered and sustained by linking social capital. One way to do this is to link social capital to economic production (Anderson 2001; Torsvik 2000), acknowledging history and the social creation of relations, as well as the fact that their relative importance may shift over time (Woolcock 1998). For example, the social protest and popular movements of the last four decades (e.g. civil rights, anti-war, women's rights, gay rights, environmentalism) brought new issues into the political arena that no doubt influence community social capital. However, reliance on any particular measures of social ties (such as Putnam's measures of voluntary participation in clubs, picnics and bowling leagues) may not capture the influence of new social movements (Boggs 2001). People may be going on fewer picnics and the membership in the Elks may be in decline, but that does not necessarily mean that social capital is less, whatever it may be. Without creating new network ties, a social movement is unlikely to have gone far.

Academic advocates of social capital initially overlooked the issue of the potential 'dark side' of social capital. But there is now broad agreement among advocates that this is a real problem. Even Putnam now speaks of not wanting to go back to the 1950s. In his standard social capital stump speech, he regularly includes the line that his point is not to ask, 'OK, would all the women in the room please report to the kitchen?'[3] He wants a kind of social capital in tune with current times. Social capital scholars have also enthusiastically received Burt's 1992 article on the distinction between 'bridging' and 'bonding' social capital as a way to distinguish between social capital that does good and social capital that does bad. Much of the recent work in social capital has been devoted to finding ways of operationalising and measuring this distinction.

Nevertheless, the critics are mostly unmoved by the distinction between 'bridging' and 'bonding' social capital, seeing it as a patch-up job on a more generally flawed theoretical contraption. As noted by Edwards *et al.* (2001), researchers continue to ignore the momentous economic changes that have profoundly affected the attitudes of citizens toward their government and larger society. We know that America has experienced a long, steady decline of real incomes. The effects of economic restructuring have hit members of the working and middle classes especially hard. These macro-level changes are transferred to local economies and can indirectly affect a community's social solidarity (Boggs 2001; Jackman and Miller 1998; Tarrow 1996). By ignoring the broader political and economic changes, social capital arguments take on an elitist stance. As Portes notes, 'responsibility for the alleged decline of social capital is put squarely on the leisure behavior of the masses, rather then on the economic and political changes wrought by the corporate and governmental establishment' (Portes 1998: 19). If social capital – again, whatever it may be – is in decline, it is not because parents are not showing up anymore at the PTA meetings at their child's school and are staying home to watch TV instead. (Television watching is often singled out in social capital research as a primary cause of social capital's decline.) It is because they are completely exhausted by the demands of two or even three jobs, and by the increase in the number of hours that one is expected to put it to keep even one job.

Thus a tautology emerges. Portes notes the logical circularity of Putnam's argument: 'As a property of communities rather than individuals, social capital is simultaneously a cause and an effect. It leads to positive outcomes . . . and its existence in inferred from the same outcomes' (1998: 19). In other words, the basic argument of social capital has the following form: we know a community has high social capital when it is doing well and when everyone speaks well of everyone else. So what does the term social capital add to the analysis of why a community is in fact doing well and speaking well of each other? It merely restates the point. For many, this blurring of the distinction between correlation and causation is a fatal flaw in social capital approach to community (e.g. Edwards and Foley 2001; Tarrow 1996).

Why so many sociologists have embraced the concept

And yet despite all these critiques of the concept of social capital, social scientists have taken to it with a will. We suspect that it is not because of the political worries of the critics, however. Most sociologists are, of course, politically left or left-leaning, and that goes for most advocates of social capital as well. To understand the power of the idea in the academe, then, we need to look further.

It has been suggested that one reason for the concept's popularity is professional narcissism, with elites subconsciously attracted to the concept because it rings true to their personal circumstances and with American's preoccupation with excesses of individualism (Schuller *et al.* 2000). For the most part, the concept focuses on positives and ignores the less attractive features of community. As Portes notes, 'It is our sociological bias to see good things emerging out of sociability; bad things are more commonly associated with behavior of homo economicus' (1998: 15). As such, social capital research highlights the 'social' part of economic relations, potentially reducing the distinction between sociological and economic perspectives while at the same time directing policy makers to non-economic solutions to community troubles.

But we suspect that deeper than any of these reasons has been precisely the left and left-leaning political inclinations of social capital's academic enthusiasts. Call it economist-envy. Sociologists have sojourned so long in the wilderness of public opinion and policy debates that there is a strong temptation to seize onto whatever means seem necessary to bring the insights of the social into public decision making. Sociologists have long sought an attractive bottle for the sociological vintage that would encourage broader sampling of, and thus perhaps greater appreciation for, what the field has to offer. If public taste has grown accustomed to labels with economic-sounding words on them, so be it: as long as they buy, for otherwise they may never buy in.

Can we save the concept as part of the rural agenda?

Seen from the point of view of marketing the social, it must be said that the term social capital is indeed very attractive. Its popularity outside the halls of the academe cannot be doubted. When development agencies and governments rank the social as equal in significance to the financial it is very tempting to shout hallelujah and to dance down those academic halls out, finally, into the streets of public opinion. We could be throwing away a major intellectual opportunity, if we cast social capital aside.

In this regard, a number of compromise positions have begun to emerge in the literature. For example, some writers have begun to switch to the language of 'social capacity' and 'civic engagement' to address many of the same issues that social capital is intended to alert the world to (see Tolbert *et al.* 1998). This perspective is noteworthy in that it addresses the influence of global market forces on local communities and attempts to move assumptions beyond neoclassical and rational choice perspectives. Much more, it seems to us, could be done with this approach. The word 'civic' may not resonate as loudly in American culture as 'capital', but it is a very resonant word nonetheless, and perhaps as well one that avoids tautology and the overlooking of inequality.

One thought that we have mulled over is that perhaps social capital could be retained as a useful concept if its scope was narrowed to the strictly economic – that is to say, it referred truly to capital, to the role of the social in wealth creation, and not, as sometimes seems the case, everything social that there is. In this way, the rationalistic and economistic cast of both the language and most of the formulations of the term could be justified. If we limit the term to being about the rationalistic and economistic dimensions of social life, then there would be nothing untoward in having a rationalistic and economistic concept for describing these dimensions. Rationalism and economism are, for better or worse, real features of human society, in rural and urban areas both. But social capital's current broad usage runs the risk of encouraging the view that everything in social life of significance can be reduced to the rational and the economic. We suspect, however, that few advocates of social capital would support an economistic and rationalistic focus on wealth creation. The very point of the term, from their perspective, is to suggest that there is something else of significance going on in life. Perhaps Audre Lourdes's famous insight is right for social capital too: you can't use the master's tools to take down the master's house.

Finally, a return to the Bourdieu's understanding of social capital may provide a light out of the dark tunnel. Bourdieu argues that there are four main forms of capital – economic, cultural, social and symbolic (1986). These forms are interchangeable resources for appropriating social energy and can be converted from one form to another according to the rules that operate in a particular social field. The forms of capital are resources which yield power and involve the capacity to exercise control over one's own future and that of others (Bourdieu 1986: 241). Social capital is:

> the aggregate of the actual or potential resources which are linked to possession of a durable network or more or less institutionalized relationships of mutual acquaintance and recognition – or in other words, to membership in a group – which provides each of its members with the backing of the collectively-owned capital, a 'credential' which entitles them to credit, in the various sense of the word (Bourdieu 1986: 248–9).

There may be promise in such a context-dependent and social structural/ relational approach, as different types of organisation can produce different types of civic behaviours (Edwards *et al.* 2001). To this end, one crucial component of a reformulated social capital would be the role of networks in which individuals are embedded. The model provided by Edwards *et al.* (2001: 278) is particularly useful in demonstrating the importance of both resources and access (networks) in the understanding of social capital as context-dependent by calling attention to the fact that resources are not equally available, nor are they uniformly utilised.

Conclusion

In 1998, Portes predicted that 'current enthusiasm for the concept [of social capital] . . . and its proliferating application to different social problems and processes in not likely to abate soon.' Its popularity is partially warranted, Portes suggested, because the concept does call attention to real and important phenomena. But it is also partially exaggerated. The set of processes encompassed by the concept are not new and have been studied under different labels in the past. Calling them 'social capital' is a means of presenting them in a more appealing conceptual garb. Also, Portes argued, there is little ground to believe that social capital will provide a ready remedy for major social problems. Indeed, mishandled, social capital could make them much worse.

How are we to evaluate the utility of social capital in terms of the rural agenda? It is hard to know and perhaps too soon to say. We suspect that sometimes rural scholars have made sociological headway using the term, while in other cases they have merely been duped into being the agents of political leaders who know that they must at least pretend to 'engage' the public and to widen our social dialogues. Also, we do need to be wary that the criticism of social capital may reflect the academic's unease with making sociology accessible – unease with putting sociology in the common language. And if the common language of the day is economistic, perhaps then we should be economistic. Maybe that would indeed result in less social inequality. But on the other hand, perhaps such language merely reinforces the very cultural trends that sociology has long sought to intervene with and change. Are we making a pact with the devil? Is Robert Putnam a modern-day Faust? This is the question of the moment as we consider the fortune of our rural visions.

Portes (1998) argues for a 'dispassionate stance' towards social capital that 'will allow analysts to consider all facets of the event in question and prevent turning the ensuing literature into an unmitigated celebration of community.' He states, 'Communitarian advocacy is a legitimate political stance; it is not good social science.' This is nearly right. Communitarian advocacy is not *necessarily* good social science. We need always to be wary that we may be damning ourselves with our own good intentions.

Notes

1. This is a direct quote from Putnam's speech, scribbled down by one of us (Bell), who was in attendance. See also Putnam (2000).
2. The full line is 'They say in Harlan County, There are no neutrals here; You'll either be a union man, Or a thug for J.H. Blair.'
3. We have heard Putnam use this line in public twice, both at his speech at the 2001 RSS annual meeting, and at a public lecture he gave at Iowa State University in 1998.

References

Anderson, C.D. 2001 'Inequality, Communities, and Networks of Power: Uneven Development of Social Capital', Iowa State University Department of Sociology Seminar, 15 March, Ames, IA.

Bell, M.M. 1998 'The dialogue of solidarities, or why the lion spared Androcles', *Sociological Focus*, **31**(2), 181–99.

Besser, T.L. and Ryan, V.D. 2000 'The impact of labor market involvement on participation in community', pp. 72–88. *Journal of the Community Development Society*, **31**(1).

Blau, P.M. 1964 *Exchange and Power in Social Life*, J. Wiley, New York.

Boggs, C. 2001 'Social capital and political fantasy: Robert Putnam's Bowling Alone', *Theory and Society*, **30**, 281–97.

Bourdieu, P. 1986 'The forms of capital', pp. 241–58 in J. Richardson (ed.), *Handbook of Theory and Research for the Sociology of Education*, Greenwood Press, New York.

Bregendahl, C., Ryan, V. and Agnitsch, K. 2000 *A Case Study of Controversy in a Close-Knit Community*. Paper presented at the Rural Sociological Society Annual Meetings Washington DC.

Burt, R.S. 1992 *Structural Holes*, Harvard University Press, Cambridge, MA.

Carney, D. (ed.) 1998 *Sustainable Rural Livelihoods: What Contributions Can We Make?* Department for International Development, London.

Coleman, J. 1988 'Social capital in the creation of human capital', *American Journal of Sociology*, **94**, 95–119.

Coleman, J. 1990 *Foundations of Social Theory*, Belknap Press of Harvard University Press, Cambridge, MA.

Coleman, J. 1993 'The rational reconstruction of society', *American Sociology Review*, **58**, 1–15.

Dyk, P.H. and Wilson, S.M. 1999 'Family-based social capital considerations as predictors of attainments among Appalachian youth', *Sociological Inquiry*, **69**(3), 477–503.

Edwards, B. and Foley, M.W. 2001 'Much ado about social capital', *Contemporary Sociology*, **30**(3), 227–30.

Edwards, B., Foley, M.W. and Diani, M. 2001 'Social capital reconsidered', pp. 266–80 in B. Edwards, M.W. Foley, and M. Diani (eds), *Beyond Tocqueville: Civil Society and the Social Capital Debate in Comparative Perspective*, University Press of New England, Hanover and London.

Etzioni, A. 2001 'Is bowling together sociologically lite?', *Contemporary Sociology*, 30(3), 223–4.

Evans, P. 1996 'Government action, social capital, and development: reviewing evidence on synergy', *World Development*, 24, 1119–32.

Fedderke, J., DeKadt, R. and Luiz, J. 1999 'Economic growth and social capital: a critical reflection', *Theory and Society*, 28(5), 709–45.

Flora, C.B. and Flora, J.L. 1993 'Entrepreneurial social infrastructure: a necessary ingredient', *The Annals of the American Academy of Political and Social Sciences*, 529, 48–58.

Forse, M. 1999 'Social capital and status attainment in contemporary France', *Tocqueville Review*, 20(1), 59–81.

Granovetter, M. 1985 'Economic action and social structure: the problem of embeddedness', *American Journal of Sociology*, 91(3), 481–510.

Grootaert, C. 1998 'Social Capital: The Missing Link', Social Capital Initiative Working Paper No. 3, April 1998. World Bank on the web: http://www.worldbank.org/poverty/scapital/wkrppr/sciwp3.pdf.

Iowa State University Extension 1996 *Social Capital and Sustainability: The Community and Managing Change in Agriculture*, Video, Iowa State University, Ames, IA.

Jackman, R.W. and Miller, R.A. 1998 'Social capital and politics', *Annual Review of Political Science*, 1998(1), 47–73.

Kawachi, I., Kennedy, B.P. and Lochner, K. 1997 'Long live community: Social capital as public health', *The American Prospect*, Nov.–Dec., 56–9.

Kolankiewicz, G. 1996 'Social capital and social change', *British Journal of Sociology*, 47, 427–39.

Lauglo, J. 1999 'Working harder to make the grade: immigrant youth in Norwegian schools', *Journal of Youth Studies*, 2(1), 77–100.

Lin, N. 1999 'Social networks and status attainment', *Annual Review of Sociology*, 25, 467–87.

Lin, N. 2000 'Inequality in social capital', *Contemporary Sociology*, 29(6), 785–95.

McNeal, R.B. Jr 1999 'Parental involvement as social capital: differential effectiveness on science achievement, truancy, and dropping out', *Social Forces*, 78(1), 117–44.

Morgan, S.L. and Sørensen, A.B. 1999 'Parental network, social closure, and mathematical learning: a test of Coleman's social capital explanation of school effects', *American Sociological Review*, 64, 661–81.

NCRCRD (North Central Regional Center for Rural Development) n.d. *Measuring Community Success and Sustainability: An Interactive Workbook*, http://www.ag.iastate.edu/centers/rdev/Community_Success/entry.html.

Petrzelka, P. and Bell, M.M. 2000 'Rationality and solidarities: The social organization of common property resources in the Imdrhas Valley of Morocco', *Human Organization*, 59(3), 343–52.

Portes, A. 1998 'Social capital: its origins and applications in modern sociology', *Annual Review of Sociology*, 22, 1–24.

Portes, A. and Landolt, P. 1996 'The downside of social capital', *The American Prospect*, May–June, 18–21, 94.

Portes, A. and MacLeod, D. 1999 'Educating the second generation: determinants of academic achievement among children of immigrants in the United States', *Journal of Ethnic and Migration Studies*, 25(3), 373–96.

Portes, A. and Sensenbrenner, J. 1993 'Embeddedness and immigration: notes on the social determinants of economic action', *American Journal of Sociology* 98,1320–50.

Putnam, R.D. 1993 *Making Democracy Work: Civic Tradition in Modern Italy*. Princeton University Press, Princeton, NJ.

Putnam, R.D. 2000 *Bowling Alone: The Collapse and Revival of American Community*, Simon & Schuster, New York.

Rich, P. 1999 'American volunteerism, social capital, and political culture', *Annals of the American Academy of Political and Social Science*, 565, 15–34.

Rotolo, T. 1999 'Trends in voluntary association participation', *Nonprofit and Voluntary Sector Quarterly*, 28(2), 199–212.

Schuller, T., Baron, S. and Field, J. 2000 'Social capital: a review and critique', pp. 1–38 in S. Baron, J. Field, and T. Schuller (eds), *Social Capital: Critical Perspectives*. Oxford University Press, New York.

Schulman, M.D. and Anderson, C.D. 1999 'The Dark Side of the Force: a case study of restructuring and social capital', pp. 351–372, *Rural Sociology*, 64, 3.

Tarrow, S. 1996 'Making social science work across space and time: a critical reflection on Robert Putnam's *Making Democracy Work*', *American Political Science Review*, 90(2), 389–97.

Tolbert, C.M., Lyson, T.A. and Irwin, M.D. 1998 'Local capitalism, civic engagement, and socioeconomic well-being', *Social Forces*, 77(2), 401–28.

Torsvik, G. 2000 'Social capital and economic development: a plea for the mechanisms', *Rationality and Society*, 12(4), 451–76.

Wall, E., Ferrazzi, G. and Schryer, F. 1998 'Getting the goods on social capital', *Rural Sociology*, 62(2), 300–22.

Warner, M.E., Hinrichs, C.C., Schneyer, J. and Lucy Joyce 1999 'Organizing communities to sustain rural landscapes: lessons from New York', pp. 178–95 *Journal of the Community Development Society*, 30(2).

Wilson, J. and Musick, M. 1998 'The contribution of social resources to volunteering', *Social Science Quarterly*, 79(4), 799–814.

Woolcock, M. 1998 'Social capital and economic development: toward a theoretical synthesis and policy framework', *Theory and Society*, 27, 151–208.

World Bank 1997 *World Development Report 1997: The State in a Changing World*, Oxford University Press, Oxford.

Applying the rural: governance and policy in rural areas

CHAPTER 14

Michael Woods and Mark Goodwin

Introduction

The practice of governing rural areas in the developed world has undergone a significant transformation in recent years, with changes not just in the emphasis and direction of rural policy, but also in the processes through which rural policy is formulated and in the institutions and mechanisms through which it is implemented. These trends have in turn stimulated a growing body of research on rural politics, policy and governance, developing what was until recently a barely explored field of academic inquiry (see Goodwin 1998; Grant 1990; Little 2001), and engaging with theories of 'governance', 'regulation' and 'governmentality' pioneered in urban and regional studies. In this chapter, we examine the application of these concepts in rural research and consider what contribution the study of rural areas may be able to make to the development of these theories in a wider context.

First, however, it may be useful to summarise the key changes in rural government and policy. For four decades from the end of the Second World War rural policy in most developed nations was characterised by three distinctive features. Firstly, there was segmentation of both policy making and policy delivery between the different sectors of state activity relating to rural areas (e.g. agriculture, conservation, economic development, welfare provision). Policy formulation within each sector was controlled by independent closed policy communities which excluded potentially dissenting voices. Secondly, despite segmentation, the interests of agriculture tended to be prioritised across all fields of operation. Representation of rural interests to central states was mediated through agricultural unions and (informally) by landowners who transcended local and national elite networks. Thirdly, policy delivery was conducted through state intervention, structured around a scalar division of labour between the central and local state. In this, the central state acted as the guarantor and supporter of agriculture, providing subsidies, regulating prices and farm incomes, and servicing the research and training needs of the industry. Central states took the lead in designating and managing protected landscapes and initiated top-down rural development programmes. Local states commonly held responsibility for the delivery of welfare services, with rural councils generally characterised by the lightness of their touch such that state provision was lesser in rural areas than in urban districts, and the tax demands on rural landowners and businesses remained relatively low.

As social and economic change in rural areas intensified in the late twentieth century, so this model of rural government became increasingly unsustainable. The declining significance of agriculture, both as a source of rural employment and as a contributor to rural gross domestic product (GDP), provoked pressures to relegate the emphasis given to agriculture in rural policy and to reduce the fiscal demand on the state. In some rural regions, counter-urbanisation has produced a majority population detached from farming, unwilling to adhere to traditional paternalist power structures, and with different expectations of the state. In others, persistent depopulation and the need to rebuild local economies hit by the collapse of traditional industries created challenges for rural development strategy. The globalisation of trade in agricultural produce has invested power in supra-national agreements such as the General Agreement on Tariffs and Trade (GATT) and in transnational corporations; while the increased connectivity of rural areas through the mobility of tourists and commuters and through cultural homogenisation, has rendered urban–rural distinctions in policy and institutional structures increasingly questionable.

Furthermore, the intensification of social and economic change coincided with the emergence of neo-liberal governments ideologically committed to the 'rolling back of the state'. The programme of state restructuring impacted on rural areas both as an indirect effect of reforms to institutions with a (partly) rural remit, and because responses to rural change were developed and delivered within the new paradigm of the 'hollowed-out' state.

Collectively, these social, economic and political influences have initiated a series of still ongoing changes in rural policy and governance. Firstly, there is a continuing trend away from sector-specific policies towards integrated rural policy. This was represented in the British 'Rural White Paper' policy documents of 1995/96 and 2000 (Hodge 1996; Lowe and Ward 2001), and in the agenda of the Australian Regional Summit, and is evident in pressures to reconfigure the EU's Common Agricultural Policy as a 'Common Rural Policy' and to develop an integrated national rural policy in the United States (Fluharty 2001).

Secondly, the shift towards integrated rural policy has been accompanied by a broadening of participation in rural policy making. Assisted by growing public concern over the environmental impact of modern agriculture and over food safety, previously excluded environmental and consumer groups have achieved greater access to rural policy makers. Events such as the Australian Regional Summit have been convened explicitly to develop inclusive approaches to rural policy; while the British government received 791 responses during the consultation phase for the 2000 English rural white paper, only 4 per cent of which came from agricultural groups (DETR 1999).

Thirdly, integrated policy has demanded coordination of policy delivery. At one level this has resulted in the reorganisation of state institutions, as witnessed in the creation of the Department of the Environment, Food and Rural Affairs (DEFRA) and the Countryside Agency in Britain. At another, it has prompted the development of partnerships between state agencies active in rural areas, as for example in the US National Rural Development Partnership and its constituent State Rural Development Councils (Radin *et al.* 1996).

Fourthly, there has been a scaling-back of state activities in rural government, as in other areas of the state's operation. In its most extreme manifestation this has included the deregulation of agriculture in New Zealand (Le Heron and Roche 1999). Elsewhere, the state has sought to disperse responsibilities through the privatisation of state-owned agencies and utility companies, and through the forging of 'partnerships' with private and voluntary sector organisations. The former has had particular significance for rural areas because of the extensive rural land ownership of many privatised corporations (e.g. water companies), and because public ownership guaranteed the subsidisation of the uneconomic delivery of services to remote rural locations. The latter is enshrined as a guiding principle of EU rural development policy and has become a commonplace feature of rural government in Britain (Edwards *et al.* 2000).

Fifthly, partnership working at a local scale has supported a renewed emphasis on community engagement and 'bottom-up' initiatives. The 'empowerment' of communities and active citizens has been promoted in the EU Cork Declaration and through schemes such as LEADER in Europe, Landcare in Australia and the Vermont Environmental Partnerships in Communities Program in the USA (Edwards 1998; Ray 2000; J. Richardson 2000; Sobels *et al.* 2001). At the same time, innovations such as the French *intercommunalité* system have developed horizontal inter-governmental partnerships at the local scale to assist smaller rural authorities in service delivery and economic development (Michel 1998). Local partnerships and grassroots innovation have been encouraged by the channelling of public funds through competitive bidding processes, which have in addition produced uneven geographies of public funding, particularly for regeneration (Edwards *et al.* 2000; Jones and Little 2000).

Sixthly, there has been in some sectors a withdrawal from specifically rural institutions and policies in favour of regional initiatives encompassing both rural and urban areas. In Britain, the Development Board for Rural Wales was incorporated into the all-Wales Welsh Development Agency in 1999, while the economic development responsibilities of the English Rural Development Corporation were transferred to new Regional Development Agencies in April 2000. Similarly, the development of the European Spatial Development Perspective has proposed the subsuming of rural areas into regional urban–rural partnerships (T. Richardson 2000).

Many of the above processes have been paralleled in urban policy and it is therefore perhaps unsurprising that rural researchers have looked to theoretical perspectives already employed in urban studies for guidance in analysing these trends. This chapter introduces a number of such perspectives and examines their application in a rural context. To illustrate these, we will periodically refer to examples drawn from our own research in rural Wales. Rural Wales has experienced many of the processes of restructuring outlined above. As a region historically dominated by agriculture, it has witnessed economic realignment as the significance of farming as an employer and income-generator has declined, and this has been reflected in the introduction of state-sponsored initiatives to promote broader-based economic development. Initially these followed a top-down state-interventionist model, through the Development Board for Rural Wales. More recently, however, the emphasis has shifted to 'bottom-up' community development strategies, driven in part by the need to meet requirements for European Union funding. Much of the region received EU funds through Objective 5b and the LEADER programme during the 1990s, and the western sector qualified for Objective 1 funding in 2000. The region has also been affected by wider processes of state restructuring. Public agencies privatised or commercialised in the 1980s and 1990s, including water boards and the Forestry Commission, are large landowners in central Wales; while the delivery of public services has been influenced by the restructuring of local government and changes such as the deregulation of public transport[1].

Understanding policy change: employing the concepts of governance and regulation in rural research

In an effort to analyse and understand these shifts in rural policy, and in the institutions charged with framing and delivering such policy, rural researchers have begun to turn to a range of new theoretical perspectives, based around the concepts of governance and regulation. In many ways these concepts have provided a means of broadening the traditional concerns of rural policy studies, which tended to be based around the twin issues of agricultural policy and land use planning (although see Cloke and Little 1990 for a notable exception). However, the use of such concepts should be tempered with caution – as Jessop stated 'It is important to distinguish words from concepts. This applies especially to regulation and governance' (1995: 308). This is a warning that perhaps has not always been well heeded in rural research where the concepts (or rather the words) have been used somewhat indiscriminately in recent years. For this reason we will spend a short while clarifying each concept, before looking at how they have been applied in research on rural Wales. We will then make suggestions as to how they might be used in the future, before moving on to consider a range of other concepts which might be drawn on to help analyse contemporary governance and policy in rural areas.

Of the two concepts, governance has been the most familiar within rural research. The term governance is now used, and accepted, in a variety of academic and practitioner contexts. There is a general agreement within these contexts that 'governance refers to the development of governing styles in which boundaries between and within public and private sectors have become blurred' (Stoker 1996: 2). Thus the concept of governance is not simply an academic synonym for government. Its increasing use signifies a concern with a change in the meaning and content of government. As Rhodes puts it (1996: 652–3), the term is now used to refer 'to a new process of governing, or a changed condition of ordered rule, or the new method by which society is governed'. Where government signals a concern with the formal institutions and structures of the state, the concept of governance is broader and draws attention to the ways in which governmental and non-governmental organisations work together, and to the ways in which political power is distributed, both internal and external to the state (Stoker 1995). In the words of Jessop, the term governance signals a shift to 'a broad concern with a wide range of governance mechanisms with no presumption that these are anchored primarily in the sovereign state' (1995: 310–11).

For those interested in understanding the shifting ways in which rural areas are governed, the concept of governance thus offers a route into examining the changing relationship between state, market and civil society. In the case of rural Wales, for instance, Edwards *et al.* (2000) have charted the growth and nature of partnership working in the field of economic regeneration. They found that partnerships are now a commonplace feature of rural regeneration strategies across Wales. Most small towns and rural districts were able to boast a plethora of groups focused on community development, civic refurbishment, training, business development, marketing, sustainability, transport or tourism – all constituted as some form of *partnership*, bringing together a range of organisations, often from across the public, private and voluntary sectors. These partnerships were responsible for regeneration policies that would once have been anchored solely in the public sector – hence the academic concern with a shift away from government towards a much more complex system of governance.

Viewing the shift away from local authorities and development boards through the conceptual lens of governance also opens up a number of questions concerning the structure of such partnerships and their operation.

The messiness and complexity of the new structures of governance, for instance, raise questions concerning legitimacy, accountability and power. Whereas the old structures of local and central government were elected, the new governance arrangements are largely appointed, and often involve voluntary and community groups in an unpaid capacity. In this context, Murdoch (1997) and Murdoch and Abram (1998) have pointed out how the rural White Papers of the mid-1990s in England, Scotland and Wales all drew on notions of self-help, self-sufficiency and community involvement to legitimise and frame a withdrawal of state support and public services, and Ward and McNicholas (1998) have studied how the European Union's rural policy also stresses ideas of self-help and the 'active' citizen. Edwards (1998) has used this perspective to explore the details of community activity in west Wales, and has pointed out that while central government policy has encouraged community participation, this call has been interpreted and responded to differently by various community interests.

The concept of governance as an interactive process between a range of organisations draws attention to the difficulties of negotiating shared goals and agendas, and to the acceptance that many intended actions will not match eventual outcomes. Most studies in this area to date have found that despite a rhetoric of inclusion and partnership, there is a considerable imbalance of power between those involved in the new rural governance. Edwards *et al.* (2001: 308) conclude from their work on Wales that as long as the new partnership structures 'have no direct accountability to the public, remain dominated by state sector representatives, funding and resourcing, and operate within structures established by state agencies, then it is the state which continues to govern governance'. Jones and Little (2000) have confirmed the continuing power of the state in rural regeneration policy, charting the difficulties of involving both private and community sectors, and have also identified considerable gender imbalances in the new rural power structures.

In sum, the work within a governance perspective has broadened our knowledge of a range of processes surrounding new forms of rural policy formulation and delivery. While this work has undoubtedly been valuable, it is true to say that it has privileged new empirical knowledge over and above conceptual and theoretical development. In this sense, rural researchers have been largely content to draw on concepts of governance developed elsewhere (often in urban-based literatures) and apply them in a rural context. What has been less in evidence is any attempt to use rural research to actually develop the concepts. It remains the case that researchers have focused on what concepts of governance can do to extend rural research, rather than investigate what such research might mean for the continued development of the concepts. Partly because of this there is a danger that the concept of governance has been applied in a rather one-dimensional manner – and used in a descriptive rather than in a conceptual sense.

In order to tackle this problem, some rural research has attempted to investigate the concept of governance rather than simply apply it. A key aspect of this move has been to take governance not as the end point of analysis, but as the beginning – in other words to ask how and why new mechanisms of governance are emerging, rather than simply taking as given, and then charting, the fact that they have. It is in this spirit that some researchers have used the concept of regulation, to seek to provide a broader framework within which the emergence of new structures of governance may themselves be situated and understood. Regulation in this sense does not mean rule-making, or legal regulation – which has been its accepted use in rural research, especially in the areas of agricultural regulation and de-regulation (see for instance Bell and Lowe 2000; Lowe *et al.* 1994; Marsden *et al.* 1990). Instead, regulation should be understood in a far broader sense, to refer to the regulation of the economy as a whole[2].

The regulation approach in this latter sense has its origins in work under-taken by a group of French economists in the mid-1970s. Put simply, these academics were concerned to analyse the 'regulation' (perhaps better translated as regularisation or normalisation) of the economy in its broadest sense, begin-ning from the insight that continued capital accumulation depends on a series of social, cultural and political supports. The approach therefore 'aims to study the changing combinations of economic *and extra-economic* institutions and practices which help to secure, if only temporarily and always in specific eco-nomic spaces, a certain stability and predictability in accumulation – despite the fundamental contradictions and conflicts generated by the very dynamic of capital itself' (Jessop 1997a: 288). As a method of analysis, then, regulation theory starts from the premise that the reproduction of capitalist social rela-tions is not guaranteed by the abstract relations that are the defining features of the capitalist mode of production. Rather, both crises in the accumulation process and phases of expanded production (when these occur) are the prod-ucts of more concrete institutional structures, political and social processes and cultural discourses. Mechanisms and institutions of governance may be viewed as part of these multiple social, cultural and institutional supports which come together in an attempt to promote and sustain economic growth.

Goodwin *et al.* (1995) have used their work on changing rural lifestyles in Wales to argue that the use of a regulationist approach to analyse rural change has the potential to open up a whole host of research questions. They state that:

> Far from closing down research by attempting to fit it into a Fordist/post-Fordist straitjacket, a regulationist inspired approach can open up new and significant avenues of enquiry for rural studies. By drawing on regulation theory we can locate and conceptualise rural change within a framework which acknowledges that this is part and parcel of more general attempts to regulate the continuing contradictions and crises of capitalism. But it is also a framework which acknow-ledges that rural change is distinctive and diverse (1995: 1258).

This work pointed, for instance, to a continuing series of economic, social and political changes that were having a wide impact on the lives of rural residents in Wales. A quarter of those in rural Wales were living in, or on the margins of, poverty, with two-fifths surviving on extremely low incomes. Agriculture was in decline as a source of employment, and instead the rural economy was based around service sector employment. The study also found a significant number of residents suffering from housing, health and mobility problems. As well as helping to dispel the persistent image of idyllic rural society, studies such as this are able to link rural change to broader sets of social and economic shifts.

Yet the reordering of society produced in rural Wales was not the same as that experienced elsewhere – Goodwin *et al.* found a rather unstable society, based around low incomes, seasonal, temporary and part-time employment and high levels of poverty and deprivation, in comparison with more favoured rural areas within England. Analysing the diversity and difference between rural areas from within a regulationist perspective can be enhanced by employing the notion of 'regulation as process', developed by Painter and Goodwin (1995; see also Goodwin and Painter 1996). Instead of looking for coherent 'modes of regulation' research can then emphasise the ebb and flow of regulatory processes through time and across space.

This leads us to thinking about the generation of regulation (or, conversely, of processes that undermine regulation) as organised in and through key *sites* and spaces. Each set of social practices that go to make up the interactions that can be identified as contributing to (or undermining) regulation has its own key sites, and those interactions are thus interactions across space. Hence, the spatiality of regulation is integral to its effectiveness, or the lack of it. In this way we can investigate issues at the rural level such as transport, housing, social polarisation, employment change and economic development and still maintain a purchase on how each of these is related both to each other and to wider sets of social, economic and political processes. Hence research can proceed without divorcing the countryside from its broader social context. Comparisons can be made, both between rural areas within the same country, and between rural areas in different nations, of sets of regulatory processes and their economic and social effects.

When used properly, a regulationist perspective has the potential to link the study of economic processes in the countryside to concerns surrounding rural policy, the state and political activity. In focusing 'on the historically contingent ensembles of complementary economic and extra-economic mechanisms and practices which enable relatively stable accumulation to occur over relatively long periods' (Jessop 1997b: 503), the regulation approach legitimately links the traditional concerns of political economy with analyses of the state and civil society. This is one of its attractions for those researching rural policy, or shifts in rural governance. The use of the regulation approach would lead to the conclusion that for those interested in local changes in, say, rural housing, planning and welfare provision, the rural state and rural governance cannot be fully understood outside their roles (both positive and negative) in the ebb and flow of regulation. However, the point should also be made that neither can they be fully understood within them. The institutions and practices of rural government have their own histories and patterns of development. Explaining their changing character thus requires a theory of governance, a theory of the state, and empirical historical and geographical research, as well as a theory of their impact on (economic) regulation. Thus, while a regulation approach can illuminate how changes in governance and policy can help (or hinder) continued accumulation and economic development, it should not be expected to explain these changes themselves. Instead we need to turn to other concepts and other theories that are more centrally concerned with issues of politics, policy and governance.

Analysing the 'micro-circuits' of rural power

Although the concepts of governance and regulation offer considerable insights into broad sets of changes in rural policy, they need to be complemented by theoretical frameworks that are able to analyse power and politics both as a set of strategic calculations and at a more local level. Guidance as to how we might understand the strategic processes that have produced changes in local governance and policy may be provided by four approaches, which we examine in this section. Two, governmentality and strategic relational state theory potentially provide an insight into the state strategies through which changes in governance and policy are framed. The second two, 'institutional thickness' and a focus on the local *politics* of rural policy and governance, may help to explain how changes in governance and policy are received and implemented within rural localities. Each of these approaches has so far gained only limited application in rural research. As such, it is again appropriate for us to briefly introduce each concept before looking at how they have been employed within rural studies, and how they may be developed in future use.

Governmentality is associated with the work of Michel Foucault and is essentially concerned with the problem of how government renders society governable (Foucault 1991; Rose 1993). 'Classical governmentality' hence involves both the description and problematisation of society, and the putting in place of techniques and mechanisms to respond to the problems identified. However, Foucault also proposed a second, more historically specific, meaning of governmentality which 'marks the emergence of a distinctly new form of thinking about and exercising power in certain societies' (Dean 1999: 19; see Foucault 1991). In this 'neo-foucauldian governmentality' the distinction between government and population becomes blurred (Thompson 2001).

The concept of governmentality is attractive to researchers concerned with changing rural policy and governance for two reasons. Firstly, in highlighting the *apparatuses of security* – including health, education, social welfare and economic management systems – that the state employs to govern a population (Dean 1999), governmentality can reveal the strategic rationalities which produce new forms of governance (see Lockie 1999; MacKinnon 2000). Theorists such as Nicholas Rose (1996a, b) have proposed that advanced western democracies have experienced a shift in the regime of governmentality from 'managed liberalism' – epitomised by the Keynesian welfare state – in which the 'social sphere' was positioned as a legitimate object of governance and in which state planning proceeded predominantly at the national scale of rationalisation, to a new governmental rationality of 'governing through communities' which 'does not seek to govern through "society"; but through the regulated choices of individual citizens, now construed as subjects of choices and aspirations to self-actualisation and self-fulfilment' (Rose 1996a: 41). In the new rationality, individuals are represented as members of heterogeneous communities of allegiance, through which governance can be organised.

Murdoch identifies this shift in the English 'Rural White Paper' of 1995, in which, he argues, the representation of the countryside as consisting of small, tightly knit communities is mobilised to justify policies devolving responsibilities to local communities, voluntary groups and 'active citizens' as part of a 'covert withdrawal of the state as the contours of governmental responsibility are redrawn' (1997: 117). However, care should be taken not to conflate 'governing through communities' with initiatives to 'empower' territorial communities. While such initiatives may form part of a strategy of 'governing through communities', both Rose and Murdoch emphasise that 'communities' refer not just to territorial units, but also to any unit of self-defining allegiance. Thus, new forms of governance which seek to develop 'partnerships' between state agencies and representatives of young people, social housing tenants, local businesses and so on; to empower user groups; or to promote self-help and mutuality, may all be positioned as part of the new regime of governmentality.

Although Murdoch's analysis focused on English policy, a similar shift can be observed in Wales. Furthermore, this is evidenced not just in policy statements, but also in the structure, organisation and objectives of rural development initiatives. Since the late 1980s, rural development strategy in Wales has been spear-headed by community-based schemes, including the EU LEADER programme, the Development Board for Rural Wales's Market Town Initiative and Powys County Council's Community Enterprise Programme. These initiatives were distinctive in engaging communities in identifying 'problems' and proposing and implementing 'solutions' – in other words, 'governing through communities'. As such, for example, the different communities participating in the Market Town Initiative adopted different constitutions and followed different programmes of action, instead of having common practice imposed from above. Moreover, while most of the community development initiatives introduced have been targeted at geographical communities, there is also evidence of 'governing through non-geographical communities'. Firstly, the National Assembly for Wales's most recent community development programme, Communities First, invites 'imaginative proposals' from non-territorially discrete communities. Secondly, entities such as 'the farming community' and 'the business community' have been enrolled into the governmental process through representation on strategic partnerships including regional economic fora and Objective 1 monitoring committees. Significantly, it is often left to these 'communities' themselves to select how that representation shall be determined and what mechanisms exist for consultation and agreement of a common view (see also Edwards et al. 2000, 2001).

The second attraction of governmentality is that by questioning how the state thinks or reflects about its territory and how it produces knowledges about that territory, the concept allows for exploration of how 'the rural' is constructed and deployed in framing policies and techniques of governance. The representation of rurality is examined from a governmentality perspective by Murdoch (1997), Murdoch and Ward (1997) and Ward and McNicholas (1998), but the potential exists to go beyond the *application* of the governmentality approach in these papers to develop an exploration of how the concept of 'rurality' serves a technique of governing that in turn may contribute to wider understanding of the spatial dimensions of governmentality. Such a project might draw connections with a parallel body of literature which, although not grounded in the governmentality approach, has employed the wider Foucauldian notion of discourse in exploring how rural space is constructed in and through policy (Dixon and Hapke forthcoming; Gray 2000; T. Richardson 2000) and political practice (Mougenot and Mormont 1988; Woods 1997).

A second set of literatures has explored issues of state power and strategy from a neo-Gramscian perspective. Neo-Gramscian state theory (see Jessop 1990, 1997c, d; Jones 1997; MacLeod and Goodwin 1999a, b) approaches a study of new state institutions and new structures of rural power in terms of the strategic political decisions of leading social forces. The institutions of the state can be understood as the site, generator and product of such strategies. Thus for Jessop,

> state power can only be assessed relationally. The state as such has no power – it is merely an institutional ensemble; it has only a set of institutional capacities and liabilities which mediate that power: the power of the state is the power of the social forces acting in and through the state (1990: 269–70).

Jessop argues that while a regulationist approach can help us interpret broad shifts from one mode of regulation to another, neo-Gramscian state theory may help to disclose the political forces and practices that activate the very constitution of any particular mode of regulation. This focus on politics and political strategy is a useful reminder that the institutions of rural governance, and the policies they pursue, are shaped by political struggle and social conflict – in other words there is nothing predetermined about the shift from government to governance, or from one mode of regulation to another. But crucially, the terrain of such struggle is not necessarily equal, and the internal organisation of the state will tend to privilege access by some interests and forces over others. In the words of Jessop:

> particular forms of state privilege some strategies over others, privilege the access by some forces over others, some interests over others, some time horizons over others, some coalition possibilities over others. A given type of state, a given state form, a given form of regime, will be more accessible to some forces than others according to the strategies they adopt to gain state power. And it will be more suited to the pursuit of some types of economic or political strategy than others because of the modes of intervention and resources which characterize that system (1990: 10).

As developed by Jessop, neo-Gramscian state theory is both strategic – the question of which groups gain access to state resources is not predetermined, but dependent on the particular strategies they pursue – and relational – the state is conceived of as a set of social relations operating in and through various institutions, rather than as merely the institutions themselves. Various authors have used strategic-relational state theory to analyse rural politics. One of the earliest examples is that of Cloke and Goodwin (1992a, b) who drew on the additional Gramscian concepts of hegemonic and historic blocs to analyse how different social forces have been able to pursue different political projects in rural areas. More recently, Goodwin and Pemberton (forthcoming) have drawn on strategic-relational theory to analyse political change in west Wales. What these authors have in common is a stress on the politically mediated nature of rural policy, and on the ways in which such policy is contested and pursued differently through different sets of institutional structures. Goodwin and Pemberton, for instance, examine the changing nature of economic development policy in west Wales following the restructuring of local government in 1996. This abolished county councils, and replaced them with smaller, single tier, unitary local authorities. The strategic relational approach allowed Goodwin and Pemberton to explore how this change in local government structure affected the nature and content of local politics – empowering some groups but making it less possible for others to pursue their chosen strategies.

While the above approaches assist in understanding the strategic context of changes to rural policy and governance, a second set of questions may be posed about the factors that influence the reception and implementation of these changes within rural localities. For example, the 'institutional thickness' approach argues that the presence of particular institutions, the interaction between institutions, and the capacity for building coalitions and common regional visions for development, can all influence regional development trajectories (Amin and Thrift 1994; Hudson 1994). This thesis was developed in the context of deindustrialising regions and its applicability to rural areas is debatable. Amin (1999) holds that lagging rural regions face a different set of impediments and that therefore the concept is not transferable; yet, Jones and Clark have contended that 'many restructuring rural regions face strongly similar, often identical, development "impediments" to lagging industrial or urban regions' (2000: 354), and have sought to apply the perspective to work on viticultural elites in the Languedoc region of France. Here they argue that both consensual institutions (shared views and interpretations of problems and solutions) and concrete institutions (the agreements, agencies and policy measures created to put these views into practice) have over time constituted locally specific notions of 'rurality' and territorial identity which have acted to enable and constrain elite responses to structural change and partnership formation as part of new structures of governance.

However, Jones and Clark's employment of institutional thickness has not entirely overcome the criticisms of abstractionism and reductionism that have been levied at the institutional thickness concept (Lovering 1999; MacLeod and Goodwin 1999b). As such, it may be more productive to focus on the broader question of how local elites and political actors engage with changes to rural governance and policy within what might be labelled the *local politics of rural change*. This umbrella title does not relate to any one coherent theoretical perspective, but rather to a body of work informed by various theoretical positions which has generally placed a greater emphasis on human agency and on the role of individual actors within the rural political system than the more structurally focused approaches outlined above.

Three main avenues of inquiry can be identified within work on the local politics of rural change. The first is concerned with the micropolitics and intra-organisational politics of new forms of governance (see, for example, Parker 1999, and Sobels *et al.* 2001). The significance of these interactions can again be illustrated with reference to Wales. As we noted in the section on governance above, the transition to a new structure of 'rural governance' in Wales has spawned a substantial number of partnerships, operating in a range of arenas including economic regeneration, health, youth policy and conservation, that bring together two or more partners from the public, private, voluntary and community sectors. The rationale for partnership formation has tended to be described in terms of 'community engagement' or 'pooling resources' or 'integrated strategic planning', but the effectiveness of partnerships in meeting these ideals is often contingent on the micropolitics of their operation. The selection of partners was frequently a political decision – one partnership in the DBRW Market Town Initiative deliberately excluded the Town Council and Chamber of Trade because it wanted to set itself up as a 'new broom'. Once enrolled, the contribution made by individual partner organisations may be similarly politically calculated – one farming union confided that it participated in a particular partnership only to guard against it trespassing on to agricultural issues. The capacity of partner representatives to participate fully is structured by their training, administrative support and familiarity with other participants. Some community representatives find themselves marginalised as the representatives of major established partners, who are used to working with each other and who control the purse strings, dominate proceedings. Conversely, individuals who sit on a number of partnership boards have become empowered by their bridging role[3].

The significance of individuals within local power networks has been explored further as part of the second avenue of inquiry, which has focused on the response of local political elites and political actors to policy reforms and the restructuring of local rural governance. Elites may, in different circumstances, attempt to resist reforms or may be proactive in using new forms of governance to their advantage; while new institutions and policy shifts may create opportunities for the emergence of new leaders (Woods 1997, 1998). How these opportunities are created and taken may be shaped by broader structural factors, but they are also frequently determined by the actions of individuals within particular places.

The third body of work has addressed issues of representation in both established and new forms of governance, notably with respect to gender (Little and Jones 2000). These include questions about whether new institutional forms are reproducing previous patterns of inequality, or whether they are creating opportunities for greater participation by previously under-represented groups; and questions about the dynamics of representation in initiatives aimed at 'community engagement'.

By focusing on the dynamics of local political engagement, these various studies have enabled some of the assumptions implicit in rural policy and governance to be challenged, helping to construct a better understanding of why the intentions of rural policy and governmental initiatives may not always be achieved on the ground.

Conclusion

These are promising times for research on rural policy and governance. Not only does the pace of continuing reform and institutional change provide a rich field of inquiry, but the engagement with theory in the analysis of these changes has proved fruitful and has contributed to the current dynamism of rural studies. However, we wish to conclude this review with two caveats: one a statement of potential, the other a word of warning.

Firstly, we can observe that theoretical concepts such as governance, regulation and governmentality tend to have been applied to rural situations rather than developed in rural contexts. There are few theoretical writings in any of these fields which draw on rural research as empirical evidence for their discussion. In contrast, we would argue that rural studies has much to contribute to the development of these theories. Indeed, given the urban genesis of most elements of these theories, rural researchers potentially have a critical role to play in assessing their wider applicability and in offering additional insights and developments that may not be readily apparent in an urban context.

Secondly, care needs to be exercised in order to ensure that these concepts are being employed in a theoretically consistent manner. No one theory discussed above is able to provide a totalising explanation for changes in rural policy and governance, and there exists the capacity for two or more concepts to be employed alongside each other to interrogate different parts of the governing process. However, if two or more concepts are to be deployed alongside each other, the onus is on the researcher to ensure that they are epistemologically complementary. Painter (1997) has pointed out how work on urban politics and policy often falls into this precise trap. He uses the example of regulation theory and regime theory to argue that there are fundamental incompatibilities that should prevent them being used in the same analysis. Regime theory is ultimately based on a rational choice model of selective incentives, whilst regulation theory rejects the idea that processes of regulation arise through individual choices (Painter 1997: 134). In contrast, Jessop has argued that regulation theory is more commensurate with strategic relational state theory, as each is grounded in an inclusive or integral understanding of economy and state respectively (1997d: 53–4). If this caution is not exercised, then there is the danger that we will end up with a combination of fundamentally incompatible theoretical frameworks, while not producing any real conceptually informed understanding of rural policy and governance.

Underlying both of these observations is the need for rural researchers to engage more directly with the original theoretical writings on governance, governmentality, regulation theory, strategic relational state theory and so on. Thus far, rural researchers have often tended to draw on authors who have translated these concepts into applied settings (usually urban-based), rather than on the original works themselves. By following the concepts back to their origins in the work of authors such as Foucault, Jessop, Gramsci and Poulantzas, rural researchers may grasp the potential not just to employ these concepts with greater epistemological clarity, but also to exploit the rural as a laboratory for work on policy and governance and thus contribute more fully to our understanding of these processes across all environments.

Notes

1. For more background on the region see Cloke *et al.* (1997), Edwards (1998) and Edwards *et al.* (2000).
2. This confusion stems from the polysemy of the English term 'regulation'. In French there is a distinction between *reglementation* and *regulation* – *reglementation* refers to regulation in the sense of rule-making (in this case by the state), while *regulation* refers to regulation in the regulation theorists' sense of contingently emerging regulatory effects operating at the level of the economy as a whole.
3. For more on these examples see Edwards *et al.* (2000, 2001).

References

Amin, A. 1999 'An institutionalist perspective on regional economic development', *International Journal of Urban and Regional Research*, **23**(2), 365–78.

Amin, A. and Thrift, N. (eds) 1994 *Globalization, Institutions and Regional Development in Europe*, Oxford University Press, Oxford.

Bell, M. and Lowe, P. 2000 'Regulated freedoms: the market and the state, agriculture and the environment', *Journal of Rural Studies*, **16**, 285–94.

Cloke, P. and Goodwin, M. 1992a 'Conceptualizing countryside change: from post-Fordism to rural structured coherence', *Transactions of the Institute of British Geographers*, **17**, 321–6.

Cloke, P. and Goodwin, M. 1992b 'The changing function and position of rural areas in Europe', *Nederlandse Geografische Studies*, **153**, 19–36.

Cloke, P. and Little, J. 1990 *The Rural State*, Oxford University Press, Oxford.

Cloke, P., Goodwin, M. and Milbourne, P. 1997 *Rural Wales: Community and Marginalization*, University of Wales Press, Cardiff.

Dean, M. 1999 *Governmentality: Power and Rule in Modern Society*, Sage, London.

DETR 1999 *Rural England: A Discussion Document – A Summary of Responses*, Department of the Environment, Transport and the Regions, London.

Dixon, D. and Hapke, H. forthcoming 'Cultivating discourse: shifting the terms of debate in the 1996 Freedom to Farm Bill'. *Annals of the Association of American Geographers*.

Edwards, B. 1998 'Charting the discourse of community action: perspectives from practice in rural Wales', *Journal of Rural Studies*, **14**(1), 63–78.

Edwards, B., Goodwin, M., Pemberton, S. and Woods, M. 2000 *Partnership Working in Rural Regeneration*, Policy Press, Bristol.

Edwards, B., Goodwin, M., Pemberton, S. and Woods, M. 2001 'Partnerships, power and scale in rural governance', *Environment and Planning C: Government and Policy*, **19**, 289–310.

Fluharty, C. 2001 'Testimony to the Sub-committee on Conservation, Credit, Rural Development and Research', US House of Representatives Committee on Agriculture, June Rural Policy Research Institute, Columbia, MO.

Foucault, M. 1991 'Governmentality', pp. 87–104 in G. Burchell, C. Gordon and P. Miller (eds), *The Foucault Effect: Studies in Governmentality*, Harvester Wheatsheaf, London.

Goodwin, M. 1998 'The governance of rural areas: some emerging research issues and agendas', *Journal of Rural Studies*, **14**(1), 5–12.

Goodwin, M. and Painter, J. 1996 'Local governance, the crisis of Fordism and the changing geographies of regulation', *Transactions of the Institute of British Geographers*, **21**, 635–48.

Goodwin, M. and Pemberton, S. forthcoming 'Rural politics, state projects and local political strategies: accumulation and hegemony in the countryside', *Journal of Rural Studies*, forthcoming.

Goodwin, M., Cloke, P. and Milbourne, P. 1995 'Regulation theory and rural research: theorising contemporary rural change', *Environment and Planning A*, **27**, 1245–60.

Gray, J. 2000 'The Common Agricultural Policy and the re-invention of the rural in the European Community', *Sociologia Ruralis*, **40**(1), 30–52.

Grant, W. 1990 'Rural politics in Britain', pp. 286–98 in P. Lowe and M. Bodiguel (eds), *Rural Studies in Britain and France*, Belhaven, London.

Hodge, I. 1996 'On penguins on icebergs: the Rural White Paper and the assumption of rural policy', *Journal of Rural Studies*, **12**(4), 331–7.

Hudson, R. 1994 'Institutional change, cultural transformation, and economic regeneration: myths and realities from Europe's old industrial regions', pp. 196–216 in A. Amin and N. Thrift, (eds), *Globalization, Institutions and Regional Development in Europe*, Oxford University Press. Oxford.

Jessop, B. 1990 *State Theory: Putting Capitalist States in their Place*, Blackwell, Oxford.

Jessop, B. 1995 'The regulation approach, governance and post-Fordism: alternative perspectives on economic and political change?', *Economy and Society*, **24**(3), 307–33.

Jessop, B. 1997a 'Survey article: the regulation approach', *Journal of Political Philosophy*, 5, 287–326.

Jessop, B. 1997b 'Twenty years of the (Parisian) regulation approach: the paradox of success and failure at home and abroad', *New Political Economy*, 2, 503–26.

Jessop, B. 1997c 'Globalization and the national state: reflections on a theme of Poulantzas', Paper presented to the Colloquium 'Miliband and Poulantzas in Retrospect and Prospect', City University of New York, pp. 1–31.

Jessop, B. 1997d 'A neo-Gramscian approach to the regulation of urban regimes', pp. 51–73 in M. Lauria (ed.), *Reconstructing Urban Regime Theory: Regulating Urban Politics in a Global Economy*, Sage, London.

Jones, A. and Clark, J. 2000 'Of vines and vignettes: sectoral evolution and institutional thickness in the Languedoc', *Transactions of the Institute of British Geographers*, 25(3), 333–54.

Jones, M. 1997 'Spatial selectivity of the state? The regulationist enigma and local struggles over economic governance', *Environment and Planning A*, 29(5), 831–64.

Jones, O. and Little, J. 2000 'Rural challenge(s): partnership and new rural governance', *Journal of Rural Studies*, 16, 171–84.

Le Heron, R. and Roche, M. 1999 'Rapid re-regulation, agricultural restructuring and the re-imagining of agriculture in New Zealand', *Rural Sociology*, 64(2), 207–18.

Little, J. 2001 'New rural governance?', *Progress in Human Geography*, 25(1), 97–102.

Little, J. and Jones, O. 2000 'Masculinity, gender and rural policy', *Rural Sociology*, 65(4), 621–39.

Lockie, S. 1999 'The state, rural environments and globalisation: "action at a distance" via the Australian Landcare program', *Environment and Planning A*, 31(4), 597–611.

Lovering, J. 1999 'Theory led by policy: the inadequacies of the new regionalism', *International Journal of Urban and Regional Research*, 23(2), 379–95.

Lowe, P. and Ward, N. 2001 'New Labour, new rural vision? Labour's rural white paper', *Political Quarterly*, 72(3), 386–90.

Lowe, P., Marsden, T. and Whatmore, S. (eds) 1994 *Regulation and Agriculture*, David Fulton, London.

MacKinnon, D. 2000 'Managerialism, governmentality and the state: a neo-Foucauldian approach to local economic governance', *Political Geography*, 19, 293–314.

MacLeod, G. and Goodwin, M. 1999a 'Space, scale and strategy: towards a re-interpretation of contemporary urban and regional governance', *Progress in Human Geography*, 23, 503–27.

MacLeod, G. and Goodwin, M. 1999b 'Reconstructing an urban and regional political economy: on the state, politics, scale and explanation', *Political Geography*, 18, 697–730.

Marsden, T., Lowe, P. and Whatmore, S. (eds) 1990 *Rural Restructuring: Global Processes and Their Responses*, David Fulton, London.

Michel, H. 1998 'Government or governance? The case of the French local political system', *West European Politics*, 21(3), 146–69.

Mougenot, C. and Mormont, M. 1988 *L'Invention du Rural: l'héritage des mouvements ruraux (de 1930 à nos jours)*, Vie Ouvrière, Brussels.

Murdoch, J. 1997 'The shifting territory of government: some insights from the rural white paper', *Area*, 29, 109–18.

Murdoch, J. and Abram, S. 1998 'Defining the limits of community governance', *Journal of Rural Studies*, **14**, 41–50.

Murdoch, J. and Ward, N. 1997 'Governmentality and territoriality: the statistical manufacture of Britain's "national farm"', *Political Geography*, **16**(4), 307–24.

Painter, J. 1997 'Regulation, regime and practice in urban politics', pp. 122–43 in M. Lauria (ed.), *Reconstructing Urban Regime Theory: Regulating Urban Politics in a Global Economy*, Sage, London.

Painter, J. and Goodwin, M. 1995 'Local governance and concrete research: investigating the uneven development of regulation', *Economy and Society*, **24**, 334–56.

Parker, G. 1999 'Rights, symbolic violence and the micropolitics of the rural: case study of the Parish Paths Partnership scheme', *Environment and Planning A*, **31**(7), 1207–22.

Radin, B., Agranoff, R., Bowman, A., Buntz, G., Ott, J.S., Romzek, B. and Wilson, R. 1996 *New Governance for Rural America*, University of Kansas Press, Lawrence, KS.

Ray, C. 2000 The EU LEADER programme: rural development laboratory, *Sociologia Ruralis*, **40**(2), 163–71.

Rhodes, R. 1996 'The new governance: governing without government', *Political Studies*, **XLIV**, 652–67.

Richardson, J. 2000 *Partnerships in Communities: Reweaving the Fabric of Rural America*, Island Press, Washington, DC.

Richardson, T. 2000 'Discourses of rurality in EU spatial policy: the European Spatial Development Perspective', *Sociologia Ruralis*, **40**(1), 53–71.

Rose, N. 1993 'Government, authority and expertise in advanced liberalism', *Economy and Society*, **22**, 283–99.

Rose, N. 1996a 'Governing "advanced liberal democracies"', pp. 37–64 in A. Barry, T. Osborne and N. Rose (eds), *Foucault and Political Reason*, UCL Press, London.

Rose, N. 1996b 'The death of the social? Re-figuring the territory of government', *Economy and Society*, **25**(3), 327–56.

Sobels, J., Curtis, A. and Lockie, S. 2001 'The role of Landcare group networks in rural Australia: exploring the contribution of social capital', *Journal of Rural Studies*, **17**(3), 265–76.

Stoker, G. 1995 'Public–private partnerships and urban governance', mimeo, available from author at Department of Government, University of Manchester.

Stoker, G. 1996 'Governance as theory: five propositions', mimeo available from author at Department of Government, University of Manchester.

Thompson, N. 2001 'Governmentality in rural studies', paper presented at the Restless Ruralities Conference, Coventry, July.

Ward, N. and McNicholas, K. 1998 'Reconfiguring rural development in the UK: Objective 5b and the new rural governance', *Journal of Rural Studies*, **14**, 27–39.

Woods, M. 1997 'Discourses of power and rurality: local politics in Somerset in the twentieth century', *Political Geography*, **16**(6), 453–78.

Woods, M. 1998 'Advocating rurality? The repositioning of rural local government', *Journal of Rural Studies*, **14**, 13–26.

Co-constructing the countryside: hybrid networks and the extensive self

CHAPTER 15

Jonathan Murdoch

Introducing hybridity

A number of the chapters in this collection have shown that the countryside is a social and cultural construction. In general, the social constructionist perspective aims to uncover the ways in which the countryside reflects prevailing socio-cultural aspirations, processes and norms. To take just one recent example, the conservative philosopher Roger Scruton (2001: 13) claims that the countryside is 'an icon of national loyalty, a symbol of what is most precious to us, and at the same time an example of the fragility of our attachments'. In proposing this perspective Scruton seems to believe that the countryside's symbolic status should be protected from those globalising and standardising forces that are threatening to disrupt the existing rural social order. He claims there is a requirement to retain (English) rurality's particular and special qualities in the face of externally imposed processes of change.

In this view, the countryside seemingly lies 'beyond' modernity; it is deemed to encompass communal and altruistic social forms that work to a quite different social calculus from those found elsewhere in modern society, notably in the city: where the city is fragmented, the countryside is organic; where the city breeds alienation, the countryside encourages belonging and affection (see Short 1991 for a summary of such views). However contrived, these social assumptions are widely held throughout contemporary society. Yet, there are other perceptions at play. For example, the countryside is also seen as a place of 'nature', a zone where some connection to biophysical rather than social processes is deemed to occur. Birdwatchers, ramblers, naturalists and other such groupings attempt to engage with a *natural*, as opposed to a *social*, order in the countryside. What marks out the countryside in their view is the degree to which it escapes from purely social relations; it is valued because it offers an immersion in a world of nature and seems to promise a genuine engagement with the 'non-human' (Macnaghten and Urry 2001).

This second perspective places limits on the first; that is, the idea that the countryside is simply a social construction, one that reflects dominant patterns of social relations, cannot adequately account for the 'natural' entities found within its boundaries. There is something beyond the 'social' at work as the countryside displays a material complexity that is not easily reducible to even the most nuanced social categories. This is not to say that such categories are redundant; it is just that, when discussing the countryside more needs to be added in. To paraphrase Sarah Whatmore (1999), the countryside 'is more than human'. Yet, when the extra, non-human 'something' is stirred into the mix, the meaning and status of the 'social' changes. Thus, it is difficult to talk about the social *plus* the non-human for the intertwining of the two appears to give rise to something new (Irwin 2001).

Another way of talking about the rural and the countryside has therefore emerged. This discursive mode combines the 'social' and the 'natural' perspectives with which people are most familiar in order to treat the countryside as a *hybrid* space, one that mixes up social and natural entities in creative combinations (cf. Matless 1998). Admittedly, this third discourse is not in common usage for it stems largely from theoretical developments in sociology and human geography. In these disciplines new theories are employed to throw light on the complex interrelationships between societies and environments so that both can be taken seriously (i.e. one should not be seen simply as the reflection of the other). Relationships between natural and social 'worlds' are now thought to be so intimate that their (artificial) separation no longer makes analytical sense. Because disciplinary boundaries have been established on the basis that the world can, to some extent, be sifted into discrete conceptual arenas, it is argued that we should now employ new hybrid forms of knowledge-making (Latour 1993). These new hybrid forms attempt to investigate the materially complex character of contemporary social, technological and natural relations. Thus despite the rather specialised provenance of the 'hybridity' repertoire, it is argued that it has the potential to capture the socio-natural complexity of the countryside more easily than traditional modes of representation (Whatmore 2002).

In this chapter I wish to explore the idea that rurality is also 'hybridity'. I want to examine whether some of the things that go on in the countryside can be thought of as 'heterogeneous' processes and consider how they might be evaluated using a perspective that celebrates, rather than marginalises, the heterogeneous diversity of rural objects and entities. In short, I want to propose that the countryside is *co-constructed* by humans and non-humans, bound together within complex interrelationships. In so doing, I will outline a conceptual approach that helps to bring processes of co-construction to the foreground of our concerns. As in earlier work (cf. Murdoch 1997, 1998, 2001), the approach is drawn from *Actor Network Theory* (ANT), a mode of analysis that investigates how social arrangements are integrated with technological and natural processes. In what follows, I will consider the extent to which this theory provokes a rethinking of such spatial categories as the 'rural' and the 'countryside'.

One interpretation of hybrid perspectives such as the actor network approach is that they force us to treat humans and non-humans in the country-side in a *symmetrical* fashion (on the notion of 'symmetry', see Callon 1986); that is, no special emphasis should be placed on the *social* domain of action because the stimulus for change may equally come from non-human entities. Therefore, any analysis of rural change must adopt an 'agnostic' attitude towards different types of actors and entities and must keep an open mind about which are likely to prevail in any given circumstance. In other words, analysis must follow *all* the actors and relations and the analyst should remain 'as undecided as possible on which elements will be tied together, on when they will start of have a common fate, on which interest will eventually win out over which' (Latour 1987: 175–6). This symmetrical approach requires that we do not adopt differing repertoires (e.g. 'social', 'natural') for entities that have still to become fully formed (that is, have still to *become* natural or social); rather, we must remain open to their hybridity, however complex it may be. In this perspective, then, the countryside is 'co-constructed' by social and natural entities.

In the first section, I will supply some illustrations drawn from recent events in the countryside that would appear to accord with this symmetrical view. However, I then go on to qualify the argument that the hybrid perspective more readily captures key processes of change by suggesting that certain overtly 'social' actions may retain their significance in the rural context. I argue that there is consequently a need to somehow align the *social constructionist* per-spective with the new concern for hybrid relationships. In this regard I wish to follow recent work by Blokland and Savage, who suggest that:

> a sensitivity to diverse kinds of networks allows us to see categories (such as class or ethnicity) as *relational*, and the various ways that categorical networks are *embedded* in physical space, and how such physical spaces are *made into* social spaces as articulations of social relations (2001: 10; emphasis added).

By bringing the heterogeneous networks of ANT to bear upon social cat-egories, it should be possible to show how *social* relations in the countryside are constructed out of more elements than those usually considered within purely *social* perspectives. Likewise, by giving the analysis of actor networks a social inclination, it should be possible to illustrate how *social processes* invariably act to order arrangements of *heterogeneous materials*. I then go on to give some indication how this dual perspective might be employed by showing how the social identities of class and gender are currently being reconstituted within and around rural objects and relations. In conclusion, I argue that, following this alignment of 'social' and 'hybrid' approaches, there is an obvious need to construct 'country visions' in theoretically 'pluralist' ways.

Hybrid events in the contemporary countryside

For purposes of clarification let us begin with an illustration of hybridity in the countryside. In early 2001, foot and mouth disease broke out in the United Kingdom. The disease was first identified at an abattoir in the east of England. Shortly thereafter its source was traced to a farm in the north of England. In rapid fashion new cases began to appear across the country, notably in Devon and Cumbria where clusters of affected farms soon became evident. Within 100 days of the outbreak, foot and mouth had been identified on 1700 farms and around 3 million animals had been slaughtered at a substantial cost to both taxpayers and rural businesses (losses to tourism alone were calculated to be over £5 billion and the dramatic decline in visitors to the countryside was thought to have put 150,000 jobs at risk). This was a countryside event of huge significance – as Peter Hetherington (2001) describes it, foot and mouth disease drove 'a huge hole in the rural economy'. It was also, I shall suggest, a 'hybrid' event, one that aligned natural, social, economic, political and technological processes within a complex and heterogeneous network of effects (see also Donaldson *et al.* 2002).

Foot and mouth is an infectious viral disease which attacks cattle, sheep, pigs and goats (along with other wild and domestic cloven-hooved animals and elephants, hedgehogs, and rats – MAFF 2001). It causes blisters to form in the mouth and on the feet of affected animals, leading them to lose both appetite and the ability to move around freely. The disease spreads through the saliva, milk and dung of animals but can also be borne on the wind. In the right climatic conditions (e.g. the cold and the damp) it remains virulent for long periods. Yet, while the disease is clearly caused by a viral agent, this agent works *within* economic, social and technological contexts. For instance, in the 2001 outbreak the spread of the disease was closely linked to the movement of animals within an increasingly centralised agricultural system. The age-old tradition of taking animals to livestock markets had been extended, with modern systems of transportation moving stock further and further to more and more distant markets (both within the United Kingdom and overseas). Once the virus reached the large markets that in the United Kingdom act as distribution centres in the livestock sector (especially significant for sheep), it quickly spread all over the country and then to mainland Europe (not surprisingly, one of the Government's first acts was to place a ban on the movement of livestock in an attempt to contain the spread of the virus).

Thus, the foot and mouth outbreak comprised a heterogeneous arrangement of linkages between viral agents, climatic conditions, styles of farming, systems of transportation and market requirements. As the crisis unfolded, however, its hybrid nature was revealed in a more sinister fashion by a strange intermingling of foot and mouth and BSE (bovine spongiform encephalopathy). In a disturbing development, a direct linkage between foot and mouth and BSE was established in the spring of 2001 when the Food Standards Agency discovered that animals at risk of carrying BSE may have been buried during the foot and mouth cull, with the consequence that the infective (prion) protein responsible for causing BSE could have entered the soil and water courses, and thus the food chain. The Agency recommended that these animals be dug up and incinerated. Foot and mouth thus resurrected fears about BSE.

To many people, the strange confluence of these two diseases conjures up a 'medieval' scenario of plague and pestilence in which unknown or unstoppable afflictions sweep through human and animal populations. Echoes of the 'medieval' also stem from a feeling that these events should have been left behind during successive rounds of industrial modernisation. Surely science, technology and the rational organisation of food systems have cast unruly, uncontrolled nature out? Surely nature is now domesticated, tamed, rendered compliant? Surely it is only a passive participant in human dominated systems of production and consumption? Apparently not: BSE and foot and mouth indicate that nature has 'boomerang' qualities; just when it seems to be under control it 'bounces back' in a fashion that escapes all attempts at containment. This 'boomerang' quality seems little changed from pre-industrial times when natural calamities were a frequent and expected occurrence.

And yet, these are not medieval times: these diseases are not 'acts of God' but, in important respects, have been 'made' by humans. The significance of key human interventions is rendered especially clear by the role played in both cases by reprocessed animal feed. It was widely reported in the press, and eventually acknowledged by Government, that the likely cause of the foot and mouth outbreak was the feeding of 'pigswill' on the farm first affected. 'Pigswill' is made up of reconstituted food products, including meat. The virus is thought to have entered the food chain via this route. A similar causal process lay at the heart of BSE. By the 1980s it had become commonplace for farmers to supplement the forage-based diet of cattle with protein concentrates bought from animal feed manufacturers (this practice was particularly widespread in the dairy industry where calves would routinely have protein concentrates included in their feed). The protein in these concentrates came from animal sources in the form of meat and bone meal (MBM), bloodmeal, feathermeal and fishmeal. As the Government Inquiry into BSE reported, 'the process of rendering animal parts to produce MBM, which is then incorporated in animal feed, will result in the pooling of material from many different animals and the wide dissemination of infection from a single infective animal' (Phillips Inquiry 2000: 6). And the more centralised and concentrated the system, the more effective and widespread the dissemination. In other words, the modern agro-food system provides a perfect ecology for disease to spread.

Foot and mouth and BSE are therefore not straightforwardly 'natural' events as they arise from interactions between human and natural systems (Hinchcliffe 2001). Thus, we can infer that there are two 'sides' to hybridity. Firstly, nature is active and can still wreak havoc in our carefully calibrated systems of control. The BSE causal agent is a prion protein that mutated within one cow and then spread along the food chain with devastating consequences.

Here a natural entity showed its ability to change shape and to act in unpredictable and uncontrollable ways. In this case, a mutated protein 'engineered' a profound restructuring of human systems. Secondly, we humans are generating new alignments of the social and the natural within our ever-expanding technological systems. In the BSE case, the feeding of reconstituted animal waste in animal food resulted from a new alignment of animals and technologies in the context of economic and political demands for cheap food products. For much of the time this alignment is hidden from view and simply appears in the form of packages of meat in supermarkets. However, the incorporation of a rogue agent into the mixture – the mutated prion protein – ruptured the alliances that had been consolidated in the food chain and rendered the system transparent. In other words, it opened up the heterogeneous relations that 'lie behind' meat commodities and highlighted the rather careless manner in which complex new hybrids are generated.

Theorising hybridity

The two aspects of hybridity outlined in the previous section are discussed more generally by Bruno Latour in his (1993) book *We Have Never Been Modern*. Here it is argued that modernity should *not* be seen as executing a gradual diminution of nature's significance (as humans gain greater control over their environments): rather, modernity itself is founded on 'hybrids', that is, economic, social and technical processes are also *heterogeneous* processes in which humans become bound ever more closely to non-humans. As modernity unfolds so heterogeneous relations proliferate. Thus, rather than escaping from nature, we are in a very real sense plunged further and further into it. But nature itself is no longer fully 'naturalised': it is 'hybridised', locked into complex sets of relations with other (social, technological) entities and systems.

Although the modern world is founded upon 'hybridity', Latour believes it is also marked by a curious inability on the part of modern humans to recognise this state of affairs. Despite the fact that our world is made up of ever more complex interrelations between humans and non-humans, we continue to assume that it is clearly marked out from the world of nature. It is through the use of binary categories (Nature, Society, Culture and so on) that, in Latour's view, we *efface* the role of hybrids: as Lee and Stenner (1999: 95) put it, 'this effacement involves a mode of thought which insists that the relations between the natural and the cultural are subject to a law of the excluded middle'.

Latour emphasises that our attempts to socially order the modern world necessarily generate further hybrids: '[The] effective exclusion of hybridity from thought and from credit is the condition of possibility for their inclusion in action and their proliferation in actuality' (Lee and Stenner 1999: 95). In other words, it is only because we divide the world up into (modernist) categories, that we can generate continuing streams of hybrids. As Lee and Stenner say:

> Modernity in this account, is founded upon a moment of systematic misrecognition: we must speak as if nature and culture are clear and distinct realms but act as if they were not. We produce the modern world by mixing natural and cultural things into productive hybrids who can then promptly be ignored thanks to purifying tendencies of modern thought (1999: 95).

So we should investigate this hybrid world not with one category – 'Natural' or 'Social' – but with concepts that somehow reflect the complexity of the 'missing middle'. Rather than standing on one side of the divide that is thought to run through modern life we should plant ourselves firmly in the hybrid 'centre ground'. The task then is to assess how the combinations or collectives get made and how they are held together (Latour 2000).

We might propose, then, that BSE and foot and mouth arise from an inability to recognise the relentless mixing of elements that goes on in modern agro-food production processes. A systematic misrecognition of the heterogeneous relations that configure this area of production has facilitated the generation of multiple hybrids that have bound economic and social food practices ever more tightly into natural processes. This promiscuous intermingling of social and natural entities in food chains has resulted in some unexpected and unwelcome consequences for humans and natural entities alike.

To fully understand contemporary trends such as ecological change or disease spread it is necessary to explore the neglected 'middle ground'. In order to explore this ground, Latour (1993) suggests we adopt a perspective – Actor Network Theory – that he argues is particularly appropriate to the study of a materially complex, 'non-modern' world. This perspective, which was first developed in the sociology of science (e.g. Latour 1987) but which is now applied more widely (e.g. Hassard and Law 1999), contends that all social forms are deeply embedded in sets of heterogeneous relations (just think, for example, of scientists producing knowledge about nature in their technologically sophisticated laboratories). The starting point is the idea that *actors* (which may be social, natural or technological entities) can only *act* because they are enmeshed within networks (that is, the laboratory itself can be seen as a 'network', one that combines differing entity types in order to generate scientific facts and artefacts). In fact, this linkage between action and relation is so close that actors *are* networks (and vice versa); thus, the term 'actor network' expresses a tension between 'the centred "actor" on the one hand and the decentred "network" on the other' (Law 1999: 5). In other words, one can act only with others; behind every action lies a network. And the networks are hybrids; they consist of differing, heterogeneous entities brought into alignments that permit actions to be conducted up and down their length (Latour 1987).

Thus, to return to the earlier example, the foot and mouth virus alone can do nothing – it can only act in relationships with other entities. And these other entities are multiple: they include animals, climates, transportation systems, farm-ing practices, disease control procedures, political regulations and economic imperatives. The foot and mouth virus thus works within a set of hetero-geneous relations. If these relations are consolidated on terms favourable to the virus then the disease will spread (as was obviously the case during much of 2001 in the UK); if these relations are disrupted then the network will break down and the spread of the disease will be curtailed (by mid-summer UK Government efforts to contain the disease by culling animals around diseased farms appeared to have limited the scope of the foot and mouth 'network' and limited the ability of the virus to forge new relations). The foot and mouth out-break, as a hybrid event, was underpinned by heterogeneous networks. The task of the hybrid perpsective in rural research is to trace these networks in all their splendid complexity.

Countryside networks

The focus on heterogeneity qualifies ANT as a 'hybrid' perspective (Murdoch 2001). In this theory, the world is made not by humans or social beings but by collectives in which non-humans exchange properties with humans so that all become modified and gain new (network) identities. If these identities hold and if the relations between the actors are stabilised then the network will have real and tangible effects. And according to the actor network theorists, the effects generated by hybrid networks are widespread. Latour (2000: 117) says just open a daily newspaper and you will be confronted by a whole array of hetero-geneous processes – genetically modified organisms, global warming, ozone depletion, all emerge as social and natural entities combine in novel ways to generate multiple effects.

Given this proliferation of actor networks, we should expect the countryside to be similarly entangled within heterogeneous matrices. And, indeed, there is growing evidence to support this view. For instance, a number of comment-ators have drawn upon ANT to argue that agriculture is 'hybridised' (Busch and Juska 1997; FitzSimmons and Goodman 1998; Goodman 1999; Whatmore 2002; Whatmore and Thorne 1997). These authors share the view that this productive sector promiscuously mixes entities of different types so that all 'exchange properties' (Latour 1999). For much of the time this 'exchange' takes place in ways that are predictable, that is, in ways that accord with the intentions of human participants. However, at other times the exchanges can spiral out of control so that hybrid entities cause unforeseen (and sometimes terrible) consequences. BSE and foot and mouth are distressing illustrations of this: the diseased entities emerge as food production systems mix nature into ever more novel sets of heterogeneous relations. Given that such 'expelling' and 'mixing' is a routine part of food production, it implies that 'nature' will always hold the potential to reassert itself (Murdoch *et al.* 2000). Sometimes this reassertion will take place in ways that are deleterious to other entities (including humans).

But it is not only the food sector that displays how hybrid networks act to reconfigure the countryside. Studies have also shown that complex sets of relations underlie expressions of 'nature' in rural areas. To cite just one example, Gareth Enticott (2001) considers the status of badgers in the United Kingdom. He shows that while the badger population overall is increasing, the main threat to badger groups comes from a purported link between the animals and bovine tuberculosis. He identifies an actor network, one that comprises the badgers, cattle, a bacterium (*Mycobacterium bovis*, the cause of bovine tuberculosis), Ministry of Agriculture vets, and farmers. Enticott describes a struggle among these groups to define both the relations between the actors in the network and the character of each enrolled entity. In particular, there is some effort to link the badgers to the bacterium, thereby consolidating a world in which badgers are seen as the cause of TB in cattle. In developing his account, Enticott emphasises that the way the relations within the network are constructed depends not just upon the motivations and strategies of human actors but also upon the behaviour of the natural entities. The badgers can behave in ways that make certain network relations possible, likewise the bacterium *M. bovis*. The 'final' network shape emerges from a 'negotiation' between all the enrolled entities; it therefore reflects more than just the aspirations of the human participants.

There are many rural relationships that might usefully be described as 'hybrids': we need to think only of development processes that reshape the landscape in line with given social desires or economic demands (Marsden *et al.* 1993); we could also consider recreational activities that rely not only on complex technologies but on particular landscapes and climates (everything from mountain-biking to hang-gliding; Macnaghten and Urry 2001); or perhaps we might examine the patterns of transportation that have markedly altered the character of rural areas, comprising as they do new human–machine relations that drive a host of associated changes in patterns of rural living (Macnaghten and Urry 1998). All these activities give the countryside a 'heterogeneous quality'.

In most conventional accounts such heterogeneity is underplayed or ignored; it is seen as a relatively benign outcrop of human action. But a full recognition of human–nonhuman relations shows that there is a 'co-evolution' between social, natural and technological aspects of the rural world (Norgaard 1994). As these systems co-evolve so they interact and give rise to novel and unexpected combinations of entities. And these combinations do not just 'reflect' the initial (social, natural, technological) ingredients: the 'exchange' of properties ensures that many networks are genuinely heterogeneous in almost all respects (Latour 1999). As foot and mouth and BSE indicate, processes of change in the countryside frequently follow because hybrids are generated by heterogeneous systems in which humans constantly seek to exercise control over other entities and processes but in so doing serve to generate more and more complex relations. While these relations usually accord with human intentions and actions (and so become 'blackboxed'), they can also frequently spiral out of control with unpredictable consequences (Beck 1992). Thus, we can conclude that, while on one level the countryside reflects human aspirations, cultural norms and modes of ordering, at another level it reflects the relentless mixing of diverse entities within networks.

The multiple spaces of hybridity

In the previous section it was argued that many aspects of country life are 'hybridised': they are composed of heterogeneous elements which have been aligned in order to produce significant and stable outcomes. These alignments testify to the network building capacities, not only of human actors, but of non-humans as well. And they configure the countryside so that at any given moment, its shape reflects the interrelations between various entities within actor networks (see Marsden *et al.* 1993: Ch. 6 for a summary of this argument). In many respects, then, the countryside might be seen as a distinctive, yet hybrid space (e.g. it combines a quite different set of elements from those found in the city). However, saying this rather undermines some of our-taken-for-granted notions of this spatial zone.

For instance, in the introduction we saw that the countryside is often regarded as a 'mirror' of social relations and this process of 'mirroring' is thought to yield particular forms of ordering in rural areas. Within this *social* perspective, the shape of the countryside is determined by (and therefore reflects) dominant structures within society (e.g. capitalism, patriarchy, class, nationality). Societal structures underpin rural structures. Yet, the hybrid approach proposes a rather different analytical starting point: it holds that because the countryside contains so many different entities, mixed together in so many varied combinations, it will have a spatial form that is heterogeneous and complex and this form is not easily captured from any one vantage point. As Kevin Hetherington (1998: 23) puts it, a heterogeneous space is 'folded and topologically complex, allowing only small glimpses rather than a full view'. What this means is that hybrid spaces are always bifurcated by networks of heterogeneous relations. These networks are potentially composed of differing entities combined in multiple ways and therefore 'mirror' a multitude of social–material formations. Thus, just as there are many network shapes, so there are many forms of spatiality.

In short, within the hybrid perspective, space is complex. It is complex both because networks interact with given or pre-existing spaces and because these networks construct their own spatial coordinates. Mol and Law (1994) suggest that we might reduce this complexity somewhat by envisaging three main spatial categories: 'regions', 'networks' and 'fluids'. The 'region' is the most familiar spatial type: it refers to spaces of relatively fixed coordinates. In this view, the countryside is a zone that is knowable from maps and other 'panoptical' mechanisms. A good illustration is the local authority development plan with its zoning techniques, development priorities and conservation areas. Such plans effectively 'regionalise' the countryside by bounding and categorising rural spaces, thereby determining the uses to which the demarcated areas can be put. As Mol and Law (1994: 647) say, regional spaces create '[n]eat divisions, no overlap. Here or there, each space is located one side of a boundary'.

Mol and Law's second type, the 'network' space, derives more squarely from ANT: it refers to relations that link together entities in ways that mark out their own space–time coordinates. As Mol and Law (1994: 649) put it, in a network space 'proximity isn't metric . . . [it] has instead to do with . . . network elements and the way they hang together'. To return to our earlier example, the consolidation of heterogeneous relations within the livestock sector provokes a greater intensity of production, the arrival of large-scale feeding lots in rural areas and the gradual diminution of animals in the fields. A spatial arrangement accompanies the construction of the network and it acts to 'fold' the rural into a set of interconnected and proximate elements, thereby detaching these elements from previously consolidated sets of relations (e.g. fields as part of landscapes and grazing animals as part of fields).

The third type – 'fluid' space – also emerges from network relations but here the links between enrolled entities are loose and unstable, so that multiple identities are possible. Rather than a single network configuration, complex shifting affiliations provoke ambivalence and instability. As Mol and Law (1994: 663) say, 'typically the objects generated within [fluid spaces] aren't well-defined. . . . In a fluid, elements may inform each other, but the way they do so may continually alter. The bonds within fluid spaces aren't stable'. We can illustrate this spatial type by reference once again to BSE. An actor network was established in the livestock sector that allowed standardised food production practices to generate an intense circulation of entities in the form of food to animals and animals to food, in the process bypassing more 'natural' and extensive modes of cattle rearing. BSE disrupts this system and, for a time at least, renders the whole network into a fluid state as a new entity (the prion protein) escapes conventional linkages and systematically undermines the relationships that had previously been consolidated within the beef network. As a consequence, there is increased instability in the network as new links between cattle, production practices and meat consumers are established.

Any discussion of these three spatial categories implies, as Mormont (1990: 34) puts it, that 'the rural is no longer one single space, but [is] a multiplicity of social spaces . . . each of them having its own logic, its own institutions, as well as its own specific network of actors'. The countryside is thus detached from any one analytical reference point. Its meanings are asserted relationally and will vary according to the socio-spatial context in which the perspective is being set. The three spaces outlined above *perform* the rural in three very different ways and generate a set of markedly varied spatial relations (see Murdoch and Pratt 1997 for a fuller consideration of the three spatial types in the rural arena).

In short, the hybrid perspective proposes that the countryside is a place where multiple processes co-exist. It therefore demands an appreciation of spatial *complexity*. To paraphrase Doreen Massey (1998), countryside places are 'meeting places', where diverse socio-spatial relations become juxtaposed with one another. Thus, rather than continuously 'regionalising' spatial relations (that is, fixing spaces as stable Euclidean 'containers'), hybrid approaches such as ANT propose that networks mark out differing space–times. In some relationships the countryside will be configured as a standardised space in which entities are lined up in accordance with formal rules and norms; in others, much more fluid sets of relations will unfold in ways that are not easily prescribed by any one network configuration (Murdoch 1998). In short, the countryside is made by varied network types and it can be seen as an aggregation of network effects.

Rethinking the 'social': rural identities and hybrid networks

The countryside is hybrid. To say this is to emphasise that it is defined by networks in which heterogeneous entities are aligned in a variety of ways. It is also to propose that these networks give rise to slightly different country*sides*: there is no single vantage point from which the whole panoply of rural or countryside relations can be seen. Thus, a 'regionalised' perspective can be adopted only in the knowledge that network and fluid spaces will escape its purview; a focus on networks and fluid spaces will disrupt the notions of easily demarcated and fixed rural spaces but will generate contrasting and sometimes contradictory understandings of rural processes.

We must, therefore, suppose that to say the countryside is 'topologically complex' (Law 2000), that it is 'folded' (Hetherington 1998), or that it is 'multiple' (Massey 1998), is to simultaneously imply that no one perspective can gain access to all the relations that are consolidated within its spatial parameters. Thus, to argue that 'social' and 'natural' perspectives are limited in their scope is also to suggest that 'hybridity' too must have its limits. In other words, despite its seemingly inclusive character, there may be occasions when the relations established within networks cannot be adequately described using only the repertoire of ANT and other such hybrid approaches. In particular, there may be times when we need to look in the 'interstices' that lie between these three general perspectives to develop a suitably nuanced account of rural change.

In what follows, I want to briefly examine interconnections between 'social' and 'hybrid' perspectives in order to consider how the social emerges *through* heterogeneous relations and how heterogeneous relations are consolidated *in line with* social categories. In considering how theories of social change might be aligned with theorisations of hybridity, I wish to firstly outline some potential problems with ANT (drawn from the discussion in Murdoch 2001). As we have seen above, this theory proposes that subjects and objects gain their shapes and their abilities to act effectively from situatedness in networks. It thus suggests that any pre-existing identities or powers held by these entities are renegotiated during the course of network construction – all, to some extent, come 'into being' within the network (e.g. foot and mouth viruses and prion proteins take shape *within* rather than *outside* networks). As Law (1999: 3) puts it, 'entities take their form and acquire their attributes as a result of their relations with other entities. In this scheme of things entities have no inherent qualities'. ANT is thus based on the (semiotic) notion that entities are 'produced in relations' and it applies this view 'ruthlessly to all materials' (1999: 4). But we might question whether this symmetrical approach is always the most appropriate way of conceptualising actors in networks (Breslau 2000). For instance, is it so surprising that the foot and mouth virus appears to act in very similar ways within diverse circumstances? And don't humans also display stable characteristics and capabilities? Are there not some features of human action, such as meaning generation and language use, that invariably emerge within (heterogeneous) networks? In other words, despite the heterogeneity of actor networks, are all entities constructed anew in each network or are some pre-existing attributes sometimes incorporated into new network relations?

I wish to briefly consider these questions here in relation to the 'human' aspects of hybrid networks. I want to suggest that, while humans are clearly enmeshed in networks of heterogeneous relations, they also retain distinctive qualities as members of such networks and these qualities can be seen, at times, as 'driving' sets of changes in the socio-natural world. In other words, I want to propose that an awareness of human distinctiveness – notably linked to the use of given social categories – might be combined with a focus on the heterogeneous matrices in which this distinctiveness is expressed. While this introduction of the 'social' into the actor network approach might seem to breach the 'symmetry' principle – that is the notion that all actors whether natural, technological or social should be given equal status (cf. Callon 1986; Latour 1987) – it might allow us to consider whether hybrid networks come, in practice, to be aligned with very human forms of social being.

In linking together social and hybrid approaches, I want to introduce the notion of the 'extensive self'. This idea is employed in order to suggest that humans are (always?) immersed in heterogeneous relations but that at certain times and in certain places these relations are constructed in ways that 'centre' (rather than 'decentre') the self (in accordance with commonly understood social categories). In so doing, I want to briefly explore a suggestion made by Karin Knorr-Cetina to the effect that major classess of individuals have tied themselves to object worlds . . . object-centred environments which situate and stabilise selves, define individual identity just as much as communities or families used to do, and which promote forms of sociality (social forms of binding self and other) that feed on and supplement the human forms of sociability studied by social scientists (1997: 1).

The countryside might be seen as such an 'object world' in that it serves to stabilise selves and acts to define individual identities. Because the countryside is, among other things, a *spatial* entity then we can speculate that it allows the 'self' to be *geographically* spread across differing object types (Matless 1997). If we adopt this view, then the most significant aspect of rural relationships is not that they are moving towards greater and greater heterogeneity, but that they function to stabilise *social* modes of being. To paraphrase Hetherington (1998), the heterogeneous relations gathered in the countryside somehow work to 'express' particular forms of social identity, such as class, ethnicity or gender.

In making this suggestion I am asserting that, yes, these selves are immersed in heterogeneous relations, but that the key feature of such relations is not that they lead to a 'hybrid', 'networked' or perhaps even more fancifully 'cyborg' self, but that they serve to *reinforce* traditional (that is, recognisably 'social') states of selfhood (see Hacking 2000 for an extended elaboration of this argument). Further, I want to argue that relations of this type are best investigated by modes of analysis that retain distinctive theoretical repertoires for human involvement. In other words, a focus on social categories (class, gender, ethnicity, etc.) is warranted because, in certain circumstances, to talk of 'hybridity' detracts from a full appreciation of the 'social self' and the role it plays in holding heterogeneous relations together (Haraway 1997). In what follows, I briefly consider two social categories – class and gender – and suggest that in the context of the countryside these aspects of social identity are often bound into sets of heterogeneous relations.

Firstly, class. It is now widely recognised that one of the most important processes of change in the countryside in recent years has been 'counter-urbanisation'. This term refers to a 'cascade' of population from cities and large towns down the settlement hierarchy towards villages and rural areas (Champion 1994). Although households continue to move into large urban areas, a larger number of moves take place in the opposite direction, towards the countryside. While counter-urbanisation can be attributed to a variety of heterogeneous factors (such as changing systems of transportation, new patterns of economic dispersal, the diminishing quality of urban life), it is generally accepted that its primary cause is the desire on the part of many households to live *in* the countryside, that is, to become immersed in rurality (Little 1986; Murdoch and Marsden 1994; Pahl 1970; Thrift 1989). From the various studies undertaken into this phenomenon, it is possible to say that, this 'immersion' has two aspects: firstly, a social aspect so that the families wish to reside in a rural community; secondly, a 'natural' aspect as counter-urbanisers seek to live within a particular kind of *material* environment, one that includes traditional buildings, open space, green fields, etc. (see Halfacree 1994, 1995).

In order to show how these two aspects combine to re-order self–object relations among rural residents, it is worth referring briefly to Michael Bell's (1994) study of the Hampshire village of 'Childerley'. Bell initially approaches this village using overtly social frameworks of analysis. Thus, he is immediately struck by the way Childerley's residents are differentiated by class. In his view, most Childerleyeans come from the 'moneyed' (i.e. middle and upper) classes, while around 40 per cent are relatively 'poor'. Yet, having established that the village is composed of differing class-related cultures or lifestyles, Bell goes on to argue that what all the villagers have in common is an affinity with the countryside itself. He proposes that Childerleyeans regard the social distinctions between moneyed and poor residents as 'morally ambiguous' (1994: 78); they recognise that such distinctions structure their lives, but they do not wish to be bound by these social identities. He says:

> Most moneyed villagers do not enjoy thinking about themselves merely as 'one of those rich people' . . . and the ordinary villagers do not enjoy thinking of themselves as merely the poor . . . What they do feel good about is being someone who lives in the country and more than that, being a 'country person', a 'village person', a 'country girl', a 'villager', or a 'countryman born and bred'.

Bell believes the security of the country identity derives from proximity to 'nature'. Through this proximity, the villagers manage to connect themselves to the natural environment in the belief that this environment is 'free from social interests' (1994: 138). Thus, through an affiliation with the countryside, both the moneyed and the poorer villagers can achieve a secure moral foundation for their lives: both gain a secure place in the 'natural order' of the countryside

In this study Bell provides an illustration of what I refer to here as the 'extensive self': social identity is realised *through* linkages with heterogeneous entities. By establishing a close relationship to the countryside, the villagers believe they can change their identities for the better; in this way they '(re)distribute' themselves across the communities and the environments that surround them. In other words, they 'extend' their identities into heterogeneous relations. And in so doing, they act to stabilise these relations (see, for instance, work which examines the link between counter-urbanisation and local environmental activism – Lowe and Goyder 1983; Murdoch and Marsden 1994). The countryside of Childerley therefore reflects a new form of sociability, in which a social group (counter-urbanisers) becomes linked to an object world (rural nature).

Turning to gender identities in the countryside, a useful illustration of a linkage between this form of identity and heterogeneous relations is provided by Alistair Bonnett (1996) in his account of men's groups operating in rural areas of the United States. In effect, these groups seek to reconstitute masculine identity *through* an engagement with nature: Bonnett (1996: 283) quotes one participant as saying, 'the beauty and rawness of nature works towards . . .

giving [a man] a larger context within which to see himself'. The groups thus organise retreats into forest camps so that 'men leave the sounds and pressures of the city and come to a place with greater contact with birds, other animals, water, the earth, fire and the rest of nature'. As Bonnett comments, the 'uncorrupted countryside' stabilises the identities of these men in ways that are simply unimaginable in the city. Yet, we should not assume that the rural simply 'reflects' underlying gender male identities; rather the assertion of manhood is made *through* and *within* rural nature. Again, social identity and natural relation are closely intertwined.

In both the cases quoted above we see a process of 'extending the self' across the countryside so that human actions are, as Cloke and Jones (2001: 649) put it, 'networked into complex social and material relations'. The examples of class and gender could be broadened in order to show how ethnic, racial and other identity categories are composed within heterogeneous relations. Nevertheless, it is possible to conclude from this brief discussion that such a process of networking is part of those 'habitual practices of humans' that 'form familiar patterns which can become landscapes or places' (2001: 652). These landscapes are, as Matless (1998: 12) emphasises, 'quasi-objects', hybrid zones that shuttle 'between fields of reference'. But they are also assemblages of 'economic, social, political and aesthetic values' (1998: 12) and these values, as Matless also shows, become linked with particular social identities (the identity that emerges in Matless's study is 'Englishness'). The extension of 'value' in the countryside is therefore also an extension of the self. But as ANT usefully indicates, these extensions take place within networks that involve the mobilisation of heterogeneous entities: thus, the 'material' make-up of rural spaces becomes inextricably bound into their 'social' make-up. In other words, the social is materially constituted.

Conclusion: towards theoretical pluralism

> Words have meanings: some words, however, also have a 'feel'. The word 'community' is one of them. It feels good: whatever the word 'community' may mean, it is good 'to have a community', 'to be in a community'. . . . Company or society can be bad; but not the community. Community, we feel, is always a good thing (Bauman 2001: 1).

This quotation neatly summarises the seemingly beneficial qualities of community but it could equally well be directed towards countryside: in fact, were the word 'countryside' to be substituted for 'community', the quotation would still make almost perfect sense. People 'feel good' about the 'countryside' for two main sets of reasons: firstly, the countryside is thought of as a 'civilised retreat' (Lowe *et al.* 1995), a place where timeless and virtuous ways of life still act as civilising influences in the increasingly insecure and frenetic world of todays global economy (cf. Scruton 2001); secondly, the countryside is a place of 'nature', and it continues to offer access, even for the most cursory visitor, to a rich array of biological processes and entities (Macnaghten and Urry 1998).

The social and environmental qualities of the countryside are things that almost everyone 'feels good' about. Yet, in many respects, these two visions of country life are incompatible: the more socialised the countryside becomes, the less 'natural' it seems; the more naturalised it is, the less room there appears to be for social entities. To most people this incompatibility is invisible: it is perfectly possible to gaze on a rural landscape and see *either* the natural features *or* the social processes – it all depends on the viewer's perceptual vantage point. However, in attempting to clarify just what the countryside 'is' this incompatibility cannot be easily ignored: we must be alert to the ways in which natural and social entities *combine* as particular countryside features emerge into view.

The repertoire of 'hybridity' focuses our attention on the zone where the two worlds of nature and society meet. In describing this zone, the hybridity repertoire concentrates on the exchange of properties between natural and social entities and shows how heterogeneous actors come into being. These actors do not confine either their actions or relations to any arbitrary division drawn between supposedly discrete 'worlds'; they simply put together network relationships in whatever ways they see fit. The consequence is that the countryside is composed of many varied relations, relations that are orchestrated according to a number of different rationalities and modes of valuation. The discourse of hybridity (evident in such theoretical approaches as ANT) is a response to this 'mixing up' of things and people in rural processes and events.

The countryside, then, is composed by heterogeneous actors – viruses, mutant proteins, conservative philosophers, farmers, fields, counter-urbanisers, men's groups, and so on. Yet, despite this heterogeneous composition, it is still possible to talk about *social* constructions of the countryside, just as it is still sensible to discuss rural *natures*. It would be foolish to argue that such words no longer have any utility in making sense of rural arrangements. In the preceding pages it has merely been suggested that another perspective might be added into the repertoire – hybridity. This perspective illuminates aspects of the countryside that were perhaps not so easily incorporated into dominant social or naturalistic perspectives (it covers the missing 'middle ground', referred to by Latour 1993).

Thus, one purpose of this chapter is to ask for theoretical tolerance or pluralism – the countryside is multiple and it therefore requires multiple modes of understanding. It is for this reason that the delineation of hybridity presented above ended with a plea for new understandings of *sociability* ('sociability with objects', to use Knorr-Cetina's 1997 phrase). The countryside continues to be shaped by social processes, it is just that these processes are *more than* social (just as the countryside continues to be shaped by natural processes that are *less than* natural). Notions such as the 'actor network' and the 'extensive self' have been introduced in order to help understand the material complexity of the social (and the social complexity of the 'natural').

In short, while any particular vision of the countryside will continue to focus upon social forms, natural entities or even hybrid objects, it will also need to be aware of the interrelationships that exist between these realms if it is to capture the full range of processes currently running through rural areas. As events such as foot and mouth and BSE remind us, the countryside is now a complex and unpredictable space. Given that this complexity is likely to increase in the future as social, technological and natural systems come into even closer contact (just think, for example, of the possibilities generated in this regard by the genetic modification of crops), then it is incumbent upon us to find ways of investigating the countryside that are capable of reflecting its elaborate and manifold character. The ideas put forward in this chapter can be read as but one part of a more general effort to develop theoretical approaches that can elucidate the variegated and heterogeneous relationships that now drive processes of change in the contemporary countryside.

References

Bauman, Z. 2001 *Community*, Polity, London.

Beck, U. 1992 *The Risk Society*, Sage, London.

Bell, M.M. 1994 *Childerley*, University of Chicago Press, Chicago, IL.

Blokland, T. and Savage, M. 2001 'Editorial: networks, class and place', *International Journal of Urban and Regional Research*, **25**, 221–6.

Bonnett, A. 1996 'The new primitives: identity, landscape and cultural appropriation in the mythopoetic men's movement', *Antipode*, **28**, 273–91.

Breslau, D. 2000 'Sociology after humanism: a lesson from contemporary science studies', *Sociological Theory*, **18**, 289–307.

Busch, L. and Juska, A. 1997 'Beyond political economy: actor–networks and the globalization of agriculture', *Review of International Political Economy*, **4**, 688–708.

Callon, M. 1986 'Some elements of a sociology of translation: domestication of the scallops and fishermen of St. Brieuc Bay', pp. 196–233 in J. Law (ed.), *Power, Action, Belief: A New Sociology of Knowledge?*, Routledge and Kegan Paul, London.

Champion, T. 1994 'Population change and migration in Britain since 1981: evidence for continuing deconcentration', *Environment and Planning A*, **26**, 1501–20.

Cloke, P. and Jones, O. 2001 'Dwelling, place, and landscape: an orchard in Somerset', *Environment and Planning A*, **33**, 649–66.

Donaldson, A., Lowe, P. and Ward, N. 2002 'Virus – crises – institutional change: the foot and mouth actor–network and the governance of rural affairs in the UK', *Sociologia Ruralis*, **42**, 201–14.

Enticott, G. 2001 'Calculating nature: the case of badgers, bovine tuberculosis and cattle', *Journal of Rural Studies*, **17**, 149–64.

FitzSimmons, M. and Goodman, D. 1998 'Incorporating nature: environmental narratives and the reproduction of food', pp. 194–220 in B. Braun and N. Castree (eds), *Remaking Reality: Nature at the Millennium*, Routledge, London.

Goodman, D. 1999 'Agro-food studies in the "Age of Ecology": nature, corporeality, bio-politics', *Sociologia Ruralis*, **39**, 17–38.

Hacking, I. 2000 *The Social Construction of What?*, Harvard University Press, London.

Halfacree, K. 1994 'The importance of "the rural" in the constitution of counterubanisation: evidence from England in the 1980s', *Sociologia Ruralis*, **34**, 164–89.

Halfacree, K. 1995 'Talking about rurality: social representations of the rural as expressed by residents of six English parishes', *Journal of Rural Studies*, **11**, 1–20.

Haraway, D. 1997 *Modest Witness at the Millennium: FemaleMan Meets Oncomouse*, Routledge, London.

Hassard, J. and Law, J. (eds) 1999 *Actor-network and After*, Routledge, London.

Hetherington, K. 1998 *Expressions of Identity*, Sage, London.

Hetherington, P. 2001 'After 100 days, a severe outbreak of cynicism', *Guardian*, **10 May**, 10.

Hinchcliffe, S. 2001 'Indeterminacy in-decisions – science, science policy and politics in the BSE (bovine spongiform encephalopathy) crisis', *Transactions of the Institute of British Geographers*, **26**, 182–204.

Irwin, A. 2001 *Sociology and the Environment: A Critical Introduction to Society, Nature and Knowledge*, Polity, London.

Knorr-Cetina, K. 1997 'Sociability with objects: social relations in postsocial societies', *Theory, Culture and Society*, **14**, 1–30.

Latour, B. 1987 *Science in Action*, Open University Press, Milton Keynes.

Latour, B. 1993 *We Have Never Been Modern*, Harvester Wheatsheaf, Hemel Hempstead.

Latour, B. 1999 *Pandora's Hope*, Harvard University Press, London.

Latour, B. 2000 'When things strike back: a possible contribution of "science studies" to the social sciences', *British Journal of Sociology*, **51**, 107–23.

Law, J. 1999 'After ANT: complexity, naming and topology', pp. 1–14 in J. Hassard, and J. Law (eds), *Actor Network and After*, Routledge, London.

Law, J. 2000 'Objects, Spaces, Others', unpublished paper available from Centre for Science Studies, Lancaster University: www.comp.lancs.ac.uk/sociology/soc027jl

Lee, N. and Stenner, P. 1999 'Who pays? Can we pay them back?', pp. 90–112 in J. Hassard, and J. Law, (eds), *Actor Network and After*, Routledge, London.

Little, J. 1986 'Social class and planning policy', pp. 62–78 in P. Lowe, and S. Wright (eds), *Deprivation and Welfare in Rural Areas*, Geo Books, Norwich.

Lowe, P. and Goyder, J. 1983 *Environmental Groups in Politics*, Allen and Unwin, London.

Lowe, P., Murdoch, J. and Cox, G. 1995 'A civilised retreat? Anti-urbanism, rurality and the making of an Anglo-centric culture', pp. 63–82 in P. Healey, *et al.* (eds), *Managing Cities: the New Urban Context*, Wiley, Chichester.

Macnaghten, P. and Urry, J. 1998 *Contested Natures*, Sage, London.

Macnaghten, P. and Urry, J. 2001 *Bodies of Nature*, Sage, London.

MAFF 2001 *Foot and Mouth Disease: Public Information Factsheet 1*, Ministry of Agriculture, Fisheries and Food, London.

Massey, D. 1998 *Power-geometries and the Politics of Space–Time: Hettner Lecture, 1998*, Department of Geography, University of Heidelberg, Heidelberg.

Marsden, T., Murdoch, J., Lowe, P., Munton, R. and Flynn, A. 1993 *Constructing the Countryside*, UCL Press, London.

Matless, D. 1997 'The geographical self, the nature of the social, and geoaesthetics: work in social and cultural geography, 1996', *Progress in Human Geography*, **21**, 393–405.

Matless, D. 1998 *Landscape and Englishness*, Reaktion, London.

Mol, A. and Law, J. 1994 'Regions, networks and fluids: anaemia and social topology', *Social Studies of Science*, 24, 641–71.

Mormont, M. 1990 'Who is rural? Or, how to be rural: towards a sociology of the rural', pp. 21–37 in T. Marsden, P. Lowe and S. Whatmore (eds), *Rural Restructuring: Global Processes and their Local Responses*, Fulton, London.

Murdoch, J. 1997 'Towards a geography of heterogeneous associations', *Progress in Human Geography*, 21, 321–37.

Murdoch, J. 1998 'The spaces of actor-network theory', *Geoforum*, 29, 357–74.

Murdoch, J. 2001 'Ecologising sociology: actor-network theory, co-construction and the problem of human exemptionalism', *Sociology*, 35, 111–33.

Murdoch, J. and Marsden, T. 1994 *Reconstituting Rurality: Class, Community and Power in the Development Process*, UCL Press, London.

Murdoch, J. and Pratt, A.C. 1997 'From the power of topography to the topography of power: a discourse on strange ruralities', pp. 51–69 in P. Cloke and J. Little (eds), *Contested Countryside Cultures: Rurality and Socio-Cultural Marginalisation*, Routledge, London.

Murdoch, J., Marsden, T. and Banks, J. 2000 'Quality, nature and embeddedness: some theoretical considerations in the context of the food sector', *Economic Geography*, 76, 107–25.

Norgaard, R. 1994 *Development Betrayed*, Routledge, London.

Pahl, R. 1970 *Readings in Urban Sociology*, Pergamon, Oxford.

Phillips Inquiry 2000 *Official Government Inquiry into BSE: Final Report*, Stationary Office, London.

Scruton, R. 2001 'A conservative view of the countryside', pp. 13–23 in Sissons, M. (ed.), *Countryside for All: the Future of Rural Britain,* Vintage, London.

Short, J. 1991 *Imagined Country*, Routledge, London.

Thrift, N. 1989 'Images of social change', pp. 8–25 in C. Hamnett, L. McDowell and P. Sarre (eds), *The Changing Social Structure*, Sage, London.

Whatmore, S. 1999 'Hybrid geographies: rethinking the "human" in human geography', pp. 22–39 in D. Massey, J. Allen and P. Sarre (eds), *Human Geography Today*, Polity, Cambridge.

Whatmore, S. 2002 *Hybrid Geographies*, Sage, London.

Whatmore, S. and Thorne, L. 1997 'Nourishing networks: alternative geographies of food', pp. 287–304 in D. Goodman and M. Watts (eds), *Globalising Food: Agrarian Questions and Global Restructuring*, Routledge, London.

'The restraint of beasts': rurality, animality, Actor Network Theory and dwelling

CHAPTER 16

Owain Jones

As Mr. McCrindle had demonstrated by his phone call, the main concern of farmers was that their fences should be tight. Without this the restraint of beasts was impossible.

(Magnus Mills, *The Restraint of Beasts*, 1998: 10)

Introduction

This chapter is about how rurality and animality[1] (Tapper 1988) are intertwined. Animals are central to how the rural is constructed in both imaginative and material terms. These constructions, of course, interconnect, and are formed out of particular presences of particular animals in particular contexts. In this chapter I explore these presences and try to open up thinking about them in a number of related ways.

I initially illustrate some of the ways in which animals are bound into cultural formations of the rural in order to show how their presences form central yet diverse and contested components. I then point out that the study of such constructions, although significant, needs to be accompanied by the acknowledgement of the very real (bodily) and often hidden presences of animals in the rural. I then trace out some of the recent trajectories of rural animal geographies and relate these to the wider context of animal geographies, which are moving in this direction and highlight key substantive and theoretical trends. Agreeing with Yarwood and Evans (2000) that there is still much to be done in the field of rural animal geographies, I then focus on two key themes, agency and ethics.

In particular I am interested in how Actor Network Theory (ANT) is increasingly used to describe animal geographies and the agency of animals (Philo and Wilbert 2000). Such approaches are now appearing in accounts of the production of the rural and in the analysis of rural processes which include the roles and positions of animals. These accounts *can* offer a new precision in describing the roles of animals in society, and in describing 'the rural'[2] as comprising particular interlocking networks or collectives (Latour 1999)[3] producing particular effects in which animals may play their part. As such these approaches do sometimes aim to show *how* animals are actors, or *actants*[4], in the production of the rural (in some form or other), or are at least networked into relational collectives which produce aspects of it.

My concern is that these animal/rural geographies which derive from ANT are drawing from a 'position' – acknowledging Law's (1999) concern of how ANT has been over-defined and fixed – that can be unsympathetic to, and neglectful of, the roles and fates of animals in collectives, and of the wider ethical/power dynamics embedded in collectives (see Bingham and Thrift 2000: 299). Analysis inspired by ANT, particularly in its more extreme relational form, can miss or deny certain characteristics that animals (generally) have, and the consequences of these characteristics that occur on their enrolment into networks. I draw upon work of Ingold (1988, 2000) on the differences between human usages of machines and human usages of animals to raises questions about the 'other' agency of animals, how exactly they are enrolled into collectives, and pressing ethical questions that stem from this.

These ideas drive my second theme, the need to pursue understanding of ethical geographies (Jones 2000; Lynn 1998a, b; Proctor 1998) arising from human–animal relations in the rural. Concerns for both agency and (un)ethical encounter (Jones 2000) involve 'opening up' the differing spaces and practices of particular animalities in particular ruralities. I suggest that the idea of dwelling, as articulated by Ingold (1993, 2000) (with certain adaptations) is a productive theorisation for considering the role of animals in the rural (or anywhere else) which can *leaven* ANT approaches that seem bereft of a sensitivity to the otherness of animals, to ethics more generally and to ideas of places and landscape.

Animality and rurality: cultural constructions and corporeal presences

I was watching television one night just as I was beginning to think about this chapter when two back-to-back prime-time BBC 1 programmes stirred my imagination in regard to the rural and animals. The first was 'Down to Earth', a 'comedy drama' about a London family – mum, dad, three kids – realising a dream (the dad's) to move to the countryside and run a smallholding.

Romantic house and plot purchased, humorous (and more serious) trials and tribulations ensue, but an underlying theme of the programme is of the imagined idyll[5], and idyll realised. At the end of a hard day the parents stand arm in arm and survey a stunning view of rolling Devon landscape, as they sigh and say, 'this is what we did it for'. In this drama, animals played a key role in setting the rural scene and moving the plot along. Tension and uncertainty are rife within the family, particularly via the teenage urbanite daughter whose lifestyle and boyfriend have remained in London. One of the first moments of harmony and signs of the promise ahead is when the cow they had bought at the local market gives birth to a calf, right outside the house, with dad with his arm inserted deep into the cow to assist. The camera plays lovingly as the calf is born, is licked by its mother, struggles to its feet, and begins the fumbling, soft muzzling search for milk. An animal magic moment. Other rural animal dynamics are hinted at when the family attend the local market and the teenage urbanite daughter shouts 'hey, don't hit the animals' angrily at stock handlers in the auction ring as they control the animals with the obviously routine use of sticks, and everyone laughs and makes comments about this (young female) outsider. The mum has trouble milking the family cow by hand, a strange awkward process at first, but then one of contact and authenticity as the milk finally flows. The younger daughter, who is bullied at her new school, sits in the sty with the piglets reading and talking to them, and is later found by her worried mum curled up asleep with them (in immaculately clean straw) and is tenderly carried to bed. This girl also craves a pony (which is beyond the meagre family means) as the contact with animals runs as a theme through this construction of rural idyll.

The very next programme happened to be the episode of 'The Vicar of Dibley' (a comedic narrative of the life of a rural female cleric) in which the vicar decides to have a service for all the local animals. The Chair of the Parish Council scoffs and is cynical, the Bishop is doubtful, even the tabloid press get onto it as an example of liberal Church of England hocus-pocus. The day of the service dawns, the vicar wonders if she has made a big mistake, the Chair of the Parish Council comes to gloat, but then a montage of shots begins, with Land-Rovers towing horse boxes bowling down country roads, riders and horses galloping over fields, farmers leading cows and sheep (show-prepared), smallholders leading goats and carrying ferrets, children carrying rabbits, guinea pigs, mice and rats, down the village lanes. These all close in on, and file into the packed church. There are owls, and dogs and cats aplenty. The owners range from sweet little old ladies to punks. The filming is in a glowing, golden, reverential style, panning around this ecclesiastical menagerie as the hymn 'All things bright and beautiful' is sung. The programme ends with the Chair of the Parish Council, heart melted and chastened, pondering what a magical and wonderful event it had been.

In these two programmes some of the density and variation of animals' presence in cultural representations of the rural were vividly depicted. Animals were shown to be at the centre of the ruralities depicted and to be key icons in ideas of rural lifestyle and ideas of idyll. But beneath these key and essentially benign constructions other issues were also hinted at: for example, issues of 'town versus country' attitudes to animals; issues of gendered attitudes to animals; how they are bound in wealth-dependent and contested recreational and sporting/hunting ruralities; how they are bound up with the productionist political economy of the rural; ideas of the (un)ethical human–animal relations which abound in the rural, with shades of the all cruelty, care, love and indifference which are present in this diversity of human–animal relations; and of animals as 'others', subjugated within, but often resistant to numerous networks of power which have, for numerous reasons (see below), come to the fore in terms of critical gaze in recent times.

There are of course a myriad other cultural texts that portray animal presences in the rural[6]. But Phillips *et al.* point out that such representations of rurality on British television are significant for three interrelated reasons. Firstly 'television constitutes a relatively dominant site of contemporary cultural production' (2001: 1). Secondly, these cultural productions have 'possible significance in the material and social reconstitution of rural, and indeed non-rural, areas' (2001: 3). And, thirdly, these cultural productions are bound up with 'the formation of highly contestable images of the countryside' (2001: 4). In terms of animals and the rural, all these three strands of analysis are possible and in fact important.

Later in the same year a whole new series of images of animals in the countryside poured from our television screens (and newspapers) as the 2001 foot and mouth epidemic took hold. These cultural discourses were resonant of animals in the rural in somewhat similar ways, in that animals were not only shown to be central to the rural/agricultural economy, but also central to regional, community, family and individual lifestyle/identity as millions of animals were removed from the fabric of the rural. But the shocking pictures of yards of dead cows, of pyres of animal bodies being assembled by heavy plant machinery, the ongoing stream of culling statistics, and description of often 'hidden' farming practices of feeding and animal transportation and so on, began to make clear the staggering numerical presence of animals in the rural, the very bulk and corporality of that presence, and some of the welfare/ethical issues which surround their enrolment into production networks. To sum up the scale and nature of these animal presences, Beavis (2002) suggests that in the UK '860 million animals are reared each year for food, usually in highly intensive systems'.

So like the other crises that have hit animal-based agriculture/cultures in the United Kingdom, particularly the BSE crisis, the Salmonella in eggs crisis, the live animal exports protests and the ongoing and bitter 'hunting wars', the foot and mouth coverage opened up many of the closed, unimagined spaces and practices of rural set human–animal relations to a wider, often critical gaze. This opening up has challenged settled (more benign) assumptions about animal presences in the rural, especially in relation to food production, where 'in representational terms, the farm animal has changed from a saviour of health and security to one associated with risk and pollution' (Franklin 1996: 127).

There are excellent accounts of how animals are present in cultures of the rural (Buller 2003; Milbourne 2003). But I am interested here in emphasising the need to go beyond cultural constructions of animals in the rural or, more precisely, to add to them accounts of animals' very corporeal presences around which questions of agency and ethics revolve. As Cloke states it is 'important not to just "read" [rural] texts but to trace their interconnections with actual practices' (1997: 372). And this also responds to Philo's concern about the dematerialised nature of much contemporary cultural geography, which ignores 'stubbornly there-in-the-world kind of matter' (2000: 33).

Rural animal geographies

So it could be suggested that 'the rural' as an 'imagined space' is a space of animals, as the television programmes previously described help to illustrate. This broad political construction of the rural as an animal space helps distinguish it as rural space in the first place and sets up contexts in which animals are regarded and treated. For example Ridley argues that 'animals represent one of the chief points of friction between town and country' (1998: 142). And, importantly, Tapper observes that 'urban-industrial society, finally, is dependent for animal products on battery – or factory-farming' (1988: 4). Thus the rural has become the space where much of the subjugation of animals on behalf of modern society takes place, and thus it becomes a space of great tension in terms of human–animal relations. Also, much of the recent hunting debate, and related protest and counter-protest, has been framed as a 'country verses town issue' where the Countryside Alliance pushes the idea that rural society has an identity built out of certain relationships with animals, which are separate, and more legitimate, than urban society's understandings of animals and human–animal relations.

Within this overarching construction of animals and rurality are other constructions which will have their own spatial, legislative and ethical dimensions. For example Seymour (1979) in *The Countryside Explained* has chapters on 'The domestic animals of the countryside' and 'The wild animals of the countryside'. This kind of distinction begins to highlight how differing collectives of animals (Jones 2000; Serpell 1995) are implicated in the rural in differing ways. Below, I expand such typologies to take in some of the key ways in which animals are present in the rural.

Agriculture

Perhaps the most obvious ways animals are and have been present in the rural is through agriculture. Sheep, cattle, pig and poultry farming have been agricultural staples, while for centuries the horse was a means of power, and other animals such as dogs and cats were working animals too. These have ensured that animals have been at the heart of the rural and, previously, the national economy and culture. The wool industry, for example, was not only central to many rural economies but a key factor in the economic, political and industrial development of the UK more generally. These multiple presences of animals, as I have discussed, have placed them at the heart of cultural constructions of the rural which are always in dynamic relationships with the shifting natures of the practices of animal husbandry in terms of new types and breeds of animals, new products which are derived from them, and new practices and technologies of production. Other (wild) animals came to be defined in relation to agricultural practices, with some being exterminated, others still subject to hunting and culling, others displaced by farmland 'ecologies', and others seen as useful allies to farming practices.

Wildlife conservation

But the wild fauna of the UK is not entirely constructed in its relation to agriculture and is another key element of animal presences and animal cultures of the rural. In her seminal *The Theft of the Countryside* Marion Shoard (1980: 183) states that 'for many people . . . the creatures and plants of our countryside have provided the key to its charms'. These presences and efforts to conserve and even enhance them are central to the idea of the rural as a space of nature and even in certain areas, as a space of wildness. Often in tension with the needs of agriculture (but not exclusively) wildlife appreciation and latterly conservation has shaped aspects of countryside legislation and countryside cultures. This has made the countryside a multi-dimensional and contested 'animal space'. Again, this is a complex and continuously unfolding cultural and ecological process, with 'native' wild animal (re)introductions on one hand, and the culling of other 'alien' invasive species on the other. (See Whatmore 2000 on the fate of the ruddy duck.)

Hunting, shooting and fishing

'For many of us, countrymanship is synonymous with the back of a horse or some other form of sport. The saddle, the rod and the gun are the sensors by which we keep contact with Nature' (Leader Comment in *Countryweek*, 12 September 1991). This pungent statement, like the vocality of the Countryside Alliance, shows the strength of feeling about the role of hunting and animal-based recreation in certain rural identities and lifestyles. Although such forms of recreation and sport are linked to agriculture, and wildlife in certain ways, they need to be seen in separate terms because they have become increasingly controversial in recent times, and are thus highlighted as key aspects on animality and rurality in both positive and negative terms. Scenes from these activities are part of the quintessential iconography of the 'traditional' countryside. In addition to this large swathes of the rural landscape are managed or part managed, to satisfy the particular needs of animals to be hunted. For example, the maintenance of woods and hedges in fox-hunt territories, the maintenance of the grouse moors in upland areas, and the growth of cover and maintenance of woods in game bird shooting territories.

Pets and other recreations and sports

It has to be added that animals in the countryside can also be pets. Indeed part of the 'rural lifestyle' may be the keeping of animals such as dogs and horses in particular ways. The boundary between the status of livestock, working animals and even wild animals and that of 'pet' can become blurred. In addition the animals of the countryside become enrolled in other perhaps more benign and less controversial recreational activities such as horse riding, animal watching, bird watching, animal breeding and showing. These are significant rather than marginal cultural manifestations. The RSPB now has over 1 million members. Recreation can spill over into sport which involves animals in competition: most obviously horses in racing, jumping and so forth, but also more 'quaint' rural activities such as sheep dog trials. The attempted removal of 'One Man and His Dog' from BBC television a few years ago caused a vociferous barrage of objections.

All these animal presences in the countryside have their spatial variations and historical particularities. Some have waxed, others waned, some have shifted from production processes to reflexive cultural processes, some have become the focus of ongoing, faltering, policy histories and others have become fiercely contested, as in hunting, but they all remain as minor or major streams of practice and symbolism in the fabric of 'the rural' which is reproduced both through ongoing production and consumption.

These presences of animals in the rural have been recognised and studied within rural geography which was very much concerned with 'agriculture' in its earlier forms, and by agricultural (economic) geography. Yarwood and Evans show how these early 'livestock geographies' were largely economic or distributional in nature, and, tying into both regional and economic perspectives, 'treated animals as "units of production"' (2000: 100), with scant concern for issues of agency, otherness and ethics. More recently, developments in agricultural geographies, rural geographies and animal geographies have opened up a much wider range of ways in which animals in the rural might be considered. This has been given added impetus by the developing concerns over, and new theorisations of environmental/ethical issues such as bioethics, animal rights and broader questionings of nature–society relations. In terms of the latter, FitzSimmons and Goodman (1998: 194) claim that 'it has been a commonplace in social theory to ignore the specific "agency" and "materiality" of nature'. The push towards animal geographies is a response to the neglect of the presences of 'nature' within the fabric of the social, and how those presences are complex and heterogeneous and thus in need of detailed study. Harvey (1996: 183) is concerned that there has been a tendency to 'homogenise the category "nature" (and [to] discuss its social meaning and constitution as a unitary category) when it should be regarded as intensely internally variegated – an unparalleled field of difference'.

In relation to these new critical concerns about nature, and driven by the ethical and philosophical imperatives emerging from environmentalism and animal rights discourses, animal geographies have developed markedly over the last half of the 1990s (see Philo and Wilbert 2000; Wolch and Emel 1998). Broadly, this movement is concerned with how animals are implicated in the social in all manner of very significant ways, and how the acknowledgement and study of these implications have been marginal(ised). Studies have now begun to delve into the many ways animals and humans are bound together in spatially and temporally variable cultural, economic, social, material, imaginative and (un)ethical ways. Approaches range between the very 'real' processes of animal product production (for example Ufkes 1998) and ways in which the humans define themselves in symbolic relation to the animal as 'other' (Anderson 2000). Studies of differing categories of animals and their related spatialities have been conducted, for example on domesticated animals (Anderson 1997), wildlife (Emel 1995; Gullo *et al.* 1998; Thorne 1998; Whatmore and Thorne 1998, 2000) and zoo animals (Anderson 1995). The range of yet other animal spatialities studied includes, animals in the city (Griffiths *et al.* 2000; Philo 1998), animals and religious spaces (Wescoat 1998), and animals being 'in place or out of place' (Griffiths *et al.* 2000; Philo 1998) in the context of how their presence is constructed as appropriate or otherwise within the spatial fabrics of the social.

New 'rural animal geographies' have developed within this broader context of animal geography (and to an extent the sociological studies of animals, e.g. Arluke and Sanders 1996; Franklin 1996), and has exchanged theoretical and substantive foci with them. Yarwood and Evans (1998, 1999, 2000; Evans and Yarwood 1995) have opened up hitherto unconsidered aspects of rural animal geographies. For example, in their rare breeds geography (2000), they chart how certain types of livestock are implicated in shifts to a 'post-productivist' rural where (tourist) consumption of animals as spectacle has become important within farm diversification. They discuss how rare breeds can retain links with local and regional identity, and how animals are bound up with diverse cultures and landscapes of the countryside. They begin to consider how animals are implicated in the constructive *production* of particular country-sides, but do not venture as far as to discuss the agency or possibly disruptive nature of animals.

Woods (1998, 2000) has also built connections between animal and rural geo-graphy, particularly through the politics of hunting and other representations of animals. Here all the powerful visual and written and performed discourses of pro- and anti-hunting movements are depicted as highlighting and destabilising the imagined and performed animal geographies of the countryside.

Woods considers the 'political marginalisation' of the animals themselves and how the agency of animals is '(unintended) agency-as-effect'. Milbourne (2003) has now taken up the relationship between hunting, nature and construction of rurality where the roles and fates of various animals are critical.

Matless offers an intriguing account of one regional culture of animal geography, showing how, in the Norfolk Broads, particular animals – the bittern and the coypu – play their roles in a region where there is 'a tight interweaving of local ecology and economy' (2000: 138). This is an important pointer to the possible density and heterogeneity of such geographies which merit further consideration. But, as in human geography more generally, Yarwood and Evans suggest that rural geography has generally paid scant attention to animal and human–animal connections in the much wider senses opened up by animal geographies, and perhaps even on its own more productionist terms, and they conclude that 'there is still much work to be done on the place of animals in the countryside' (2000: 99).

ANT and rural animal geographies

One way in which the roles and positions of animals in the rural are being studied is through ANT perspectives. This again is set in wider contexts of animal geography studies, and given the influence this approach now has[7] this is like to be a developing trend. Philo and Wilbert (2000) in their comprehensive account of human–animal relations and new animal geographies, focus on ANT as 'sophisticated intellectual innovation' which is useful for developing the discussion of the agency of animals, and they conclude that 'Latour's pioneering experiments open up "a space" for contemplating the agency of non-humans, animals included, and for speculating about them taking their seats in his envisaged parliament of things' (2000: 17). Wilbert (1999) has also deployed ANT approaches to study the agency of animals and it is one of the theorisations which inform the work on wildlife by Whatmore and Thorne (1998, 2000). In terms of the rural, Cloke (1997) has argued that both the hybridity approach of Haraway (1991), and the ANT approaches of Latour (1993) and Callon et al. (1986), have been important for researchers looking at ideas of nature and at representations of the countryside – 'the "easiest" or most "obvious" spatializations of nature' (Cloke 1997: 369).

There are two forms of ANT-based rural (animal) geography. These are specific rural geographies which adopt an ANT approach, and other geographies such as hybrid geographies which consider 'rural' issues, but without particular reference to the rural. Lowe et al. (1997) and Woods (1998, 2000) are examples of the former where ANT is deployed to follow human and non-human actants in rural networks and to account for the precise outcome of relational interactions at work in both agricultural production and hunting. Whatmore (1997) and Fitzsimmons and Goodman (1998) are examples of the latter where networks of food production and the role of animals (and plants) as ' "quasi-objects, quasi-subjects" ' (Fitzsimmons and Goodman 1998: 209) within them are considered in ways which inevitably address 'the rural' as a network context.

Animals and the actant network approach

ANT approaches have been so influential because, as Thrift (1996) has said, they offer a powerful re-examination of the nature and locus of agency and thus of the way the world is ordered as it continuously unfolds. ANT is very much about achievements maintained over time by networks of things and beings enrolled to that effect. Enrolment is how actants are recruited and bound into networks where they then translate input and output within the network. The ongoing effort that courses through networks is a kind of electricity which hold the various actants together through translation. As Law (1999) has recently reasserted, this approach is about the 'relational materiality' and the 'performativity' of this process.

In terms of animals in the 'rural', (most obviously) the cows that produce milk or meat, the hens that produce eggs, the boars and sows that produce meat and other pigs for meat, the horse that learns to jump, the dog that learns to control sheep, or hunt, and so on, are, *in relation* with humans, technology, information and science, productive actants who contribute vital *affordences* to achievements of one kind or another emanating from networks. These are important conceptualisations which, as in the examples above begin to place animals more visibly and precisely in these achievements (e.g. Whatmore 1997). But as I outlined at the outset, I have a number of concerns about the status of animals as actants in ANT. How can ANT consider animals as they play complex roles in the rural, how are they enrolled into shifting agricultural networks (or other networks) and how might they resist and create 'other' non-human networks? To explore this I want to reconsider ANT in three ways.

Symmetry, extreme relationality and technology

ANT is highlighted for its symmetry (see Philo and Wilbert 2000) because of how it resists classifying and treating different actants such as human or non-human in the old set categories which were given special characteristics worthy of distinct study, and which generally saw the social as subject and the non-social as object. As Fitzsimmons and Goodman (1998: 216) state 'the principle of symmetry, and its importance in overcoming modern polarities and silences, is that consideration is given to non-human and human entities equally, with no prior assumption of privilege, rank or order'. Thus humans, machines, texts and animals can all be considered in the same way. The problem, which in a way parallels some feminist responses to poststructuralism (McNay 1992), is that here is a theoretical approach which in one way liberates, or brings out from the shadows, oppressed subjectivities, while at the same time, in other ways undermines their identity as distinct subjects worthy of epistemological, political and ethical distinction.

My second concern is that some versions of ANT, in relation to the idea of symmetry, take on what I call an extreme relational view. In this view the natures and identities of actants are not only subordinate to the relational connections and output of the network they may be in, but are actually *formed by* the relational position they are held in. This is shown in Law's assertion that 'entities take their form and acquire their attributes as a result of their relations with other entities. In this scheme of things entities have *no inherent qualities*' (1999: 3; emphasis added). It is also shown by the notion of 'blankness' where 'the agency of things does not come from within but from the "inscriptions" generated by a heterogeneous network upon . . . [its] blankness' (Hetherington 1997: 214, cited by Brown and Capdevila 1999: 40).

So these approaches seem to deny that certain entities do have some 'internal agency', can have 'inherent characteristics', and have form that is other to and resistant to the network identity inscribed upon them. I argue that differing actants are enrolled into hybrid networks *precisely because they have inherent qualities*; what would be the point of hybridity otherwise? This problem with the extreme relational view is highlighted by Lee and Stenner (1999: 110) who claim that if we 'render everything "networky" we will become insensitive to complexity and heterogeneity'. Whatmore (1999: 26) suggests that agency should be seen as 'a relational achievement, involving the *creative* presence of organic beings, technological devices and discursive codes' (my emphasis). This is particularly so in relation to nature wherein lies great complexity and heterogeneity (see also Cloke and Jones 2001; Jones and Cloke 2002), and in relation to animals who do have inherent qualities which do need to be taken into account. What is the nature of that 'creativity' which such 'beings' bring to relational processes (such as being able to turn grass to milk, and grassland into habitat), how can that be accounted for in relational accounts and what are the means and consequences of enrolment?

Thirdly ANT also does seem to stress the roles and agencies of technological objects and to shy away from confronting natural organic beings. There are exceptions to this (e.g. Callon 1986) but ANT does have a 'technical inflection' to use Whatmore and Thorne's (2000: 186) term, who also point out the 'socio-technical emphasis [within ANT] is real enough', that its focus 'is primarily [on] the panoply of devices, inventions, and inscriptions that pass through our hands' (2000: 186), and that this can be usefully contrasted to 'the more visceral preoccupations of feminist analyses with the corporeal configuration of energies and elements particularised in the experiential fabric of diverse *living beings*' (2000: 186; my emphasis). Technology *is* critical because it is 'society made durable' as Latour's telling phrase has it, and is, in a way, what distinguishes human network building from, say, that of baboon network building (see Philo and Wilbert 2000: 16). But this means animals remain a 'ghostly populous' (Whatmore and Thorne 2000: 186) whose many and various positions in techno-organic networks need further accounting for.

Animals as 'others': their enrolment, intentionality and resistance

So I want to respond to these concerns by asking a series of questions. Is it reasonable to treat animals symmetrically, as blanks, as things that take their identity from their relational interconnectivities alone? How are animals enrolled into networks and what are the spatialities and ethical implications of this? And how do these questions resonate in the particular contexts of rural set animal–human encounters?

Ingold suggests:

> to regard the animal as a mere tool is to deny its capacity for autonomous movement (Reed 1988); tools cannot 'act back' or *literally* interact with their users, they only conduct the users' action on the environment (Cohen 1978: 3–44). Evidently then the human 'handling' of animals is quite different from the handling of tools (2000: 307).

No doubt some ANT approaches would question the dismissive word 'mere' to describe tools, but Ingold's observation points not only to the difference in human *usages* of tools and animals, but also to the differences in *enrolling* animals and tools into networks. As already touched upon, enrolling in ANT is critical because it is the way that '*a nonhuman is seduced, manipulated, or induced into the collective*' (Latour 1999: 194; my emphasis).

Consider further the difference between a designed artefact and an animal. Consider a key. It will, if all is well, fit its lock very nicely and do its job well. The translation through brain, arm, hand, key, lock mechanism, to the opening of a door may be perfect. A lot of care has been invested to ensure that this is so. Artefacts can have this tendency of ease of enrolment and perfection of translation if made well and used properly or expertly. A huge effort over time goes into the developing design of artefacts (and into the creation of new artefacts for new functions), and developing the skills to use them, to try to ensure such perfect (or not) enrolments. Animal breeding and control does this to an extent, but there are also major differences.

As Ingold intimates, animals have forms of intentionality, agency and otherness which generate certain effects in relation to their ongoing enrolment into networks. Any denying of autonomous agency and being to animals flies in the face of reassessments of the capacities and status of animals coming from environmental philosophy. Writers such as Peterson (2001) and Plumwood (2002) are the latest in a long line of thinkers who have been attempting to challenge the moral discounting of animals (e.g. Regan 1998; Singer 1993) and nature by pointing out how the world is a relational achievement, and that natural beings in the form of plants and animals are thus meaningful actants worthy of inclusion in the ethical community. Peterson states that 'rethinking human nature means not only dethroning humans but also liberating other animals from their passive and mechanistic portrayal by Western rationalism' (2001: 223), and as a source of means of doing so, turns to world views which 'portray nonhuman animals, even other natural objects, as intentional agents' (2001: 222).

Elsewhere Ingold (1995) too has pressed for such reworked appreciations of the nature and capacities of animals. Part of doing this depends on dealing with the 'otherness' of animals. Peterson asks of 'the worldviews of other species – their knowledge of a given landscape, their own construction of reality. . . . We ought to ask whether there are nonhuman ways of being conscious, of having a mind, of acting morally' (2001: 223). And Plumwood asserts that the behaviours of certain animals

> require sophisticated higher-order intentionality; there are so many examples of this kind, which so many people experience, that one has to wonder whether theorists who strive to dismiss them have any knowledge of animals outside the laboratory (2002: 182).

Even if these views are discounted, animals are clearly extremely complex (far more so than any technological device) evolved entities 'saturated with being' (Whatmore and Thorne 2000: 186), with patterns of instinctive behaviour which have to be dealt with when they are being enrolled into networks. Animals are not, as yet, artefacts, fully designed and formed by humans so as they fit into networks perfectly. Animals (and plants) took their form to suit other relational connections, and they have tendencies and directions of their own, which makes their enrolment in agential networks different and more problematic in practical and ethical terms.

As Jones and Cloke (2002) and Cloke and Jones (2001) point out, natural artefacts (animals – or even trees) are enrolled in part by *working with(in) their (pre) existing tendencies*, thus *their* habits and tendencies shape the technologies and practices which in turn shape and control them. Animal husbandry practices and agricultural technologies have been adapted – to an extent – to the life cycles and habits of animals. The domestication of animals over time, through selective breeding, and now the possibilities of genetic modification, can be seen as attempts to make animals into artefacts that fit networks as exactly as possible, but this has been by no means a complete pro-cess of transformation. The consequence of this is that the otherness of animals often has to be harshly controlled as they are treated as artefacts and enrolled into collectives.

'The restraint of beasts'

The post and wire fences built by the 'heroes' of Magnus Mills's novel (see opening quote) can be seen as parts of ANT assemblages to enrol animals. The resistance and subversion of animals will often require significant degrees of force and maintenance to secure their enrolment. Thus the forms of much of the English countryside – its fields, hedges, stone walls, its buildings old and new, the location and layouts of farms, agricultural markets, slaughter houses and market towns – are dictated by the need to ensure the successful enrolment of domesticated animals into human-driven networks. And other forms of enrolments, such as that of sporting animals, hunting/hunted animals, even conserved animals brings other material arrangements to the rural. These enrolments (particularly in agricultural terms) have been so successful that the resistance of animals seems a rather strange idea. Only when such 'escapes' as the 'Tamworth Two'[8] and similar cases occur does this become more clear. But Philo and Wilbert (2000: 16) discuss such situations where animals 'often end up evading the places to which humans seek to allot them'. In such 'transgressions', it is 'animals themselves who inject what might be termed their own agency into the scene [and] forge their own 'other spaces'. Thus they can adapt their environment, subvert and even resist human (spatial) orderings (Philo and Wilbert 2000).

Cows, pigs, horses, poultry and sheep often have to be coerced by violent means into rural production networks. As Ingold shows, dealing with animals has produced a whole range of 'tools of coercion, such as the whip or the spur, designed to inflict physical force and very often acute pain' (2000: 307). The means of enrolling pigs into traditional agricultural production collectives shown in Malcolmson and Mastoris (1998) (Figure 16.1) are very much tools of coercion where attachment devices were stapled into the sensitive parts of the pig's body (snout) which could then be connected to handling tools. Such enrolment technologies have not remained static, but have gone though transformations that echo Foucault's accounts of shifts in discipline from the infliction of pain to the imposition of surveillance. Franklin (1996: 127) shows how 'the former relationship between farmer and farmed has changed: the microchip and process system has taken over almost most of the caring, monitoring and management of animals to the extent that the farmers have become technicians, often dependent on expert back-up from system suppliers'.

These modern enrolling techniques have also removed animals from public gaze. 'Today pigs are infrequently seen by most people, until a generation or two ago, by contrast, pigs were part of everyday life. They were included in the normal landscape of human experience' (Malcolmson and Mastoris 1998). More generally Wolch and Emel (1998: xi) state that the use of (and plight) of animals 'is mostly obscured by the progressive elimination of animals from everyday human experience of animals', and this is the cue to turn to considerations of ethics and spaces of ethics.

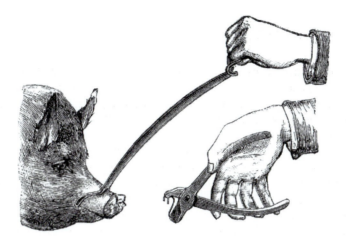

Figure 16.1 Pig-ringing. An example of coercive technology for enrolling farm animals into agricultural production collectives. Is this assemblage of human, technology and animal 'symmetrical'?

ANT and ethics: networks and spaces of (un)ethical practice

Within animal geographies issues of ethics and animal welfare and rights are often prominent (Jones 2000; Wolch and Emel 1998). Indeed Matless (2000) sees these as the chief motivating forces of much of this work. Thus theoretical approaches such as ANT used to consider the positions of animals must retain or acquire a means of ethical analysis. But what are ANT's credentials for doing this? It is somewhat ironic that when ANT talks of the 'excluded masses' it is often not animals (or plants) which are in mind, but technological devices. Laurier and Philo (1999) and Philo and Wilbert (2000) interrogate Latour's treatment of an artefact (a prototype rapid personal system) to which Philo and Wilbert (2000) ascribe 'thought-and-action' and 'a capacity for agency' (p. 17). They feel that Latour's work 'illuminates shadowy dimensions of the machinic thing-world all too easily forgotten by conventional social science' (p. 18), and that this does open up the space for thinking about animals as well. But ANT can be criticised for its lack concern for the fate of actants enrolled into networks, Bingham and Thrift (2000: 299) in their elucidation of the geographies of ANT, admit that it is open to the accusation that it 'ignores "the quite real effectivity of victimisation" [quoting Wise 1997: 39] it is studiously neutral and, as a result, *it bypasses questions of unequal power*' (my emphasis).

But there are accounts of ANT that are trying to argue it into a more overtly ethical trajectory. The victimisation of nature and the unequal power relations between modernity and nature forged a social contract which excluded non-humans, as ethical, agential, significant others (Serres 1995), while at the same time enrolling them as things into the monstrous hybrids (e.g. modern industrial agriculture) which Latour depicts. Lee and Stenner in an effort to prompt the ethical potentials of ANT write

> We are morally enraged by banishment – by the idea of sacrificing someone or something else for the sake of the maintenance of our order, and by the idea of parasitism: that we live like vampires, only because we kill and eat the flesh, plant or animal, of those we kill. If we're good people, we set about exposing such banishments (1999: 101).

To do this Lee and Stenner turn to the work of Serres where they find sentiments more open to the otherness of nature and more interested in balances of power between nature and the social:

> For Serres the Otherness of nature screams out in it own terms, from its own world, and the issue, on pain of life and death, concerns balance and reciprocity – the maintenance of an order not dictated solely by our terms (1999: 109)

Furthermore they see in Serres recognition of 'other' non-human networks, separate from but in collision with the social:

> For Serres [unlike Latour] the natural or worldwide world and the human world or worldly world of culture and politics, *far from being part of the same network*, have always had a violent and antagonistic relationship 'a combat that has lasted since prehistory' (1999: 107; my emphasis).

Human networks have tangled with, conflicted with, co-opted, extended and exterminated these other non-human networks and the beings in them. Often, within this, the enrolment of animals across the divide into social networks has been brutal and total. Over time the selective breeding of animals (and plants) has been a process of evolving enrolment where animals have been modified to better match their niche in the (evolving) network. Yet they are not as yet artefacts but are treated as such. Other forms of enrolment may be more empathetic. The notion of symbiosis is important here, where animals enter relationships with other animals, plants, humans, in a way where both parties are enrolling each other to their own ends but in ways that benefit the other's ends. Such relationships, particularly those between animal and human, again open up questions and possibilities in terms of treating animals as actants in human networks, and may point to more empathetic forms of enrolment. But as I have already raised, the material orders of the rural, and the coercive devices of animal husbandry are part of this ongoing 'violent and antagonistic relationship'.

As well as the example shown in Figure 16.1, many animal handlers use sticks, whips and leads; bulls have rings inserted into their noses so they can be led around and tied up if needed; cattle farms have cattle crushes; male animals are routinely castrated, most animals are incarcerated in some way or other.

This could be a very long list. But the point is that all this subjugation para-phernalia is required to ensure the successful enrolment of these animals into networks or collectives of one kind or another. And often it is trying to make animals as much like artefacts as possible so they can be stably incorporated into networks. Beavis (2002) notes that a key moment in the development of the farm animal welfare movement was the publication of Ruth Harrison's 1964 book *Animal Machines*, which exposed the conditions of 'factory farm-ing'. Ingold (1988: 15), in considering Tapper's account of the shift from a hunter economy to pastoralism and further into modernity in the form of 'modern factory farming', feels that within this process 'the animal moves from being a strange person to a familiar thing'. In other words, their being and otherness are lost sight of as they are rendered into common artefacts:

> To mint animals for *human* time (read economy) required fencing and tethering, fodder and shelter and protection again predation, very likely the detention of the newborn as means of controlling the mother, clocking estrus, as selective breed-ing for desirable traits through manipulation of the mating process. One can quite properly label the process detention, forced breeding, and patronization (fodder, shelter, protection) – these constituting of course, the precise terms of slavery (Martin 1993: 57–8).

Serpell also charts the historical development of agriculture and states:

> the entire system depends on the subjugation of nature, and the domination and manipulation of living creatures. If the record of civilisation is anything to go by, it was the most ruthless cultures – the ones with the most effective distancing devices – who prospered most of all (1996: 218).

Conclusions: bitter and benign dwellings

There is a need to unpack the geographies of animal–human relations and the geoethics that shadow them (Jones 2000; Lynn 1998a,b). This in part will be driven by perusing ideas of relational agency, the placed (un)ethics of encounter which may be associated with that agency, and an effort to sense somehow the otherness of animals. As I have argued elsewhere (Jones 2000) the encounters that make up the world are shadowed by a geography of ethics which resonate through material and imagined spaces. This needs to be unpacked with a sensitivity to situatedness (Thrift 1996) and uncertainty (Bauman 1993) if we are to deal with the huge diversity of complex encounters. We need to try to see other bodies, other scales, other spaces (water – fish farm-ing) and their life as meaningfully other, meaninglessly other. These demands apply to, and take particular form in, 'the rural' and the spaces and kinds of encounters that constitute the rural.

I have shown that there are clear sensitivities to the otherness of nature within ANT approaches, as in the work of Serres, but there are also concerns about how the natures, roles and fates of animals may be conceptualised from an ANT perspective. The rural is an 'animal space' in certain senses, but more importantly is an arena where many types of human–animal encounters occur. Rural geographies of wild animals and domestic animals can be constructed, but also geographies of particular animals in particular settings within and between these. One way of conceptualising these animal presences and the geoethics that shadow them is through the idea of dwelling. This is a concept partly developed through considerations of animals' lives (see Ingold 1995, 2000) but is often applied to how humans live in landscapes (Macnaghten and Urry 1998). It offers opportunities to think about non-human agency, but in a way more sensitive to the place of encounter, the body, the otherness of animals, ideas of agency and finally the ethical dimension.

Thrift (1999) acknowledges that ANT provides a convincing account of how all manner of things constantly combine and recombine in the formation of the functioning social world, but it does not recognise how these comings together can have qualities, or have qualities brought to them, which resonate of place. In his view, 'Latour and other actor network theorists . . . fail to see the importance of place because they are reluctant to ascribe different competencies to different aspects of the network or to understand the role of common ground in how networks echo back and forth, often unwittingly' (1999: 313). Animals are networked into all manner of productive connections in the rural but their presence in material landscapes (of one kind of the other) and their presence in imaginative geographies of the rural contribute to the formation of the rural as a place and to places within the rural.

With its phenomenological associations (see Ingold 1993), dwelling also acknowledges the importance of the body, the senses, and the body in (relational) motion which places one in the world. This opens up opportunities for sensitivity to the other-sensed ways by which animals inhabit their worlds. The bulk of animal presences, their movement, which humans can either constrain and contest, or value and celebrate in some way (as in animal/bird watching, horse riding), their social interaction through movement, the differing capacities of their senses, and the marks they leave on the landscapes, are all about animal bodies dwelling in landscapes in differing relations to humans.

In terms of the otherness of animals, Ingold (1995) points out that they, and even plants, build and dwell in the world in *creative* ways which are outside human enrolment and often in conflict with its networks. The resistance of domesticated animals to their enrolment, and the adaptation of wild animals to farmed landscapes are examples of the otherness of animals disrupting and refolding (human) spaces, orders and networks to their own ends.

I have discussed the concept of 'transgression' (see Philo and Wilbert 2000) where domesticated animals persistently (but often unsuccessfully) resist and subvert the places set out for them in human orderings, this creates a 'background noise' of otherness in rural spaces. Wild animals can also render the rural as 'other'. Deer, foxes, badgers, birds and other animals make light of the striated space of the productive countryside and render it smooth again by their ability to move through, round and over fences, hedges, settlements and roads (with some danger to both wild and social networks). There has been a tendency to see Britain's nature/wildlife as 'semi-domesticated' because 'it' lives in a substantially adapted landscape rather than in a 'natural' habitat. To imagine true nature and wilderness (if any remains), far-off 'uninhabited' spaces are conjured. Under this construction of 'wildlife', a deer, say, becomes less wild, less natural (and maybe a pest) if it leaves an area of woodland to graze on growing crops. I would prefer to say that the deer makes that space wild as she breaks into a domesticated production network and renders it other. Dwelling is much concerned with breaking down this binary of natural/social orders, spaces and lives and acknowledges them to be all mixed up together (see Franklin 2002) in ways much in sympathy with some new accounts of human–nature relationships (Cronon 1996). Dwelling needs to be seen in terms of the dense, intimate relationships in a given landscape[9] as Lopez evocatively illustrates as he describes the movement of a black-throated sparrow landing on a thin branch, and the relational movement between the resilient give of the branch and the fluttering and balancing of the settling bird (see Harris 1998: 262).

There are also other 'othernesses' of animals which merit consideration in terms of shaping the countryside or the rural. Animals, even domesticated ones, are ecological by nature. Therefore their existence in the countryside, their particular agencies have creative spin-offs, making cultures, landscapes, places and habitats. For example, many of the wild ecologies of our landscapes are dependent on the ongoing grazing by domesticated animals and the management of that landscape for those animals. These could be said to be *wild extensions* of production networks. It is easy to see the rural in such relational terms. In the 2001 foot and mouth crisis, when landscapes such as the Brecon Beacons and the Lake District were cleared of sheep, news comment was often along the lines of, without the sheep, these landscapes are not sustainable and will never be the same again. These connections and interweavings driven by both human and non-human agency chime more with ideas of dwelling, common ground and the ecology of place(s) (Thrift 1996) than with a strictly networked view.

So like ANT, dwelling does allow for ideas of non-human agency. Ingold talks of the world as an achievement of process, 'a world that is . . . in motion, continually coming into being through the combined action of human and non-human agencies' (2000: 155). Dwelling, in animal terms, according to Ingold, is thus the expression of their agency and their creative intentionality. Franklin (2002) sees that to accept Ingold's notion of dwelling as deployed by Macnaghten and Urry (1998) 'is to recognise the truth of Latour's claim (that seems implicit in the notion of dwelling), that modernity did not and, indeed, cannot separate the natural, the cultural/human, there can only be hybrids and networks of humans and non-humans' (2002: 58).

So finally we turn back to ideas of ethics. If dwelling is the expression of animal intentionality and agency, then the denying of their ability to do this is what has now become to be seen as the unethical treatment of animals, particularly those enrolled into human collectives such as food production, or tourist spectacle. Beavis (2002) sketches the evolution of the 'Five Freedoms' which now underpin animal welfare campaigning. These are freedom from hunger and thirst; from discomfort; from pain, injury and disease; from fear and distress; and to express normal behaviour. In other words these freedoms represent a call not to enrol animals as machines, fitting exactly into intensive systems (the most obvious example being battery hens) but to enrol animals by letting them dwell in their environment in a way that gives some freedom to their agency and intentionality. The idea of giving animals more freedom to move, to forage for food, to socialise, to establish their own space (as in some versions of free range husbandry) is in effect allowing them to dwell as beings rather than exist as machines.

Cloke and Jones (2001) have considered that to dwell, in the sense of being embedded in the world, is not necessarily a romantic, authentic, or even positive process, and we suggest the idea of more bitter and contested dwellings (because all beings are always embedded in the world). In the case of animals these 'bitter dwellings' are lives where some or all of the five freedoms are denied and pain or the adoption of repetitive, unnatural (self or other damaging) behaviour, replaces the more benign activities of autonomous dwelling.

Within concerns about food quality; sustainable rural economies, cultures and environments; nature conservation; animal welfare; the rural as an aesthetic (tourist friendly) experience, the questions of how animals are enrolled into various networks which constitute the rural is a critical issue. This will remain the focus of much debate, conflict and legislation particularly in relation to hunting, domestic animal welfare and wildlife presences. Consequently these interweavings between rurality and animality will remain a central concern of rural studies. ANT approaches can help to open up the precise relations at work in this, but account needs to be taken of the otherness of animals, the (un)ethical geographies of those relations, and the ways in which animals can live out bitter or more benign dwellings.

Notes

1. I take the term animality from Tapper (1988) who concerns himself in 'definitions of "humanity" and "animality"' and how these are defined and define each other.

2. I am aware that 'the rural' is a term which has been problematised and even questioned. This calling into question may be exacerbated by ANT approaches which challenge 'traditional' views of space (Murdoch 1997, 1998; Thrift 2000) but I support Whatmore's (1993) account of how the rural has a robust and lively existence in popular imagination and everyday reality which defies academic limits and concerns.

3. ANT has entered a phase of self-review (Law and Hassard 1999) and there is a tendency for the word collective (Latour 1999) or collectif (Callon and Law 1995) to

represent hybrid groups of heterogeneous actants which generate and maintain effects through their relational agency. This term seems to supersede the idea of network to some extent and in this paper both terms are used.

4. ANT has turned to the term 'actant' to describe what might be termed actors in order to step away from the anthropocentric resonance of the latter term. Actant(s) rather than actor(s) will be used through this chapter.

5. I am conscious that there have been calls for 'rural geography' to move on from the shorthand of idyll (see Little 1999). But as it is a notion and a shorthand still used profusely in British culture, is it our place to decide to 'move on' or to keep thinking about this powerful way in which the rural is imagined?

6. In art – from the fabulous horse paintings of Stubbs, Bewick's woodcuts of animals and farm scenes, the endless mushy Victorian paintings of peasant life (with animals), to even more mushy contemporary (but commercially successful) work by Gordon Beningfield – 'Britain's leading countryside artist' – animals, and animals and humans together has been a key theme of rural depictions. In literature – from the high romanticism of Mary Webb (*Gone to Earth*) to the satire of Stella Gibbons (*Cold Comfort Farm*), to the contemporary fiction of Miles quoted at the outset, and in the extended agriculture/nature focus of Ted Hughes's poetry; the wild, the domestic, the loved and the disregarded are all present in a synthesised way and this hints at how the 'animality' of rurality in the end depends on the richness of these imagined presences. This also has it outlets in other popular culture from the rural soaps to the incredibly successful James Herriott rural vet stories, where animals quietly or noisily populate depictions of rural life. In the history of children's literature the rural and animals (in the rural) have had a dominating presence. As Bunce (1994: 65) has it 'for generations of young children animals are country folk – the real inhabitants of villages, woods, fields and the river banks, with adult human beings either nowhere in sight or at the best hostile figures in an alien world'.

7. As indicated in note 3 above ANT has undergone a certain amount of revision, but it has now a considerable presence in some significant social theory stances, for example in that of Thrift (1996) who uses certain aspects of ANT approach in his heterogeneous theoretical orientations, and is thus likely to remain a viable theoretical orientation for some time to come.

8. The Tamworth Two' were two Tamworth pigs which escaped while in transit to an abattoir for slaughter in the United Kingdom in 1998. They evaded capture for a week by when they had come to the attention of national and international media. A National Newspaper eventually paid for them to live out their lives in an animal sanctuary (see Ford 1998).

9. This is not to say they any given landscape is spatially bounded and isolated, connections (networks) will flow in and out of any space and contribute to the elements folded together therein and elsewhere (see Cloke and Jones 2001).

References

Anderson, K. 1995 'Culture and nature at the Adelaide Zoo: at the frontiers of "human" geography', *Transactions of the Institute of British Geographers*, NS 20, 275–94.

Anderson, K. 1997 'A walk on the wild side: a critical geography of domestication', *Progress in Human Geography*, **21**(4), 463–85.

Anderson, K. 2000 'The beast within: race, humanity and animality', *Environment and Planning D: Society and Space*, **18**, 301–20.

Arluke, A. and Sanders, C.R. 1996 *Regarding Animals*, Temple University Press, Philadelphia.

Bauman, Z. 1993 *Postmodern Ethics*, Blackwell, Oxford.

Beavis, S. 2002 'Creature comforts', in Farming Today? (Supplement), *Guardian*, 28 June.

Bingham, N. and Thrift, N. 2000 'Some new instructions for travellers: the geography of Bruno Latour and Michel Serres', pp. 281–301 in M. Crang and N. Thrift (eds), *Thinking Space*, Routledge, London.

Brown S.D. and Capdevila R. 1999 '*Perpetum Mobile*: substance, force and the sociology of translation', pp. 26–50 in J. Law and J. Hassard (eds), *Actor Network Theory and After*, Blackwell, Oxford.

Buller, H. 2003 'Where the wild things are: reflexions on the evolving iconography of rural fauna', *Journal of Rural Studies*, forthcoming.

Bunce, M. 1994 *The Countryside Ideal: Anglo-American Images of Landscape*, Routledge, London.

Callon, M. 1986 'Some elements of a sociology of translation; domestication of the scallops and the fishermen of St Brieux Bay', pp. 196–223 in J. Law (ed.), *Power, Action and Belief: A New Sociology of Knowledge?*, Routledge & Kegan Paul, London.

Callon, M. and Law, J. 1995 'Agency and the Hybrid Collectif', *The South Atlantic Quarterly*, **94**(2), 481–507.

Callon, M., Law, J. and Rip, A. (eds) 1986 *Mapping the Dynamics of Science and Technology*, Macmillan, London.

Cloke, P. 1997 'Country backwater to virtual village? Rural studies and the cultural turn', *Journal of Rural Studies*, **13**(4), 367–75.

Cloke, P. and Jones, O. 2001 'Dwelling, place, and landscape: an orchard in Somerset', *Environment and Planning A*, **33**, 649–66.

Cohen, G.A. 1978 *Karl Marx's Theory of History: A Defence*, Oxford, Clarendon Press.

Cronon, W. 1996 'The trouble with wilderness, or, getting back to the wrong of nature', pp. 69–90 in W. Cronon (ed.), *Uncommon Ground: Rethinking the Human Place in Nature*, W.W. Norton and Co., New York.

Emel, J. 1995 'Are you man enough, big enough and bad enough? Ecofeminism and wolf eradication in the USA', *Environment and Planning D: Society and Space*, **13**, 707–34.

Evans, N. and Yarwood, R. 1995 'Livestock and landscape', *Landscape Research*, **20**, 141–6.

Fitzsimmons, M. and Goodman, D. 1998 'Incorporating nature: environmental narratives and the reproduction of food', pp. 194–220 in B. Braun and N. Castree (eds), *Remaking Reality: Nature at the Millennium*, Routledge, London.

Ford, C. 1998 'A tail of two pigs', *The Spark*, **13**, 30.

Franklin A. 1996 *Animals and Modern Cultures. A Sociology of Human–Animal Relations in Modernity*, Sage, London.

Frankin, A. 2002 *Social Nature*, Sage, London.

Griffiths, D., Poulter, I. and Sibley, D. 2000 'Feral cats in the city', pp. 56–70 in C. Philo and C. Wilbert (eds), *Animal Spaces, Beastly Spaces: New Geographies of Human–Animal Relations*, Routledge, London.

Gullo, A., Lassiter, U. and Wolch, J. 1998 'The Cougar's tale', pp. 139–161 in J. Wolch and J. Emel (eds), *Animal Geographies: Place, Politics and Identity in the Nature–Culture Borderlands*, Verso, London.

Haraway, D. 1991 *Simians, Cyborgs, and Women: The Reinvention of Nature*, Chapman & Hall, New York.

Harris, M.S. 1998 'Being homesick, writing home', pp. 253–64 in P. Banting (ed.), *Fresh Tracks: Writing the Western Landscape*, Polestar Books, Victoria.

Harrison, R. 1964 *Animal Machines: The New Factory Farming Industry*, New York, Ballantine Books.

Harvey, D. 1996 *Justice, Nature, and the Geography of Difference*, Blackwell, Oxford.

Hetherington, K. 1997 'Museum topology and the will to connect', *Journal of Material Culture*, **2**(2), 199–218.

Ingold, T. (ed.) 1988 *What is an Animal?* London, Unwin Hyman.

Ingold, T. 1993 'The temporality of landscape', *World Archaeology*, **25**, 152–74.

Ingold, T. 1995 'Building, dwelling, living: how people and animals make themselves at home in the world', pp. 57–80 in M. Strathern (ed.), *Shifting Contexts: Transformations in Anthropological Knowledge*, Routledge, London.

Ingold, T. 2000 *The Perception of the Environment: Essays in Livelihood, Dwelling and Skill*, Routledge, London.

Jones, O. 2000 'Inhuman geographies: (un)ethical spaces of human non-human relations', pp. 268–91 in C. Philo and C. Wilbert (eds), *Animal Geographies: New Geographies of Human–Animal Relations*, Routledge, London.

Jones, O. and Cloke, P. 2002 *Tree Culture: The Place of Trees, and Trees in their Place*, Berg, Oxford.

Latour, B. 1993 *We Have Never Been Modern*, Harvester Wheatsheaf, Hemel Hempstead.

Latour, B. 1999 *Pandora's Hope: Essays on the Reality of Science Studies*, Harvard University Press, Cambridge.

Laurier, E. and Philo, C. 1999 ' "X" morphising: review essay of Bruno Latour's Aramis or the Love of Technology', *Environment and Planning A*, **31**, 1047–71.

Law, J. 1999 'After ANT: complexity, naming and topology', pp. 1–14 in J. Law and J. Hassard (eds), *Actor Network Theory and After*, Blackwell, Oxford.

Law, J. and Hassard, J. 1999 *Actor Network Theory and After*, Oxford, Blackwell.

Lee, N. and Stenner, P. 1999 'Who pays? Can we pay them back?' pp. 90–112 in J. Law, and J. Hassard (eds), *Actor Network Theory and After*, Blackwell, Oxford.

Little, J. 1999 'Otherness, representation and the cultural construction of rurality', *Progress in Human Geography*, **23**, 437–42.

Lowe, P., Clark, J., Seymour, S. and Ward, N. 1997 *Moralizing the Environment: Countryside Change, Farming and Pollution*, University of London Press, London.

Lynn, W.S. 1998a 'Animal, ethics and geography', pp. 280–97 in J. Wolch and J. Emel (eds), *Animal Geographies: Place, Politics and Identity in the Nature–Culture Borderlands*, Verso, London.

Lynn, W.S. 1998b 'Contested moralities: animals and moral value in the Dear/Symanski debate', *Ethics, Place and Environment*, **1**(2), 223–44.

Macnaghten, P. and Urry, J. 1998 *Contested Natures*, Sage, London.

Malcolmson, R. and Mastoris, S. 1998 *The English Pig: A History*, Hambledon Press, London.

Martin, C.L. 1993 *In the Spirit of the Earth*, Johns Hopkins University Press, Baltimore.

Matless, D. 2000 'Versions of animal–human: Broadland, c 1945–1970', pp. 115–40 in C. Philo and C. Wilbert (eds), *Animal Geographies: New Geographies of Human–Animal Relations*, Routledge, London.

McNay, L. 1992 *Foucault and Feminism: Power, Gender and the Self*, Polity Press, Cambridge.

Milbourne, P. 2003 'Hunting ruralities: nature, society and culture in "hunt countries" of England and Wales', *Journal of Rural Studies*, forthcoming.

Mills, M. 1998 *The Restraint of Beasts*, London, Flamingo Books.

Murdoch, J. 1997 'Inhuman/nonhuman/human: actor-network theory and the potential for a non-dualistic and symmetrical perspective on nature and society', *Environment and Planning D, Society and Space*, **15**, 731–56.

Murdoch, J. 1998 'The spaces of actor-network theory', *Geoforum*, **29**(4), 357–74.

Peterson, A.L. 2001 *Being Human: Ethics, Environment, and Our Place in the World*, University of California Press, Berkeley, CA.

Phillips, M., Fish, R. and Agg, J. 2001 'Putting together ruralities: towards a symbolic analysis of rurality in the British mass media', *Journal of Rural Studies*, **17**, 1–27.

Philo, C. 1998 'Animals, geography, and the city: notes on inclusions and exclusions', pp. 51–71 in J. Wolch and J. Emel (eds), *Animal Geographies: Place, Politics and Identity in the Nature–Culture Borderlands*, Verso, London.

Philo, C. 2000 'More words more worlds: reflections on the "cultural turn" and human geography', pp. 26–53 in I. Cook, D. Crouch, S. Naylor and J.R. Ryan (eds), *Cultural Turns/Geographical Turns: Perspectives on Cultural Geography*, Prentice Hall, Harlow.

Philo, C. and Wilbert, C. 2000 'Animal spaces, beastly places: an introduction', pp. 1–34 in C. Philo and C. Wilbert (eds), *Animal Spaces, Beastly Spaces: New Geographies of Human–Animal Relations*, Routledge, London.

Plumwood, V. 2002 *Environmental Culture: The Ecological Crisis of Reason*, Routledge, London.

Proctor, J.D. 1998 'Ethics in geography: giving moral form to the geographical imagination', *Area*, **30**(1), 8–18.

Reed, E. 1988 'The affordances of the animate environment: social science from the ecological point of view', pp. 110–26 in T. Ingold (ed.), *What is an Animal?*, London, Unwin Hyman.

Regan, T. 1998 'The case for animal rights', pp. 821–8 in S.M. Cahn and P. Markie (eds), *Ethics: History, Theory and Contemporary Issues*, Oxford University Press, Oxford.

Ridley, J. 1998 'Animals in the countryside', pp. 142–52 in A. Barnett and R. Scruton (eds), *Town and Country*, Jonathan Cape, London.

Serpell, J. 1995 'A consideration of policy implications: a panel discussion', *Social Research, In the Company of Animals*, **62**(3), 821–6.

Serpell, J. 1996 *In the Company of Animals: A Study of Human–Animal Relations*, Cambridge University Press, Cambridge.

Serres, M. 1995 *The Natural Contract*, The University of Michigan Press, Michigan.

Seymour, J. 1979 *The Countryside Explained*, Penguin, Harmondsworth.

Shoard, M. 1980 *The Theft of the Countryside*, Maurice Temple Smith, London.

Singer, P. 1993 *Practical Ethics* (2nd edn), Cambridge University Press, Cambridge.

Tapper, R. 1988 'Animality, humanity, morality, society', pp. 47–62 in T. Ingold (ed.), *What is An Animal?*, Unwin Hyman, London.

Thorne, L. 1998 'Kangaroos: the non-issue', *Society and Animals*, **6**(2), 167–82.

Thrift, N. 1996 *Spatial formations*, Sage, London.

Thrift, N. 1999 'Steps to an ecology of place', pp. 295–352 in D. Massey, P. Sarre and J. Allen (eds), *Human Geography Today*, Polity, Oxford.

Thrift, N. 2000 'Afterwords', *Environment and Planning D, Society and Space*, **18**(2), 213–56.

Ufkes, F.M. 1998 'Building a better pig: fat profits in lean meat', pp. 241–58 in J. Wolch and J. Emel (eds), *Animal Geographies: Place, Politics and Identity in the Nature–Culture Borderlands*, Verso, London.

Wescoat, J.L. 1998 'The "right of thirst" for animals in Islamic law: a comparative approach', pp. 259–79 in J. Wolch and J. Emel (eds), *Animal Geographies: Place, Politics and Identity in the Nature–Culture Borderlands*, Verso, London.

Whatmore, S. 1993 'On doing rural research (or breaking the boundaries)', *Environment and Planning A*, **25**(2), 605–7.

Whatmore, S. 1997 'Dissecting the autonomous self: hybrid cartographies for a relational ethics', *Environment and Planning D: Society and Space*, **15**, 37–53.

Whatmore, S. 1999 'Rethinking the "human" in human geography', in D. Massey, P. Sarre and J. Allen (eds), *Human Geography Today*, Polity, Oxford.

Whatmore, S. 2000 'Heterogeneous geographies: reimagining the spaces of nature', in I. Cook, D. Crouch, S. Naylor and J.R. Ryan (eds), *Cultural Turns/Geographical Turns: Perspectives on Cultural Geography*, Prentice Hall, Harlow.

Whatmore, S. and Thorne, L. 1998 'Wild(er)ness: reconfiguring the geographies of wildlife', *Transactions of the Institute of British Geographers*, NS **23**(4), 435–54.

Whatmore, S. and Thorne, L. 2000 'Elephants on the move: spatial formations of wildlife exchange', *Environment and Planning D: Society and Space*, **18**, 185–203.

Wilbert, C. 1999 'Anti-this-against-that: resistances along a human–non-human axis', pp. 238–55 in P. Routledge, C. Philo, and R. Paddison (eds), *Entanglements of Power, Geographies of Domination/Resistance*, Routledge, London.

Wise, J.M. 1997 *Explaining Technology and Social Space*, Sage, London.

Wolch, J. and Emel, J. 1995 'Bringing the animals back in', *Environment and Planning D: Society and Space*, **13**, 632–6.

Wolch, J. and Emel, J. (eds) 1998 *Animal Geographies: Place, Politics and Identity in the Nature–Culture Borderlands*, Verso, London.

Woods, M. 1998 'Researching rural conflicts: hunting, local politics and actor-networks', *Journal of Rural Studies*, **14**, 321–40.

Woods, M. 2000 'Fantastic Mr. Fox? Representing animals in the hunting debate', pp. 182–202 in C. Philo and C. Wilbert (eds), *Animal Geographies: New Geographies of Human–Animal Relations*, Routledge, London.

Yarwood, R. and Evans, N. 1998 'New places for "Old Spots": the changing geographies of domestic livestock animals', *Society and Animals*, **6**, 137–66.

Yarwood, R. and Evans, N. 1999 'The changing geography of rare livestock breeds in Britain', *Geography*, **84**, 80–87.

Yarwood, R. and Evans, N. 2000 'Taking stock of farm animals and rurality', pp. 98–114 in C. Philo and C. Wilbert (eds), *Animal Geographies: New Geographies of Human–Animal Relations*, Routledge, London.

Still life in nearly present time: the object of nature

CHAPTER 17

Nigel Thrift

Introduction

The problem that writing on the countryside faces is that it still tends to work with a romantic version of complexity in which there is a basic wholeness – a kind of organic circuitry – that makes up a 'natural' world (Kwa 2002). However, nowadays there is a growing tendency to try to think of the countryside in terms of a baroque view of complexity in which the sensuous materiality of the 'natural' does not add up. Instead, it flows in many directions and can produce many novel combinations out of what might sometimes seem a rather limited set of elements, a set of worlds-in-themselves which may partially connect to each other but do not add up to a natural whole. In turn, binaries such as nature/society, macro/micro and organic/inorganic become impossible to sustain, not least because the human sensorium is continually adding body parts as it invents new ways to inhabit, 'creative transformations', to use a Whiteheadian term. So we obtain a fragmented and dissonant 'nature', a heap of highly significant fragments rather than a seamless web (Benjamin 1985) in which the links are of reciprocal reference rather than connection. The struggle now is to allow this baroque view of nature to gain a foothold and to put aside the romantic view and its associated symbols – which so limits our ability to think – in favour of something less certain: a contingent, complex and creative nature (Kwa 2002).

In this chapter, I will try to achieve this goal through a consideration of concepts which are not symbols but allegorical narratives which contain their own images of the world. But what I also want to show is how these images of the world are continually being revised by the evolution of the human sensorium. What we see is the continual addition of new body parts (Hinchliffe 2002; Latour 2001) which produce new relations of reciprocal reference and so redefine what counts as 'natural', from new colours (Garfield 2000; Harvey 1995; Pastoureau 2002) to the new times that I will document below. My intent, then, is to show that country visions do quite literally change, producing new spaces of opportunity and event that were not able to be experienced before, new sensations and sensitivities that produce constitutive fluctuations in the world which we might perhaps best think of as new pathways along which we move/sequence differently and which show up the world in ways that were not available to us before.

In a sense, what I want to do is to restate some of the current concerns of the turn to a vitalist conception of the world. But I want to do so in a way that goes beyond the general and sometimes rather portentous philosophical statements about time, the body and becoming which have now become so familiar (e.g. Grosz 1999) by connecting with understandings of body practices from the social sciences – and capitalist business.

Using these resources, I want to argue that a suitably recast nature has become a, and perhaps even the, key site of contemplation and mysticism in the modern world as a result of the evolution of a set of body practices which, as they have taken hold, have produced an expanded awareness of present time. My problem in making such an argument is that contemplation and mysticism are not practices much associated with an enhanced grasp of the modern world; they are more usually associated with figures from times of yore like hermits and monks. How can such practices of slowness make sense in an increasingly frantic capitalist world, a ferocious jumble of signals, journeys and screens which has squeezed out or is likely to squeeze out such sedate activity once and for all (see just most recently, Bertman 1998; Brand 1999; Flaherty 1999; Kovach and Rosenstiel 1999; Speak 1999)? Surely it is all quick, quick and no slow.

In order to refute such easy characterisation, I will therefore make an argument in six stages, each of which corresponds to a particular part of the chapter. The first part therefore begins by setting out some theoretical aspirations, aspirations that all attempt to escape the traps of representational thinking of the kind that wants, for example, to understand nature as simply a project of cultural inscription (as in many writings on 'landscape') in favour of the kind of thinking that understands nature as a complex virtuality (Cache 1995; Rajchman 1998). With an account distilled from these thoughts, in the second part, I will argue that a go-faster world, in which time takes on an increasingly frenetic future-oriented quality, has been balanced by a series of contemplative practices – many of them to do with a heightened awareness of movement – which have, in fact, produced an expansion of awareness of the present. The third part of the paper follows on. It concerns the classical idea that the world has been disenchanted. My argument here is to the contrary. In fact, the mystical qualities of the world remain in place. Assured by a whole series of body practices, some old and some new, these practices have produced an expansion of awareness of present time. The fourth part of the paper then argues that the experience of these two sets of *immersive* body practices account for a large part of what we attend to as 'Nature'; they define much of what we cleave to as a 'natural' experience by setting up a *background of expectation*. The fifth part of the paper then suggests that these body practices can be seen as part of a larger biopolitical project which is an attempt to renovate and value 'bare life'. But 'bare life' is not bare. It is most of what there is. Then, the sixth part of the paper offers some words of warning. Another such project of renovation of bare life is already in motion, but it is being undertaken by business and its goal is a narrow one. The paper concludes with some further clarifications.

Becoming there

My thinking on nature, the body and time in this paper is based upon four different but quite clearly associated sources of inspiration which, when taken together, make it possible to construct an emergent account of emergent body practice which is the base of the rest of the chapter. The first of these is the work of biological philosophers and philosophical biologists such as Clark (1997), Deleuze (1988), Margulis (1998) and Ansell Pearson (1997, 1999) who want to argue for a reconfigured ethology in which bodies become means of transporting 'instincts'[1] which are best thought of as particular territories of becoming, maps mapping out 'populations' of identities and forces, zones and gradients, through differentiation, divergence and creation:

> Behaviour can no longer be localised in individuals conceived as preformed homunculi; but has to be treated epigenetically as a function of complex material systems which cut across individuals (assemblages) and which transverse phyletic lineages and organismic boundaries (rhizomes). This requires the articulation of a distributed conception of agency. The challenge is to show that nature consists of a field of multiplicities, assemblages of heterogeneous components (human, animal, viral, molecular, etc) in which 'creative evolution' can be shown to involve blocks of becoming (Ansell Pearson 1999: 171).

Maps are their own practitioners, in other words.

The second source of inspiration is the revival of interest in the non-cognitive dimensions of embodiment. Probably 95 per cent of embodied thought is non-cognitive, yet probably 95 per cent of academic thought has concentrated on the cognitive dimension of the conscious 'I'. Without in any way diminishing the importance of cognitive thought (though certainly questioning its exact nature), we can conceive of non-cognitive thought as a set of embodied dispositions ('instincts' if you like) which have been biologically wired-in or culturally sedimented (the exact difference between the two being a fascinating question in itself), action-oriented 'representations' which simultaneously describe aspects of the world and prescribe possible actions. There has, of course, been a considerable amount of work on body practices stemming from the work of authors as different as Mauss, Benjamin, Wittgenstein,

Merleau-Ponty and Bourdieu (e.g. Taussig 1994), which recognises that much of human life is lived in a non-cognitive world. But I think it is fair to say that its implications are only now being worked through, most especially in areas such as performance studies, feminist theory and non-representational geographies. In particular, when we say that human beings act to think or that they learn by doing, we need to refigure what we count as thought and knowledge. In particular, much cognitive thought and knowledge may, indeed, be only a kind of *post hoc* rumination; 'to be aware of an experience means that it has passed' (Norretranders 1998: 128). For example, most of the time, an action is in motion before we decide to perform it; our average 'readiness potential' is about 0.8 seconds, although cases of up to 1.5 seconds have been recorded[2].

As McCrone (1999: 135) makes clear, none of this means that conscious awareness is just along for the ride. Rather, we can say that the non-conscious comes to be more highly valued – the 'not properly conscious impulses, inklings, automotisms and reflexive action' can no longer be regarded as trivial. And, at the same time, conscious awareness is repositioned as a means of scrutinising and focusing these actions. To put it another way, what has been found is that the body has a number of ways of conjuring with time that work through structures of *anticipation*, the something to be known which is very often the result of the body's own movements, which leave 'some aspect of the movement standing proud' (McCrone 1999: 158). Why? Because:

> The brain was never really designed for contemplating images. Our ability to imagine and fantasise is something that has to piggyback on a processing hierarchy designed first and foremost for the business of perception. And to do perception well, the brain needs a machinery that comes up with a fresh wave of prediction at least a couple of times a second, or about as fast as we can make a substantial shift in our conscious point of view. . . . it would be unnatural for the brain to linger and not move on.

In turn, such work points to the pivotal importance of emotions as the key means the body has of sorting the non-cognitive realm through a range of different sensory registers, including the interoceptive (including not only the viscera but also the skin), the proprioceptive (based on musculoskeletal investments) and fine touch which involves the conduct of the whole body and not just the brain.

> Note that, depending on the object, there may be different proportions of musculoskeletal and emotional accompaniment, but both are always present. The presence of all these signals . . . describes both the object as it looms towards the organism and part of the reaction of the organism towards the object. . . . (Damasio 1999: 147).

Which brings us to the third source of inspiration – the much greater emphasis that is being placed on the object. To begin with, the body is objectified as a composite of biological-cultural 'instincts' which enable and in many ways constitute thought as a result of the development of particular organs. For example, the development of the hand, with all the possibilities it presents, was an impetus to the redesign, or reallocation of the brain's circuitry so that the hand speaks to the brain just as much as the brain speaks to the hand (Wilson 1998). Then, these organs are closely linked with particular objects (Sudnow 1993). Organs like the hand become as one with tools they relate to.

> The idea of 'becoming one' with a [mechanical] back hoe is no more exotic than the idea of a rider becoming one with a horse or a carpenter becoming one with a hammer, and this phenomenon may itself take its origin from countless monkeys who spent countless eons becoming one with tree branches. The mystical feel comes from the combination of a good mechanical marriage and something in the nervous system that can make an object external to the body feel as if it had sprouted from the hand, foot, or (rarely) some other place on the body where your skin makes contact with it (Wilson 1998: 63).

Then again, objects do not just constitute an extension of bodily capacities; they themselves are a vital element in distributed ecology of thought, so that 'what used to look like internalisation (of thought and subjectivity) now appears as a gradual propagation of organised functional properties across a set of malleable media' (Hutchins 1995: 312); 'the true engine of reason . . . is bounded neither by skin nor skull' (Clark 1997: 69). Thus, as Hayles (1999: 290) puts it

> no longer is human will seen as the source from which emanates the mystery necessary to dominate and control the environment. Rather, the distributed cognition of the emergent human subject correlates with – in Bateson's phrase, becomes a metaphor for – the distributed cognitive system as a whole, in which thinking is done by both human and nonhuman actors.

Not only do objects make thought doable e.g. (Latour and Hermant 1998) but they also very often make thought possible. In a sense, then, as parts of networks of effectivity, objects think. We might even go still further, by arguing that 'everything that is resounds' (Lingis 1998: 99):

> It is not that things barely show themselves, behind illusory appearances fabricated by our subjectivity; it is that things are exorbitantly exhibitionist. The landscape resounds; facades, caricatures, halos, shadows, dance across it. Under the sunlight extends the pageantry of things. The twilight does not put an end to their histrionics. In the heart of the night the pulse of the night summons still their ghosts (Lingis 1998: 100).

The fourth source of inspiration is the genealogy of the body practices which must be a large part of an ethology of 'instincts'. These are now, finally, coming under intense scrutiny. Grouped around terms such as 'performance', and around theorists such as Bourdieu and Foucault, researchers in the social sciences and humanities have, over the last 20 years, begun to produce a history of particular organs (e.g. Hillman and Mazzio 1997; Jordanova 1994) and particular body practices – from drill to dance. But it is true to say that we still understand very little of how the body practices that constitute 'us' have come down to and inhabit us, passing into our being, passing our being back and forth between bodies and passing our being on (Hayles 1999)[3].

These four sources of inspiration allow us to begin to sense, through this combination of work in areas as diverse as biology, philosophy and performance studies, what an understanding of that little space of time that much of what we are is, a space not so much at the edge of action as lighting the world. I will call this domain 'bare life' after Aristotle's notion of *zoé*, a 'simple natural sweetness' (Agamben 1998). Of course, it is not really bare; bare life pulses with action. And it is not simple. And it is not preturnatural. But what such a notion allows us to do is to point beyond the grand notions of bodily hexis such as *habitus* towards something more specific and more open to description. And it does two more things. One is to begin to understand qualities such as anticipation and intuition as not just spirits but material orientations. And the other is to understand that this little space of time is a vast biopolitical domain, that blink between actor and performance in which the world is pre-set by biological and cultural instincts which bear both extraordinary geneological freight – *and* a potential for potentiality.

How might we begin to understand the structure of this domain of flourishing? One manageable and usable account has been offered by Gil (1998). Gil argues, as I would (see Thrift 1996, 1997, 1998, 2000), that we need to escape the constructionist notion of the body as simply an inscribed surface, in which the body is reduced to what Gil (1998) calls a 'body image', an individual unitary, organismic body which can act as a surface upon which society can construct itself. This interpretation is mistaken in at least three ways. First, the body becomes a static signified to be filled with signs of society. Second, the body is divorced from other things, from the object world. Third, the body is located *in* space, it does not produce space. But, there is another, non-representational view (Thrift 1997, 2000). In this view, the body is 'not about signs and meanings but about a mechanics of space' (Gil 1998: 126) brought about by the relation between bodies and things. Thus

> the space of the body has limits that are not those of the body image, if we understand by that the limits of the body lived in a unitary fashion. The limits of the space of the body are in things. In movement, for example, the body places changing limits on these things. To the extent that they are 'subjective', these limits constitute the end result of the integration into the body of the relations (of distance, form, and so on) that it holds with things in objective space. To the extent that they can be pinned down topologically, these limits are no longer 'lived' but are properties of space itself (Gil 1998: 125).

In turn, and following a Deleuzian interpretation,

the body 'lives' in space, but not like a sphere with a closed continuous surface. On the contrary, its movements, limbs and organs determine that it has regular relations with things in space, relations that are individually integrated for the decoder. These relations imply *exfoliations* of the space of the body that can be treated separately. Relations to a tree, a prey, a star, an enemy, a loved object or desired nourishment set into motion certain privileged organs including precise spaces of the body. Exfoliation is the essential way the body 'turns on to' things, onto objective space, onto living things. Here there is a type of communication that is always present, but only makes itself really visible in pathological or marginal experiences. Nevertheless the ordinary experience of relations to things also implies this mode of communication. Being in space means to establish diverse relationships with the things that surround our bodies. Each set of relations is determined by the action of the body that accompanies an investment of desire in a particular being or particular object. Between the body (and the organs in use) and the things is established a connection that immediately affects the form and space of the body; between the one and the other a privileged spatial relation emerges that defines the space uniting them as 'near' or 'far', resistant, thick, wavy, vertiginous, smooth, prickly (Gil 1998: 127)[4].

In other words, the space of the body consists of a series of 'leaves', each of which 'contains' the relations of the body to things and each of which is more or less related to other spaces. Correspondences are not, at least initially, conceptual but result 'from the work done by the body spatialising space' (Gil 1998: 130). Thus,

Analogy, similitude, opposition, and dissimilitude are given in the forms of the space of the body before being thought of as concepts. In the same ways as the 'concrete science' which establishes classification on the basis of sensorial differences found in 'primitive thought', the recording-body gathers up, brings together, unites, dislocates, spreads, and separates things to the spatial forms that contain in themselves (because they bring them about) the properties of unification and division (Gil 1998: 130).

It follows that in what follows body practices are *not* to be thought of, at least in the first instance, as cognitive. This would be a first-order mistake. For, to reiterate, we know that 'consciousness is a measure of but a very small part of what our senses perceive' (Norretranders 1998: 127).

Conscious thought is the tip of an enormous iceberg. It is the rule of thumb among cognitive scientists that unconscious thought is 95 per cent of all thought – and that may be a serious underestimate. Moreover the 95 per cent below the surface of conscious awareness shapes and structures all conscious thought. If the cognitive unconscious were not doing this shaping, there could be no conscious thought.

The cognitive unconscious is vast and intricately structured. It includes not only all our automatic cognitive operations, but also all our implicit knowledge. All of our knowledge and beliefs are formed in terms of a conceptual system that resides mostly in the cognitive unconscious.

> Our unconscious cognitive system functions like 'a hidden hand' that shapes how we conceptualise all aspects of our experience. This hidden hand gives form to the metamorphosis that is built into our ordinary conceptual system. It creates the entities that inhabit the cognitive unconscious – abstract entities like friend-ships, bargains, failures and lies – that we use in ordinary unconscious reasoning. It thus shapes how we automatically and unconsciously comprehend what we experience. It constitutes our unreflective common sense (Lakoff and Johnson 1998: 13).

And this cognitive unconscious rises out of the layerings and interleavings of body practices and things which we might frame as 'instincts' or, more accur-ately, as structured *anticipations*. For neither is conscious awareness just going for the ride on the back of the cognitive unconscious. Rather every moment is processed as a prior intent, style or tone which arises from perception-in-movement, every moment is the fleeting edge of a sensory forecast (McCrone 1999), quite literally a stance to the world.

With these 'thoughts in mind' (how easily we use these questionable phrases), we can now move to a consideration of how body practices show up in the modern world and how the modern world shows up in them. To do this, we first need to clear away some tired old pictures of the world.

The go-faster world

Elsewhere (Thrift 1995, 1996, 1997), I have criticised the notion that we live in a speeded-up world in which friction has been lost and everyday life skids along on the plane of velocity. Much of the literature which enforces this notion is based upon a simple technological determinism which unproblemat-ically maps the apparent powers of things onto subjects. While it is undeniable that people and messages now move faster than they did, old practices have been adjusted, and new practices have been invented, which make it impos-sible to simply read off this physical fact on to culture. Further, it is possible to argue that speed is itself in part a cultural creation, a classical modernist trope now in general cultural circulation (see Kern 1983) as a series of metaphors and analogies and as a rhetoric of 'speedy' things[5]. This cultural creation of speed itself depends upon the depiction of certain places, things and people as slow-moving, most particularly those places, things and people connected with nature, countryside, and so on.

This is, of course, a very strange opposition since one might just as well argue – precisely through the instruments available to measure speed – that nature is actually very fast. The speed of light is, well, the speed of light. Chemical reactions can work at astounding speeds. Even that slow old thing, the human body, works reasonably fast. Though in our brains, nerve impulses only tend to crawl along – at between 2 and 20 miles per hour – along the heavily myelinated nerves (such as muscle and the sensory nerves) nerve impulses travel at up to 240 miles per hour (McCrone 1999; Norretranders 1998).

But, more than this, the opposition ignores a general reconstruction of time that has taken place (quite literally) over the last 150 years, a sense of body practices which constitute and value the *present moment*, rather than spearing into the future. Ironically, these body practices have all taken shape around the increasing awareness of kinaesthesia, a sixth sense based on the interactive *movement* and subsequent awareness of body parts:

> we obtain a sense of our own movement not only from specialised receptors in the inner ear, joints, tendons and muscles but also from what we can see, hear and feel . . . vision, 'for instance', is kinaesthetic in that it registers movements of the body, just as much as do the vestibular receptors and those in the muscles, joints and skin (Reason 1982: 233). Contrary to Sherrington's direct correlation of sensory experience with the activation of specific receptors and their nerves of different cellular levels, the kinaesthetic sense is a gestalt emerging from the inter-action of all the other senses. After Gibson we can speak of kinaesthesia in terms of its muscular, articular, vestibular, cutaneous, auditory and visual modalities (Gibson 1996: 36–8). In this view kinaesthesia is the ground to our consciousness (Stewart 1998: 44).

I think it can be argued that greater awareness of movement has in turn pro-duced a set of resources that enable us to separate out and value a present-oriented stillness, thus promoting a 'politics' based in intensified attention to the present and unqualified affectivity. Where might this present orientation have come from? I would argue that its history is borne out of a number of developments which, taken together, constitute a genealogy of the present.

The first of these developments is practices of contemplation. Foucault and others have highlighted the significance of confession as a model for recent practices of the technology of the self. I think an argument can be made for a similar kind of history based in practices of contemplation understood as 'aptitudes of performance' (Asad 1993), rather than explicit belief. This history might touch upon certain forms of prayer, the practices of some rituals, and other religious technologies which concentrate time.

Whatever the case, there seems no doubt that extant practices of contempla-tion were gradually transmuted by a whole series of developments in the nineteenth century and thereafter (Segel 1998). The first of these was the devel-opment of a series of body practices that stressed sensory appreciation through a more complete control of the body in order to provide more harmonious rela-tions with the environment. A good example of these developments is the rise of various body techniques such as the Alexander Technique, the Feldenkrais technique, Bioenergetics and Body–Mind Centring which teach movement awareness and the reorganisation of movement sensation (Feldenkrais 1972;

Hartley 1995; Lowen 1975; MacDonald 1998; McGowan 1997a, b). Felden-krais (1972), for example, argued that cultivation of certain bodily practices could enhance our ability to 'know' the world through systematic correction of what he called the 'body image'.

The second development is the rise of systematic knowledge of body measurement, based on increasing the efficiency of the body. From Marey's and Muybridge's study of the physiology of movement through to Gilbreth and Taylor's time-and-motion studies through to modern ergonomics and sports science, the study and articulation of minute human movement has become a key to producing human comportment (Dagognet 1992; Mattelart 1996). In turn, it can be argued that the increasingly fine grain of the many bodily movements built out of this study has made its mark on how time is constructed by the body[6].

The third development is the fixing of a still, contemplative gaze, which is able to capture transience. Such a gaze is found in art from the eighteenth century on but reaches a kind of technological fulfilment in the photograph, especially with the growth of popular photography from the end of the nineteenth century onwards. Crawshaw and Urry (1998) argue that popular photography consists of a set of socially organised rituals which fix a place, a 'language' of material objects through which we understand and appreciate the environment (and the material objects themselves) and a means of organising time itself. In each case, what is being described is a set of practices that momentarily fix the body and other things in spaces and times by producing spaces and times in which they can be fixed[7].

The fourth development is the forging of a body of knowledge about social interaction as the distillation of detailed body practices. Such knowledge can already be found in the nineteenth century and early twentieth century (for example, in the development of various movement notations) but it reaches a peak in the twentieth century with the rise of various knowledges of body practice from work on the psychology of body language and gesture, though work on bodily intonations of space, as in Hall's 'proxemics' (Hall 1990), through to the detailed conversational analysis of symbolic interactionism, ethno-methodology and the like to be found in the work of Goffman, Garfinkel, Sacks and so on (e.g. Burns 1992). In turn, this knowledge, much of which was developed in academia and other relatively formal arenas, has gradually seeped out into everyday life as a whole new corporeal curriculum of expressive competence, for example through courses on body language (now being given, for example, to checkout operators in some supermarket chains), cultural awareness trainings, and all manner of trainings in self-presentation (cf. Giddens 1991; Thrift 1997). Thus what was quite specific knowledge has become general and routine.

Each of these four developments of body practice stretches out the moment, most especially by paying detailed attention to it. They expand, if you like, the 'size' of consciousness, allowing each moment to be more carefully attended to and invested with more of its context. Taken together, they may be seen as constructing a slow-down of perception, as much as a speed-up.

Re-enchantment

These developments have to be taken in concert with others to complete my argument. One of the most damaging ideas that has swept the social sciences and humanities has been the idea of a disenchanting modernity (Thrift 1996). This act of purification has radically depopulated thinking about western societies as whole sets of delegates and intermediaries have been consigned to oblivion as extinct impulses, those delegates and intermediaries which might appear to be associated with forces of magic, the sacred, ritual, affect, trance and so on. Now, however, the contemporary turn towards vitalist ways of thinking (cf. Watson 1998b) has made it much easier to see that the magic has not gone away. Western societies, like all others, are full of these forces (Dening 1996; Muecke 1999). They can be seen as concentrating, in particular, in a set of practices which can be described as 'mystical'. Like practices of contemplation, with which they are intimately linked, they can be seen as the result of a number of overlapping processes of animation and play which allow forces and intensities to be focused and channelled: it is *stimulation* that produces tranquility and it is *stimulation* that produces trance.

First, then, there is the importance of various forms of mystical communication, mental and physical techniques that 'fix the conditions of possibility of an encounter or dialogue with the other (method of prayer, meditation, concentration)' (de Certeau 1992: 5). Current forms of practice have a long genealogy in Western cultures and stem from traditions as different as the Christian (both Anglican and Catholic); the nature mysticisms of Romanticism as found in various forms of the sublime, the numerous forms of Eastern thinking which have been imported into the West, especially in the nineteenth century, and the cathartic elements of many types of performance. More recently, there has been the growth of New Age religions, nearly all of which contain an explicitly mystical component (for example, following on from sources as diverse as the writings of Gurdijeff or Hopi Indian practices). Not least, in all of these traditions can be found, to a greater or lesser degree, an approach to nature as both the focus and the object of mystical energies. For example, New Age thinking often stresses grids of power such as ley lines, nature goddesses, and the like, as well as the importance of particular sites as magical territories able to conjure up communication with the other.

This brings us to the second process, the importance of ritual, understood as practices which offer a heightened sense of involvement in our involvements through various performative technologies (Hughes-Freeland 1998; Schechner 1995). There may actually have been a multiplication of these performative spaces of affirmation, in which mystical experiences can be brought forth and animated through the power of body postures, repetitive movements, schedules of recall and spatial juxtapositions. Western societies have evolved more and more bodily practices which are a means of amplifying passions and producing 'oceanic' experiences: music, dance, theatre, mime, art and so on which very large numbers of the population participate in; rather more than is often thought (see, for example, Finnegan 1989). These practices have at least the potential to provide mystical experiences[8] – the trance state of some kinds of dance (Malbon 1999), the 'high' of listening to a piece of music, and so on[9].

Last, but not least, there has been the rise of varying forms of body therapy which, though they often rest on various psychological and psychiatric principles, have quite clear links to not only contemplative but mystical body practice. These are the various forms of dance therapy (e.g. Roth 1998), music therapy, massage therapy, variants of bioenergetics (e.g. Lowen 1975), autogenic therapy, body–mind centring, and so on, which try to harness and work with emotional energy on the grounds that movement causes emotion, rather than vice versa.

These body practices again allow the present to be intensified since they produce both an intensified sense of body movement and, at the same time, focus and enhance that movement. They are tempos of involvement without any necessary intention or initiative. They 'flow' time through the minute particulars of body movements that both have effects and yield experiences. They are 'performed dreams' (Schechner 1995), 'virtual actualisations' of time which allow consciousness to become acute without necessarily being directed by drawing on the non-cognitive.

Nature as background

What I want to argue next is that these contemplative and mystical developments which, taken as a whole, are widespread in modern western societies, constitute a *background* within which Nature is apprehended and which provides quite particular experiences of what Nature is. They form, if you like, an embodied 'unconscious', a set of basic exfoliations of the body through which Nature is constructed, planes of affect attuned to particular body parts (and senses) and corresponding elements of Nature (from trees and grass, to river and sky) (Massumi 1996), 'the sense and recognisability of things . . . do not lie in conceptual categories in which we mentally place them but in their positions and orientations which our postures address' (Lingis 1998: 59).

Following on from this point, I want to argue, very tentatively, that these immersive practices are producing a new form of vitalism (Watson 1998a, b), a stance to *feeling* life (in the doubled sense of both a grasp of life, and emotional attunement to it) which explain many of the strong, sometimes even fanatical, investments that are placed on the 'natural'. The very ways in which, through these practices of contemplation and mysticism, embodiment is reproduced in the West have produced an increasing bias towards framing life as a moving force, as push. In other words, the forms of embodiment I have set out in this chapter constitute a biopolitical domain arising out of a heightened awareness of particular forms of embodiment which, in turn, allow certain forms of signification to be grasped 'instinctively'.

This biopolitical domain has been strengthened by three developments. The first of these is the turning of certain body practices into privileged kinaesthetic spaces, and the privileged kinaesthetic spaces into body practices. I am thinking here especially of *walking* which since the nineteenth century, precisely in association with greater mobility (Wallace 1993), has produced a new experience of nature. This is not walking as travel, but walking for itself. As walking becomes a natural practice to be indulged in for its own sake, so, against the background I have outlined, it can become a means to contact the Earth, to be at one with 'nature', even to be deemed therapeutic. It becomes a means of gathering still, without having to stay still, a means of contemplation and mystical communion to be found within the body. Lingis (1998: 70) captures what I take to be a culturally particular investment particularly well:

> when we go out for a walk, our look is not continually *interested*, surveying the environment for landmarks and objectives. Even when we are on our way somewhere, for something, once launched we shift into just enjoying – or ending – the walk or the ride. Our gaze that prises beyond things is not situating on coordinates. It surveys across things, drawn to the distance when it fuses into the tone and mists of space. . . . The perception of things, the apprehension of their content and of their forms, is not an appropriation of them, but an expropriation of our forces into them, and ends in engagement.

Of course, none of this is to deny the cultural industry that has grown up around the practice of walking – the vast literature of books and guides, the special clothing, and so on all of which enhance or expand the range of affordances that inhere in any setting – but it is to suggest that the power of the meanings circulated by this industry is founded in the intensification of present experience coded in the body practices set out above. The background has allowed this foreground of symbolic delegates to develop.

The second development is, as the example of walking shows, the style of the body's location in space. What has developed has been both overall body stance and the formation of certain sequences of bodily experiences which, in their virtualised nature, produce an *expectation, an anticipation,* of a 'natural' experience: 'it is the way in which the body sits in space that allows signification to be grasped' (Gil 1998: 109). For example, travel to a 'natural' place sets up the body to fall into a 'natural' stance to the world. There is, if you like, a genetics of movement which the body slips into through constant practice. There are 'dance floors of nature' (Lingis 1998: 87).

The third development is similar but different. The body attends to configurations of objects which are in line with its expectations and which produce particular exfoliations/spaces and times. The body produces spaces and times through the things of nature which, in turn, inhabit the body through that production. Thus, for example, trees do not so much *mean* nature (Rival

1998) as they are present as evidence of a natural configuration that embodiment itself has produced: our bodies know themselves in such thinking. Thus trees become flesh by being bound up in a practical field. And, in the intensified present time I have described, that presence becomes its own justification. There *is*. Nature, in a sense, becomes more natural.

In turn, of course, nature, understood as body practices such as walking, expectations and configurations of objects pushes back in confirmation. For example, our experience of walking is validated by its effects on the body – from sweat to heart rate to muscles stretching – which are a function of a *resistance* on certain planes which confirms the *existence* of other planes. So nature speaks in us as 'an infralanguage' (Gil 1998) of movement which, through the articulations and micro-articulations of the body-in-encounter, fixes 'symbolic' thought as affect, mood, emotions and feelings[10] (thus as self-evidently present and numinous). Nature observes and writes us, bumping intensities into our thought[11] (understood especially as unconscious thought), rather as Deleuze would have it:

> [Deleuze's] projection of virtual elements too fast and multiple for conscious inspection or close third-person explanation meshes with his exploration of how differential degrees of intensity in thought moves it in some directions rather than others, open up lines of flight through which new concepts are introduced into being, and render thinking too layered and unpredictable to be captured by a juridical model in the Kantian tradition. He translates the story of juridical recognition in which Kant encloses thought in the last instance into one in which thinking is periodically nudged, frightened or terrorised into action by strange encounters. Recognition is a secondary formation often taken by consciousness in its innocence to be primary or apodictic, but thinking sometimes disturbs or modifies an established pattern of thought (Connolly 1999: 24).

'May I not be Separated from Thee'[12]

In an important book, Giorgio Agamben (1998) manages to conjure up a depiction of 'bare life' (*zoé*) immured. Through the development of a whole set of governmental templates in a manner familiar to those who read Foucault or study the totalitarian state, bare life has become 'a life that has been deadened and mortified into juridical role' (Agamben 1998: 187), a life 'naturalised' (to use a bitterly ironic term) from birth. Thus:

> the Foucauldian thesis will have to be corrected or, at least, completed, in the sense that what characterises modern politics is not so much the illusion of *zoé* in the polis – which is, in itself, absolutely ancient – not simply the fact that life as such becomes a principal object of the projections and calculations of state power. Instead the decisive fact is that, together with the process by which the

exception everywhere becomes the rule, the realm of bare life – which is originally situated at the margins of the political order – gradually begins to coincide with the political realm, and exclusion and inclusion, outside and inside, *bios* and *zoé*, right and fact, enter into a zone of incredible indistinction. At once excluding bare life from and capturing it within the political order, the state of exception actually constituted, in its very separateness, the hidden foundation on which the entire political system rested. When its borders began to be blurred, the bare life that dwelt there frees itself in the city and becomes both subject and object of the political order, the one place for both the organisation of state power and emancipation from it. Everything happens as if, along with the disciplinary process by which state power makes man as a living being into its own specific object, another process is set in motion that in large measure corresponds to the birth of modern democracy, in which man as a living being presents himself no longer as an *object* but as the *subject* of political power. These processes which in many ways oppose and (at least apparently) bitterly conflict with each other – nevertheless converge insofar as both concern the bare life of the citizen, the new biopolitical body of humanity (Agamben 1998: 8–9).

For Agamben, one of the questions is how to produce a notion of bare life that constitutes a politics but does not weigh it down with state imperatives. But his answer is pessimistic. Such a revitalisation of bare life cannot be born:

Bare life remains included in politics in the form of an exception, that is, as something that is included solely through an exclusion. How is it possible to 'politicize' the 'natural sweetness' of *zoé*? And first of all does *zoé* really need to be politicized, or is politics not already contained in *zoé* as its most priceless centre? The biopolitics of both modern totalitarianism and the society of mass hedonism and consumerism certainly constitute answers to these questions. Nevertheless, until a completely new politics – that is, a politics no longer founded on the *exception* of bare life – is at hand, every theory and every praxis will remain improvised and immobile and the 'beautiful day' of life will be given citizenship only either through blood and death or in the perfect senselessness to which the society of the spectacle condemns it (Agamben 1998: 11).

What Agamben seems to argue for, in part, is a revitalisation of the body in new forms of life: 'we are not only, in Foucault's words, animals whose life as living beings is at issue in their politics, but also – inversely – citizens whose very politics is at issue in their natural body' (Agamben 1998: 188). What this chapter has argued is that such an emancipatory politics of bare life, founded in practices such as contemplation and mysticism, both already exists – and continues to come into existence in new ways – a politics founded especially but not only in a 'nature' which is a 'product of the double investment of the body by space (the information coming from the physical world) and the investment of space by the body (as a certain kind of receiver-encoder of information)' (Gil 1998: 28). This is a politics of enhancement of the anticipation and conduct of certain bodily skills which, at the same time, contains its own premises though the effects of those skills.

This 'politics of the half-second delay' has the potential to expand the biopolitical domain, to make it more than just the site of investment by the state or investments by transnational capitalism. It may well explain the deep affective investments that are made by so many in a politics of nature, investments that move far beyond the cognitive and which are often figured as a restitution of all that has been lost. Perhaps, though, as this chapter has argued, the outcome might be more accurately figured as new appreciations and anticipations of spaces of embodiment, best understood as a form of magic dependent upon new musics of stillness and silence able to be discovered in a world of movement.

But: 'Step inside the great outdoors'[13]

But, let's not overdo this. There are powerful contra-forces. For there is another politics of bare life which I have so far only touched on. This is the politics that arises out of the enormous efforts currently being made to foreground the background of bare life – to make it comprehensible and therefore able to be apprehended and so *made more of* – across a range of different interests and arenas. And of these interests and arenas the most powerful and, in many ways, the most advanced is capitalist business: Agamben's mass consumerism.

Capitalist firms are drawing on the various knowledges of bare life they are producing to produce new products, products which animate – 'turn on' – the body by producing an engaging and compelling ethology of the senses.

This is the rise of an 'experience economy' (Pine and Gilmore 1999), a new genre of economic output which can construct experiences in order to produce added value. What have been the chief knowledges of bare life from which this experience economy has grown? There are four. The first has been tourism. Since the 1960s a new kind of tourism has emerged based upon the theming of spaces. Relying on the experience of running museums, heritage centres, theme parks and certain kinds of themed retailing (Gottdiener 1997) it has gradually constructed knowledge of how to produce spaces that can grip the senses. Of late, the kinaesthetic element of tourism has accordingly been amplified. For example, there are all the postcolonial forms of adventure including: house boating, portaging, mountain-biking, cattle driving, bobsledding, tall-ship sailing, tornado-chasing, canyon orienteering, wagon training, seal viewing, iceberg tracking, racing car driving, hot-air ballooning, rock climbing, spelunking, white-water rafting, canoeing, heli-hiking, hut-to-hut hiking, whale kissing, llama trekking, barnstorming, land yachting, historic battle re-enactments, iceboating, polar bearing and dog-sledding. The second knowledge, one clearly linked to the former, is sport and exercise. Sport and exercise have become key elements in modern experience economies, through their ability to influence bodily comportment (including specialised precision knowledges) through the specialised spaces that are constructed to serve them, and through the connections to the mass media (Abercrombie and Longhurst 1998).

A second knowledge has been of performance. Since the 1960s again, knowledge of performance – which is, after all, extensive – has moved out from the stage to fill all manner of venues – from corporate presentations to the street. Buoyed up by mass media which have, in all probability, made the population at large more performative (Abercrombie and Longhurst 1998), the art of performance has become a general art which concentrates especially on the conduct of the now and which can be appropriated. The fourth knowledge has been from education. Pedagogy has become a more and more active affair. Bolstered by findings from fields such as cognition and consciousness, learning is now universally practised as active, even sensuous.

Capitalist firms have taken these knowledges and produced a series of purchases on the world. The first of these has been advertising. Advertising companies have become alive to an approach that takes in all the senses. Companies such as St Lukes have led the way towards advertising which is meant to tug at bare life by emphasising kinaesthetic qualities. Another purchase is through sensorialising goods – producing goods that will richly engage the senses:

> Doing so requires awareness of which senses most affect customers, focuses on those senses and the sensations they experience, and the corporate redesign of the good to make it more appealing. Automakers, for example, now spend millions of dollars on every model to make sure that car doors sound *just so* when they close. Publishers greatly enhance the covers and interiors of books, and magazines with a number of tactile innovations (embossed lettering, scratching, bumpy or ultrasmooth surfaces) and sight sensations (translucent covers, funky fonts, clear photographs, three-dimensional graphics). Even presentation markers aren't just coloured anymore; Sanford scents them as well (liquorice for black, cherry for red, etc) (Pine and Gilmore 1999: 18).

Even quite simple goods are being designed which can feed back to the senses. For example, 'radar' baseballs make it possible to know how fast a ball was thrown, and generates social interaction since the catcher has to relay the speed back to the thrower.

The third purchase is the growth of packaged experiences which rely on theming contexts, so as to produce enhanced sensory experiences. This packaging can range all the way from the increasing outsourcing of children's parties from the home to companies to the most elaborate virtual environments, which are virtually self-contained ethologies:

> Companies that want to stage compelling capacities should . . . determine the theme of the experience as well as the impressions that will convey the theme to guests. Many times, experience stagers develop a list of impressions they wish guests to store away and then think creatively about different themes and storylines that will bring the impressions together in the cohesive narrative. Then they winnow

the impressions down to a manageable number – only and exactly those which truly devote the chosen theme. Next they focus on the animate and inanimate cues that could connote each impression, following the simple guidelines of accentuating the positive and eliminating the negative. They then must meticulously map out the effect each cue will have on the five senses – sight, sound, taste, touch and smell – taking care not to overwhelm guests with too much sensory input. Finally, they add memorabilia to the total mix, extending the experience in the customer's mind over time. Of course, embracing these principles remains, for now, an art form. But those companies which figure out how to design experiences that are compelling, engaging, memorable – and rich – will be the ones leading the way into the emerging Experience Economy (Pine and Gilmore 1999: 61).

The fourth purchase is on objects that will produce kinaesthetic experiences, on the grounds that these experiences are usually the most compelling and the most memorable. What is fascinating is the speed with which this kinaesthetic purchase on the world is now expanding its grip, as knowledge of movement becomes engineered in institutions as different as film animation and special effects houses, virtual reality games, exponents of light shows, producers of extreme sports, and those who construct theme park rides. Increasingly, in particular, this knowledge is projected through objects that are based on maximising movement experiences through the application of particular sequences of movement which engage the visceral sense as well as the proprioceptive and fine touch, rather like hieroglyphs of the kind found in dance and other performing arts (Thrift 2000). For example, roller coasters are now often described in specifically choreographic terms.

Then a final purchase is, as already prefaced, memorabilia. Memorabilia both encapsulates and strings out experiences. Most experienced businesses mix memorabilia into what they offer. Memorabilia is becoming more sophisticated as objects are increasingly able to be customised. For example, guest's credit card signatures can be digitised and transferred to objects such as clothing, sports equipment and photographs, often next to the signatures of appropriate celebrities. And, increasingly, memorabilia are being played for affective capacity. For example:

Hillenbrand Industries of Butestaffe, Indiana, developed a new memorabilia capacity for the funeral industry. The concept emerged from the practice in many funeral homes of producing memory books for display at viewing and memorial services. Hillenbrand sought to bring greater efficiencies to the process but also to preserve the kind of one-of-a-kind collages families now put together to commemorate the lives of lost loved ones. Hillenbrand does this by developing a proprietary system to digitise, merge and print mass customised collages to both paper and video output media. But these life space collages serve merely as a prop for the experience Hillenbrand really offers. A self-guided kit that walks a family, group of friends or co-workers through a series of steps to create their own memories. 'What we sell', says Gary Bonnie, who handled the initiative, 'is the life scaping experience of gathering with others, rummaging through old photographs and other mementos, and recalling fond memories. The collage gift happens to be the outcome; the value is experienced in going through the process we've helped script.' Accordingly, Hillenbrand charges for the kit experience, whether or not people actually buy the collage (Pine and Gilmore 1999: 58).

So, what we see is bare life laid bare, and atomised, and put together again as saleable, immersive experiences. Through history, of course, landscapes have been constructed and experiences have been put up for sale but I think the new developments which, by engaging all the senses, produce new realms of experience for exchange to exchange should give us pause. It may be that 'the history of economic progress consists of charging a fee for what once was free' (Pine and Gilmore 1999: 67). Alternatively, this maxim can be seen as simply another rationalisation of the neoliberal order, one that entails a significant broadening and deepening of economic relations through much more sophistic-ated means of interpellation[14].

In particular, of course, it involves a stance to Nature, one which by *re-embodying* natural ethologies, using the examples gleaned from museums, theatre and theme parks, sets aside the immersive practices of contemplation and mysticism based on make-believe for immersion of a different kind based on make-us-believe (Walton 1990). This is play without play, if you like[15] – play without the kind of anticipations that make live – that can produce an enhanced Nature:

> In 1996 Ogden [Corporation] committed $100 million to create eight attractions called the American Wilderness Experience. There it immerses guests in nature scenes that feature the live animals, foliage, scents, and climates indigenous to various locales. The company's first American Wilderness Experience opened in late 1997 in the Ontario Malls Mill in San Bernadino, California. The company charges an admission fee of $9.95 for adults to take in five 'biomes' depicting various aspects of California's natural environment: Redwoods, sierras, deserts, coasts and valleys. These exhibits are inhabited by 160 wild animals, across 60 distinct species, including snakes, bobcats, scorpions, jelly fish and porcupines. Guests begin their journey with a motion-based attraction, called the Wild Ride Theater, that lets them experience the world through the eyes of various animals – moving like a mountain lion, buzzing like a bee – and then tour live animal exhibits and enjoy nature discussions with costumed Wilderness rangers. Of course, once guests pay to participate in the American Wilderness Experience, Ogden also makes money on the food service at its Wilderness Grill and the memorabilia at its Nature Untamed retail store (Pine and Gilmore 1999: 23–4).

Conclusion

The stakes are high. Should we move towards a capitalist super-nature, tuning our bodies to an economy of naturalised experiences, or to something more modest, more fluid and less market-driven? Unlike Agamben, I think there is hope, precisely born out of the heightened participations in bare life, shown up by movement, that I have tried to show in this chapter. To begin with, there are the myriad activities that exist at the edge of the economic system which travel all the way from those who are simply looking for simple forms of exercise to those who are trying to sense something different. Then, there is the realm of the performance studies and arts which, since at least the 1960s, have, through techniques as different as dance and performance art, been attempting to stimulate new corporeal sensibilities (e.g. Jones and Stephenson 1999). And, last, there is the more general move towards a philosophy which can incorporate the body and so think thought differently (Shusterman 1999).

Taken together, these alternative forms of biopolitics continue to allow a different time to inhabit the moment and even to flourish. Though they may be a small thing they are not insignificant: sometimes a little can be a lot.

Acknowledgements

This chapter is a partly rewritten version of a paper that appeared in *Body and Society* (2000), 6, 34–57 and is reprinted with permission.

Notes

1. I use the word 'instincts' here to signal my intention to try to transcend humanist approaches to nature, though many of these 'instincts' are complex biological-cultural constructions.

2. 'Then when we say "information" in everyday life, we spontaneously think of information as the result of a discarding of information. We do not consider the fact that there is more information in an experience than in an account of it. It is the *account* that we consider to be information. But the whole basis of such an account is information that is discarded. Only after information has been discarded can a situation become an event people can talk about. The total situation we find ourselves in at any given time is precisely one we cannot provide an account of: we can give an account of it only when it has "collapsed" into an event through the discarding of information' (Norretranders 1998: 109).

3. Many of these bodily practices necessarily contain improvisational elements, since they are always performative, instantiated in the capacities of particular bodies and content-specific (see Hayles 1999; Thrift 2000). Think only of the face with its potent muscular geography (cf. Brothers 1997; McNeil 1998; Taussig 1998).

4. This is a very different notion of metaphor from that employed by Lakoff and Johnson (1998) which seems to me to over-determine both the idea of metaphor and the process of metaphorisation.

5. In other words, the notion of speed is part of the rhetoric of how Euro-American societies go on.

6. There are interesting connections here with all kinds of earlier body practices from drill to dance which could be brought out and which are brought together in the twentieth century city in the work of writers such as Laban (see Thrift 2000).

7. The practice of photography, in other words, is as important for its *process of doing* as for its results (photographs which are normally rarely looked at).

8. Aided, in certain cases, by stimulants like drugs.

9. All these practices are heightened by the growing sense, stimulated by the media, of audience (see Abercrombie and Longhurst 1998); we now constantly see and take in other body practices: ways of walking and the like. This mundane anthropology is becoming more and more important.

10. Thus, for example, 'when we approach a great fir on the crest of a mountain, we stand tall or our eyes travel upward to the clouds and eagles, when we approach a willow our gaze sweeps in languid arcs across the backs of lime branches rippling over the lake. When we come upon a fallen tree, we have difficulty seeing it is a willow or a pine or a tree; if appears as a thicket about a log, in a confused layout inviting closer scrutiny (Lingis 1998: 53).

11. Note also Derrida's thoughts on nature as a form of writing (see Kirby 1997).

12. Ancient Christian Prayer cited in de Certeau (1992: 1).

13. The main marketing slogan of the American Wilderness Experience.

14. So think of the following quotation as a business proposition: 'To recognise a person is to recognise a typical way of addressing tasks, of envisaging landscapes, of advancing hesitantly and cautiously or ironically, of playing exuberantly down the paths to us. Someone we know is someone we relate to posturally, someone we walk in step with, someone who maintains a certain style of positioning himself or herself and gesticulating in conversation and with whom we take up a compromising position as we talk' (Lingis 1998: 53).

15. I realise that this section might be read as a Baudrillardean account of the rise of simulacra. This is not, however, the way I would want it read. Baudrillard's accounts are far too sweeping for me, and lack any but a stylised historical sense.

References

Abercrombie, N. and Longhurst, B. 1998 *Audiences. A Sociological Theory of Performance and Imagination*, Sage, London.

Agamben, G. 1998 *Homo Sacer. Sovereign Power and Bare Life*, Stanford University Press, Stanford.

Ansell Pearson, K. 1997 *Viroid Life. Perspections on Nietzsche and the Transhuman Condition*, Routledge, London.

Ansell Pearson, K. 1999 *Germinal Life. The Difference and Repetition of Deleuze*, Routledge, London.

Asad, T. 1993 *Genealogy of Religion*, Johns Hopkins University Press, Baltimore, MD.

Benjamin, W. 1985 *The Origin of German Tragic Drama*, Verso, London.

Bertman, S. 1998 *Hyperculture. The Human Cost of Speed*, Praeger, New York.

Brand, S. 1999 *The Clock of the Long Now*, Phoenix, London.

Brothers, L. 1997 *Friday's Footprint. How Society Shapes the Human Mind*, Oxford University Press, New York.

Burns, T. 1992 *Erving Goffman*, Routledge, London.

Cache, B. 1995 *Earth Moves. The Furnishing of Territories*, MIT Press, Cambridge, MA.

de Certeau, M. 1992 *The Mystic Fable. Volume One. The Sixteenth and Seventeenth Centuries*, University of Chicago Press, Chicago, IL.

Clark, A. 1997 *Being There. Putting Brain, Body, and World Together Again*, MIT Press, Cambridge, MA.

Connolly, W.E. 1999 'Brain wars, transcendental fields and techniques of thought', *Radical Philosophy*, **94**, 19–28.

Crawshaw, C. and Urry, J. 1998 'Tourism and the photographic eye', pp. 176–95 in C. Rojek and J. Urry (eds), *Touring Cultures. Transformations of Travel and Theory*, Routledge, London.

Dagognet, F. 1992 *Etienne-Jules Marey. A Passion for the Trace*, Zone Books, New York.

Damasio, A. 1999 *The Feeling of What Happens*, Heinemann, London.

Deleuze, G. 1988 *Bergsonism*, Zone Books, New York.

Dening, G. 1996 *Performances*, University of Chicago Press, Chicago, IL.

Feldenkrais, M. 1972 *Awareness through Movement. Health Exercises for Personal Growth*, Harper and Row, New York.

Finnegan, R. 1989 *The Hidden Musicians*, Cambridge University Press, Cambridge.

Flaherty, M.G. 1988 *A Watched Pot. How We Experience Time*, New York University Press, New York.

Flaherty, M.G. 1999 *A Watched Pot. How We Experience Time*, New York University Press, New York.

Foucault, M. 1984 'On the genealogy of ethics: an overview of work in progress', in P. Rabinow (ed.), *The Foucault Reader*, Pantheon, New York.

Garfield, S. 2000 *Mauve*, Faber and Faber, London.

Gibson, J.T. 1996 *The Senses Considered as Perceptual Systems*, Houghton Mifflin, Boston.

Giddens, A. 1991 *Modernity and Self-identity*, Polity Press, Cambridge.

Gil, J. 1998 *Metamorphoses of the Body*, University of Minnesota Press, Minneapolis.

Gottdiener, M. 1997 *The Theming of America. Dreams, Visions and Commercial Spaces*, Westview Press, Boulder, CO.

Grosz, E. (ed.) 1999 *Becomings. Explorations in Time, Memory and Futures*, Cornell University Press, Ithaca, NY.

Hall, E.T. 1990 *The Hidden Dimension*, Anchor Doubleday, New York.

Hartley, L. 1995 *Wisdom of the Body Moving. An Introduction to Body–Mind Centreing*, North Atlantic Books, Berkeley, CA.

Harvey, J. 1995 *Men in Black*, Reaktion, London.

Hayles N.K. 1999 *How We Became Posthuman. Virtual Bodies in Cybernetics, Literature and Informatics*, University of Chicago Press, Chicago, IL.

Hillman, D. and Mazzio, D. 1997 *The Body in Parts. Fantasies of Corporeality in Early Modern Europe*, Routledge, New York.

Hinchliffe, S. 2002 'Inhabiting. Landscapes and natures', in K. Anderson, M. Domosh, S. Pile and N.J. Thrift (eds), *The Handbook of Cultural Geography*, Sage, London.

Hughes-Freeland, F. (ed.) 1998 *Ritual, Performance, Media*, Routledge, London.

Hutchins, E. 1995 *Cognition in the Wild*, MIT Press, Cambridge, MA.

Jones, A. and Stephenson, A. (eds) 1999 *Performing the Body. Performing the Text*, Routledge, London.

Jordanova, L. 1994 'The hand', pp. 252–9 in L. Taylor (ed.), *Visualizing Theory*, Routledge, New York.

Kern, S. 1983 *The Culture of Space and Time, 1880–1914*, University of California Press, Berkeley.

Kirby, V. 1997 *Thinking Flesh*, Routledge, London.

Kovach, B. and Rosenstiel, T. 1999 *Warp Speed. American in the Age of Mixed Media*, Century Press, New York.

Kwa, C. 2002 'Romantic and baroque conceptions of complex wholes in the sciences', pp. 23–52 in J. Law and A. Mol (eds), *Complexities. Social Studies of Knowledge Practices*, Duke University Press, Durham, NC.

Lakoff, G. and Johnson, M. 1998 *Philosophy in the Flesh. The Embodied Mind and its Challenge to Western Thought*, Basic Books, New York.

Latour, B. 2001 'Good and bad science: the Stengers-Deprest falsification principle', unpublished.

Latour, B. and Hermant, E. 1998 *Paris Ville Invisible*, La Decouverte: Institut Synthelabo, Paris.

Lingis, A. 1998 *The Imperative*, Indiana University Press, Bloomington.

Lowen, A. 1975 *Bioenergetics*, Penguin/Arkana, Harmondsworth.

MacDonald, G. 1998 *The Complete Illustrated Guide to the Alexander Technique*, Element Books, Shaftesbury.

Malbon, B. 1999 *Clubbing*, Routledge, London.

Margulis, L. 1998 *The Symbiotic Planet*, Weidenfeld and Nicolson, London.

Margulis, L., Sagan, D. and Schwartz, W. 1999 *Slanted Truths. Essays on Gaia, Symbiosis and Evolution*, Springer Verlag, Berlin.

Massumi, M. 1996 'The autonomy of affect', pp. 217–39 in P. Patton (ed.), *Deleuze: A Cultural Reader*, Blackwell, Oxford.

Mattelart, A. 1996 *The Invention of Communication*, University of Minnesota Press, Minneapolis.

McCrone, J. 1999 *Going Inside. A Tour Round a Single Moment of Consciousness*, Faber and Faber, London.

McGowan, D. 1997a *Alexander Technique. Original Writings of F.M. Alexander*, Larsons Publications, Burdett, NY.

McGowan, D. 1997b *Constructive Awareness. Alexander Technique and the Spiritual Quest*, Larsons Publications, Burdett, NY.

McNeil, D. 1998 *The Face*, Hamish Hamilton, London.

Muecke, S. 1999 'Travelling the subterranean river of blood: philosophy and magic in cultural studies', *Cultural Studies*, **13**, 1–17.

Norretranders, T. 1998 *The User Illusion. Cutting Consciousness Down to Size*, Viking, New York.

Pastoureau, M. 2002 *Blue*, Princeton University Press, Princeton.

Pine, J. and Gilmore, J.H. 1999 *The Experience Economy*, Harvard Business School Press, Boston, MA.

Reason, J.T. 1982 'Sensory processes' pp. 218–52 in A. Taylor (ed.), *Introducing Psychology*, Penguin, Harmondsworth.

Rival, L. (ed.) 1998 *The Social Life of Trees. Anthropological Perspectives on Tree Symbolism*, Berg, Oxford.

Roth, G. 1989 *Maps to Ecstasy*, Harper Collins, London.

Roth, G. 1998 *Sweat Your Prayers. Movement as Spiritual Practice*, Harper Collins, London.

Schechner, R. 1995 *The Future of Ritual. Writings on Culture and Performance*, Routledge, New York.

Segel, H.B. 1998 *Modernism and the Physical Imperative*, Johns Hopkins University Press, Baltimore, MD.

Serres, M. 1995 *Angels. A Modern Myth*, Flammarion, Paris.

Shusterman, R. 1999 'Somaesthetics: a disciplinary proposal', *Journal of Aesthetics and Art Criticism*, 57, 299–313.

Speak, D. 1999 *The End of Patience*, Indiana University Press, Bloomington, IN.

Stewart, N. 1998 'Relanguaging the body: phenomenological descriptions and the body image', *Performance Research*, 3, 42–58.

Sudnow, D. 1993 *Ways of the Hand*, MIT Press, Cambridge, MA.

Taussig, M. 1994 'Physiognomic aspects of visual words', pp. 205–12 in L. Taylor (ed.), *Visualising Theory*, Routledge, New York.

Taussig, M. 1998 'Crossing the face', pp. 224–43 in P. Spyer (ed.), *Border Fetishisms. Material Objects in Unstable Spaces*, Routledge, New York.

Thrift, N.J. 1995 'A hyperactive world', in R.J. Johnston, P.J. Taylor and M. Watts (eds), *Geographies of Global Transformation*, Blackwell, Oxford.

Thrift, N.J. 1996 *Spatial Formations*, Sage, London.

Thrift, N.J. 1997 'The still point: resistence, expressive embodiment and dance', in S. Pile and M. Keith (eds), *Geographies of Resistance*, Routledge, London.

Thrift, N.J. 1998 'Steps to an ecology of place', in D. Massey, J. Allen and P. Sarre (eds), *Human Geography Today*, Polity Press, Cambridge.

Thrift, N.J. 2000 'Afterwords', *Environment and Planning D: Society and Space*, 18(2), 213–56.

Wallace, A.C. 1993 *Walking, Literature, and English Culture. The Origins and Uses of Peripatetic in the Nineteenth Century*, Clarendon Press, Oxford.

Walton, K.L. 1990 *Mimesis as Make-Believe. On the Foundations of the Representational Arts*, Harvard University Press, Cambridge, MA.

Watson, S. 1998a 'The neurobiology of sorcery: Deleuze and Guattari's brain', *Biology and Society*, 4.

Watson, S. 1998b 'The new Bergsonism', *Radical Philosophy*, 92, 1–23.

Weiss, B. 1996 *The Making and Unmaking of the Haya Lived World. Consumption, Commodification and Everyday Practice*, Duke University Press, Durham, NC.

Wilson, F.R. 1998 *The Hand. How Its Use Shapes the Brain, Language and Culture*, Pantheon, New York.

Index